D1190320

Wallace Library

DUE DATE (stamped in blue)
RETURN DATE (stamped in black)

THE EVE OF
THE REFORMATION

THE EVE OF THE REFORMATION

STUDIES IN THE
RELIGIOUS LIFE AND THOUGHT OF THE ENGLISH
PEOPLE IN THE PERIOD PRECEDING THE
REJECTION OF THE ROMAN JURIS-
DICTION BY HENRY VIII

BY

FRANCIS AIDAN GASQUET, D.D., O.S.B.

KENNIKAT PRESS
Port Washington, N. Y./London

THE EVE OF THE REFORMATION

First published in 1900
Reissued in 1971 by Kennikat Press
Library of Congress Catalog Card No: 75-118522
ISBN 0-8046-1144-0

Manufactured by Taylor Publishing Company   Dallas, Texas

CONTENTS

THE EVE OF
THE REFORMATION

CHAPTER I

INTRODUCTION

THE English Reformation presents a variety of problems to the student of history. Amongst them not the least difficult or important is the general question, How are we to account for the sudden beginning and the ultimate success of a movement which, apparently at least, was opposed to the religious convictions and feelings of the nation at large? To explain away the difficulty, we are asked by some writers to believe that the religious revolution, although perhaps unrecognised at the moment when the storm first burst, had long been inevitable, and indeed that its issue had been foreseen by the most learned and capable men in England. To some, it appears that the Church, on the eve of the Reformation, had long lost its hold on the intelligence and affection of the English people. Discontented with the powers claimed by the ecclesiastical authority, and secretly disaffected to much of the mediæval teaching of religious truth and to many of the traditional religious ordinances, the laity were, it is suggested, only too eager to seize upon the first opportunity of emancipating themselves from a thraldom which in practice had become intolerable. An increase of knowledge, too, it is supposed, had inevitably led men to view as false and superstitious many of the practices of religion which had been acquiesced in and followed without doubt or question in earlier and more simple days. Men, with the increasing light, had come to see, in the support given to these practices by the clergy, a determination to keep people at large in ignorance, and to make capital out of many of these objectionable features of mediæval worship.

Moreover, such writers assume that in reality there was little or no practical religion among the mass of the people for some considerable time before the outbreak of the religious difficulties in the sixteenth century. According to their reading of the facts, the nation, as such, had long lost its interest in the religion of its forefathers. Receiving no instruction in faith and morals worthy of the name, they had been allowed by the neglect of the clergy to grow up in ignorance of the teachings, and in complete neglect of the duties, of their religion. Ecclesiastics generally, secular as well as religious, had, it is suggested, forfeited the respect and esteem of the laity by their evil and mercenary lives ; whilst, imagining that the surest way to preserve the remnants of their former power was to keep the people ignorant, they had opposed the literary revival of the fifteenth century by every means at their command. In a word, the picture of the pre-Reformation Church ordinarily drawn for us is that of a system honeycombed with disaffection and unbelief, the natural and necessary outcome of an attempt to maintain at all hazards an effete ecclesiastical organisation, which clung with the tenacity of despair to doctrines and observances which the world at large had ceased to accept as true, or to observe as any part of its reasonable service.

In view of these and similar assertions, it is of interest and importance to ascertain, if possible, what really was the position of the Church in the eyes of the nation at large on the eve of the Reformation, to understand the attitude of men's minds to the system as they knew it, and to discover, as far as may be, what in regard to religion they were doing and saying and thinking about, when the change came upon them. It is precisely this information which it has hitherto been difficult to get, and the present work is designed to supply some evidence on these matters. It does not pretend in any sense to be a history of the English Reformation, to give any consecutive narrative of the religious movements in this country during the sixteenth century, or to furnish an adequate account of the causes which led up to them. The volume in reality presents to the reader merely a series of separate studies which, whilst joined together by a certain connecting thread, must not be taken as claiming to present any complete picture of the period immediately preceding the Reformation, still less of that movement itself.

This is intentional. Those who know most about this portion of our national history will best understand how impossible it is as yet for any one, however well informed, to write the history of the Reformation itself or to draw for us any detailed and accurate picture of the age that went before that great event, and is supposed by some to have led up to it. The student of this great social and religious movement must at present be content to address himself to the necessary work of sifting and examining the many new sources of information which the researches of late years have opened out to the inquirer.   For example, what a vast field of work is not supplied by the *Calendar of Papers, Foreign and Domestic, of the Reign of Henry VIII.* alone!   In many ways this monumental work may well be considered one of the greatest literary achievements of the age.   It furnishes the student of this portion of our national history with a vast catalogue of material, all of which must be examined, weighed, and arranged, before it is possible to pass a judgment upon the great religious revolution of the sixteenth century.   And, though obviously affording grounds for a reconsideration of many of the conclusions previously formed in regard to this perplexing period, it must in no sense be regarded as even an exhaustive calendar of the available material. Rolls, records, and documents of all kinds exist in public and private archives, which are not included in these State Papers, but which are equally necessary for the formation of a sound and reliable opinion on the whole story.   Besides this vast mass of material, the entire literature of the period demands careful examination, as it must clearly throw great light on the tone and temper of men's minds, and reveal the origin and growth of popular views and opinions.

Writers, such as Burnet, for example, and others, have indeed presented their readers with the story of the Reformation as a whole, and have not hesitated to set out at length, and with assurance, the causes which led up to that event.   Whether true or false, they have made their synthesis, and taking a comprehensive view of the entire subject, they have rendered their story more plausible by the unity of idea it was designed to illustrate and confirm.   The real value of such a synthesis, however, must of course entirely depend on the data upon which it rests. The opening up of new sources of information and the examination of old sources in the critical spirit now demanded in all historical investigations have fully proved, however, not merely this or that fact to be wrong, but that whole lines of argument are without justification, and general deductions without reasonable basis. In other words, the old synthesis has been founded upon false facts and false inferences.

Whilst, however, seeing that the old story of the Reformation in England is wrong on some of the main lines upon which it depended, it is for reasons just stated impossible at present to substitute a new synthesis for the old. However unsatisfactory it may appear to be reduced to the analysis of sources and the examination of details, nothing more can safely be attempted at the present time. A general view cannot be taken until the items that compose it have been proved and tested and found correct. Till such time a provisional appreciation at best of the general subject is alone possible. The present volume then is occupied solely with some details, and I have endeavoured mainly by an examination of the literature of the period in question to gather some evidence of the mental attitude of the English people towards the religious system which prevailed before the rejection of the Roman jurisdiction by Henry VIII.

In regard to the general question, one or two observations may be premised.

At the outset it may be allowed that in many things there was need of reform in its truest sense. This was recognised by the best and most staunch sons of Holy Church ; and the Council of Trent itself, when

we read its decrees and measure its language, is sufficient proof that by the highest authorities it was
acknowledged that every effort must be made to purify
the Church from abuses, superstitions, and scandals
which, in the course of the long ages of its existence,
had sprung from its contact with the world and through
the human weaknesses of its rulers and ministers. In
reality, however, the movement for reform did not in
any way begin with Trent, nor was it the mere outcome
of a terror inspired by the wholesale defection of
nations under the influence of the Lutheran Reformation. The need had long been acknowledged by the
best and most devoted sons of the Church. There
were those, whom M. Eugène Müntz has designated
the " morose cardinals," who saw whither things were
tending, and strove to the utmost of their power to
avert the impending catastrophe. As Janssen has
pointed out, in the middle of the fifteenth century, for
instance, Nicholas of Cusa initiated reforms in Germany, with the approval — if not by the positive
injunctions—of the Pope. It was, however, a true
reform, a reform founded on the principle "not of
destruction, but of purification and renewal." Holding that " it was not for men to change what was holy;
but for the holy to change man," he began by reforming himself and preaching by example. He restored
discipline and eagerly welcomed the revival of learning
and the invention of printing as the most powerful
auxiliaries of true religion. His projects of general
ecclesiastical reforms presented to Pius II. are admir-
able. Without wishing to touch the organisation of the
Church, he desired full and drastic measures of "reformation in head and members." But all this was entirely

different from the spirit and aim of those who attacked the Church under the leadership of Luther and his followers. Their object was not the reform and purification of abuses, but the destruction and overthrow of the existing religious system. Before, say, 1517 or even 1521, no one at this period ever dreamt of wishing to change the basis of the Christian religion, as it was then understood. The most earnest and zealous sons of the Church never hesitated to attack this or that abuse, and to point out this or that spot, desiring to make the edifice of God's Church, as they understood it, more solid, more useful, and more like Christ's ideal. They never dreamt that their work could undermine the edifice, much less were their aims directed to pulling down the walls and digging up the foundations; such a possibility was altogether foreign to their conception of the essential constitution of Christ's Church. To suggest that men like Colet, More, and Erasmus had any leaning to, or sympathy with, "the Reformation" as we know it, is, in view of what they have written, absolutely false and misleading.

The fact is, that round the true history of the Reformation movement in England, there has grown up, as Janssen has shown had been the case in Germany, a mass of legend from which it is often difficult enough to disentangle the truth. It has been suggested, for instance, that the period which preceded the advent of the new religious ideas was, to say the least, a period of stagnation. That, together with the light of what is called the Gospel, came the era of national prosperity, and that the golden age of literature and art was the outcome of that liberty and freedom of spirit which was the distinct product of the Protestant Reformation. And yet what are the facts? Was the age immediately

before the religious upheaval of the sixteenth century
so very black, and was it the magic genius of Luther
who divined how to call forth the light out of the
" void and empty darkness " ?   Luther, himself, shall
tell us his opinion of the century before the rise of
Protestantism.   " Any one reading the chronicles," he
writes, " will find that since the birth of Christ there is
nothing that can compare with what has happened in
our world during the last hundred years.   Never in any
country have people seen so much building, so much
cultivation of the soil.   Never has such good drink,
such abundant and delicate food, been within the reach
of so many.   Dress has become so rich that it cannot
in this respect be improved.   Who has ever heard of
commerce such as we see it to-day ?   It circles the
globe ; it embraces the whole world !   Painting, engrav-
ing—all the arts—have progressed and are still improving.   More than all, we have men so capable, and so
learned, that their wit penetrates everything in such a
way, that nowadays a youth of twenty knows more
than twenty doctors did in days gone by." [1]

In this passage we have the testimony of the German reformer himself that the eve of the Reformation
was in no sense a period of stagnation.   The world was
fully awake, and the light of learning and art had already
dawned upon the earth.   The progress of commerce and
the prosperity of peoples owed nothing to the religious
revolt of the sixteenth century.   Nor is this true only
for Germany.   There is evidence to prove that Luther's
picture is as correct in that period for England.   Learning, there can be no question, in the fifteenth century,
found a congenial soil in this country.   In its origin, as

---

[1] *Opera* (ed. Frankfort), tom. x. p. 56, quoted by Janssen.

well as in its progress, the English revival of letters, which may be accurately gauged by the renewal of Greek studies, found its chief patrons in the fifteenth and early sixteenth centuries among the clergy and the most loyal lay sons of the Church. The fears of Erasmus that the rise of Lutheranism would prove the death-blow of solid scholarship were literally fulfilled. In England, no less than in Germany, amid the religious difficulties and the consequent social disturbances, learning, except in so far as it served to aid the exigencies of polemics or meet the controversial needs of the hour, declined for well-nigh a century ; and so far from the Reformation affording the congenial soil upon which scholarship and letters flourished, it was in reality—to use Erasmus's own favourite expression about the movement—a " catastrophe," in which was overwhelmed the real progress of the previous century. The state of the universities of Oxford and Cambridge, before and after the period of religious change, is an eloquent testimony as to its effect on learning in general ; whilst the differences of opinion in religious matters to which the Reformation gave rise, at once put a stop to the international character of the foreign universities. English names forthwith disappeared from the students' lists at the great centres of learning in France and Italy, an obvious misfortune, which had a disastrous effect on English scholarship ; the opening up of the schools of the reformed churches of Germany in no wise compensating for the international training hitherto received by most English scholars of eminence.

In art and architecture, too, in the second half of the fifteenth century and the beginning of the sixteenth, there was manifested an activity in England which is

without a parallel.   There never was a period in which
such life and energy was displayed in the building and
adornment of churches of all kinds as on the very eve
of the Reformation.   Not in one part of the country
only, nor in regard only to the greater churches, was
this characteristic activity shown, but throughout the
length and breadth of England the walls of our great
cathedrals and minsters, and well-nigh those of every
little parish church in the land, still bear their testimony
to what was done out of love for God's house during
the period in question by the English people.   Moreover, by the aid of the existing accounts and inventories
it can be proved to demonstration that it was a work
which then, more than at any other period of our
national existence, appealed to the people at large and
was carried out by them.   No longer, as in earlier
times, was the building and beautifying of God's house
left in this period to some great noble benefactor or
rich landowner.   During the fifteenth century the
people were themselves concerned with the work,
initiated it, found the means to carry it out, and super-
intended it in all its details.

The same may be said of art.   The work of adorn-
ing the walls of the churches with paintings and frescoes,
the work of filling in the tracery of the windows with
pictured glass, the work of setting up, and carving, and
painting, and decorating ; the making of screens, and
stalls, and altars, all during this period, and right up to
the eve of the change, was in every sense popular.   It
was the people who carried out these works, and evidently for the sole reason because they loved to beautify
their churches, which were, in a way now somewhat
difficult to realise, the centre no less of their lives than of

their religion. Popular art grows, and only grows luxuri-
antly, upon a religious soil ; and under the inspiration
of a popular enthusiasm the parish churches of England became, if we may judge from the evidence of the
wills, accounts, and inventories which still survive, not
merely sanctuaries, but veritable picture galleries, teaching the poor and unlettered the history and doctrine of
their religion. Nor were the pictures themselves the
miserable daubs which some have suggested. The
stained-glass windows were not only multiplied in the
churches of England during this period, but by those
best able to judge, the time between 1480 and 1520
has been regarded as the golden age of the art ; and as
regards the frescoes and decorations themselves, there
is evidence of the existence in England of a high proficiency, both in design and execution, before the
Reformation. Two examples may be taken to attest
the truth of this : the series of paintings against which
the stalls in Eton College Chapel are now placed, and
the pictures on the walls of the Lady Chapel at Winchester, now unfortunately destroyed by the whitewash
with which they had been covered on the change of
religion. Those who had the opportunity of examining
the former series, when many years ago they were un-
covered on the temporary removal of the stalls, have
testified to their intrinsic merit. Indeed, they appeared
to the best judges of the time as being so excellent in
drawing and colour that on their authority they were
long supposed to have been the work of some unknown
Italian artist of the school of Giotto. By a fortunate
discovery of Mr. J. Willis Clarke, however, it is now
known that both these and the Winchester series were
in reality executed by an Englishman, named Baker.

The same is true with regard to decoration and carving work. In screen - work, the Perpendicular period is allowed to have excelled all others, both in the lavish amount of the ornament as well as in the style of decoration. One who has paid much attention to this subject says : " During this period, the screen - work was usually enriched by gilding and painting, or was ' depensiled,' as the phrase runs, and many curious works of the limner's art may still be seen in the churches of Norfolk and Suffolk. In Sussex, the screens of Brighton and Horsham may be cited as painted screens of beauty and merit, both having been thus ornamented in a profuse and costly manner, and each bore figures of saints in their panels." [1]   The churchwardens' accounts, too, show that the work of thus decorating the English parish churches was in full operation up to the very eve of the religious changes. In these truthful pictures of parochial life, we may see the people and their representatives busily engaged in collecting the necessary money, and in superintending the work of setting up altars and statues and paintings, and in hiring carvers and decorators to enrich what their ancestors had provided for God's house. It was the age, too, of organ-making and bell-founding, and there is hardly a record of any parish church at this time which does not show considerable sums of money spent upon these. From the middle of the fifteenth century to the period described as "the great pillage," music, too, had made great progress in England, and the renown of the English school had spread over Europe. Musical compositions had multiplied in a wonderful way, and before the close of the fifteenth century " prick song,"

[1] J. L. Andre, in *Sussex Archæological Journal*, xxxix. p. 31.

or part music, is very frequently found in the inventories of our English parish churches. In fact, it has been recently shown that much of the music of the boasted school of ecclesiastical music to which the English Reformation had been thought to have given birth, is, in reality, music adapted to the new English services, from Latin originals, which had been inspired by the ancient offices of the Church. Most of the "prick song" masses and other musical compositions were destroyed in the wholesale destruction which accompanied the religious changes, but sufficient remains to show that the English pre-Reformation school of music was second to none in Europe. The reputation of some of its chief masters, like Dunstable, Tallis, and Bird, had spread to other countries, and their works had been used and studied, even in that land of song, Italy.

A dispassionate consideration of the period preceding the great religious upheaval of the sixteenth century will, it can hardly be doubted, lead the inquirer to conclude that it was not in any sense an age of stagnation, discontent, and darkness. Letters, art, architecture, painting, and music, under the distinct patronage of the Church, had made great and steady progress before the advent of the new ideas. Moreover, those who will examine the old parish records cannot fail to see that up to the very eve of the changes, the old religion had not lost its hold upon the minds and affections of the people at large. And one thing is absolutely clear, that it was not the Reformation movement which brought to the world in its train the blessings of education, and the arts of civilisation. What it did for all these is written plainly enough in the history of that period of change and destruction.

CHAPTER II

THE REVIVAL OF LETTERS IN ENGLAND

THE story of the English literary revival in the fifteenth and sixteenth centuries is of no little interest and importance. The full history of the movement would form the fitting theme of an entire volume ; but the real facts are so contrary to much that is commonly believed about our English renaissance of letters, that some brief account is necessary, if we would rightly understand the attitude of men's minds on the eve of the Reformation. At the outset, it is useful to recall the limits of this English renaissance. Judged by what is known of the movement in Italy, the land of its origin, the word "renaissance" is usually understood to denote not only the adoption of the learning and intellectual culture of ancient Greece and Rome by the leaders of thought in the Western World during the period in question, but an almost servile following of classical models, the absorption of the pagan spirit and the adoption of pagan modes of expression so fully, as certainly to obscure, if it did not frequently positively obliterate, Christian sentiment and Christian ideals. In this sense, it is pleasing to think, the renaissance was unknown in England. So far, however, as the revival of learning is concerned, England bore its part in, if indeed it may not be said to have been in the forefront of, the movement.

14

This has, perhaps, hardly been realised as it should be. That the sixteenth century witnessed a remarkable awakening of minds, a broadening of intellectual interests, and a considerable advance in general culture, has long been known and acknowledged. There is little doubt, however, that the date usually assigned both for the dawning of the light and for the time of its full development is altogether too late ; whilst the circumstances which fostered the growth of the movement have apparently been commonly misunderstood, and the chief agents in initiating it altogether ignored. The great period of the reawakening would ordinarily be placed without hesitation in post-Reformation times, and writers of all shades of opinion have joined in attributing the revival of English letters to the freedom of minds and hearts purchased by the overthrow of the old ecclesiastical system, and their emancipation from the narrowing and withering effects of mediævalism.

On the assumption that the only possible attitude of English churchmen on the eve of the great religious changes would be one of uncompromising hostility to learning and letters, many have come to regard the one, not as inseparably connected with the other, but the secular as the outcome of the religious movement. The undisguised opposition of the clergy to the " New Learning" is spoken of as sufficient proof of the Church's dislike of learning in general, and its determination to check the nation's aspirations to profit by the general classical revival. This assumption is based upon a complete misapprehension as to what was then the meaning of the term " New Learning." It was in no sense connected with the revival of letters, or with what is now understood by learning and culture; but it was in the Reformation days a well-recognised expression used to denote the novel religious teachings of Luther and his followers.[1] Uncompromising hostility to such novelties, no doubt, marked the religious attitude of many, who were at the same time the most strenuous advocates of the renaissance of letters. This is so obvious in the works of the period, that were it not for the common misuse of the expression at the present day, and for the fact that opposition to the " New Learning " is assumed on all hands to represent hostility to letters, rather than to novel teachings in religious matters, there would be no need to furnish examples of its real use in the period in question. As it is, some instances taken from the works of that time become almost a necessity, if we would understand the true position of many of the chief actors at this period of our history.

Roger Edgworth, a preacher, for instance, after speaking of those who " so arrogantly glory in their learning, had by study in the English Bible, and in these seditious English books that have been sent over from our English runagates now abiding with Luther in Saxony," praises the simple-hearted faith that was accepted unquestioned by all " before this wicked 'New Learning' arose in Saxony and came over into England amongst us." [2]

[1] The use of the expression "New Learning" as meaning the revival of letters is now so common that any instance of it may seem superfluous. Green, for example, in his *History of the English People*, vol. ii. constantly speaks of it. Thus (p. 81), " Erasmus embodied for the Teutonic peoples the quickening influence of the New Learning during the long scholar-life which began at Paris and ended amidst sorrow at Basle." Again (p. 84), " the group of scholars who represented the New Learning in England." Again (p. 86), " On the universities the influence of the New Learning was like a passing from death to life." Again (p. 125), "As yet the New Learning, though scared by Luther's intemperate language, had steadily backed him in his struggle."   [2] *Sermons*. London : Robert Caly, 1557, p. 36.

From the preface of *The Praier and Complaynte of the Ploweman*, dated February 1531, it is equally clear that the expression "New Learning" was then understood only of religious teaching. Like the Scribes and Pharisees in the time of Our Lord, the author says, the bishops and priests are calling out : "What 'New Learning' is it ?   These fellows teach new learning : these are they that trouble all the world with their new learning ? . . . Even now after the same manner, our holy bishops with all their ragman's roll are of the same sort. . . . They defame, slander, and persecute the word and the preachers and followers of it, with the selfsame names, calling it 'New Learning' and them 'new masters.'"[1]

The same meaning was popularly attached to the words even after the close of the reign of Henry VIII. A book published in King Edward's reign, to instruct the people "concerning the king's majesty's proceedings in the communion," bears the title, *The olde Faith of Great Brittayne and the new learning of England.* It is, of course, true, that the author sets himself to show that the reformed doctrines were the old teachings of the Christian Church, and that, when St. Gregory sent St. Augustine over into England, "the new learning was brought into this realm, of which we see much yet remaining in the Church at the present day."[2]   But this fact rather

---

[1] *The Praier and Complaynte of the Ploweman unto Christ*, sig. Aij.

[2] R.V. *The olde Faith of Great Brittayne, &c.*—The style of the book may be judged by the following passages :—"How say you (O ye popish bishops and priests which maintain Austen's dampnable ceremonies)—For truly so long as ye say masse and lift the bread and wine above your heads, giving the people to understand your mass to be available for the quick and the dead, ye deny the Lord that bought you ; therefore let the mass go again to Rome, with all Austen's trinkets, and cleave to the Lord's Supper " . . . Again :—"Gentle reader: It is not unknown what an occasion of sclander divers have taken in that the king's majesty hath with his honourable council

emphasises than in any way obscures the common understanding of the expression "New Learning," since the whole intent of the author is to show that the upholders of the old ecclesiastical system were the real maintainers of a "New Learning" brought from Rome by St. Augustine, and not the Lutherans. The same appears equally clearly in a work by Urbanus Regius, which was translated and published by William Turner in 1537, and called *A comparison betwene the old learnynge and the newe*. As the translator says at the beginning—

> " Some ther be that do defye
> All that is newe and ever do crye
> The olde is better, away with the new
> Because it is false, and the olde is true.
> Let them this booke reade and beholde,
> For it preferreth the learning most olde."

As the author of the previous volume quoted, so Urbanus Regius compares the exclamation of the Jews against our Lord : "What new learning is this ? " with the objection, "What is this new doctrine ?" made by the Catholics against the novel religious teaching of Luther and his followers. "This," they say, " is the new doctrine lately devised and furnished in the shops

gone about to alter and take away the abuse of the communion used in the mass . . . The ignorant and unlearned esteem the same abuse, called the mass, to be the principal point of Christianity, to whom the altering thereof appears very strange . . . Our popish priests still do abuse the Lord's Supper or Communion, calling it still a new name of *Missa* or Mass." The author strongly objects to those like Bishop Gardiner and Dr. Smythe who have written in defence of the old doctrine of the English Church on the Blessed Sacrament : "Yea, even the mass, which is a derogation of Christ's blood. For Christ left the sacrament of his body and blood in bread and wine to be eaten and drunk in remembrance of his death, and not to be looked upon as the Israelites did the brazen serpent . . . Paul saith not, as often as the priest lifts the bread and wine above his shaven crown, for the papists to gaze at." All this, as "the New Learning" brought over to England by St. Augustine of Canterbury, the author would send back to Rome from whence it came.

and workhouses of heretics. Let us abide still in our old faith . . . Wherefore," continues the author, " I, doing the office of Christian brother, have made a comparison between the ' New Learning ' and the olden, whereby, dear brother, you may easily know whether we are called worthily or unworthily the preachers of the ' New Learning.' For so did they call us of late." He then proceeds to compare under various headings what he again and again calls " the New Learning " and " the Old Learning." For example, according to the former, people are taught that the Sacraments bring grace to the soul ; according to the latter, faith alone is needful. According to the former, Christ is present wholly under each kind of bread and wine, the mass is a sacrifice for the living and the dead, and " oblation is made in the person of the whole church " ; according to the latter, the Supper is a memorial only of Christ's death, " and not a sacrifice, but a remembrance of the sacrifice that was once offered up on the cross," and that "all oblations except that of our Lord are vain and void."[1]

In view of passages such as the above, and in the absence of any contemporary evidence of the use of the expression to denote the revival of letters, it is obvious that any judgment as to a general hostility of the clergy to learning based upon their admitted opposition to what was then called the " New Learning " cannot seriously be maintained. It would seem, moreover, that the religious position of many ecclesiastics and laymen has been completely misunderstood by the meaning now so commonly assigned to the expression. Men like Erasmus, Colet, and to a great extent, More himself,

---

[1] Urbanus Regius, *A comparison betwene the old learnynge and the newe*, translated by William Turner. Southwark : Nicholson, 1537, sig. Aij to Cvij.

have been regarded, to say the least, as at heart very lukewarm adherents of the Church, precisely because of their strong advocacy of the movement known as the literary revival, which, identified by modern writers with the " New Learning," was, it is wrongly assumed, condemned by orthodox churchmen. The Reformers are thus made the champions of learning ; Catholics, the upholders of ignorance, and the hereditary and bitter foes of all intellectual improvement. No one, however, saw more clearly than did Erasmus that the rise of Lutheran opinions was destined to be the destruction of true learning, and that the atmosphere of controversy was not the most fitting to assure its growth. To Richard Pace he expressed his ardent wish that some kindly *Deus ex machinâ* would put an end to the whole Lutheran agitation, for it had most certainly brought upon the humanist movement unmerited hatred.[1] In subsequent letters he rejects the idea that the two, the Lutheran and the humanist movements, had anything whatever in common ; asserting that even Luther himself had never claimed to found his revolt against the Church on the principles of scholarship and learning. To him, the storm of the Reformation appeared —so far as concerned the revival of learning—as a catastrophe. Had the tempest not risen, he had the best expectations of a general literary renaissance and of witnessing a revival of interest in Biblical and patristic studies among churchmen. It was the breath of bitter and endless controversy initiated in the Lutheran revolt and the consequent misunderstandings and enmities which withered his hopes.[2]

There remains, however, the broader question as

---

[1] *Opera* (ed. Le Clerc), Ep. 583.   [2] Ibid., Ep. 751.

to the real position of the ecclesiastical authorities generally, in regard to the revival of learning. So far as England is concerned, their attitude is hardly open to doubt in view of the positive testimony of Erasmus, which is further borne out by an examination of the material available for forming a judgment. This proves beyond all question, not only that the Church in England on the eve of the change did not refuse the light, but that, both in its origin and later development, the movement owed much to the initiative and encouragement of English churchmen.

It is not necessary here to enter very fully into the subject of the general revival of learning in Europe during the course of the fifteenth century. At the very beginning of that period what Gibbon calls " a new and perpetual flame " was enkindled in Italy. As in the thirteenth century, so then it was the study of the literature and culture of ancient Greece that re-enkindled the lamp of learning in the Western World. Few things, indeed, are more remarkable than the influence of Greek forms and models on the Western World. The very language seems as if destined by Providence to do for the Christian nations of Europe what in earlier ages it had done for pagan Rome. As Dr. Döllinger has pointed out, this is " a fact of immense importance, which even in these days it is worth while to weigh and place in its proper light," since " the whole of modern civilisation and culture is derived from Greek sources. Intellectually we are the offspring of the union of the ancient Greek classics with Hellenised Judaism." One thing is clear on the page of history : that the era of great intellectual activity synchronised with re-awakened interests in the Greek classics and Greek language in such a way that the study of Greek may conveniently be taken as representing a general revival of letters.

By the close of the fourteenth century, the ever-increasing impotence of the Imperial sway on the Bosphorus, and the ever-growing influence of the Turk, compelled the Greek emperors to look to Western Christians for help to arrest the power of the infidels, which, like a flood, threatened to overwhelm the Eastern empire.   Three emperors in succession journeyed into the Western world to implore assistance in their dire necessity, and though their efforts failed to save Constantinople, the historian detects in these pilgrimages of Greeks to the Courts of Europe the providential influence which brought about the renaissance of letters. "The travels of the three emperors," writes Gibbon, "were unavailing for their temporal, or perhaps their spiritual salvation, but they were productive of a beneficial consequence, the revival of the Greek learning in Italy, from whence it was propagated to the last nations of the West and North."

What is true of Italy may well be true of other countries and places.   The second of these pilgrim emperors, Manuel, the son and successor of Palæologus, crossed the Alps, and after a stay in Paris, came over the sea into England.   In December 1400 he landed at Dover, and was, with a large retinue of Greeks, entertained at the monastery of Christchurch, Canterbury.   It requires little stretch of imagination to suppose that the memory of such a visit would have lingered long in the cloister of Canterbury, and it is hardly perhaps by chance that it is here that half a century later are to be found the first serious indications of a revival of Greek studies. Moreover, it is evident that other Greek envoys followed in subsequent times, and even the great master and prodigy of learning, Manuel Chrysoloras himself, found his way to our shores, and it is hardly an assumption, in view of the position of Canterbury—on the high-road from Dover to London —to suppose to Christchurch also.[1] It was from his arrival in Italy, in 1396, that may be dated the first commencement of systematic study of the Greek classics in the West. The year 1408 is given for his visit to England.[2]

There are indications early in the fifteenth century of a stirring of the waters in this country. Guarini, a pupil of Chrysoloras, became a teacher of fame at Ferrara, where he gathered round him a school of disciples which included several Englishmen. Such were Tiptoft, Earl of Worcester;[3] Robert Fleming, a learned ecclesiastic; John Free, John Gundthorpe, and William Gray, Bishop of Ely; whilst another Italian, Aretino, attracted by his fame another celebrated Englishman, Humphrey, Duke of Gloucester, to his classes. These, however, were individual cases, and their studies, and even the books they brought back, led to little in the way of systematic work in England at the old classical models. The fall of Constantinople in 1453 gave the required stimulus here, as in Italy. Among the fugi-

---

[1] Remigio Sabbadini, *La Scuola e gli studi di Guarino Guarini Veronese,* pp. 217-18.

[2] R. Sabbadini, *Guarino Veronese et il suo epistolario,* p. 57.

[3] The Earl was a confrater and special friend of the monks of Christchurch, Canterbury. In 1468-69, Prior Goldstone wrote to the Earl, who had been abroad "on pilgrimage" for four years, to try and obtain for Canterbury the usual jubilee privileges of 1470. In his Obit in the Canterbury *Necrology* (MS. Arund. 68 f. 45d) he is described as "vir undecumque doctissimus, omnium liberalium artium divinarumque simul ac secularium litterarum scientia peritissimus."

tives were many Greek scholars of eminence, such as Chalcocondylas, Andronicus, Constantine and John Lascaris, who quickly made the schools of Italy famous by their teaching. Very soon the fame of the new masters spread to other countries, and students from all parts of the Western World found their way to their lecture-halls in Rome and the other teaching centres established in the chief cities of Northern Italy.

First among the scholars who repaired thither from England to drink in the learning of ancient Greece and bring back to their country the new spirit, we must place two Canterbury monks named Selling and Hadley. Born somewhere about 1430, William Selling became a monk at Christchurch, Canterbury, somewhere about 1448. There seems some evidence to show that his family name was Tyll, and that, as was frequently, if not generally, the case, on his entering into religion, he adopted the name of Selling from his birthplace, some five miles from Faversham in Kent.[1] It is probable that Selling, after having passed through the claustral school at Canterbury, on entering the Benedictine Order was sent to finish his studies at Canterbury College, Oxford. Here he certainly was in 1450, for in that year he writes a long and what is described as an elegant letter as a student at Canterbury College to his Prior, Thomas Goldstone, at Christchurch

---

[1] Leland (*De Scriptoribus Britannicis*, 482) calls him Tillœus, and this has been generally translated as Tilly. In the *Canterbury Letter Books* (Rolls Series, iii. 291) it appears that Prior Selling was greatly interested in a boy named Richard Tyll. In 1475, Thomas Goldstone, the warden of Canterbury Hall, writes to Prior Selling about new clothes and a tunic and other expenses "scolaris tui Ricardi Tyll." In the same volume, p. 315, is a letter of fraternity given to "Agnes, widow of William Tyll," and on February 7, 1491, she received permission to be buried where her husband, William Tyll, had been interred, "juxta tumbam sancti Thomæ martyris."

Canterbury.[1] He was ordained priest, and celebrated his first mass at Canterbury in September 1456.[2]

In 1464 William Selling obtained leave of his Prior and convent to go with a companion, William Hadley, to study in the foreign universities for three years,[3] during which time they visited and sat under the most celebrated teachers at Padua, Bologna, and Rome.[4] At Bologna, according to Leland, Selling was the pupil of the celebrated Politian, "with whom, on account of his aptitude in acquiring the classical elegance of ancient tongues, he formed a familiar and lasting friendship." [5] In 1466 and 1467 we find the monks, Selling and his companion Hadley, at Bologna, where apparently the readers in Greek then were Lionorus and Andronicus,[6] and where, on the 22nd March 1466, Selling took his degree in theology, his companion taking his in the March of the following year.[7]

Of this period of work, Leland says :—" His studies progressed. He indeed imbued himself with Greek ; everywhere he industriously and at great expense collected many Greek books. Nor was his care less in procuring old Latin MSS., which shortly after he took with him, as the most estimable treasures, on his return to Canterbury." [8]

[1] *Canterbury Letters* (Camden Soc.), pp. 13, 15.

[2] C. C. C. C. MS. **417** f. 54d : "Item hoc anno videlicet 6 Kal. Oct. D. Willms Selling celebravit primam suam missam et fuit sacerdos summæ missæ per totam illam ebdomadam."

[3] *Literæ Cantuar.* (Rolls Series), iii. 239.

[4] Leland, *De Scriptoribus Britannicis*, p. 482. *Cf.* also *Canterbury Letters* (Camden Soc.), p. xxvii.

[5] Leland, *ut supra.*

[6] Umberto Dallari, *I rotuli dei Lettori*, &c., *dello studio Bolognese dal 1384 al 1799*, p. 51.

[7] Serafino Mazzetti, *Memorie storiche sopra l'università di Bologna*, p. 308.

[8] Leland, *ut supra.*

His obituary notice in the Christchurch Necrology recites not only his excellence in learning, classical and theological, but what he had done to make his monastery at Canterbury a real house of studies. He decorated the library over the Priests' Chapel, adding to the books, and assigned it "for the use of those specially given to study, which he encouraged and cherished with wonderful watchfulness and affection." The eastern cloister also he fitted with glass and new desks, "called carrels," for the use of the studious brethren." [1]

After the sojourn of the two Canterbury monks in Italy, they returned to their home at Christchurch. Selling, however, did not remain there long, for on October 3, 1469, we find him setting out again for Rome [2] in company with another monk, Reginald Goldstone, also an Oxford student. This visit was on business connected with his monastery, and did not apparently keep him long away from England, for there is evidence that sometime before the election of Selling to the Priorship at Canterbury, which was in 1472, he was again at his monastery. Characteristically, his letter introducing William Worcester, the antiquary, to a merchant of Lucca who had a copy of Livy's *Decades* for sale, manifests his great and continued interest in classical literature. [3]

---

[1] B. Mus. Arundel MS. 68, f. 4. The Obit in Christchurch MS. D. 12, says: "Sacræ Theologiæ Doctor. Hic in divinis agendis multum devotus et lingua Græca et Latina valde eruditus. . . . O quam laudabiliter se habuit opera merito laudanda manifesto declarant."

[2] In the Canterbury Registers (Reg. R.) there is a record which evidently relates to Selling's previous stay in Rome as a student. On October 3, 1469, the date of Selling's second departure for Rome, the Prior and convent of Christchurch granted a letter to Pietro dei Milleni, a citizen of Rome, making him a *confrater* of the monastery in return for the kindness shown to Dr. William Selling, when in the Eternal City. This letter, doubtless, Selling carried with him in 1469.

[3] *The Old English Bible and other Essays*, p. 306.

At Canterbury, Selling must have established the teaching of Greek on systematic lines, and it is certainly from this monastic school as a centre, that the study spread to other parts of England. William Worcester, keenly alive to the classical revival, as his note-books show, tells us of "certain Greek terminations as taught by Doctor Selling of Christchurch, Canterbury," and likewise sets down the pronunciation of the Greek vowels with examples evidently on the same authority.[1]

Selling's long priorship, extending from 1472 to 1495, would have enabled him to consolidate the work of this literary renaissance which he had so much at heart.[2] The most celebrated of all his pupils was, of course, Linacre. Born, according to Caius, at Canterbury, he received his first instruction in the monastic school there, and his first lessons in the classics and Greek from Selling himself. Probably through the personal interest taken in this youth of great promise by Prior Selling, he was sent to Oxford about 1480. Those who have seriously examined the matter believe that the first years of his Oxford life were spent by Linacre at the Canterbury College, which was connected with Christchurch monastery, and which, though primarily intended for monks, also afforded a place of quiet study to others who were able to obtain admis-

---

[1] B. Mus. Cotton MS. Julius F. vii., f. 118.

[2] One of Prior Selling's first acts of administration was apparently to procure a master for the grammar school at Canterbury. He writes to the Archbishop : "Also please it your good faderhood to have in knowledge that according to your commandment, I have provided for a schoolmaster for your gramerscole in Canterbury, the which hath lately taught gramer at Wynchester and atte Seynt Antonyes in London. That, as I trust to God, shall so guide him that it shall be worship and pleasure to your Lordship and profit and encreas to them that he shall have in governance."—*Hist. MSS. Com.* 9th Report, App. p. 105.

sion.[1]   Thus, in later years, Sir Thomas More, no doubt through his father's connection with the monastery of Christchurch, Canterbury, of which house he was a "confrater," became a student at the monks' college at Oxford.   In later years Sir Thomas himself, when Chancellor of England, perpetuated the memory of his life-long connection with the monks of Canterbury by enrolling his name also on the fraternity lists of that house.

Linacre, in 1484, became a Fellow of All Souls' College, but evidently he did not lose touch with his old friends at Canterbury, for, in 1486, Prior Selling being appointed one of the ambassadors of Henry VII. to the Pope, he invited his former pupil to accompany him to Italy, in order to profit by the teaching of the great humanist masters at the universities there.   Prior Selling took him probably as far as Florence, and introduced him to his own old master and friend, Angelo Politian, who was then engaged in instructing the children of Lorenzo de Medici.   Through Selling's interest, Linacre was permitted to share in their lessons, and there are letters showing that the younger son, when in after years he became Pope, as Leo X., was not unmindful of his early companionship with the English scholar.[2]   From Politian, Linacre acquired a

---

[1] I. Noble Johnson, *Life of Linacre*, p. 11. Among the great benefactors to Canterbury College, Oxford, was Doctor Thomas Chaundeler, Warden of New College. In 1473, the year after the election of Prior Selling, the Chapter of Christchurch, Canterbury, passed a resolution that, in memory of his great benefits to them, his name should be mentioned daily in the conventual mass at Canterbury, and that at dinner each day at Oxford he should be named as founder.

[2] Galeni, *De Temperamentis libri tres, Thoma Linacro interpretante*, is dedicated to Pope Leo X., with a letter from Linacre dated 1521. "The widow's mite was approved by Him whose vicar on earth" Pope Leo is, so this book is only intended to recall common studies, though in itself of little interest to one having the care of the world.

purity of style in Latin which makes him celebrated even among the celebrated men of his time.   Greek he learnt from Demetrius Chalcocondylas, who was then, like Politian, engaged in teaching the children of Lorenzo de Medici.[1]

From Florence, Linacre passed on to Rome, where he gained many friends among the great humanists of the day.   One day, when examining the manuscripts of the Vatican Library for classics, and engaged in reading the *Phædo* of Plato, Hermolaus Barbarus came up and politely expressed his belief that the youth had no claim, as he had himself, to the title Barbarus, if it were lawful to judge from his choice of a book. Linacre at once, from the happy compliment, recognised the speaker, and this chance interview led to a life-long friendship between the Englishman and one of the great masters of classical literature.[2]

After Linacre had been in Italy for a year or more, a youth whom he had known at Oxford, William Grocyn, was induced to come and share with him the benefit of the training in literature then to be obtained only in Italy.   On his return in 1492, Grocyn became lecturer at Exeter College, Oxford, and among his pupils in Greek were Sir Thomas More[3] and Erasmus.   He was a graduate in theology, and was chosen by Dean Colet to give lectures at St. Paul's and subsequently appointed

---

[1] G. Lilii, *Elogia*, ed. P. Jovii, p. 91.   [2] Ibid., lxiii. p. 145.

[3] Sir Thomas More writing to Colet says : "I pass my time here (at Oxford) with Grocyn, Linacre, and our (George) Lilly : the first as you know the only master of my life, when you are absent ; the second, the director of my studies ; the third, my dearest companion in all the affairs of life" (J. Stapleton, *Tres Thomæ*, p. 165.) Another constant companion of More at Oxford was Cuthbert Tunstall, one of the most learned men of his day, afterwards in succession Bishop of London and Durham.   Tunstall dedicated to More his tract *De arte supputandi*, which he printed at Paris in 1529.

by Archbishop Warham, Master or Guardian of the collegiate church of Maidstone.[1]   Erasmus describes him as "a man of most rigidly upright life, almost superstitiously observant of ecclesiastical custom, versed in every nicety of scholastic theology, by nature of the most acute judgment, and, in a word, fully instructed in every kind of learning." [2]

Linacre, after a distinguished course in the medical schools of Padua, returned to Oxford, and in 1501 became tutor to Prince Arthur.   On the accession of Henry VIII. he was appointed physician to the court, and could count all the distinguished men of the day, Wolsey, Warham, Fox, and the rest, among his patients; and Erasmus, Sir Thomas More, and Queen Mary among his pupils in letters.   In his early life, entering the clerical state, he had held ecclesiastical preferment ; in advanced years he received priest's orders, and devoted the evening of his life to a pious preparation for his end.[3]

Grocyn and Linacre are usually regarded as the pioneers of the revival of letters.   But, as already pointed out, the first to cross the Alps from England in search for the new light, to convey it back to England, and to hand it on to Grocyn and Linacre, were William Selling, and his companion, William Hadley. Thus, the real pioneers in the English renaissance were the two monks of Christchurch, and, some years after, the two ecclesiastics, Grocyn and Linacre.

Selling, even after his election to the priorship of Canterbury, continued to occupy a distinguished place both in the political world and in the world of letters.

---

[1] Reg. Warham, in Knight's *Erasmus*, p. 22 *note.*
[2] Encyclop. Brit. *sub nomine.*   [3] Ibid.

He was chosen, though only the fifth member of the embassy sent by Henry VII. on his accession to the Pope, to act as orator, and in that capacity delivered a Latin oration before the Pope and Cardinals.[1]

He was also and subsequently sent with others by Henry on an embassy to the French king, in which he also fulfilled the function of spokesman, making what is described as " a most elegant oration."

That as Prior, Selling kept up his interest in the literary revival is clear from the terms of his obituary notice. There exists, moreover, a translation made by him after his return from his embassy to Rome, when he took his youthful protégé, Linacre, and placed him under Chalcocondylas and Politian in Florence, which seems to prove that the renewal of his intimacy with the great humanist masters of Italy had inspired him with a desire to continue his literary work. Even in the midst of constant calls upon him, which the high office of Prior of Canterbury necessitated, he found time to translate a sermon of St. John Chrysostom from the Greek, two copies of which still remain in the British Museum.[2] This is dated 1488 ; and it is probably the first example of any Greek work put into Latin in England in the early days of the English renaissance of letters. The very volume (Add. MS. 15,673) in which one copy of this translation is found shows by the style of the writing, and other indications, the Italian influences at work in Canterbury in the time

---

[1] Ugo Balzani, *Un' ambasciata inglese a Roma*, Società Romana di storia patria, iii. p. 175 *seqq.* Of this an epitome is given in Bacon's *Henry VII.*, p. 95. Count Ugo Balzani says : "Il prior di Canterbury sembra essere veramente stato l'anima dell' ambasciata." Burchardus, *Rerum Urbanarum Commentarii* (ed. Thuasne), i. p. 257, gives a full account of the reception of this embassy in Rome and by the Pope.

[2] Harl. MS. 6237, and Add. MS. 15,673.

of Selling's succession at the close of the fifteenth century ; and also the intercourse which the monastery there kept up with the foreign humanists.[1]

It is hardly necessary to say more about the precious volumes of the classics and the other manuscripts which Selling collected on his travels.   Many of them perished, with that most rare work, Cicero's *De Republica,* in the fire caused by the carelessness of some of Henry VIII.'s visitors on the eve of the dissolution of Selling's old monastery at Canterbury.   Some, like the great Greek commentaries of St. Cyril on the Prophets, were rescued half burnt from the flames ; " others, by some good chance," says Leland, "had been removed ; amongst these were the commentaries of St. Basil the Great on Isaias, the works of Synesius and other Greek codices."[2] Quite recently it has been recognised that the complete Homer and the plays of Euripides in Corpus Christi College library at Cambridge, which tradition had associated with the name of Archbishop Theodore in the seventh century, are in reality both fifteenth-century manuscripts ; and as they formed, undoubtedly, part of the library at Christchurch, Canterbury, it is hardly too much to suppose that they were some of the treasures brought back by Prior Selling from Italy.   The same may probably be said of a Livy, a fifteenth-century Greek Psalter, and a copy of the Psalms in Hebrew and Latin, in Trinity College Library.[3]

---

[1] In the same beautifully written volume is a printed tract addressed to the Venetian Senate in 1471 against princes taking church property. The tract had been sent to the Prior of Christchurch by Christopher Urswick, with a letter, in which, to induce him to read it, he says it is approved by Hermolaus Barbarus and Guarini.   Christopher Urswick was almoner to Henry VII., and to him Erasmus dedicated three of his works.

[2] Leland, *De Scriptoribus Britannicis,* 482.

[3] This information I owe to the kindness of Dr. Montague James.

Prior Selling's influence, moreover, extended beyond the walls of his own house, and can be traced to others besides his old pupil, and, as some think, relative, Linacre.   Among the friendships he had formed whilst at Padua was that of a young ecclesiastical student, Thomas Langton, with whom he was subsequently at Rome. Langton was employed in diplomatic business by King Edward IV., and whilst in France, through his friendship for Prior Selling, obtained some favour from the French king for the monastery of Canterbury.   In return for this the monks offered him a living in London.[1]   Prior Selling, on one occasion at least, drafted the sermon which Dr. Langton was to deliver as prolocutor in the Convocation of the Canterbury Province.[2]   In 1483 Langton became Bishop of Winchester, and " such was his love of letters" that he established in his own house a *schola domestica* for boys, and himself used to preside in the evening at the lessons. One youth especially attracted his attention by his music.   This was Richard Pace, afterwards renowned as a classical scholar and diplomatist.   Bishop Langton recognised his abilities, and forthwith despatched him to Italy, paying all his expenses at the universities of Padua and Rome.[3]   At the former place, he says:

[1] *Canterbury Letters* (Camden Soc.), p. xxvii.

[2] Ibid., p. 36, a letter in which Dr. Langton asks Prior Selling to "attend to the drawing of it."   The draft sermon is in Cleop. A. iii.

[3] Richard Pace, *De Fructu*, p. 27.   The work *De Fructu* was composed at Constance, where Pace was ambassador, and where he had met his old master, Paul Bombasius.   He dedicates the tract to Colet, who had done so much to introduce true classical Latin into England, in place of the barbarous language formerly used.   The work was suggested to him by a conversation he had in England two years before, on his return from Rome, with a gentleman he met at dinner, who strongly objected to a literary education for his children, on the ground that he disapproved of certain expressions made use of by Erasmus.   The tract shows on what a very intimate footing Pace was with Bombasius.

" When as a youth I began to work at my humanities, I was assisted by Cuthbert Tunstall and William Latimer, men most illustrious and excelling in every branch of learning, whose prudence, probity, and integrity were such that it were hard to say whether their learning excelled their high moral character, or their uprightness their learning." [1]

At this university he was taught by Leonicus and by Leonicenus, the friend and correspondent of Politian : " Men," he says, as being unable to give higher praise, " like Tunstall and Latimer." [2]   Passing on to Bologna he sat at the feet of Paul Bombasius, " who was then explaining every best author to large audiences."   Subsequently, at Rome, he formed a lasting friendship with William Stokesley, whom he describes as " his best friend on earth ; a man of the keenest judgment, excellent, and indeed marvellous, in theology and philosophy, and not only skilled in Greek and Latin, but possessed of some knowledge of Hebrew," whose great regret was that he had not earlier in life realised the power of the Greek language.[3]   At Ferrara, too, Pace first met Erasmus, and he warmly acknowledges his indebtedness to the influence of this great humanist.

In 1509, Richard Pace accompanied Cardinal Bainbridge to Rome, and was with him when the cardinal died, or was murdered, there in 1514.   Whilst in the Eternal City, " urged to the study by that most upright and learned man, William Latimer," he searched the Pope's library for books of music, and found a great number of works on the subject.   The cardinal's death

---

[1] *De Fructu*, p. 99.   Pace published at Venice in 1522, *Plutarchi Cheronei Opuscula*, and dedicated the work to Bishop Tunstall.   He reminds the bishop of their old student days, and says the translation has been examined by their " old master, Nicholas Leonicus."   [2] Ibid.   [3] Ibid.

put a stop to his investigations; but he had seen sufficient to be able to say that to study the matter properly
a man must know Greek and get to the library of the
Pope, where there were many and the best books on
music. "But," he adds, "I venture to say this, our
English music, if any one will critically examine into
the matter, will be found to display the greatest subtlety
of mind, especially in what is called the introduction of
harmonies, and in this matter to excel ancient music." [1]

It is unnecessary to follow in any detail the story
of the general literary revival in England. Beginning
with Selling, the movement continued to progress down
to the very eve of the religious disputes. That there was
opposition on the part of some who regarded the stirring of the waters with suspicion was inevitable. More
especially was this the case because during the course
of the literary revival there rose the storm of the great
religious revolt of the sixteenth century, and because the
practical paganism which had resulted from the movement in Italy was perhaps not unnaturally supposed by
the timorous to be a necessary consequence of a return
to the study of the classics of Greece and Rome. The
opposition sprung generally from a misunderstanding,
and "not so much from any hostility to Greek itself as
from an indifference to any learning." This Sir Thomas
More expressly declares when writing to urge the Oxford authorities to repress a band of giddy people who,
calling themselves Trojans, made it their duty to fight
against the *Grecians*. It is true also that the pulpit was
at times brought into requisition to decry "not only
Greek and Latin studies," but liberal education of

----

[1] Ibid., p. 51. "Quas vocant proportionum inductiones . . . antiquitatem
superasse."

any kind.[1]   But, so far as England is concerned, this
opposition to the revival of letters, even on the score of
the danger likely to come either to faith or morals, was,
when all is said, slight, and through the influence of
More, Fisher, and the king himself, easily subdued.[2]
The main fact, moreover, cannot be gainsaid, namely,
that the chief ecclesiastics of the day, Wolsey, Warham,
Fisher, Tunstall, Langton, Stokesley, Fox, Selling,
Grocyn, Whitford, Linacre, Colet, Pace, William Latimer, and Thomas Lupset,[3] to name only the most

[1] More to the University of Oxford, in Knight's *Erasmus*, p. 31.

[2] Bishop Fisher's love and zeal for learning is notorious. He did all in his
power to assist in the foundation of schools of sound learning at Cambridge,
and especially to encourage the study of Greek. Richard Croke, the protégé
of Archbishop Warham and Bishop Fisher, after teaching Greek in 1516 at
Leipzig, was sent by Fisher in 1519 to Cambridge to urge the utility of Greek
studies at that university. In the *Orationes* he delivered there, after speaking
of the importance of Greek for all Biblical study, he says that Oxford had
taken up the work with great avidity, since "they have there as their patrons
besides the Cardinal (Wolsey), Canterbury (Warham), and Winchester, all
the other English bishops except the one who has always been your great stay
and helper, the Bishop of Rochester, and the Bishop of Ely." It was entirely
owing to Bishop Fisher's generosity, and at his special request, that Croke had
gone to Cambridge rather than to Oxford, whither his connection with Warham,
More, Linacre, and Grocyn would have led him, in order to carry on the work
begun by Erasmus.

[3] Thomas Lupset was educated by Colet, and learnt his Latin and Greek
under William Lilly, going afterwards to Oxford. There he made the acquaintance of Ludovico Vives, and at his exhortation went to Italy. He joined
Reginald Pole in his studies at Padua, and on his return, after acting as
Thomas Winter's tutor in Paris, he held a position first as a teacher and then in
Cardinal Wolsey's household. In his *Exhortation to Young Men*, persuading
them to a good life, "written at More, a place of my Lord Cardinal's," in 1529,
he gives a charming account of his relation with a former pupil. "It hap-
peneth," he says, "at this time (my heartily beloved Edmund) that I am in
such a place where I have no manner of books with me to pass the time after
my manner and custom. And though I had here with me plenty of books, yet
the place suffereth me not to spend in them any study. For you shall understand that I lie waiting on my Lord Cardinal, whose hours I must observe,
to be always at hand lest I be called when I am not bye, which would be
straight taken for a fault of great negligence. I am well satiated with the beholding of these gay hangings that garnish here every wall." As a relief he
turns to address his young friend Edmund. Probably Edmund doesn't under-

distinguished, were not only ardent humanists, but thorough and practical churchmen. Of the laymen, whether foreigners or Englishmen, whose names are associated with the renaissance of letters in this country, such as, for example, the distinguished scholar Ludovico Vives, the two Lillys, Sir Thomas More, John Clement,[1] and other members of More's family, there can be no shadow of doubt about their dispositions towards the ancient ecclesiastical régime. A Venetian traveller, in 1500, thus records what he had noticed as to the attitude of ecclesiastics generally towards learning:—"Few,

stand his affection, because he had always acted on the principle he has "been taught, that the master never hurteth his scholar more than when he utteıeth and sheweth by cherishing and cokering the love he beareth to his scholars." Edmund is now " of age, and also by the common board of houseling admitted into the number of men, and to be no more in the company of children," and so now he can make known his affection. "This mind had I to my friend Andrew Smith, whose son Christopher, your fellow, I ever took for my son. . . . If you will call to your mind all the frays between you and me, or me and Smith, you will find that they were all out of my care for ' your manners.' When I saw certain fantasies in you or him that jarred from true opinions, the which true opinions, above all learning, I would have masters ever teach their scholars. Wherefore, my good withipol, take heed of my lesson."

   [1] John Clement, a protégé of Sir Thomas More, was afterwards a doctor of renown not only in medicine but in languages. He had been a member of More's household, which Erasmus speaks of as "schola et gymnasium Christianæ religionis." He is named at the beginning of the *Eutopia*, and Sir Thomas, in writing to Erasmus,'says that Linacre declared that he had had no pupil at Oxford equal to him. John Clement translated several ancient Greek authors into Latin, amongst others many letters of St. Gregory Nazianzen and the Homilies of Nicephorus Callistus on the Saints of the Greek Calendar. Stapleton, in his *Tres Thomæ* (p. 250), says he had himself seen and examined with the originals these two voluminous translations at the request of John Clement himself. He had married Margaret, the ward of Sir Thomas More, and in the most difficult places of his translation he was helped by his wife, who, with the daughters of Sir Thomas, had been his disciple and knew Greek well. Mary Roper, More's grand-daughter, and the daughter of Margaret Roper, translated Eusebius's *History* from Greek into Latin, but it was never published, because Bishop Christopherson had been at work on a similar translation. On the change of religion in Elizabeth's reign, John Clement and his wife, with the Ropers, took refuge in the Low Countries. Paulus Jovius, in his *Descriptio Britanniæ*, p. 13, speaks of all three daughters of Sir Thomas More being celebrated for their knowledge of Latin.

excepting the clergy, are addicted to the study of letters, and this is the reason why any one who has any learning, though he may be a layman, is called a *clerk*. And yet they have great advantages for study, there being two general universities in the kingdom, Oxford and Cambridge, in which there are many colleges founded for the maintenance of poor scholars. And your magnificence (the Doge of Venice) lodged at one named Magdalen, in the University of Oxford, of which, as the founders having been prelates, so the scholars also are ecclesiastics."

It was in England, and almost entirely among the ecclesiastics of England, that Erasmus found his chief support. " This England of yours," he writes to Colet in 1498, " this England, dear to me on many accounts, is above all most beloved because it abounds in what to me is the best of all, men deeply learned in letters." [1] Nor did he change his opinion on a closer acquaintance. In 1517, to Richard Pace he wrote from Louvain in regret at leaving a country which he had come to regard as the best hope of the literary revival:— " Oh, how truly happy is your land of England, the seat and stronghold of the best studies and the highest virtue ! I congratulate you, my friend Pace, on having such a king, and I congratulate the king whose country is rendered illustrious by so many brilliant men of ability. On both scores I congratulate this England of yours, for though fortunate for many other reasons, on this score no other land can compete with it." [2]

When William Latimer said in 1518 that Bishop Fisher wished to study Greek for Biblical purposes, and that he thought of trying to get a master from Italy,

[1] Erasmi *Opera* (ed. 1703), Col. 40.   [2] Ibid., Ep. 241.

Erasmus, whilst applauding the bishop's intention as likely to encourage younger men to take up the study, told Latimer that such men were not easy to find in Italy. "If I may openly say my mind," he adds, "if I had Linacre, or Tunstall, for a master (for of yourself I say nothing), I would not wish for any Italian."[1]

Not to go into more lengthy details, there is, it must be admitted, abundant evidence to show that there was in the religious houses of England, no less than in the universities, a stirring of the waters, and a readiness to profit by the real advance made in education and scholarship. The name of Prior Charnock, the friend of Colet and Erasmus at Oxford, is known to all. But there are others with even greater claim than he to be considered leaders in the movement. There is distinct evidence of scholarship at Reading, at Ramsey, at Glastonbury, and elsewhere.[2] The last-named house, Glastonbury, was ruled by Abbot Bere, to whose criticism Erasmus desired to submit his translation of the New Testament from the Greek. Bere himself had passed some time, with distinction, in Italy, had been sent on more than one embassy by the king, and had been chosen by Henry VII. to invest the Duke of Urbino with the Order of the Garter, and to make the required oration on that occasion.[3] He had given other evidence also of the way the new spirit that had

---

[1] Ibid., Ep. 363.

[2] To take one example, Thomas Millyng, who as Bishop of Hereford died in 1492, had studied at Gloucester Hall, Oxford, as a monk of Westminster. During the old age of Abbot Fleet, of Westminster, he governed the monastery, and became its abbot in 1465. He was noted for his love of studies, and especially for his knowledge of Greek. This, says the writer of his brief life in the *National Biographical Dictionary*, was "a rare accomplishment for *monks* in those days." He might have added, and for any one else !

[3] Dennistoun, *Memorials of the Dukes of Urbino*, iii., pp. 415 *seqq.*

been enkindled in Italy had entered into his soul. It was through Abbot Bere's generosity that Richard Pace, whom Erasmus calls "the half of his soul," was enabled to pursue his studies in Italy.[1] Glastonbury was apparently a soil well prepared for the seed-time, for even in the days of Abbot Bere's predecessor, Abbot John Selwood, there is evidence to show that the religious were not altogether out of touch with the movement. The abbot himself presented one of the monks with a copy of John Free's translation from the Greek of *Synesius de laude Calvitii*. The volume is written by an Italian scribe, and contains in the introductory matter a letter to the translator from Omnibonus Leonicensis, dated at Vicenza in 1461, as well as a preface or letter by Free to John Tiptoft, Earl of Worcester.[2]

At St. Augustine's, Canterbury, also, we find, even amid the ruins of its desolation, traces of the same spirit which pervaded the neighbouring cloister of Christchurch. The antiquary Twyne declares that he had been intimately acquainted with the last abbot, whom he knew to have been deeply interested in the literary movement. He describes his friend as often manifesting in conversation his interest in and knowledge of the ancient classical authors. He says that

[1] Erasmus to Abbot Bere. *Opera*, Ep. 700.

[2] MS. Bodl. 80. It is the autograph copy of Free, *cf.* J. W. Williams, *Somerset Mediæval Libraries*, p. 87. It was Abbot Bere who, in 1506, presented John Claymond, the learned Greek scholar, to his first benefice of Westmonkton, in the county of Somerset. In 1516 Claymond became first President of Corpus Christi College, Oxford, often after signing himself, *Eucharistiæ servus*. Dr. Claymond procured for his college several Greek manuscripts which had belonged to Grocyn and Linacre, which are still possessed by it. At the end of MS. XXIII., which is a volume containing ninety homilies of St. John Chrysostom in Greek, is an inscription stating that this, and MS. XXIV., were copied in the years 1499 and 1500 by a Greek from Constantinople, named John Serbopylas, then living and working at Reading.

this monk was the personal friend of Ludovico Vives, and that he sent over the sea one of his subjects at St. Augustine's, John Digon, whom he subsequently made prior of his monastery, to the schools of Louvain, in order that he might profit by the teaching of that celebrated Spanish humanist.[1]

Beyond the foregoing particular instances of the real mind of English ecclesiastics towards the revival of studies, the official registers of the Universities of Oxford and Cambridge furnish us with evidence of the general attitude of approval adopted by the Church authorities in England. Unfortunately, gaps in the Register of Graduates at Oxford for the second half of the fifteenth century do not enable us to gauge the full extent of the revival, but there is sufficient evidence that the renaissance had taken place. In the eleven years, from A.D. 1449 to A.D. 1459, for which the entries exist, the average number of degrees taken by all students was 91.5. From 1506, when the registers begin again, to 1535, when the commencement of operations against the monastic houses seemed to indicate the advent of grave religious

---

[1] Ludovico Vives had been invited over to England by Cardinal Wolsey to lecture on rhetoric at Oxford. He lived at Corpus Christi College, then ruled by Dr. John Claymond, whom in his tract *De conscribendis Epistolis* he calls his "father." The fame of this Spanish master of eloquence drew crowds to his lectures at the university, and amongst the audience Henry and Queen Katherine might sometimes be seen. For a time he acted also as tutor to the Princess Mary, and dedicated several works to the queen, to whose generosity he says he owed much. He took her side in the " divorce " question, and was thrown into prison for some weeks for expressing his views on the matter. Fisher, More, and Tunstall were this constant friends in England, and of Margaret Roper he writes, "from the time I first made her acquaintance I have loved her as a sister." Among his pupils at Louvain, besides the above-named Canterbury monk, John Digon, he mentions with great affection Nicholas Wotton, whom the antiquary Twyne speaks of as returning to England with Digon and Jerome Ruffaldus, who calls Vives his " Jonathan," and who subsequently became abbot of St. Vaast, Arras.

changes, the average number of yearly degrees granted was 127. In 1506 the number had risen to 216, and only in very few of the subsequent years had the average fallen below 100. From 108 in 1535, the number of graduates fell in 1536 to only 44; and the average for the subsequent years of the reign of Henry VIII. was less than 57. From 1548 to 1553, that is, during the reign of Edward VI., the average of graduates was barely 33, but it rose again, whilst Mary was on the throne, to 70.

If the same test be applied to the religious Orders, it will be found that they likewise equally profited by the new spirit. During the period from 1449 to 1459 the Benedictine Order had a yearly average of 4 graduates at Oxford, the other religious bodies taken together having 5. In the second period of 1506–1539 the Benedictine graduates number 200, and (allowing for gaps in the register) the Order had thus a yearly average of 6.75, the average of the other Orders during the same period being 5.2. If, moreover, the number of the religious who took degrees be compared with that of the secular students, it will be found that the former seem to have more than held their own. During the time from 1449 to 1459 the members of the regular Orders were to the rest in the proportion of 1 to 9.5. In the period of the thirty years immediately preceding the general dissolution it was as 1 to 9. Interest in learning, too, was apparently kept up among the religious Orders to the last. Even with their cloisters falling on all sides round about them, in the last hour of their corporate existence, that is in the year 1538–39, some 14 Benedictines took their degrees at Oxford.

In regard to Cambridge, a few notes taken from the

interesting preface to a recent " History of Gonville and Caius College " will suffice to show that the monks did not neglect the advantages offered to them in the sister university.[1] Gonville Hall, as the college was then called, was by the statutes of Bishop Bateman closely connected with the Benedictine Cathedral Priory of Norwich. Between 1500 and 1523 the early bursars' accounts give a list of " pensioners," and these " largely consisted of monks sent hither from their respective monasteries for the purpose of study." These " pensioners paid for their rooms and their commons, and shared their meals with the fellows. All the greater monasteries in East Anglia, such as the Benedictine Priory at Norwich, the magnificent foundation of Bury, and (as a large landowner in Norfolk) the Cluniac House at Lewes, seem generally to have had several of their younger members in training at our college. To these must be added the Augustinian Priory of Westacre, which was mainly frequented (as Dr. Jessopp tells us) by the sons of the Norfolk gentry." [2]

The Visitations of the Norwich Diocese (1492–1532), edited by Dr. Jessopp for the Camden Society, contain many references to the monastic students at the university. In one house, for example, in 1520, the numbers are short, because " there were three in the university." In another case, when a religious house was too poor to provide the necessary money to support a student during his college career, it was found by friends of the monastery, until a few years later, when, on the funds improving, the house was able to meet the expenses. This same house, the Priory of Butley,

---

[1] J. Venn, *Gonville and Caius College* (1349–1897), Vol. I.
[2] Ibid., p. xvi.

" had a special arrangement with the authorities of Gonville Hall for the reservation of a suitable room for their young monks." One object of sending members of a monastery to undergo the training of a university course " was to qualify for teaching the novices at their own house " ; for after they have graduated and returned to their monastery, we not infrequently find them described as " *idoneus preceptor pro confratribus* " ; " *idoneus pro noviciis et junioribus*," &c. Moreover, the possession of a degree on the part of a religious, as an examination of the lists will show, often in after life meant some position of trust or high office in the monastery of the graduate.

Nor was the training then received any light matter of form ; it meant long years of study, and the possession of a degree was, too, a public testimony to a certain proficiency in the science of teaching. Thus, for example, George Mace, a canon of Westacre, who became a pensioner at Gonville Hall in 1508, studied arts for five years and canon law for four years at the university, and continued the latter study for eight years in his monastery.[1] William Hadley, a religious of the same house, had spent eleven years in the study of arts and theology ;[2] and Richard Brygott, who took his B.D. in 1520, and who subsequently became Prior of Westacre, had studied two years and a half in his monastery, two years in Paris, and seven in Cambridge.[3]

" With the Reformation, of course, all this came to an end," writes Mr. Venn, and we can well understand that this sudden stoppage of what, in the aggre-

[1] Ibid., p. 18. [2] Ibid., p. 23.
[3] Ibid., p. 21.

gate, was a considerable source of supply to the university, was seriously felt. On the old system, as we have seen, the promising students were selected by their monasteries, and supported in college at the expense of the house. As the author of the interesting account of Durham Priory says: " If the master did see that any of them (the novices) were apt to learning, and did apply his book and had a pregnant wit withal, then the master did let the prior have intelligence. Then, straightway after he was sent to Oxford to school, and there did learn to study divinity." [1]

Moreover, it should be remembered that it was by means of the assistance received from the monastic and conventual houses that a very large number of students were enabled to receive their education at the universities at all. The episcopal registers testify to this useful function of the old religious corporations. The serious diminution in the number of candidates for ordination, and the no less lamentable depletion of the national universities, consequent upon the dissolution of these bodies, attest what had previously been done by them for the education of the pastoral clergy. This may be admitted without any implied approval of the monastic system as it existed. The fact will be patent to all who will examine into the available evidence ; and the serious diminution in the number of clergy must be taken as part of the price paid by the nation for securing the triumph of the Reformation principles. The state of Oxford during, say, the reign of Edward VI., is attested by the degree lists. In the year 1547 and in the year 1550 no student at all graduated, and the historian of

[1] Ibid., p. xviii.

the university has described the lamentable state to which the schools were reduced. If additional testimony be needed, it may be found in a sermon of Roger Edgworth, preached in Queen Mary's reign. Speaking of works of piety and pity, much needed in those days, the speaker advocates charity to the poor students at the two national universities. " Very pity," he says, " moves me to exhort you to mercy and pity on the poor students in the universities of Oxford and Cambridge. They were never so few in number, and yet those that are left are ready to run abroad into the world and give up their study for very need. Iniquity is so abundant that charity is all cold. A man would have pity did he but hear the lamentable complaints that I heard lately when amongst them. Would to God I were able to relieve them. This much I am sure of : in my opinion you cannot bestow your charity better." He then goes on to instance his own case as an example of what used to be done in Catholic times to help the student in his education. " My parents sent me to school in my youth, and my good lord William Smith, sometime Bishop of Lincoln, (was) my bringer up and ' exhibitour,' first at Banbury in the Grammar School with Master John Stanbridge, and then at Oxford till I was a Master of Arts and able to help myself."

He pleads earnestly that some of his hearers may be inspired to help the students in the distress to which they are now reduced, and so help to restore learning to the position from which it had fallen in late years.[1]

Of the lamentable decay of scholarship as such, the inevitable, and perhaps necessary, consequence of the

[1] *Sermons* (1557), f. 54.

religious controversies which occupied men's minds and thoughts to the exclusion of all else, it is, of course, not the place here to dwell upon.   All that it is necessary to do is to point out that the admitted decay and decline argues a previous period of greater life and vigour.   Even as early as 1545 the Cambridge scholars petitioned the king for an extension of privileges, as they feared the total destruction of learning.   To endeavour to save Oxford, it was ordered that every clergyman, having a benefice to the amount of £100, should out of his living find at least one scholar at the university. Bishop Latimer, in Edward VI.'s reign, looked back with regret to past times "when they helped the scholars," for since then "almost no man helpeth to maintain them."   "Truly," he said, "it is a pitiful thing to see the schools so neglected.   Schools are not maintained, scholars have not exhibitions. . . . Very few there be that help poor scholars. . . . It would pity a man's heart to hear what I hear of the state of Cambridge ; what it is in Oxford I cannot tell. . . . I think there be at this day (A.D. 1550) ten thousand students less than there were within these twenty years."   In the year 1550, it will be remembered, there was apparently no degree of any kind taken at the university of Oxford.

This fact appears patent on this page of history ; that from the time when minds began to exercise themselves on the thorny subjects which grew up round about the "great divorce" question, the bright promises of the revival of learning, which Erasmus had seen in England, faded away.   Greek, it has been said, may conveniently stand for learning generally ; and Greek studies apparently disappeared in the religious turmoils which distracted England. With Mary's accession, some attempt was made to recover lost ground, or at least re-enkindle the lamp of learning. When Sir Thomas Pope refounded Durham College at Oxford under the name of Trinity, he was urged by Cardinal Pole, to whom he submitted the draft of his statutes, " to order Greek to be more taught there than I have provided. This purpose," he says, " I like well, but I fear the times will not bear it now. I remember when I was a young scholar at Eton, the Greek tongue was growing apace, the study of which is now of late much decayed." [1]

The wholesale destruction of the great libraries in England is an indirect indication of the new spirit which rose at this time, and which helped for a time to put an end to the renaissance of letters. When Mary came to the throne, and quieter times made the scheme possible, it was seriously proposed to do something to preserve the remnant of ancient and learned works that might be left in England after the wholesale destruction of the preceding years. The celebrated Dr. Dee drew up a supplication to the queen, stating that "among the many most lamentable displeasures that have of late happened in this realm, through the subverting of religious houses and the dissolution of other assemblies of godly and learned men, it has been, and among all learned students shall for ever be, judged not the least calamity, the spoil and destruction of so many and so notable libraries wherein lay the treasure of all antiquity, and the everlasting seeds of continual excellency in learning within this realm. But although in those days many a pre-

---

[1] A. Chalmers, *History of the Colleges, &c. of Oxford*, ii. p. 351.

cious jewel and ancient monument did utterly perish (as at Canterbury that wonderful work of the sage and eloquent Cicero, *De Republica*, and in many other places the like), yet if in time great and speedy diligence be showed, the remnants of such incredible a store, as well of writers theological as in all the other liberal sciences, might yet be saved and recovered, which now in your Grace's realm being dispersed and scattered, yea, and many of them in unlearned men's hands, still even yet (in this time of reconciliation) daily perish ; and perchance are purposely by some envious person enclosed in walls or buried in the ground."

The scheme which accompanied this letter in 1556 was for the formation of a national library, into which were to be gathered the original manuscripts still left in England, which could be purchased or otherwise obtained, or at least a copy of such as were in private hands, and which the owners would not part with. Beyond this, John Dee proposes that copies of the best manuscripts in Europe should be secured. He mentions specially the libraries of the Vatican, and of St. Mark's, Venice, those at Florence, Bologna, and Vienna, and offers to go himself, if his expenses are paid, to secure the transcripts.[1] The plan, however, came to nothing, and with Mary's death, the nation was once more occupied in the religious controversies, which again interfered with any real advance in scholarship.

One other point must not be overlooked. Before the rise of the religious dissensions caused England to isolate herself from the rest of the Catholic world, English students were to be found studying in considerable numbers at the great centres of learning in Europe.

---

[1] Hearne, *John of Glastonbury*, ii. p. 490 ; from MS. Cott. Vitellius c. vii.

An immediate result of the change was to put a stop to this, which had served to keep the country in touch with the best work being done on the Continent, and the result of which had been seen in the able English scholars produced by that means on the eve of the Reformation.

Taking a broad survey of the whole movement for the revival of letters in England, it would appear then certain that whether we regard its origin, or the forces which contributed to support it, or the men chiefly concerned in it, it must be confessed that to the Church and churchmen the country was indebted for the successes achieved.   What put a stop to the humanist movement here, as it certainly did in Germany, was the rise of the religious difficulties, which, under the name of the " New Learning," was opposed by those most conspicuous for their championship of true learning, scholarship, and education.

CHAPTER III

THE TWO JURISDICTIONS

THE Reformation found men still occupied with questions as to the limits of ecclesiastical and lay jurisdiction, which had troubled their minds at various periods during the previous centuries. It is impossible to read very deeply into the literature of the period without seeing that, while on the one hand, all the fundamental principles of the spiritual jurisdiction of the Church were fully and freely recognised by all; on the other, a number of questions, mainly in the broad borderland of debatable ground between the two, were constantly being discussed, and not infrequently gave cause for disagreements and misunderstandings. As in the history of earlier times, so in the sixteenth century ecclesiastics clung, perhaps not unnaturally, to what they regarded as their strict rights, and looked on resistance to encroachment as a sacred duty. Laymen on the other part, even when their absolute loyalty to the Church was undoubted, were found in the ranks of those who claimed for the State power to decide in matters not strictly pertaining to the spiritual prerogatives, but which chiefly by custom had come to be regarded as belonging to ecclesiastical domain. It is the more important that attention should be directed in a special manner to these questions, inasmuch as it will be found, speaking broadly, that the ultimate success or ill-success of the strictly doctrinal changes raised in the sixteenth century was determined by the issue of the discussions raised on the question of mixed jurisdiction. This may not seem very philosophical, but in the event it is proved to be roughly correct. The reason is not very far to seek. In great measure at least, questions of money and property, even of national interest and prosperity, were intimately concerned in the matter in dispute. They touched the people's pocket ; and whether rightly or wrongly, those who found the money wished to have a say in its disposal. One thing cannot fail to strike an inquirer into the literature of this period : the very small number of people who were enthusiasts in the doctrinal matters with which the more ardent reformers occupied themselves.

We are not here concerned with another and more delicate question as to the papal prerogatives exercised in England. For clearness' sake in estimating the forces which made for change on the eve of the Reformation, this subject must be examined in connection with the whole attitude of England to Rome and the Pope in the sixteenth century. It must, consequently, be understood that in trying here to illustrate the attitude of men's minds at this period to these important and practical questions, a further point as to the claims of the Roman Pontiffs in regard to some or all of them has yet to be considered. Even in examining the questions at issue between the authorities—lay and ecclesiastical—in the country, the present purpose is to record rather than to criticise, to set forth the attitude of mind as it appears in the literature of the period, rather than to weigh the reasons and judge between the contending parties.

The lawyer, Christopher Saint-German, is a contemporary writer to whom we naturally turn for information upon the points at issue. He, of course,
takes the layman's side as to the right of the State
to interfere in all, or in most, questions which arise as
to the dues of clerics, and other temporalities, such as
tithes, &c., which are attached to the spiritual functions
of the clergy. Moreover, beyond claiming the right
for the State so to interfere in the regulation of all
temporalities and kindred matters, Saint-German also
held that in some things in which custom had given
sanction to the then practice, it would be for the good
of the State that it should do so. In his *Dyalogue between
a Student of Law and a Doctor of Divinity*,[1] his views are
put clearly ; whilst the Doctor states, though somewhat
lamely perhaps, the position of the clergy.

To take the example of " mortuaries," upon which
the Parliament had already legislated to the dismay
of some of the ecclesiastical party, who, as it appears,
on the plea that the law was unjust and beyond the
competence of the State authority, tried in various
ways to evade the provisions of the Act, which was
intended to relieve the laity of exactions that, as
they very generally believed, had grown into an abuse.
Christopher Saint-German holds that Parliament was
quite within its rights. The State could, and on occasion should, legislate as to dues payable to the clergy,
and settle whether ecclesiastics, who claim articles in
kind, or sums of money by prescriptive right, ought

---

[1] Saint-German was born 1460. He was employed by Thomas Cromwell
on some business of the State, and died in 1540. The *Dyalogue* was printed
apparently first in Latin, but subsequently in English. It consisted ·of three
parts (1) published by Robert Wyer, (2) by Peter Treveris, 1531, and (3) by
Thomas Berthalet, also in 1531.

in fact to be allowed them. There is, he admits, a difficulty ; he does not think that it would be competent for the State to prohibit specific gifts to God's service, or to say that only "so many tapers shall be used at a funeral," or that only so many priests may be bidden to the burial, or that only so much may be given in alms. In matters of this kind he does not think the State has jurisdiction to interfere. " But it has," he says, "the plain right to make a law, that there shall not be given above so many black gowns, or that there shall be no herald of arms " present, unless it is the funeral of one " of such a degree," or that " no black cloths should be hung in the streets from the house where the person died, to the church, as is used in many cities and good towns, or the prohibition of such other things as are but worldly pomps, and are rather consolations to the friends that are alive, than any relief to the departed soul." In these and such like things, he says : " I think the Parliament has authority to pass laws, so as to protect the executors of wills, and relieve them from the necessity of spending so much of the inheritance of the deceased man's heirs." [1]

In like manner the lawyer holds that in all strictly temporal matters, whatever privilege and exemption the State may allow and has allowed the clergy, it still possesses the radical power to legislate where and when it sees fit. It does not in fact by lapse of time lose the ordinary authority it possesses over all subjects of the realm in these matters. Thus, for example, he holds that the State can and should prohibit all lands in mortmain passing to the Church ;

---

[1] *Dyalogue, ut sup.*, 3rd part, f. 2.

and that, should it appear to be a matter of public policy, Parliament might prohibit and indeed break the appropriations of benefices already made to monasteries, cathedrals, and colleges, and order that they should return to their original purposes. "The advowson," he says, "is a temporal inheritance, and as such is under the Parliament to order it as it sees cause." This principle, he points out, had been practically admitted when the Parliament, in the fourth year of Henry IV., cancelled all appropriations of vicarages which had been made from the beginning of Richard II.'s reign. It is indeed "good," he adds, "that the authority of the Parliament in this should be known, and that it should cause them to observe such statutes as are already made, and to distribute some part of the fruits (of the benefices) among poor parishioners according to the statute of the twentieth year of King Richard II."

In the same way, and for similar reasons, Saint-German claims that the State has full power to determine questions of "Sanctuary," and to legislate as to "benefit of clergy." Such matters were, he contends, only customs of the realm, and in no sense any point of purely spiritual prerogative. Like every other custom of the realm, these were subject to revision by the supreme secular authority. "The Pope by himself," he adds, "cannot make any Sanctuary in this realm." This question of "Sanctuary" rights was continually causing difficulties between the lay and the ecclesiastical authorities. To the legal mind the custom was certainly dangerous to the well-being of the State, and made the administration of justice unnecessarily complicated, especially when ecclesiastics pleaded their privileges, and strongly resisted any attempt on the part of legal officials to ignore them.   Cases were by no means infrequent in the courts in the reigns of Henry VII. and Henry VIII., which caused more or less friction between the upholders of the two views.[1]   To illustrate the state of conflict on this, in itself a very minor matter, a trial which took place in London in the year 1519 is here given in some detail.   One John Savage in that year was charged with murder.   At the time of his arrest he was living in St. John Street (Clerkenwell), and when brought to trial pleaded that he had been wrongfully arrested in a place of Sanctuary belonging to the Priory of St. John of Jerusalem.   To justify his contention and obtain his liberty, he called on the Prior of the Knights of St. John to maintain his rights and privileges, and vindicate this claim of Sanctuary.   The prior appeared and produced the grant of Pope Urban III., made by Bull dated in 1213, which had been ratified by King Henry III.   He also cited cases in which he alleged that in the reign of the late King Henry VII. felons, who had been seized within the precincts, had been restored to Sanctuary, and he therefore argued that this case was an infringement of the rights of his priory.

---

[1] One of the first Acts of King Henry VII. on his accession, was to obtain from the Pope a Bull agreeing to some changes in the Sanctuary customs. Prior Selling of Canterbury was despatched as King's Orator to Rome with others to Pope Innocent VIII. in 1487, and brought back the Pope's approval of three points in which the king proposed to change these laws. *First*, that if any person in Sanctuary went out at night and committed mischief and trespass, and then got back again, he should forfeit his privilege of Sanctuary. *Secondly*, that though the person of a debtor might be protected in Sanctuary, yet his goods out of the precincts were not so protected from his creditors. *Thirdly*, that where a person took Sanctuary for treason, the king might appoint him keepers within the Sanctuary.

Savage also declared that he was in St. John Street within the precincts of the priory " pur amendement de son vie, durant son vie," when on the 8th of June an officer, William Rotte, and others took him by force out of the place, and carried him away to the Tower. He consequently claimed to be restored to the Sanctuary from which he had been abducted.   Chief-Justice Fineux, before whom the prisoner had been brought, asked him whether he wished to " jeopardy " his case upon his plea of Sanctuary, and, upon consultation, John Savage replied in the negative, saying that he wished rather to throw himself upon the king's mercy. Fineux on this, said : " In this you are wise, for the privileges of St. John's will not aid you in the form in which you have pleaded it.   In reality it has no greater privilege of Sanctuary than every parish church in the kingdom ; that is, it has privileges for forty days and no more, and in this it partakes merely of the common law of the kingdom, and has no special privilege beyond this."

Further, Fineux pointed out that even had St. John's possessed the Sanctuary the prior claimed, this right did not extend to the fields, &c., but in the opinion of all the judges of the land, to which all the bishops and clergy had assented, the bounds of any Sanctuary were the church, cloister, and cemetery.   Most certain it was that the *ambitus* did not extend to gardens, barns, and stables, and in his (Fineux's) opinion, not even to the pantry and buttery.   He quotes cases in support of his opinion.   In one instance a certain William Spencer claimed the privilege of Sanctuary when in an orchard of the Grey Friars at Coventry.   In spite of the assertion of the guardian that the Pope had extended the privilege to the whole enclosure, of which the place the friars had to recreate themselves in was certainly a portion, the plea was disallowed, and William Spencer was hanged.

In regard to the privilege of the forty days, Fineux declared that it was so obviously against the common good and in derogation of justice, that in his opinion it should not be suffered to continue, and he quoted cases where it had been set aside. In several cases where Papal privileges had been asserted, the judges had held " quant à les Bulles du pape, le pape sans le Roy ne ad power de fayre sanctuarie." In other words, Fineux rejected the plea of the murderer Savage. But the case did not stop here, both the prior and Savage, as we should say, " appealed," and the matter was heard in the presence of Cardinal Wolsey, Fineux, Brudnell, and several members of the inner Star Chamber. Dr. Potkyn, counsel for the Prior of St. John, pleaded the " knowledge and allowance of the king " to prove the privilege. No decision was arrived at, and a further sitting of the Star Chamber was held on November 11, 1520, in the presence of the king, the cardinal, all the judges, and divers bishops and canonists, as well as the Prior of St. John and the Abbot of Westminster. Before the assembly many examples of difficulties in the past were adduced by the judges. These difficulties they declared increased so as to endanger the peace and law of the country, by reason of the Sanctuaries of Westminster and St. John's. To effect a remedy was the chief reason of the royal presence at the meeting. After long discussion it was declared that as St. John's Sanctuary was made, as it had been shown, by Papal Bull, it was consequently void even if confirmed by the king's patent, and hence that the priory had no privilege at all except the common one of forty days. The judges and all the canonists were quite clear that the Pope's right to make a Sanctuary had never been allowed in England, and that every such privilege must come from the king. On the other hand, the bishops present and all the clergy were equally satisfied that the general forty days' privilege belonged by right to every parish church. The Abbot of Westminster then proved by the production of charters and other indubitable evidence that the Sanctuary of Westminster had its origin in the grants of various kings, and had only been blessed by the Pope.

Fineux pointed out that Sanctuary grants had always been made to monasteries and churches "to the laud and honour of God," and that it was not certainly likely to redound to God's honour when men could commit murder and felony, and trust to get into the safe precinct of some Sanctuary ; neither did he believe that to have bad houses in Sanctuaries, and such like abuses, was either to the praise of God or for the welfare of the kingdom. Further, that as regards Westminster, the abbot had abused his privileges as to the *ambitus* or precincts which in law must be understood in the restricted sense. The cardinal admitted that there had been abuses, and a Commission was proposed to determine the reasonable bounds. Bishop Voysey, of Exeter, suggested that if a Sanctuary man committed murder or felony outside, with the hope of getting back again, the privilege of shelter should be forfeited ; but the majority were against this restriction. On the whole, however, it was determined that for the good of the State the uses of these Sanctuaries should be curtailed, and that none should be allowed in law but such as could show a grant of the privilege from the crown.[1]

In the opinion of many, of whom Saint-German was the spokesman, to go to another matter, Parliament might assign " all the trees and grass in churchyards either to the parson, to the vicar, or to the parish," as it thought fit ; for although the ground was hallowed, the proceeds, such as "trees and grass, are mere temporals, and as such must be regulated by the power of the State."

Moreover, according to the same view, whilst it would be outside the province of the secular law to determine the cut of a priest's cassock or the shape of his tonsure, it could clearly determine that no priest should wear cloth made out of the country, or costing above a certain price ; and it might fix the amount of salary to be paid to a chaplain or curate.[2]

There were circumstances, too, under which, in the opinion of Saint-German, Parliament not only could interfere to legislate about clerical duties, but would be bound to do so. At the time when he was writing, the eve of the Reformation, many things seemed to point to this necessity for State interference. There were signs of wide-spread religious differences in the world. " Why then," he asks, "may not the king and his Parliament, as well to strengthen the faith and give health to the souls of many of his subjects, as to save his realm being noted for heresy, seek for the reason of the division now in the realm by diversity of sects and opinions ? . . . They shall have great reward before God that set their hands to prevent the

[1] Robert Keilway, *Relationes quorundam casuum*, f. 188, *seqq.*
[2] *Dyalogue, ut sup.*, f. 12.

great danger to many souls of men as well spiritual as temporal if this division continue long. And as far as I have heard, all the articles that are misliked (are aimed) either against the worldly honour, worldly power, or worldly riches of spiritual men. To express these articles I hold it not expedient, and indeed if what some have reported be true, many of them be so far against the truth that no Christian man would hold them to be true, and they that do so do it for some other consideration." [1]

As an example, our author takes the question of Purgatory, which he believes is attacked because men want to free themselves from the money offerings which belief in the doctrine necessitates. And indeed, " if it were ordained by law," he continues, " that every curate at the death of any of their parishioners should be bound to say publicly for their souls *Placebo, Dirige* and mass, without taking anything for (the service): and further that at a certain time, to be assigned by Parliament, as say, once a month, or as it shall be thought convenient, they shall do the same and pray for the souls of their parishioners and for all Christian souls and for the king and all the realm : and also that religious houses do in like manner, I fancy in a short time there would be few to say there was no purgatory." [2]

In some matters Saint-German considered that the State might reasonably interfere in regard to the religious life. The State, he thinks, would have no right whatever to prohibit religious vows altogether ; but it would be competent for the secular authority to lay down conditions to prevent abuses and generally pro-

[1] *Dyalogue*, f. 23   [2] Ibid.

tect society where such protection was needed. "It would be good," for example, he writes, "to make a law that no religious house should receive any child below a certain age into the habit, and that he should not be moved from the place into which he had been received without the knowledge and assent of friends." This would not be to prohibit religious life, which would not be a just law, but only the laying down of conditions. In the fourth year of Henry IV. the four Orders of Friars had such a law made for them ; "when the four Provincials of the said four Orders were sworn by laying their hands upon their breasts in open Parliament to observe the said statute." [1]

In the same way the State may, Saint-German thinks, lay down the conditions for matrimony, so long as there was no "interference with the sacrament of marriage." Also, "as I suppose," he says, "the Parliament may well enact that every man that makes profit of any offerings (coming) by recourse of pilgrims shall be bound under a certain penalty not only to set up certain tables to instruct the people how they shall worship the saints, but also cause certain sermons to be yearly preached there to instruct the people, so that through ignorance they do not rather displease than please the saints." [2]

The State "may also prohibit any miracle being noised abroad on such slight evidence as they have been in some places in times past ; and that they shall not be set up as miracles, under a certain penalty, nor reported as miracles by any one till they have been proved such in such a manner as shall be appointed by Parliament. And it is not unlikely that many per-

[1] Ibid., f. 23.   [2] Ibid., f. 21.

sons grudge more at the abuse of pilgrimages than at the pilgrimages themselves." Parliament, he points out, has from time to time vindicated its right to act in matters such as these. For example: "To the strengthening of the faith it has enacted that no man shall presume to preach without leave of his diocesan except certain persons exempted in the statute" (2 Henry IV.).[1]

There are, Saint-German notes, many cases where it is by no means clear whether they are strictly belonging to spiritual jurisdiction or not. Could the law, for example, prohibit a bishop from ordaining any candidate to Holy Orders who was not sufficiently learned? Could the law which exempted priests from serving on any inquest or jury be abrogated? These, and such like matters in the borderland, are debatable questions; but Saint-German makes it clear that, according to his view, it is a mistake for clerics to claim more exemptions from the common law than is absolutely necessary. That there must be every protection for their purely spiritual functions, he fully and cordially admits; but when all this is allowed, in his opinion, it is a grave mistake for the clergy, even from their point of view, to try and stretch their immunities and exemptions beyond the required limit. The less the clergy were made a "caste," and the more they fell in with the nation at large, the better it would be for all parties in the State.

On the question of tithe, Saint-German took the laymen's view. To the ecclesiastics of the period tithes were spiritual matters, and all questions arising out of them should be settled by archbishop or bishop in

[1] Ibid., f. 21.

spiritual courts. The lawyer, on the other hand, maintained that though given to secure spiritual services, in themselves tithes were temporal, and therefore should fall under the administration of the State. Who, for example, was to determine what was payable on new land, and to whom ; say on land recovered from the sea ? In the first place, according to the lawyer, it should be the owner of the soil who should apportion the payment, and failing him, the Parliament, and not the spirituality.

In another work[1] Saint-German puts his view more clearly. A tithe that comes irregularly, say once in ten or twenty years, cannot be considered necessary for the support of the clergy. That people were bound to contribute to the just and reasonable maintenance of those who serve the altar did not admit of doubt, but, he holds, a question arises as to the justice of the amount in individual cases. " Though the people be bound by the law of reason, and also the law of God, to find their spiritual ministers a reasonable portion of goods to live upon, yet that they shall pay precisely the tenth part to their spiritual ministers in the name of that portion is but the law of man." If the tithe did not at any time suffice, " the people would be bound to give more" in order to fulfil their Christian duty. Some authority must determine, and in his opinion as a lawyer and a layman, the only authority competent to deal with the matter, so far as the payment of money was concerned, was the State ; and consequently Parliament might, and at times ought, to legislate about the payment of tithes.[2]

---

[1] *A treatyse concerning the power of the clergie and the laws of the realme.* London, J. Godfray.   [2] *A treatyse,* &c., *ut supra,* cap. 4.

In a second *Treatise concerning the power of the clergy and the laws of the realm*, Saint-German returns to this subject of the relation between the two jurisdictions. This book, however, was published after Henry VIII. had received his parliamentary title of Supreme Head of the Church, and by that time the author's views had naturally become somewhat more advanced on the side of State power. In regard to the king's " Headship," he declares that in reality it is nothing new, but if properly understood would be recognised as implied in the kingly power, and as having nothing whatever to do with the spiritual prerogatives as such. He has been speaking of the writ, *de excommunicato capiendo*, by which the State had been accustomed to seize the person of one who had been excommunicated by the Church for the purpose of punishment by the secular arm, and he argues that if the Parliament were to abrogate the law, such a change would in no sense be a derogation of the rights of the Church. Put briefly, the principle upon which he bases this opinion is one which was made to apply to many other cases besides this special one. It is this : that for a spiritual offence no one ought in justice to be made to suffer in the temporal order.[1] Whilst insisting on this, moreover, the lawyer maintained that there were many things which had come to be regarded as spiritual, which were, in reality, temporal, and that it would be better that these should be altogether transferred to the secular arm of the State. Such, for example, were, in his opinion, the proving and administration of wills, the citation and consideration of cases of slander and libel and other matters of this nature. " And there

---

[1] *A treatyse*, &c., *ut supra*, cap. xii.

is no doubt," he says, " but that the Parliament may with a cause take that power from them (*i.e.* the clergy), and might likewise have done so before it was recognised by the Parliament and the clergy that the king was Head of the Church of England ; for he was so before the recognition was made, just as all other Christian princes are in their own realms over all their subjects, spiritual and temporal." [1]

Moreover, as regards this, " it lieth in princes to appease all variances and unquietness that shall arise among the people, by whatsoever occasion it rise, spiritual or temporal. And the king's grace has now no new authority in that he is confessed by the clergy and authorised by Parliament to be the Head of the Church of England. For it is only a declaration of his first power committed by God to kingly and regal authority and no new grant. Further, that, for all the power that he has as Head of the Church, he has yet no authority to minister any sacraments, nor to do any other spiritual thing whereof our Lord gave power to His apostles and disciples only. . . . And there is no doubt that such power as the clergy have by the immediate grant of Christ, neither the king nor his Parliament can take from them, although they may order the manner of the doing." [2]

The question whether for grave offences the clergy could be tried by the king's judges was one which had long raised bitter feeling on the one side and the other. In 1512, Parliament had done something to vindicate the power of the secular arm by passing a law practically confining the immunity of the clergy to those in sacred orders. It ordained " that all persons hereafter

---

[1] *A treatyse*, &c., *ut supra*, cap. xii.   [2] Ibid., cap. xiii.

committing murder or felony, &c., should not be admitted to the benefit of clergy." This act led to a great
dispute in the next Parliament, held in 1515. The
clergy as a body resented the statute as an infringement
upon their rights and privileges, and the Abbot of
Winchcombe preached at St. Paul's Cross to this effect,
declaring that the Lords Spiritual who had assented
to the measure had incurred ecclesiastical censures. He
argued that all clerks were in Holy Orders, and that they
were consequently not amenable to the secular tribunals.

The king, at the request of many of the Temporal
Lords and several of the Commons, ordered the case to
be argued at a meeting held at Blackfriars at which
the judges were present. At this debate, Dr. Henry
Standish, a Friar Minor, defended the action of Parliament, and maintained that it was a matter of public
policy that clerks guilty of such offences should be
tried by the ordinary process of law. In reply to
the assertion that there was a decree or canon for-
bidding it, and that all Christians were bound by the
canons under pain of mortal sin, Standish said : " God
forbid ; for there is a decree that all bishops should
be resident at their cathedrals upon every festival day,
and yet we see the greater part of the English bishops
practise the contrary." Moreover, he maintained that
the right of exemption of clerks from secular jurisdiction had never been allowed in England. The bishops
were unanimously against the position of Standish,
and there can be little doubt that they had put forward
the Abbot of Winchcombe to be their spokesman at
St. Paul's Cross. Later on, Standish was charged
before Convocation with holding tenets derogatory to
the privileges and jurisdiction of ecclesiastics. He

claimed the protection of the king, and the Temporal Lords and judges urged the king at all costs to maintain his right of royal jurisdiction in the matters at issue.

Again a meeting of judges, certain members of Parliament, and the king's council, spiritual and temporal, were assembled to deliberate on the matter at the Blackfriars. Dr. Standish was supposed to have said that the lesser Orders were not Holy, and that the exemption of clerks was not *de jure divino*. These opinions he practically admitted, saying with regard to the first that there was a great difference between the greater Orders and the lesser ; and in regard to the second, " that the summoning of clerks before temporal judges implied no repugnance to the positive law of God." He further partially admitted saying that "the study of canon law ought to be laid aside, because being but ministerial to divinity it taught people to despise that nobler science." The judges decided generally against the contention of the clergy, and they, with other lords, met the king at Baynard's Castle to tender their advice on the matter. Here Wolsey, kneeling before the king, declared " that he believed none of the clergy had any intention to disoblige the prerogative royal, that for his part he owed all his promotion to his Highness' favour, and therefore would never assent to anything that should lessen the rights of the Crown." But " that this business of conventing clerks before temporal judges was, in the opinion of the clergy, directly contrary to the laws of God and the liberties of Holy Church, and that both himself and the rest of the prelates were bound by their oath to maintain this exemption. For this reason he entreated the king, in the name of the clergy, to refer the matter for decision to the Pope." Archbishop Warham added that in old times some of the fathers of the Church had opposed the matter so far as to suffer martyrdom in the quarrel. On the other hand, Judge Fineux pointed out that spiritual judges had no right by any statute to judge any clerk for felony, and for this reason many churchmen had admitted the competence of the secular courts for this purpose.

The king finally replied on the whole case. " By the Providence of God," he said, " we are King of England, in which realm our predecessors have never owned a superior, and I would have you (the clergy) take notice that we are resolved to maintain the rights of our crown and temporal jurisdiction in as ample manner as any of our progenitors." In conclusion, the Archbishop of Canterbury petitioned the king in the name of the clergy for the matter to rest till such time as they could lay the case before the See of Rome for advice, promising that if the non-exemption of clerks was declared not to be against the law of God, they would willingly conform to the usage of the country.

On this whole question, Saint-German maintained that the clergy had been granted exemption from the civil law not as a right but as a favour. There was, in his opinion, nothing whatever in the nature of the clerical state to justify any claim to absolute exemption, nor was it, he contended, against the law of God that the clergy should be tried for felony and other crimes by civil judges. In all such things they, like the rest of his people, were subject to their prince, who, because he was a Christian, did not, for that reason, have any diminished authority over his subjects. " Christ," he remarks, " sent His apostles," as appears from the said words, " to be teachers in spiritual matters, and not to be like princes, or to take from princes their power." [1]   Some, indeed, he says, argue that since the coming of our Lord " Christian princes have derived their temporal power from the spiritual power," established by Him in right of His full and complete dominion over the world.   But Saint-German not only holds that such a claim has no foundation in itself, but that all manner of texts of Holy Scripture which are adduced in proof of the contention are plainly twisted from their true meaning by the spiritual authority.   And many, he says, talk as if the clergy were the Church, and the Church the clergy, whereas they are only one portion, perhaps the most important, and possessed of greater and special functions ; but they were not the whole, and were, indeed, endowed with these prerogatives for the use and benefit of the lay portion of Christ's Church.

Contrary to what might have been supposed, the difficulty between the clergy and laity about the exemption of clerics from all lay jurisdiction did not apparently reach any very acute stage.   Sir Thomas More says that " as for the conventing of priests before secular judges, the truth is that at one time the occasion of a sermon made the matter come to a discussion before the king's Highness.   But neither at any time since, nor many years before, I never heard that there was any difficulty about it, and, moreover, that matter

[1] Ibid., cap. vi.

ceased long before any word sprang up about this great general division." [1]

One question, theoretical indeed, but sufficiently practical to indicate the current of thought and feeling prevalent at the time, was as to the multiplication of holidays on which no work was allowed to be done by ecclesiastical law. Saint-German, in common with other laymen of the period, maintained that the king, or Parliament, as representing the supreme will of the State, could refuse to allow the spiritual authority to make new holidays. About the Sunday he is doubtful, though he inclines to the opinion that so long as there was one day in the week set apart for rest and prayer, the actual day could be determined by the State. The Sunday, he says, is partly by the law of God, partly by the law of man. " But as for the other holidays, these are but ceremonies, introduced by the devotion of the people through the good example of their bishops and priests." And " if the multitude of the holidays is thought hurtful to the commonwealth, and tending rather to increase vice than virtue, or to give occasion of pride rather than meekness, as peradventure the synod ales and particular holidays have done in some places, then Parliament has good authority to reform it. But as for the holidays that are kept in honour of Our Lady, the Apostles and other ancient Saints, these seem right necessary and expedient." [2]

In his work, *Salem and Bizance*, which appeared in 1533 as a reply to Sir Thomas More's *Apology*, Saint-German takes up the same ground as in his more strictly legal tracts. He holds that a distinction

---

[1] *English Works* (ed. 1557), p. 1017.
[2] *A treatyse*, &c., *ut sup.*, cap. vi., sig. E. i.

between the purely spiritual functions of the clergy and their position as individuals in the State ought to be allowed and recognised. The attitude of ecclesiastics generally to such a view was, perhaps not unnaturally, one of opposition, and where the State had already stepped in and legislated, as for instance in the case of " mortuaries," their action in trying to evade the prescription of the law, Saint-German declared was doing much harm, in emphasising a needless conflict between the ecclesiastical and secular jurisdiction. " As long," he writes, " as spiritual rulers will pretend that their authority is so high and so immediately derived from God that people are bound to obey them and to accept all that they do and teach without argument, resistance, or murmuring against them " there will be discord and difficulty.[1]

Christopher Saint-German's position was not by any means that of one who would attack the clergy all along the line, and deprive them of all power and influence, like so many of the foreign sectaries of the time. He admitted, and indeed insisted on, the fact that they had received great and undoubted powers by their high vocation, having their spiritual jurisdiction immediately from God. Their temporalities, however, he maintained they received from the secular power, and were protected by the State in their possession. He fully agreed "that such things as the whole clergy of Christendom teach and order in spiritual things, and which of long time have been by long custom and usage in the whole body of Christendom ratified,

----

[1] *Salem and Bizance, a dialogue betwixte two Englishmen, whereof one was called Salem and the other Bizance* (Berthelet, 1533), f. 76.

agreed, and confirmed, by the spirituality and temporality, ought to be received with reverence." [1]

To this part of Saint-German's book Sir Thomas More takes exception in his *Apology*. The former had said, that as long as the spiritual rulers will pretend that their authority is so high and so immediately derived from God that the people are bound to obey them and accept all that they do and teach "there would certainly be divisions and dissensions." "If he mean," replies More, "that they speak thus of all their whole authority that they may now lawfully do and say at this time : I answer that they neither pretend, nor never did, that all their authority is given them immediately by God. They have authority now to do divers things by the grant of kings and princes, just as many temporal men also have, and by such grants they have such rights in such things as temporal men have in theirs." [2]

Some authority and power they certainly have from God, he says, "For the greatest and highest and most excellent authority that they have, either God has Himself given it to them, or else they are very presumptuous and usurp many things far above all reason. For I have never read, or at least I do not remember to have read, that any king granted them the authority that now not only prelates but other poor plain priests daily take on them in ministering the sacraments and consecrating the Blessed Body of Christ." [3]

Another popular book of the period, published by Berthelet, just on the eve of the Reformation, is the anonymous *Dialogue between a Knight and a Clerk con-*

[1] Ibid., f. 84. [2] *English Works*, p. 892. [3] Ibid.

cerning the power spiritual and temporal. We are not here concerned with the author's views as to the power of the Popes, but only with what he states about the attitude of men's minds to the difficulties consequent upon the confusion of the two jurisdictions. *Miles* (the Knight), who, of course, took the part of the up-holder of the secular power, clearly distinguished, like Saint-German, between directly spiritual prerogatives and the authority and position assured to the clergy by the State. "God forbid," he says, "that I should deny the right of Holy Church to know and correct men for their sins. Not to hold this would be to deny the sacrament of Penance and Confession altogether."[1] Moreover, like Saint-German, this author, in the person of *Miles*, insists that the temporality "are bound to find the spirituality that worship and serve God all that is necessary for them. For so do all nations."[2] But the direction of such temporalities must, he contends, be in the hands of the State. "What," asks the con-servative cleric, in the person of *Clericus*, "What have princes and kings to do with the governance of our temporalities? Let them take their own and order their own, and suffer us to be in peace with ours."

"Sir," replies *Miles*, "the princes must in any wise have to do therewith. I pray you, ought not men above all things to mind the health of our souls? Ought not we to see the wills of our forefathers ful-filled? Falleth it not to you to pray for our fore-fathers that are passed out of this life? And did not our fathers give you our temporalities right plentifully, to the intent that you should pray for them and spend it all to the honour of God? And ye do nothing so;

[1] *A Dialogue*, &c., *ut sup.*, f. 8.   [2] Ibid., f. 11.

but ye spend your temporalities in sinful deeds and vanities, which temporalities ye should spend in works of charity, and in alms-deeds to the poor and needy. For to this purpose our forefathers gave ' great and huge dominions.' You have received them ' to the intent to have clothes and food . . . and all overplus besides these you ought to spend on deeds of mercy and pity, as on poor people that are in need, and on such as are sick and diseased and oppressed with misery.' " [1]

Further, *Miles* hints that there are many at that time who were casting hungry eyes upon the riches of the Church, and that were it not for the protecting power of the State, the clergy would soon find that they were in worse plight than they think themselves to be. And, in answer to the complaints of *Clericus* that ecclesiastics are taxed too hardly for money to be spent on soldiers, ships, and engines of war, he tells him that there is no reason in the nature of things why ecclesiastical property should not bear the burden of national works as well as every other kind of wealth. " I pray you hold your noise," he exclaims somewhat rudely ; " stop your grudging and grumbling, and listen patiently. Look at your many neighbours round about you in the land, who, wanting the wherewith to support life, gape still after your goods. If the king's power failed, what rest should you have ? Would not the gentlemen such as be needy, and such as have spent their substance prodigally, when they have consumed their own, turn to yours, and waste and destroy all you have ? Therefore, the king's strength is to you instead of a strong wall, and you wot well that the

[1] Ibid., f. 14.

king's peace is your peace, and the king's safeguard is your safeguard." [1]

The foregoing pages represent some of the practical difficulties which were being experienced on the eve of the Reformation between the ecclesiastical and lay portion of the State in the question of jurisdiction. Everything points to the fact that the chief difficulty was certainly not religious. The ecclesiastical jurisdiction in matters spiritual was cordially admitted by all but a few fanatics. What even many churchmen objected to, were the claims for exemption put forward by ecclesiastics in the name of religion, which they felt to be a stretching of spiritual prerogatives into the domain of the temporal sovereign. History has shown that most of these claims have in practice been disallowed, not only without detriment to the spiritual work of the Church, but in some instances at least it was the frank recognition of the State rights, which, under Providence, saved nations from the general defection which seemed to threaten the old ecclesiastical system. Most of the difficulties which were, as we have seen, experienced and debated in England were unfelt in Spain, where the sovereign from the first made his position as to the temporalities of the Church clearly understood by all. In Naples, in like manner, the right of State patronage, however objectionable to the ecclesiastical legists, was strictly maintained. In France, the danger which at one time threatened an overthrow of religion similar to that which had fallen on Germany, and which at the time was looming dark over England, was averted by the celebrated Concordat between Leo X. and Francis I.

[1] *A Dialogue*, &c., *ut sup.*, p. 17.

By this settlement of outstanding difficulties between the two jurisdictions, all rights of election to ecclesiastical dignities was swept away with the full and express sanction of the Pope. The nomination of all bishops and other dignitaries was vested in the king, subject, of course, to Papal confirmation. All appeals were, in the first place, to be carried in ordinary cases to immediate superiors acting in the fixed tribunals of the country, and then only to the Holy See. The Papal power of appointment to benefices was by this agreement strictly limited ; and the policy of the document was generally directed to securing the most important ecclesiastical positions, including even parish churches in towns, to educated men. It is to this settlement of outstanding difficulties, the constant causes of friction—a settlement of difficulties which must be regarded as economic and administrative rather than as religious—that so good a judge as M. Hanotaux, the statesman and historian, attributes nothing less than the maintenance of the old religion in France. In his opinion, this Concordat did in fact remove, to a great extent, the genuine grievances which had long been felt by the people at large, which elsewhere the Reformers of the sixteenth century skilfully seized upon, as likely to afford them the most plausible means for furthering their schemes of change in matters strictly religious.

CHAPTER IV

ENGLAND AND THE POPE

NOTHING is more necessary for one who desires to appreciate the true meaning of the English Reformation than to understand the attitude of men's minds to the Pope and the See of Rome on the eve of the great change. As in the event, the religious upheaval did, in fact, lead to a national rejection of the jurisdiction of the Roman Pontiff, it is not unnatural that those who do not look below the surface should see in this act the outcome and inevitable consequence of long-continued irritation at a foreign domination. The renunciation of Papal jurisdiction, in other words, is taken as sufficient evidence of national hostility to the Holy See. If this be the true explanation of the fact, it is obvious that in the literature of the period immediately preceding the formal renunciation of ecclesiastical dependence on Rome, evidence more or less abundant will be found of this feeling of dislike, if not of detestation, for a yoke which we are told had become unbearable.

At the outset, it must be confessed that any one who will go to the literature of the period with the expectation of collecting evidence of this kind is doomed to disappointment. If we put on one side the diatribes and scurrilous invectives of advanced reformers, when the day of the doctrinal Reformation

had already dawned, the inquirer in this field of knowledge can hardly fail to be struck by the absence of
indications of any real hostility to the See of Rome in
the period in question.   So far as the works of the age
are concerned : so far, too, as the acts of individuals
and even of those who were responsible agents of the
State go, the evidence of an unquestioned acceptance
of the spiritual jurisdiction of the Pope, as Head of
the Christian Church, is simply overwhelming.   In
their acceptance of this supreme authority the English
were perhaps neither demonstrative nor loudly protesting, but this in no way derogated from their loyal
and unquestioning acceptance of the supremacy of the
Holy See.   History shows that up to the very eve
of the rejection of this supremacy the attitude of
Englishmen, in spite of difficulties and misunderstandings, had been persistently one of respect for the
Pope as their spiritual head.   Whilst other nations of
Christendom had been in the past centuries engaged in
endeavours by diplomacy, and even by force of
arms, to capture the Pope that they might use him
for their own national profit, England, with nothing
to gain, expecting nothing, seeking nothing, had never
entered on that line of policy, but had been content to
bow to his authority as to that of the appointed Head
of Christ's Church on earth.   Of this much there can
be no doubt.   They did not reason about it, nor sift
and sort the grounds of their acceptance, any more
than a child would dream of searching into, or
philosophising upon, the obedience he freely gives to
his parents.

That there were at times disagreements and quarrels
may be admitted without in the least affecting the real

attitude and uninterrupted spiritual dependence of England on the Holy See. Such disputes were wholly the outcome of misunderstandings as to matters in the domain rather of the temporal than of the spiritual, or of points in the broad debatable land that lies between the two jurisdictions. It is a failure to understand the distinction which exists between these that has led many writers to think that in the rejection by Englishmen of claims put forward at various times by the Roman curia in matters wholly temporal, or where the temporal became involved in the spiritual, they have a proof that England never fully acknowledged the spiritual headship of the See of Rome.

That the Pope did in fact exercise great powers in England over and above those in his spiritual prerogative is a matter of history. No one has more thoroughly examined this subject than Professor Maitland, and the summary of his conclusions given in his *History of English Law* will serve to correct many misconceptions upon the matter. What he says may be taken as giving a fairly accurate picture of the relations of the Christian nations of Christendom to the Holy See from the twelfth century to the disintegration of the system in the throes of the Reformation. " It was a wonderful system," he writes. " The whole of Western Europe was subject to the jurisdiction of one tribunal of last resort, the Roman curia. Appeals to it were encouraged by all manner of means, appeals at almost every stage of almost every proceeding. But the Pope was far more than the president of a court of appeal. Very frequently the courts Christian which did justice in England were courts which were acting under his supervision and carrying out his written instructions. A very large part, and by far the most permanently important part, of the ecclesiastical litigation that went on in this country came before English prelates who were sitting not as English prelates, not as 'judges ordinary,' but as mere delegates of the Pope, commissioned to hear and determine this or that particular case. Bracton, indeed, treats the Pope as the ordinary judge of every Englishman in spiritual things, and the only ordinary judge whose powers are unlimited."

The Pope enjoyed a power of declaring the law to which but very wide and very vague limits could be set. Each separate church might have its customs, but there was a *lex communis,* a common law, of the universal Church. In the view of the canonist, any special rules of the Church of England have hardly a wider scope, hardly a less dependent place, than have the customs of Kent or the bye-laws of London in the eye of the English lawyer.[1]

We have only to examine the *Regesta* of the Popes, even up to the dawn of difficulties in the reign of Henry VIII., to see that the system as sketched in this passage was in full working order ; and it was herein that chiefly lay the danger even to the spiritual prerogatives of the Head of the Church. Had the Providence

---

[1] *History of English Law,* i., p. 93-4. Mr. James Gairdner, in a letter to *The Guardian,* March 1, 1899, says : "There were, in the Middle Ages, in every kingdom of Europe that owned the Pope's jurisdiction, two authorities, the one temporal and the other spiritual, and the head of the spiritual jurisdiction was at Rome. The bishops had the rule over their clergy, even in criminal matters, and over the laity as well in matters of faith. Even a bishop's decision, it is true, might be disputed, and there was an appeal to the Pope ; nay, the Pope's decision might be disputed, and there was an appeal to a general council. Thus there was, in every kingdom, an *imperium in imperio,* but nobody objected to such a state of matters, not even kings, seeing that they could, as a rule, get anything they wanted out of the Popes—even some things, occasionally, that the Popes ought not to have conceded."

of God destined that the nations of the world should have become a Christendom in fact—a theocracy presided over by his Vicar on earth—the system elaborated by the Roman curia would not have tended doubtless to obscure the real and essential prerogatives of the spiritual Head of the Christian Church. As it was by Providence ordained, and as subsequent events have shown, claims of authority to determine matters more or less of the temporal order, together with the worldly pomp and show with which the Popes of the renaissance had surrounded themselves, not only tended to obscure the higher and supernatural powers which are the enduring heritage of St. Peter's successors in the See of Rome ; but, however clear the distinction between the necessary and the accidental prerogatives might appear to the mind of the trained theologian or the perception of the saint, to the ordinary man, when the one was called in question the other was imperilled. And, as a fact, in England popular irritation at the interference of the spirituality generally in matters not wholly within the strictly ecclesiastical sphere was, at a given moment, skilfully turned by the small reforming party into national, if tacit, acquiescence in the rejection of even the spiritual prerogatives of the Roman Pontiffs.

It is necessary to insist upon this matter if the full meaning of the Reformation movement is to be understood. Here in England, there can be no doubt, on the one hand, that no nation more fully and freely bowed to the spiritual supremacy of the Holy See ; on the other, that there was a dislike of interference in matters which they regarded, rightly or wrongly, as outside the sphere of the Papal prerogative. The national feeling had grown by leaps and bounds in the early years of the sixteenth century. But it was not until the ardent spirits among the doctrinal reformers had succeeded in weakening the hold of Catholicity in religion on the hearts of the people that this rise of national feeling entered into the ecclesiastical domain, and the love of country could be effectually used to turn them against the Pope, even as Head of the Christian Church. With this distinction clearly before the mind, it is possible to understand the general attitude of the English nation to the Pope and his authority on the eve of the overthrow of his jurisdiction.

To begin with some evidence of popular teaching as to the Pope's position as Head of the Church. It is, of course, evident that in many works the supremacy of the Holy See is assumed and not positively stated. This is exactly what we should expect in a matter which was certainly taken for granted by all. William Bond, a learned priest, and subsequently a monk of Syon, with Richard Whitford, was the author of a book called the *Pilgrimage of Perfection*, published by Wynkyn de Worde in 1531. It is a work, as the author tells us, " very profitable to all Christian persons to read " ; and the third book consists of a long and careful explanation of the Creed. In the section treating about the tenth article is to be found a very complete statement of the teaching of the Christian religion on the Church. After taking the marks of the Church, the author says : " There may be set no other foundation for the Church, but only that which is put, namely, Christ Jesus. It is certain, since it is founded on the Apostles, as our Lord said to Peter, ' I have prayed that thy faith fail not.' And no more it shall ; for (as St. Cyprian says) the Church of Rome was never yet the root of heresy.   This Church Apostolic is so named the Church of Rome, because St. Peter and St. Paul, who under Christ were heads and princes of this Church, deposited there the tabernacles of their bodies, which God willed should be buried there and rest in Rome, and that should be the chief see in the world ; just as commonly in all other places the chief see of the bishop is where the chief saint and bishop of the see is buried.   By this you may know how Christ is the Head of the Church, and how our Holy Father the Pope of Rome is Head of the Church.   Many, because they know not this mystery of Holy Scripture, have erred and fallen to heresies in denying the excellent dignity of our Holy Father the Pope of Rome." [1]

In the same way Roger Edgworth, a preacher in the reign of Henry VIII., speaking on the text " *Tu vocaberis Cephas*," says :   " And by this the error and ignorance of certain summalists are confounded, who take this text as one of their strongest reasons for the supremacy of the Pope of Rome.   In so doing, such summalists would plainly destroy the text of St. John's Gospel to serve their purpose, which they have no need to do, for there are as well texts of Holy Scripture and passages of ancient writers which abundantly prove the said primacy of the Pope." [2]

When by 1523 the attacks of Luther and his followers on the position of the Pope had turned men's minds in England to the question, and caused them to examine into the grounds of their belief, several books on the subject appeared in England.   One in particular, intended to be subsidiary to the volume

---

[1] William Bond, *The Pilgrymage of perfeccyon*, 1531, f. 223.
[2] Roger Edgworth, *Sermons*, 1557, fol. 102

published by the king himself against Luther, was
written by a theologian named Edward Powell, and
published by Pynson in London. In his preface,
Powell says that before printing his work he had
submitted it to the most learned authority at Oxford
(*eruditissimo Oxoniensium*). The first part of the book
is devoted to a scientific treatise upon the Pope's
supremacy, with all the proofs from Scripture and the
Fathers set out in detail. "This then," he concludes,
"is the Catholic Church, which, having the Roman
Pontiff, the successor of Peter, as its head, offers the
means of sanctifying the souls of all its members, and
testifies to the truth of all that is to be taught." The
high priesthood of Peter "is said to be Roman, not
because it cannot be elsewhere, but through a certain
congruity which makes Rome the most fitting place.
That is, that where the centre of the world's government
was, there also should be placed the high priesthood of
Christ. Just as of old the summus Pontifex was in
Jerusalem, the metropolis of the Jewish nation, so now
it is in Rome, the centre of Christian civilisation." [1]

We naturally, of course, turn to the works of
Sir Thomas More for evidence of the teaching as to
the Pope's position at this period ; and his testimony
is abundant and definite. Thus in the second book
of his *Dyalogue*, written in 1528, arguing that there
must be unity in the Church of Christ, he points out
that the effect. of Lutheranism has been to breed diversity of faith and practice. "Though they began so
late," he writes, "yet there are not only as many sects
almost as men, but also the masters themselves change

[1] Edward Powell, *Propugnaculum summi sacerdotii*, &c., *adversus M.
Lutherum*, 1523, fol. 22 and fol. 35.

their minds and their opinions every day. Bohemia
is also in the same case : one faith in the town, another
in the field ; one in Prague, another in the next town ;
and yet in Prague itself, one faith in one street, another
in the next.   And yet all these acknowledge that they
cannot have the Sacraments ministered but by such
priests as are made by authority derived and conveyed
from the Pope who is, under Christ, Vicar and head of
our Church." [1]   It is important to note in this passage
how the author takes for granted the Pope's supreme
authority over the Christian Church.   To this subject
he returns, and is more explicit in a later chapter of
the same book.   The Church, he says, is the " company and congregation of all nations professing the
name of Christ."   This church " has begun with Christ,
and has had Him for its head and St. Peter His Vicar
after Him, and the head under Him ; and always since,
the successors of him continually.   And it has had His
holy faith and His blessed Sacraments and His holy
Scriptures delivered, kept, and conserved therein by
God and His Holy Spirit, and albeit some nations fall
away, yet just as no matter how many boughs whatever fall from the tree, even though more fall than
be left thereon, still there is no doubt which is the
very tree, although each of them were planted again in
another place and grew to a greater than the stock it
first came off, in the same way we see and know well
that all the companies and sects of heretics and schis-
matics, however great they grow, come out of this Church
I speak of ; and we know that the heretics are they
that are severed, and the Church the stock that they all
come out of." [2]   Here Sir Thomas More expressly gives

[1] *English Works*, p. 171.   [2] Ibid., p. 185.

communion with the successors of St. Peter as one of the chief tests of the true Church.

Again, in his *Confutation of Tyndale's Answer*, written in 1532 when he was Lord Chancellor, Sir Thomas More speaks specially about the absolute necessity of the Church being One and not able to teach error. There is one known and recognised Church existing throughout the world, which "is that mystical body be it never so sick." Of this mystical body "Christ is the principal head"; and it is no part of his concern, he says, for the moment to determine "whether the successor of St. Peter is his vicar-general and head under him, as all Christian nations have now long taken him." [1] Later on he classes himself with "poor popish men," [2] and in the fifth book he discusses the question "whether the Pope and his sect" (as Tyndale called them) "is Christ's Church or no." On this matter More is perfectly clear. "I call the Church of Christ," he says, "the known Catholic Church of all Christian nations, neither gone out nor cut off. And although all these nations do now and have long since recognised and acknowledged the Pope, not as the bishop of Rome but as the successor of St. Peter, to be their chief spiritual governor under God and Christ's Vicar on earth, yet I never put the Pope as part of the definition of the Church, by defining it to be the common known congregation of all Christian nations under one head the Pope."

I avoided this definition purposely, he continues, so as not "to entangle the matter with the two questions at once, for I knew well that the Church being proved this common known Catholic congregation of

<hr />

[1] Ibid., p. 528.   [2] Ibid., p. 538.

all Christian nations abiding together in one faith, neither fallen nor cut off ; there might, peradventure, be made a second question after that, whether over all this Catholic Church the Pope must needs be head and chief governor and chief spiritual shepherd, or whether, if the unity of the faith was kept among them all, every province might have its own spiritual chief over itself, without any recourse unto the Pope. . . .

" For the avoiding of all such intricacies, I purposely abstained from putting the Pope as part of the definition of the Church, as a thing that was not necessary ; for if he be the necessary head, he is included in the name of the whole body, and whether he be or not is a matter to be treated and disputed of besides " (p. 615). As to Tyndale's railing against the authority of the Pope because there have been " Popes that have evil played their parts," he should remember, says More, that " there have been Popes again right holy men, saints and martyrs too," and that, moreover, the personal question of goodness or badness has nothing to say to the office.[1]

In like manner, More, when arguing against Friar Barnes, says that like the Donatists " these heretics call the Catholic Christian people papists," and in this they are right, since " Saint Austin called the successor of Saint Peter the chief head on earth of the whole Catholic Church, as well as any man does now." He here plainly states his view of the supremacy of the See of Rome.[2] He accepted it not only as an antiquarian fact, but as a thing necessary for the preservation of the unity of the Faith. Into the further question whether

---

[1] *English Works*, p. 616.   [2] Ibid., p. 798.

the office of supreme pastor was established by Christ Himself, or, as theologians would say, *de jure divino*, or whether it had grown with the growth and needs of the Church, More did not then enter. The fact was sufficient for him that the only Christian Church he recognised had for long ages regarded the Pope as the *Pastor pastorum*, the supreme spiritual head of the Church of Christ. His own words, almost at the end of his life, are the best indication of his mature conclusion on this matter. "I have," he says, "by the grace of God, been always a Catholic, never out of communion with the Roman Pontiff ; but I have heard it said at times that the authority of the Roman Pontiff was certainly lawful and to be respected, but still an authority derived from human law, and not standing upon a divine prescription. Then, when I observed that public affairs were so ordered that the sources of the power of the Roman Pontiff would necessarily be examined, I gave myself up to a diligent examination of that question for the space of seven years, and found that the authority of the Roman Pontiff, which you rashly—I will not use stronger language—have set aside, is not only lawful to be respected and necessary, but also grounded on the divine law and prescription. That is my opinion, that is the belief in which, by the grace of God, I shall die." [1]

Looking at More's position in regard to this question in the light of all that he has written, it would seem to be certain that he never for a moment doubted that the Papacy was necessary for the Church. He accepted this without regard to the reasons of the faith that was in him, and in this he was not different from

[1] *Henry VIII. and the English Monasteries* (popular edition), p. 367.

the body of Englishmen at large. When, in 1522, the book by Henry VIII. appeared against Luther, it drew the attention of Sir Thomas specially to a consideration of the grounds upon which the supremacy of the Pope was held by Catholics. As the result of his examination he became so convinced that it was of divine institution that " my conscience would be in right great peril," he says, "if I should follow the other side and deny the primacy to be provided of God." Even before examination More evidently held implicitly the same ideas, since in his Latin book against Luther, published in 1523, he declared his entire agreement with Bishop Fisher on the subject. That the latter was fully acquainted with the reasons which went to prove that the Papacy was of divine institution, and that he fully accepted it as such, is certain.[1]

When, with the failure of the divorce proceedings, came the rejection of Papal supremacy in England, there were plenty of people ready to take the winning side, urging that the rejection was just, and not contrary to the true conception of the Christian Church. It is interesting to note that in all the pulpit tirades against the Pope and what was called his " usurped supremacy," there is no suggestion that this supremacy had not hitherto been fully and freely recognised by all in the country. On the contrary, the change was regarded as a happy emancipation from an authority

[1] In his work against Luther, Bishop Fisher teaches the supremacy of the Pope without any ambiguity. In the *Sermon had at Paulis* against Luther and his followers, he also put his position perfectly clearly. The Church that has a right to the name *Catholic* has derived the right from its communion with the See of Peter. Our Lord called Cephas, Peter, or rock, to signify that upon him as a rock He would build His church. Unto Peter He committed His flock, and " the true Christian people which we have at this day was derived by a continual succession from the See of Peter " (fol. e. 4. d.).

which had been hitherto submitted to without question or doubt. A sermon preached at St. Paul's the Sunday after the execution of the Venerable Bishop Fisher, and a few days before Sir Thomas More was called to lay down his life for the same cause, is of interest, as specially making mention of these two great men, and of the reasons which had forced them to lay down their lives in the Pope's quarrel. The preacher was one Simon Matthew, and his object was to instruct the people in the new theory of the Christian Church necessary on the rejection of the headship of the Pope. "The diversity of regions and countries," he says, "does not make any diversity of churches, but a unity of faith makes all regions one Church." "There was," he continued, "no necessity to know Peter, as many have reckoned, in the Bishop of Rome, (teaching) that except we knew him and his holy college, we could not be of Christ's Church. Many have thought it necessary that if a man would be a member of the Church of Christ, he must belong to the holy church of Rome and take the Holy Father thereof for the supreme Head and for the Vicar of Christ, yea for Christ Himself, (since) to be divided from him was even to be divided from Christ." This, the preacher informs his audience, is "damnable teaching," and that "the Bishop of Rome has no more power by the laws of God in this realm than any foreign bishop."

He then goes on to speak of what was, no doubt, in everybody's mind at the time, the condemnation of the two eminent Englishmen for upholding the ancient teachings as to the Pope's spiritual headship. "Of late," he says, "you have had experience of some, whom neither friends nor kinsfolk, nor the judgment of both universities, Cambridge and Oxford, nor the universal consent of all the clergy of this realm, nor the laws of the Parliament, nor their most natural and loving prince, could by any gentle ways revoke from their disobedience, but would needs persist therein, giving pernicious occasion to the multitude to murmur and grudge at the king's laws, seeing that they were men of estimation and would be seen wiser than all the realm and of better conscience than others, justifying themselves and condemning all the realm besides. These being condemned and the king's prisoners, yet did not cease to conceive ill of our sovereign, refusing his laws, but even in prison wrote to their mutual comfort in their damnable opinions. I mean Doctor Fisher and Sir Thomas More, whom I am as sorry to name as any man here is to hear named : sorry for that they, being sometime men of worship and honour, men of famous learning and many excellent graces and so tenderly sometime beloved by their prince, should thus unkindly, unnaturally, and traitorously use themselves. Our Lord give them grace to be repentant ! Let neither their fame, learning, nor honour move you loving subjects from your prince ; but regard ye the truth."

The preacher then goes on to condemn the coarse style of preaching against the Pope in which some indulged at that time. " I would exhort," he says, " such as are of my sort and use preaching, so to temper their words that they be not noted to speak of stomach and rather to prate than preach. Nor would I have the defenders of the king's matters rage and rail, or scold, as many are thought to do, calling the Bishop of Rome the 'harlot of Babylon' or 'the beast of Rome,' with many such other, as I have heard some say ; these be meeter to preach at Paul's Wharf than at Paul's Cross." [1]

The care that was taken at this time in sermons to the people to decry the Pope's authority, as well as the abuse which was hurled at his office, is in reality ample proof of the popular belief in his supremacy, which it was necessary to eradicate from the hearts of the English people. Few, probably, would have been able to state the reason for their belief ; but that the spiritual headship was fully and generally accepted as a fact is, in view of the works of the period, not open to question. Had there been disbelief, or even doubt, as to the matter, some evidence of this would be forthcoming in the years that preceded the final overthrow of Papal jurisdiction in England.

Nor are direct declarations of the faith of the English Church wanting. To the evidence already adduced, a sermon preached by Bishop Longland in 1527, before the archbishops and bishops of England in synod at Westminster, may be added. The discourse is directed against the errors of Luther and the social evils to which his teaching had led in Germany. The English bishops, Bishop Longland declares, are determined to do all in their power to preserve the English Church from this evil teaching, and he exhorts all to pray. that God will not allow the universal and chief Church—the Roman Church —to be further afflicted, that He will restore liberty to the most Holy Father and high-priest now impiously

---

[1] Simon Matthew, *Sermon made in the Cathedrall Church of Saynt-Paule,* 27 *June* 1535 (Berthelet, 1535).

imprisoned, and in a lamentable state; that He Himself will protect the Church's freedom threatened by a multitude of evil men, and through the pious prayers of His people will free it and restore its most Holy Father. Just as the early Christians prayed when Peter was in prison, so ought all to pray in these days of affliction. "Shall we not," he cries, "mourn for the evil life of the chief Church (of Christendom)? Shall we not beseech God for the liberation of the primate and chief ruler of the Church? Let us pray then; let us pray that through our prayers we may be heard. Let us implore freedom for our mother, the Catholic Church, and the liberty, so necessary for the Christian religion, of our chief Father on earth—the Pope." [1]

Again, Dr. John Clark, the English ambassador in Rome, when presenting Henry's book against Luther to Leo X. in public consistory, said that the English king had taken up the defence of the Church because in attacking the Pope the German reformer had tried to subvert the order established by God Himself. In the *Babylonian Captivity of the Church* he had given to the world a book "most pernicious to mankind," and before presenting Henry's reply, he begged to be allowed to protest "the devotion and veneration of the king towards the Pope and his most Holy See." Luther had declared war "not only against your Holiness but also against your office; against the ecclesiastical hierarchy, against this See, and against that Rock established by God Himself." England, the speaker continued, "has never been behind other nations in the worship of God and the Christian faith, and in obedience to the Roman Church." Hence

---

[1] Joannis Longlondi *Tres conciones* (R. Pynson), f. 45.

"no nation" detests more cordially "this monster (Luther) and the heresies broached by him." For he has declared war " not only against your Holiness but against your office ; against the ecclesiastical hierarchy, against this See, that Rock established by God Himself." [1]

Whilst the evidence goes to show the full acceptance by the English people of the Pope's spiritual headship of the Church, it is also true that the system elaborated by the ecclesiastical lawyers in the later Middle Ages, dealing, as it did, so largely with temporal matters, property, and the rights attaching thereto, opened the door to causes of disagreement between Rome and England, and at times open complaints and criticism of the exercise of Roman authority in England made themselves heard. This is true of all periods of English history. Since these disagreements are obviously altogether connected with the question, not of spirituals, but of temporals, they would not require any more special notice but for the misunderstandings they have given rise to in regard to the general attitude of men's minds to Rome and Papal authority on the eve of the Reformation. It is easy to find evidence of this. As early as 1517, a work bearing on this question appeared in England. It was a translation of several tracts that had been published abroad on the debated matter of Constantine's donation to the Pope, and it was issued from the press of Thomas Godfray in a well-printed folio. After a translation of the Latin version of a Greek manuscript of Constantine's gift, which had been found in the Papal library

---

[1] *Assertion of the Seven Sacraments against Luther* (translation by J. W., 1687), f. a. i.

by Bartolomeo Pincern, and published by order of
Pope Julius II., there is given in this volume the
critical examination of this gift by Laurence Valla,
the opinion of Nicholas of Cusa, written for the Council of Basle, and that of St. Antoninus, Archbishop of
Florence.   The interest of the volume for the present
purpose chiefly consists in the fact of the publication in England at this date of the views expressed
by Laurence Valla.   Valla had been a canon of the
Lateran and an eminent scholar, who was employed
by Pope Nicholas V. to translate Thucydides and
Herodotus.   His outspoken words got him into difficulties with the Roman curia, and obliged him to
retire to Naples, where he died in 1457.   The tract
was edited with a preface by the leader of the reform
party in Germany, Ulrich von Hutten.   In this introduction von Hutten says that by the publication of
Pincern's translation of the supposed donation of
Constantine Julius II. had "provoked and stirred up
men to war and battle," and further, he blames the
Pontiff because he would not permit Valla's work
against the genuineness of the gift to be published.
With the accession of Leo X. von Hutten looked,
he declares, for better days, since " by striking as it
were a cymbal of peace the Pope has raised up the
hearts and minds of all Christian people."   Before
this time the truth could not be spoken.   Popes
looked "to pluck the riches and goods of all men
to their own selves," with the result that " on the
other side they take away from themselves all that
belongs to the succession of St. Peter."

Valla, of course, condemns the supposed donation
of Constantine to the Pope as spurious, and declares

against the temporal claims the See of Rome had founded upon it. He strongly objects to the "temporal as well as the spiritual sword" being in the hands of the successors of St. Peter. "They say," he writes, "that the city of Rome is theirs, that the kingdom of Naples is their own property : that all Italy, France, and Spain, Germany, England, and all the west part of the world belongs to them. For all these nations and countries (they say) are contained in the instrument and writ of the donation or grant."

The whole tract is an attack upon the temporal sovereignty of the head of the Christian Church, and it was indeed a bold thing for Ulrich von Hutten to publish it and dedicate it to Pope Leo X. For the present purpose it is chiefly important to find all this set out in an English dress, whilst so far and for a long while after, the English people were loyal and true to the spiritual headship of the Pope, and were second to no other nation in their attachment to him. At that time recent events, including the wars of Julius II., must certainly have caused men to reflect upon the temporal aspect of the Papacy ; and hearts more loyal to the successor of St. Peter than was that of Von Hutten would probably have joined fervently in the concluding words of his preface as it appeared in English. "Would to God I might (for there is nothing I do long for more) once see it brought to pass that the Pope were only the Vicar of Christ and not also the Vicar of the Emperor, and that this horrible saying may no longer be heard: 'the Church fighteth and warreth against the Perugians, the Church fighteth against the people of Bologna.' It is not the Church that fights and wars against Christian men ; it is the Pope that

does so. The Church fights against wicked spirits in
the regions of the air. Then shall the Pope be called,
and in very deed be, a Holy Father, the Father of all
men, the Father of the Church. Then shall he not
raise and stir up wars and battles among Christian men,
but he shall allay and stop the wars which have been
stirred up by others, by his apostolic censure and papal
majesty." [1]

Evidence of what, above, has been called the probable searching of men's minds as to the action of
the Popes in temporal matters, may be seen in a book
called a *Dyalogue between a knight and a clerk, concerning
the power spiritual and temporal*.[2] In reply to the complaint of the clerk that in the evil days in which their
lot had fallen "the statutes and ordinances of bishops
of Rome and the decrees of holy fathers" were disregarded, the knight exposes a layman's view of the
matter. "Whether they ordain," he says, "or have
ordained in times past of the temporality, may well be
law to you, but not to us. No man has power to
ordain statutes of things over which he has no lordship,
as the king of France may ordain no statute (binding)
on the emperor nor the emperor on the king of England.
And just as princes of this world may ordain no statutes
for your spirituality over which they have no power;
no more may you ordain statutes of their temporalities
over which you have neither power nor authority.
Therefore, whatever you ordain about temporal things,
over which you have received no power from God, is
vain (and void). And therefore but lately, I laughed

---

[1] *A treatise of the donation or gift and endowment of possessions given* (by Constantine) *with the judgement of certain great men*, 1517, Thomas Godfray.
[2] London, Thomas Berthelet.

well fast, when I heard that Boniface VIII. had made a new statute that he himself should be above all secular lords, princes, kings, and emperors, and above all kingdoms, and make laws about all things : and that he only needed to write, for all things shall be his when he has so written : and thus all things will be yours. If he wishes to have my castle, my town, my field, my money, or any other such thing he needed, nothing but to will it, and write it, and make a decree, and wot that it be done, (for) to all such things he has a right."

The clerk does not, however, at once give up the position. You mean, he says in substance, that in your opinion the Pope has no power over your property and goods. " Though we should prove this by our law and by written decrees, you account them for nought. For you hold that Peter had no lordship or power over temporals, but by such law written. But if you will be a true Christian man and of right belief, you will not deny that Christ is the lord of all things. To Him it is said in the Psalter book : ' Ask of me, and I will give you nations for thine heritage, and all the world about for thy possession ' (Ps. ii.). These are God's words, and no one doubts that He can ordain for the whole earth."

Nobody denies God's lordship over the earth, replied the knight, " but if be proved by Holy Writ that the Pope is lord of all temporalities, then kings and princes must needs be subject to the Pope in temporals as in spirituals." So they are, in effect, answered the clerk. Peter was made " Christ's full Vicar," and as such he can do what his lord can, " especially when he is Vicar with full power, without any withdrawing of power, and he thus can direct all Christian nations in temporal matters." But, said the knight, "Christ's life plainly shows that He made no claim whatever to temporal power. Also in Peter's commission He gave him not the keys of the kingdom of the earth, but the keys of the kingdom of heaven. It is also evident that the bishops of the Hebrews were subjects of the kings, and kings deposed bishops ; but," he adds, fearing to go too far, "God forbid that they should do so now." Then he goes on to quote St. Paul in the Epistle to the Hebrews to prove that St. Peter was Christ's Vicar only in "the godly kingdom of souls, and that though some temporal things may be managed by bishops, yet nevertheless it is plain and evident that bishops should not be occupied in the government of the might and lordship of the world." And indeed, he urges, "Christ neither made St. Peter a knight nor a crowned king, but ordained him a priest and bishop." If the contention that "the Pope is the Vicar of God in temporal matter be correct," then of necessity you must also grant that "the Pope may take from you and from us all the goods that you and we have, and give them all to whichever of his nephews or cousins he wills and give no reason why : and also that he may take away from princes and kings principalities and kingdoms, at his own will, and give them where he likes." [1]

This statement by the layman of the advanced clerical view is somewhat bald, and is probably intentionally exaggerated ; but that it could be published even as a caricature of the position taken up by some ecclesiastics, shows that at this time some went very

[1] *A dyalogue, ut sup.*, ff. 3–7.

far indeed in their claims.   It is all the more remarkable that the argument is seriously put forward in
a tract, the author of which is evidently a Catholic
at heart, and one who fully admits the supreme jurisdiction of the Pope in all matters spiritual.   Of course,
when the rejection of Papal jurisdiction became im-
minent, there were found many who by sermons and
books endeavoured to eradicate the old teaching from
the people's hearts, and then it was that what was called,
" the pretensions " of the successors of St. Peter in
matters temporal were held up to serve as a convenient
means of striking at the spiritual prerogatives.   As a
sample, a small book named a *Mustre of scismatyke
bysshops of Rome* may be taken.   It was printed in
1534, and its title is sufficient to indicate its tone.
The author, one John Roberts, rakes together a good
many unsavoury tales about the lives of individual
Popes, and in particular he translates the life of
Gregory VII. to enforce his moral.   In his preface
he says, " There is a fond, foolish, fantasy raging in
many men's heads nowadays, and it is this : the
Popes, say they, cannot err.   This fantastical blindness was never taught by any man of literature, but
by some peckish pedler or clouting collier : it is so
gross in itself."   And I " warn, advise, beseech, and
adjure all my well-beloved countrymen in England
that men do not permit themselves to be blinded with
affection, with hypocrisy, or with superstition.   What
have we got from Rome but pulling, polling, picking,
robbing, stealing, oppression, blood-shedding, and
tyranny daily exercised upon us by him and his." [1]

[1] f. A. ii. ; c. i. ; c. iiij.   The author recommends those who would understand the Pope's power to " resort unto *The glasse of truth* or to the book named

Again, as another example of how the mind of the people was stirred up, we may take a few sentences from *A Worke entytled of the olde God and the new.* This tract is one of the most scurrilous of the German productions of the period. It was published in English by Myles Coverdale, and is on the list of books prohibited by the king in 1534. After a tirade against the Pope, whom he delights in calling " anti-Christ," the author declares that the Popes are the cause of many of the evils from which people were suffering at that time. In old days, he says, the Bishop of Rome was nothing more "than a pastor or herdsman," and adds : " Now he who has been at Rome in the time of Pope Alexander VI. or of Pope Julius II., he need not read many histories. I put it to his judgment whether any of the Pagans or of the Turks ever did lead such a life as did these." [1]

The same temper of mind appears in the preface

the *Determinations of the universities.*" The book named here *A glasse of truth* is written in favour of the divorce. " Some lawyers," the author says, "attribute too much to the Pope—at length there shall be no law, but only his will." The work was published by Berthelet anonymously, but Richard Croke, in a letter written at this period (Ellis, *Historical Letters*, 3rd series, ii. 195), says that the book was written by King Henry himself. It was generally said that Henry had written a defence of his divorce ; but Strype did not think it was more than a State paper. Croke (p. 198) says that people at Oxford, " Mr. John Roper and others," did not believe that the king was really the author. He says that the tract has done more than anything else to get people to take the king's side.

[1] *Of the olde God and the new*, B. 1. As another sample of what was at this time said about the Popes, we may take the following : Rome, says the author, " was by Justinian restored from ruin and decay, from whence also came the riches of the Church. At the coming of these riches, forthwith the book of the gospel was shut up, and the Bishops of Rome, instead of evangelical poverty, began to put forth their heads garnished with three crowns." This is taken from the preface of Hartman Dulechin, who claims to have "taught the book to speak Latin." It was originally printed and published in German. The English version is a translation of the Latin.

of a book called *The Defence of Peace*, translated into English by William Marshall and printed in 1535. The work itself was written by Marsilius of Padua about 1323, but the preface is dated 1522. The whole tone is distinctly anti-clerical, but the main line of attack is developed from the side of the temporalities possessed by churchmen. Even churchmen, he says, look mainly to the increase of their worldly goods. "Riches give honour, riches give benefices, riches give power and authority, riches cause men to be regarded and greatly esteemed." Especially is the author of the preface severe upon the temporal position which the Pope claims as inalienably united with his office as head of the Church. Benedict XII., he says, acted in many places as if he were all powerful, appointing rulers and officers in cities within the emperor's dominions, saying, "that all power and rule and empire was his own, for as much as whosoever is the successor of Peter on earth is the only Vicar or deputy of Jesus Christ the King of Heaven." [1]

In the body of the book itself the same views are expressed. The authority of the primacy is said to be "not immediately from God, but by the will and mind of man, just as other offices of a commonwealth are," and that the real meaning and extent of the claims put forward by the Pope can be seen easily. They are temporal, not spiritual. "This is the meaning of this title among the Bishops of Rome, that as Christ had the fulness of power and jurisdiction over all kings, princes, commonwealth, companies, or

---

[1] *The Defence of Peace, written in Latin more than 200 years ago, and set forth in the English tongue by Wyllyam Marshall.* R. Wyer, 1535, folio.

fellowships, and all singular persons, so in like manner they who call themselves the Vicars of Christ and Peter, have also the same fulness of enactive jurisdiction, determined by no law of man," and thus it is that "the Bishops of Rome, with their desire for dominion, have been the cause of discords and wars." [1]

Lancelot Ridley, in his *Exposition of the Epistle of Jude*, published in 1538 after the breach with Rome, takes the same line. The Pope has no right to have " exempted himself " and " other spiritual men from the obedience to the civil rulers and powers." Some, indeed, he says, " set up the usurped power of the Bishop of Rome above kings, princes, and emperors, and that by the ordinance of God, as if God and His Holy Scripture did give to the Bishop of Rome a secular power above kings, princes, and emperors here in this world. It is evident by Scripture that the Bishop of Rome has no other power but at the pleasure of princes, than in the ministration of the Word of God in preaching God's Word purely and sincerely, to reprove by it evil men, and to do such things as become a preacher, a bishop, a minister of God's Word to do. Other power Scripture does not attribute to the Bishop of Rome, nor suffer him to use. Scripture wills him to be a bishop, and to do the office of a bishop, and not to play the prince, the king, the emperor, the lord, and so forth." [2]   It is important to note in this passage that the writer was a reformer,

---

[1] *The Defence of Peace*, f. 42. The well-known anti-papal opinions of Marsilius of Padua are, of course, of no interest in themselves, but their publication at this time in English shows the methods by which it was hoped to undermine the Papal authority in the country.

[2] *Exposition*, &c., *ut supra*, f. i.

and that he was expressing his views after the jurisdiction of the Holy See had been rejected by the king
and his advisers.   The ground of the rejection, according to him—or at any rate the reason which it was
desired to emphasise before the public—would appear
to be the temporal authority which the Popes had
been exercising.

In the same year, 1538, Richard Morysine published a translation of a letter addressed by John
Sturmius, the Lutheran, to the cardinals appointed by
Pope Paul III. to consider what could be done to
stem the evils which threatened the Church.   As the
work of this Papal commission was then directly
put before the English people, some account of it is
almost necessary.   The commission consisted of four
cardinals, two archbishops, one bishop, the abbot of
San Giorgio, Venice, and the master of the Sacred
Palace, and its report was supposed to have been
drafted by Cardinal Caraffa, afterwards Pope Paul IV.
The document thanks God who has inspired the Pope
"to put forth his hand to support the ruins of the
tottering and almost fallen Church of Christ, and to
raise it again to its pristine height."   As a beginning,
the Holy Father has commanded them to lay bare to
him "those most grave abuses, that is diseases, by
which the Church of God, and this Roman curia
especially, is afflicted," and which has brought about
the state of ruin now so evident.   The initial cause
of all has been, they declare, that the Popes have
surrounded themselves with people who only told them
what they thought would be pleasant to them, and who
had not the honesty and loyalty to speak the truth.
This adulation had deceived the Roman Pontiffs about

many things. "To get the truth to their ears was always most difficult. Teachers sprung up who were ready to declare that the Pope was the master of all benefices, and as master might by right sell them as his own." As a consequence, it was taught that the Pope could not be guilty of simony, and that the will of the Pope was the highest law, and could override all law. "From this source, Holy Father," they continue, "as from the Trojan horse, so many abuses and most grievous diseases have grown up in the Church of God." Even pagans, they say, scoff at the state of the Christian Church as it is at present, and they, the commissioners, beg the Pope not to delay in immediately taking in hand the correction of the manifest abuses which afflict and disgrace the Church of Christ. "Begin the cure," they say, "whence sprung the disease. Follow the teaching of the Apostle St. Paul: 'be a dispenser, not a lord.'"

They then proceed to note the abuses which to them are most apparent, and to suggest remedies. We are not concerned with these further than to point out that, as a preliminary, they state that the true principle of government is, that what is the law must be kept, and that dispensations should be granted only on the most urgent causes, since nothing brings government to such bad repute as the continual exercise of the power of dispensation. Further, they note that it is certainly not lawful for the Vicar of Christ to make any profit (*lucrum*) by the dispensations he is obliged to give.

Sturmius, in his preface, says he had hopes of better things, now that there was a Pope ready to listen.

"It is a rare thing, and much more than man could hope for, that there should come a Bishop of Rome who would require his prelates upon their oath to open the truth, to show abuses, and to seek remedies for them." He is pleased to think that these four cardinals, Sadolet, Paul Caraffa, Contarini, and Reginald Pole had allowed fully and frankly that a great portion of the difficulty had come from the unfortunate attitude of the Popes in regard to worldly affairs. "You acknowledge," he says, "that no lordship is committed to the Bishop of Rome, but rather a certain cure by which he may rule things in the church according to good order. If you admit this to be true and will entirely grant us this, a great part of our (*i.e.* Lutheran) controversy is taken away; granting this also, that we did not dissent from you without great and just causes." The three points the cardinals claimed for the Pope, it may be noted, were: (1) that he was to be Bishop of Rome; (2) that he was to be universal Bishop; and (3) that he should be allowed temporal sovereignty over certain cities in Italy.[1] Again we find the same view put before the English people in this translation: the chief objection

---

[1] Johann Sturmius, *Epistle sent to the cardinals and prelates that were appointed by the Bishop of Rome to search out the abuses of the Church.* Translated by Richard Morysine. Berthelet, 1538.

A later copy of the *Concilium de emendanda Ecclesia*, printed by Sturmius with his letter in 1538, in the British Museum, formerly belonged to Cecil. The title-page has his signature, "Gulielmus Cecilius, 1540," and there are marks and words underlined, and some few observations from his pen in the margin. It is interesting to note that what struck the statesman as a youth were just the points which could be turned against the temporal claims of the Roman See.

The special evils needing correction which the committee of cardinals note, and which they call *abuses*, are collected under 22 headings, some of which are the following:—

(1) Ordination of priests without cure of souls, not learned, of lower order in life, and too young and of doubtful morals: They suggest that each diocese

to the admission of Papal prerogatives was the "lord-ship" which he claimed over and above the spiritual powers he exercised as successor of St. Peter. On

should have a *magistrum* to see that candidates are properly instructed—none to be ordained except by their own bishop.

(2) Benefices, and in particular, episcopal sees, are given to people with interest, and not because their elevation would be good for the church. They suggest that the best man should be chosen, and residence should be insisted on, and consequently "non Italo conferendum est beneficium in Hispania aut in Britannia aut ex contra."

(3) *Pensions* reserved from Benefices. Though the Pope, "who is the universal dispenser of the goods of the church," may reserve a part for a pious use, *e.g.* for the poor, &c., still not to reserve sufficient for the proper purpose of the beneficiary, and still more to give a pension out of a benefice to one rich enough without, is wrong.

(4) Change of benefices for the sake of gain, and handing on benefices by arrangement or always assigning episcopal sees to coadjutors, is the cause of outcry against the clergy, and is in reality making private property out of what is public.

(5) Permission to clergy to hold more than one benefice.

(6) Cardinals being allowed to hold sees. They ought to be counsellors to the Pope in Rome, and when holding sees they are more or less dependent on the will of the kings, and so cannot give independent advice and speak their minds.

(7) Absence of bishops from their sees.

(8) Such religious houses as needed correction should be forbidden to profess members, and when they die out, their places should be taken by fervent religious. Confessors for convents must be approved by the ordinaries of the place.

(9) The use of the keys ought never, under any pretext, to be granted for money.

(10) Questors of the Holy Spirit, St. Anthony, &c., who foster superstition among the poor people, should be prohibited.

(11) Confessional privileges and use of portable altars to be very rarely allowed.

(12) No indulgences to be granted except once a year, and in the great cities only.

Finally they say of Rome: "Hæc Romana civitas et ecclesia mater est et magistra aliarum ecclesiarum," and hence it should be a model to all. Foreigners, however, who come to St. Peter's find that priests "sordidi, ignari, induti paramentis et vestibus quibus nec in sordidis ædibus honeste uti possent, missas celebrant."

Cardinal Sadolet, on receiving a copy of Sturmius's letter, replied in kindly terms. He had, he declared, a high opinion of "Sturmius, Melanchthon, and Bucer, looking on them as most learned men, kindly disposed, and cordially friendly to him. He looked upon it as the peculiar characteristic of Luther this point we find preachers and writers of the period insisting most clearly and definitely. Some, of course, attack the spiritual jurisdiction directly, but most commonly such attacks are flavoured and served up for general consumption by a supply of abuse of the temporal assumptions and the wordly show of the Popes. This appealed to the popular mind, and to the growing sense of national aims and objects, and the real issue of the spiritual headship was obscured by the plea of national sentiment and safeguards.

To take one more example: Bishop Tunstall, on Palm Sunday, 1539, preached before the king and court. His object was to defend the rejection of the Papal supremacy and jurisdiction. He declaimed against the notion that the Popes were to be considered as free from subjection to worldly powers, maintaining that in this they were like all other men. "The Popes," he says, "exalt their seat above the stars of God, and ascend above the clouds, and will be like to God Almighty. . . . The Bishop of Rome offers his feet to be kissed, shod with his shoes on. This I saw myself, being present thirty-four years ago, when Julius, the Bishop of Rome, stood on his feet and one of his chamberlains held up his skirt because it stood not, as he thought, with his dignity that he

to try and overwhelm all his opponents with shouts and attacks." He speaks of the great piety of Pope Clement from personal knowledge. His wars were, he said, rather the work of his adversaries than his own (*De consilio*, ed. J. G. Schelhorn, 1748, p. 91).

He also, in 1539, penned the *De Christiana Ecclesia* (in *Specilegium Romanum*, ii. p. 101 *seqq.*), sending it to Cardinal Salicati, and asking him to pass it on to Cardinal Contarini. It was the outcome of conversations about the troubles of the Church, and the result of the movement was the Council of Trent, to restore, as Sadolet says, ecclesiastical discipline "quæ nunc tota pæne nobis e manibus elapsa est."

should do it himself, that his shoes might appear, whilst a nobleman of great age prostrated himself upon the ground and kissed his shoes." [1]

To us, to-day, much that was written and spoken at this time will appear, like many of the above passages, foolish and exaggerated ; but the language served its purpose, and contributed more than anything else to lower the Popes in the eyes of the people, and to justify in their minds the overthrow of the ecclesiastical system which had postulated the Pope as the universal Father of the Christian Church. Each Sunday, in every parish church throughout the country, they had been invited in the bidding prayer, as their fathers had been for generations, to remember their duty of praying for their common Father, the Pope. When the Pope's authority was finally rejected by the English king and his advisers, it was necessary to justify this serious breach with the past religious practice, and the works of the period prove beyond doubt that this was done in the popular mind by turning men's thoughts to the temporal aspect of the Papacy, and making them think that it was for the national profit and honour that this foreign yoke should be cast off. Whilst this is clear, it is also equally clear in the works of the time that the purely religious aspect of the question was as far as possible relegated to a secondary place in the discussions. This was perhaps not unnatural, as the duty of defending the rejection of the Papal supremacy can hardly have been very tasteful to those who were forced by the strong arm of the State to justify it before the people. As late as 1540 we are told by a contemporary writer that the spirituality under the bishops

---

[1] *Sermon on Palm Sunday*, Berthelet, 1539.

"favour as much as they dare the Bishop of Rome's laws and his ways."[1]

Even the actual meaning attached to the formal acknowledgment of the king's Headship by the clergy was sufficiently ambiguous to be understood, by some at least, as aimed merely at the temporal jurisdiction of the Roman curia. It is true it is usually understood that Convocation by its act, acknowledging Henry as sole supreme Head of the Church - of England, gave him absolute spiritual jurisdiction. Whatever may have been the intention of the king in requiring the acknowledgment from the clergy, it seems absolutely certain that the ruling powers in the Church considered that by their grant there was no derogation of the Pope's spiritual jurisdiction.

A comparison of the clauses required by Henry with those actually granted by Convocation makes it evident that any admission that the crown had any cure of souls, that is, spiritual jurisdiction, was specifically guarded against. In place of the clause containing the words, " cure of souls committed to his Majesty," proposed in the king's name to his clergy, they adopted the form, " the nation committed to his Majesty." The other royal demands were modified in the same manner, and it is consequently obvious that all the insertions proposed by the crown were weighed with the greatest care by skilled ecclesiastical jurists in some two and thirty sessions, and the changes introduced by them with the proposals made on behalf of the king throw considerable light upon the meaning which Convocation intended to give to the *Supremum Caput* clause. In one

---

[1] Lancelot Ridley, *Commentary in Englyshe on Sayncte Paule's Epystle to the Ephesians,* L. 4.

sense, perhaps not the obvious one, but one that had *de facto* been recognised during Catholic ages, the sovereign was the Protector—the *advocatus*—of the Church in his country, and to him the clergy would look to protect his people from the introduction of heresy and for maintenance in their temporalities.   So that whilst, on the one hand, the king and Thomas Crumwell may well have desired the admission of Henry's authority over "the English Church, whose Protector and supreme Head he alone is," to cover even spiritual jurisdiction, on the other hand, Warham and the English Bishops evidently did intend it to cover only an admission that the king had taken all jurisdiction in temporals, hitherto exercised by the Pope in England, into his own hands.

Moreover, looking at what was demanded and at what was granted by the clergy, there is little room for doubt that they at first deliberately eliminated any acknowledgment of the Royal jurisdiction.   This deduction is turned into a certainty by the subsequent action of Archbishop Warham.   He first protested that the admission was not to be twisted in "derogation of the Roman Pontiff or the Apostolic See," and the very last act of his life was the drafting of an elaborate exposition, to be delivered in the House of Lords, of the impossibility of the king's having spiritual jurisdiction, from the very nature of the constitution of the Christian Church.   Such jurisdiction, he claimed, belonged of right to the Roman See.[1]

That the admission wrung from the clergy in fact formed the thin end of the wedge which finally severed

---

[1] This important paper was printed for the first time in the *Dublin Review,* April 1894, pp. 390–420.

the English Church from the spiritual jurisdiction of the Holy See is obvious.   But the " thin end " was, there can be hardly any doubt, the temporal aspect of the authority of the Roman See ; and that its insertion at all was possible may be said in greater measure to be due to the fact that the exercise of jurisdiction in temporals by a foreign authority had long been a matter which many Englishmen had strongly resented.

CHAPTER V

CLERGY AND LAITY

IT is very generally asserted that on the eve of the Reformation the laity in England had no particular love or respect for churchmen. That there were grave difficulties and disagreements between the two estates is supposed to be certain. On the face of it, however, the reason and origin of what is frequently called " the grudge " of laymen against the ecclesiastics is obviously much misunderstood. Its extent is exaggerated, its origin put at an earlier date than should be assigned to it, and the whole meaning of the points at issue interpreted quite unnecessarily as evidence of a popular and deep-seated disbelief in the prevailing ecclesiastical system. To understand the temper of people and priest in those times, it is obviously necessary to examine into this question in some detail. We are not without abundant material in the literature of the period for forming a judgment as to the relations which then existed between the clerical and lay elements in the State. Fortunately, not only have we assertions on the one side and on the other as to the questions at issue, but the whole matter was debated at the time in a series of tracts by two eminent laymen. This discussion was carried on between an anonymous writer, now recognised as the lawyer, Christopher Saint–German, and Sir Thomas More himself.

Christopher Saint-German, who is chiefly known as the writer of a *Dyalogue in English between a Student of Law and a Doctor of Divinity*, belonged to the Inner Temple, and was, it has already been said, a lawyer of considerable repute. About the year 1532, a tract from his pen called *A treatise concerning the division between the spiritualtie and temporaltie* appeared anonymously. To this Sir Thomas More, who had just resigned the office of Chancellor, replied in his celebrated *Apology*, published in 1533. Saint-German rejoined in the same year with *A Dyalogue between two Englishmen, whereof one is called Salem and the other Bizance*, More immediately retorting with the *Debellacyon of Salem and Bizance*. In these four treatises the whole matter of the supposed feud between the clergy and laity is thrashed out, and the points at issue are clearly stated and discussed.

Christopher Saint-German's position is at first somewhat difficult to understand. By some of his contemporaries he was considered to have been tainted by "the new teaching" in doctrinal matters, which at the time he wrote was making some headway in England. He himself, however, professes to write as a loyal believer in the teaching of the Church, but takes exception to certain ecclesiastical laws and customs which in his opinion are no necessary part of the system at all. In these he thinks he detects the cause of the "division that had risen between the spiritualtie and the temporaltie." Sir Thomas More, it may be remarked, is always careful to treat the writer as if he believed him to be a sincere Catholic, though mistaken in both the extent of the existing disaffection to the Church and altogether impracticable in the remedies he suggested.   In some things it must, however, be confessed, granting Saint-German's facts, that he shows weighty grounds for some grievance against the clergy on the part of the laity.

The treatise concerning the division begins by expressing regret at the unfortunate state of things which the author pre-supposes as existing in England when he wrote in 1532, contrasting it with what he remembered before. "Who may remember the state of this realm now in these days," he writes, "without great heaviness and sorrow of heart? For whereas, in times past, there has reigned charity, meekness, concord, and peace, there now reigns envy, pride, division, and strife, and that not only between laymen and churchmen, but also between religious and religious, and between priests and religious, and what is more to be lamented also between priests and priests. This division has been so universal that it has been a great (cause of) disquiet and a great breach of charity through all the realm." [1]

It must be confessed that if this passage is to be taken as it stands, the division would appear to have been very widely spread at the time. Sir Thomas More, whilst denying that the difficulty was so great as Saint-German would make out, admits that in late years the spirit had grown and was still growing apace.   He holds, however, that Saint-German's reasons for its existence are not the true ones, and that his methods will only serve to increase the spirit of division.   As regards the quarrels between religious, at which Saint-German expresses his indignation, he says: " Except this man

[1] *A treatise concerning the division between the spiritualtie and temporaltie.* London : Robert Redman, f. 2.

means here by religious folk, either women and children with whose variances the temporality is not very much disturbed, or else the lay brethren, who are in some places of religion, and who are neither so many nor so much esteemed, that ever the temporality was much troubled at their strife, besides this there is no variance between religious and religious with which the temporality have been offended." [1] Again: "Of some particular variance among divers persons of the clergy I have indeed heard, as sometimes one against another for his tithes, or a parson against a religious place for meddling with his parish, or one place of religion with another upon some such like occasions, or sometime some one religious (order) have had some question and dispute as to the antiquity or seniority of its institution, as (for instance) the Carmelites claim to derive their origin from Elias and Eliseus: and some question has arisen in the Order of Saint Francis between the Observants and the Conventuals (for of the third company, that is to say the Colettines, there are none in this realm). But of all these matters, as far as I have read or remember, there were never in this realm either so very great or so many such (variances) all at once, that it was ever at the time remarked through the realm and spoken of as a great and notable fault of the whole clergy." Particular faults and petty quarrels should not be considered the cause of any great grudge against the clergy at large. "And as it is not in reason that it should be, so in fact it is not so, as may be understood from this:" . . . "if it were the case, then must this

[1] *English Works*, p. 871. In the quotations made from the works of Sir Thomas More and other old writings, for the sake of the general reader the modern form of spelling has been adopted, and at times the words transposed to ensure greater clearness.

grudge of ours against them have been a very old thing, whereas it is indeed neither so great as this man maketh out, nor grown to so great (a pass) as it is, but only even so late as Tyndale's books and Frith's and Friar Barnes' began to go abroad."[1]

Further, in several places Sir Thomas More emphatically asserts that the talking against the clergy, the hostile feeling towards them, and the dissensions said to exist between them and lay folk generally, were only of very recent origin, and were at worst not very serious. " I have, within these four or five years (for before I heard little talk of such things)," he writes, "been present at such discussions in divers good companies, never talking in earnest thereof (for as yet I thank God that I never heard such talk), but as a passtime and in the way of familiar talking, I have heard at such times some in hand with prelates and secular priests and religious persons, and talk of their lives, and their learning, and of their livelihood too, and as to whether they were such, that it were better to have them or not to have them. Then touching their livelihood (it was debated), whether it might be lawfully taken away from them or no ; and if it might, whether it were expedient for it to be taken, and if so for what use."[2]

To this Saint-German replies at length in his *Salem and Bizance*, and says that Sir Thomas More must have known that the difficulties had their origin long before the rise of the new religious views, and were not in any sense founded upon the opinions of the modern heretics.[3]   More answers by reasserting his position that

[1] Ibid., p. 875.   [2] Ibid., p. 882.
[3] *Salem and Bizance.   A dialogue betwixte two Englishmen, whereof one was called Salem and the other Bizance.*   London : Berthelet, 1533, f. 5.

" the division is nothing such as this man makes it, and is grown as great as it is only since Tyndale's books and Frith's and Friar Barnes' began to be spread abroad." And in answer to Saint-German's suggestion that he should look a little more closely into the matter, he says : " Indeed, with better looking thereon I find it somewhat otherwise. For I find the time of such increase as I speak of much shorter than I assigned, and that by a great deal. For it has grown greater " by reason of " the book upon the division," which Saint-German with the best of intentions had circulated among the people.[1]

Putting one book against the other, it would appear then tolerably certain that the rise of the anti-clerical spirit in England must be dated only just before the dawn of the Reformation, when the popular mind was being stirred up by the new teachers against the clergy. There seems, moreover, no reason to doubt the positive declaration of Sir Thomas More, who had every means of knowing, that the outcry was modern—so modern indeed that it was practically unknown only four or five years before 1533, and that it originated undoubtedly from the dissemination of Lutheran views and teachings by Tyndale and others. It is useful to examine well into the grounds upon which this anti-clerical campaign was conducted, and to note the chief causes of objection to the clergy which are found set forth by Saint-German in his books. In the first place : " Some say," he writes, that priests and religious " keep not the perfection of their order," and do not set that good example to the people " they should do." Some also work for " their own honour, and call it the

---

[1] *English Works*, p. 934.

honour of God, and rather covet to have rule over the people than to profit the people." Others think more about their " bodily ease and worldly wealth and meat and drink," and the like, even more than lay people do. Others, again, serve God " for worldly motives, to obtain the praise of men, to enrich themselves and the like, and not from any great love of God."

Such is the first division of the general accusations which Saint-German states were popularly made against the clergy in 1532. Against these may be usefully set Sir Thomas More's examination of the charges, and his own opinion as to the state of the clergy. In his previous works he had, he says, forborne to use words unpleasant either to the clergy or laity about themselves, though he had " confessed what is true, namely, that neither were faultless." But what had offended "these blessed brethren," the English followers of Luther, was that " I have not hesitated to say, what I also take for the very truth, that as this realm of England has, God be thanked, as good and praiseworthy a temporality, number for number, as any other Christian country of equal number has had, so has it had also, number for number, compared with any other realm of no greater number in Christendom, as good and as commendable a clergy. In both there have never been wanting plenty of those who have always been ' naught ' ; but their faults have ever been their own and should not be imputed to the whole body, neither in the spirituality nor temporality." [1]

Turning to the special accusation made by Saint-German that ecclesiastics " do not keep the perfection of their order," More grants that this may " not be

[1] Ibid., p. 870.

much untrue." For " Man's duty to God is so great
that very few serve Him as they should do." . . . " But,
I suppose, they keep it now at this day much after
such a good metely manner as they did in the years
before, during which this division was never dreamed
of, and therefore those who say this is the cause have
need to go seek some other."[1] To the second point
his reply is equally clear. It is true, More thinks,
that some ecclesiastics do look perhaps to their own
honour and profit, but, he asks, " were there never
any such till so lately as the beginning of this division,
or are all of them like this now ? " No doubt there
are some such, and " I pray God that when any new
ones shall come they may prove no worse. For of
these, if they wax not worse before they die, those who
shall live after them may, in my mind, be bold to say
that England had not their betters any time these forty
years, and I dare go for a good way beyond this too.
But this is more than twenty years, and ten before this
division " (between the clergy and laity) was heard of.[2]
Further, as far as his own opinion goes, although there
may be, and probably are, some priests and religious
whom the world accounts good and virtuous, who are
yet at heart evil-minded, this is no reason to despise
or condemn the whole order. Equally certain is it
that besides such there are " many very virtuous, holy
men indeed, whose holiness and prayer have been, I
verily believe, one great special cause that God has
so long held His hand from letting some heavier stroke
fall on the necks of those whether in the spirituality
or temporality who are naught and care not." [3]

[1] Ibid., p. 877.   [2] Ibid., p. 877.
                [3] Ibid., p. 878.

In his *Apology*, Sir Thomas More protested against the author of the work on the *Division* translating a passage from the Latin of John Gerson, about the evil lives of priests; and on Saint-German excusing himself in his second book, More returns to the point in *The Debellation of Salem and Bizance*. More had pleaded that his opponent had dragged the faults of the clergy into light rather than those of the laity, because if the priests led good lives, as St. John Chrysostom had said, the whole Church would be in a good state; "and if they were corrupt, the faith and virtue of the people fades also and vanishes away." "Surely, good readers," exclaims More, "I like these words well." They are very good, and they prove "the matter right well, and very true is it, nor did I ever say the contrary, but have in my *Apology* plainly said the same: that every fault in a spiritual man is, by the difference of the person, far worse and more odious to God and man than if it were in a temporal man." And indeed the saying of St. Chrysostom "were in part the very cause that made me write against his (*i.e.* Saint-German's) book. For assuredly, as St. Chrysostom says: 'If the priesthood be corrupt, the faith and virtue of the people fades and vanishes away.' This is without any question very true, for though St Chrysostom had never said it, our Saviour says as much himself. 'Ye are (saith He to the clergy) the salt of the earth.' . . . But, I say, since the priesthood is corrupted it must needs follow that the faith and virtue of the people fades and vanishes away, and on Christ's words it must follow that, if the spirituality be nought, the temporality must needs be worse than they. I, upon this, conclude on the other side against this 'Pacifier's' book, that since this realm has (as God be thanked indeed it has) as good and as faithful a temporality (though there be a few false brethren in a great multitude of true Catholic men) as any other Christian country of equal size has, it must needs, I say, follow that the clergy (though it have some such false evil brethren too) is not so sorely corrupted as the book of *Division* would make people think, but on their side they are as good as the temporality are on theirs.[1]

On one special point Saint-German insists very strongly. As it is a matter upon which much has been said, and upon which people are inclined to believe the worst about the pre-Reformation clergy, it may be worth while to give his views at some length, and then take Sir Thomas More's opinion also on the subject. It is on the eternal question of the riches of the Church, and the supposed mercenary spirit which pervaded the clergy. "Some lay people say," writes Saint-German, "that however much religious men have disputed amongst themselves as to the pre-eminence of their particular state in all such things as pertain to the maintenance of the worldly honour of the Church and of spiritual men, which they call the honour of God, and in all such things as pertain to the increase of the riches of spiritual men, all, religious or secular, agree as one." For this reason it is found that religious men are much more earnest in trying to induce people to undertake and support such works as produce money for themselves, such as trentals, chantries, obits, pardons, and pilgrimages, than in insisting upon the payments of debts, upon restitution for wrong done, or upon works of mercy "to their

[1] Ibid., pp. 937, 938.

neighbours poor and needy—sometimes in extreme necessity."[1]

Sir Thomas More replies that those who object in this way, object not so much because the trentals, &c., tend to make priests rich, but because they "hate" the things themselves. Indeed, some of these things are not such that they make priests so very rich, in fact, as to induce them to use all endeavour to procure them. The chantries, for example, "though they are many, no one man can make any very great living out of them ; and that a priest should have some living of such a mean thing as the chantries commonly are, no good man will find great fault." As for pilgrimages, "though the shrines are well garnished, and the chapel well hanged with wax (candles), few men nowadays, I fear, can have much cause to grudge or complain of the great offerings required from them. Those men make the most ado who offer nothing at all." And with regard to "pardons," it should be remembered that they were procured often "by the good faithful devotion of virtuous secular princes, as was the great pardon purchased for Westminster and the Savoy" by Henry VII. "And in good faith I never yet perceived," he says, "that people make such great offerings at a pardon that we should either much pity their expense or envy the priests that profit."

"But then the trentals ! Lo, they are the things, as you well know, by which the multitude of the clergy and specially the prelates, all get an infinite treasure each year." For himself, Sir Thomas More hopes and "beseeches God to keep men devoted to the trentals and obits too." But where this "Pacifier" asserts that

---

[1] *A treatise concerning the division*, f. 8.

"some say that all spiritual men as a body induce people to pilgrimages, pardons, chantries, obits, and trentals, rather than to the payment of their debts, or to restitution of their wrongs, or to deeds of mercy to their neighbours that are poor and needy, and sometimes in extreme necessity, for my part, I thank God," he says, "that I never heard yet of any one who ever would give that counsel, and no more has this ' Pacifier' himself, for he says it only under his common figure of ' some say.' " [1]

In his second reply, More returns to the same subject. Saint-German speaks much, he says, about "restitution." This, should there be need, no reasonable man would object to. "But now the matter standeth all in this way : this man talks as if the spirituality were very busy to procure men and induce people (generally) to give money for trentals, to found chantries and obits, to obtain pardons and to go on pilgrimages, leaving their debts unpaid and restitution unmade which should be done first, and that this was the custom of the spirituality. In this," says More, "standeth the question." The point is not whether debts and restitution should be satisfied before all other things, which all will allow, but whether the "multitude of the clergy, that is to say either all but a few, or at least the most part, solicit and labour lay people to do these (voluntary) things rather than pay their debts or make restitution for their wrongs. . . . That the multitude of priests do this, I never heard any honest man for very shame say. For I think it were hard to meet with a priest so wretched, who, were he asked his advice and counsel on that point, would not in so plain

_____
[1] *English Works*, p. 880.

a matter, though out of very shame, well and plainly counsel the truth, and if perchance there were found any so shameless as to give contrary counsel, I am very sure they would be by far the fewer, and not as this good man's first book says, the greater part and multitude." What, therefore, More blames so much is, that under pretext of an altogether " untrue report " the clergy generally are held up to obloquy and their good name slandered.[1] If he thinks that " I do but mock him to my poor wit, I think it somewhat more civility in some such points as this to mock him a little merrily, than with odious earnest arguments to discuss matters seriously with him."

In some things even Saint-German considers the outcry raised against the clergy unreasonable. But then, as he truly says, many " work rather upon will than upon reason," and though possessed of great and good zeal are lacking in necessary discretion. Thus some people, seeing the evils that come to the Church from riches, " have held the opinion that it was not lawful for the Church to have any possessions." Others, " taking a more mean way," have thought that the Church ought not to have " that great abundance that " it has, for this induces a love of riches in churchmen and " hinders, and in a manner strangles, the love of God." These last would-be reformers of churchmen advocate taking away all that is not necessary. Others, again, have gone a step further still, " and because great riches have come to the Church for praying for souls in Purgatory, have affirmed that there is no Purgatory." In the same way such men would be against pardons, pilgrimages, and chantries. They outwardly appear

[1] Ibid., p. 951.

"to rise against all these . . . and to despise them, and yet in their hearts they know and believe that all such things are of themselves right good and profitable, as indeed they are, if they are ordered as they should be."[1]

Sir Thomas More truly says that what is implied in this outcry against the riches of the clergy is that as a body they lead idle, luxurious, if not vicious lives. It is easy enough to talk in this way, but how many men in secular occupations, he asks, would be willing to change? There might be "some who would, and gladly would, have become prelates (for I have heard many laymen who would very willingly have been bishops), and there might be found enough to match those that are evil and naughty secular priests, and those too who have run away from the religious life, and these would, and were able to, match them in their own ways were they never so bad. Yet, as the world goes now, it would not be very easy, I ween, to find sufficient to match the good, even though they be as few as some folk would have them to be."

In the fifteenth chapter of his book on the *Division*, Saint-German deals specially with the religious life and with what in his opinion people think about it, and about those who had given up their liberty for a life in the cloister. The matter is important, and considerable extracts are necessary fully to understand the position. "Another cause" of the dislike of the clergy by the laity is to be sought for in the "great laxity and liberty of living that people have seen in religious men. For they say, that though religious men profess obedience and poverty, yet many of them have and will have their

---

[1] *A treatise concerning the division*, f. 3.

own will, with plenty of delicate food in such abundance that no obedience or poverty appears in them. For this reason many have said, and yet say to the present day, that religious men have the most pleasant and delicate life that any men have. And truly, if we behold the holiness and blessed examples of the holy fathers, and of many religious persons that have lived in times past, and of many that now live in these days, we should see right great diversity between them. For many of them, I trow, as great diversity as between heaven and hell." Then, after quoting the eighteenth chapter of *The Following of Christ*, he proceeds : "Thus far goeth the said chapter. But the great pity is that most men say that at the present day many religious men will rather follow their own will than the will of their superior, and that they will neither suffer hunger nor thirst, heat nor cold, nakedness, weariness nor labour, but will have riches, honour, dignities, friends, and worldly acquaintances, the attendance of servants at their commands, pleasure and disports, and that more liberally than temporal men have. Thus, say some, are they fallen from true religion, whereby the devotion of the people is in a manner fallen from them."

"Nevertheless, I doubt not that there are many right good and virtuous religious persons. God forbid that it should be otherwise. But it is said that there are many evil, and that in such a multitude that those who are good cannot, or will not, see them reformed. And one great cause that hinders reform is this : if the most dissolute person in all the community, and the one who lives most openly against the rules of religion, can use this policy, namely, to extol his (form of) religious life above all others, pointing them out as not being so perfect as that to which he belongs, anon he shall be called a good fervent brother, and one that supports his Order, and for this reason his offences shall be looked on the more lightly."

"Another thing that has caused many people to mislike religious has been the great extremity that has been many times witnessed at the elections of abbots, priors, and such other spiritual sovereigns. And this is a general ground, for when religious men perceive that people mislike them, they in their hearts withdraw their favour and devotion again from them. And in this way charity has waxed cold between them."

"And verily, I suppose, that it were better that there should be no abbot or prior hereafter allowed to continue over a certain number of years, and that these should be appointed by the authority of the rulers, rather than have such extremities at elections, as in many places has been used in times past.

"And verily, it seems to me, one thing would do great good concerning religious Orders and all religious persons, and that is this : that the Rules and Constitutions of religious bodies should be examined and well considered, whether their rigour and straightness can be borne now in these days as they were at the beginning of the religious Orders. For people be nowadays weaker, as to the majority of men, than they were then. And if it is thought that they (*i.e.* the Rules) cannot now be kept, that then such relaxations and interpretations of their rules be made, as shall be thought expedient by the rulers. Better it is to have an easy rule well kept, than a strict rule broken without correction. For, thereof followeth a boldness to offend, a quiet heart in

an evil conscience : a custom in sin, with many an ill
example to the people.   By this many have found fault
at all religious life, where they should rather have found
fault at divers abuses against the true religion.   Certain
it is that religious, life was first ordained by the holy
fathers by the inspiration of the Holy Ghost, keep it
who so may." [1]

Much of this criticism on the state of the religious
orders on the eve of the Reformation is obviously only
very general, and would apply to all states of society,
composed, as such bodies are, of human members.
With much that Saint-German suggests, it is impossible
not to agree in principle, however difficult the attainment of the ideal may be in practice.   Sir Thomas
More, whilst admitting that there were undoubtedly
things requiring correction in the religious life of the
period, maintains most strongly that in practical working it was far better than any one would gather from
the assertions and suggestions of Saint-German, and
that in reality, with all their carping at laxity and world-
liness, none of the critics of the monks would be willing
to change places with them.   "As wealthy," he writes,
"and as easy and as glorious as some tell 'the pacifier' religious life is, yet if some other would say to them : 'Lo
sirs, those folks who are in religion shall out, come you
into religion in their steads ; live there better than they
do, and you shall have heaven,' they would answer, I fear
me, that they are not weary of the world.   And even if
they were invited into religion another way, and it was
said to them, 'Sir, we will not bid you live so straight
in religion as these men should have done ; come on
enter, and do just as they did, and then you will have a

---

[1] *A treatise concerning the division,* f. 41.

good, easy, and wealthy life, and much worldly praise for it,—I ween for all that, a man would not get them to go into it. But as easy as we call it, and as wealthy too—and now peradventure when our wives are angry we wish ourselves therein—were it offered . . . I ween that for all our words, if that easy and wealthy life that is in religion were offered to us, even as weary as we are of wedding, we would rather bear all our pain abroad than take a religious man's life of ease in the cloister." [1]

With some of the accusations of Saint-German, or rather with some of his explanations of the supposed "grudge" borne by the laity to the clergy, More has hardly the patience to deal. They, the clergy, and above all religious, should, the former says, "give alms and wear hair (shirts), and fast and pray that this division may cease." " Pray, wear hair, fast, and give alms," says the latter ; " why, what else do they do as a rule ? Some may not ; but then there were some negligent in those matters for the past thousand years, and so the present negligence of a few can't be the cause of the dissension now." " But this 'pacifier,' perceiving that what one man does in secret another cannot see, is therefore bold to say they do not do all those things he would have them do ; that is to say, fast, pray, wear hair (shirts), and give alms. For he says 'that they do all these things it appears not.'"

Now, " as to praying, it appears indeed that they do this ; and that so much that they daily pray, as some of us lay men think it a pain (to do) once a week ; to rise so soon from sleep and to wait so long fasting, as on a Sunday to come and hear out their matins. And

[1] *English Works*, p. 884.

yet the matins in every parish is neither begun so early nor so long in the saying as it is in the Charter house you know well ; and yet at the sloth and gluttony of us, who are lay people, he can wink and fan himself asleep. But as soon as the lips of the clergy stop moving he quickly spies out that they are not praying."

And "now as touching on alms: Is there none given, does he think, by the spirituality ?   If he say, as he does, that it does not appear that they do give alms, I might answer again that they but follow in this the counsel of Christ which says : 'Let not the left hand see what thy right hand doeth.' . . . But as God, for all that counsel, was content that men should both pray and give to the needy and do other works both of penance and of charity openly and abroad, where there is no desire of vain glory, but that the people by the sight thereof might have occasion therefore to give laud and praise to God, so I dare say boldly that they, both secretly and openly too, . . . give no little alms in the year, whatsoever this 'pacifier' do say.   And I somewhat marvel, since he goes so busily abroad that there is no 'some say,' almost in the whole realm, which he does not hear and repeat it ; I marvel, I say, not a little that he neither sees nor hears from any 'some say' that there is almsgiving in the spirituality ; I do not much myself go very far abroad, and yet I hear 'some say' that there is ; and I myself see sometimes so many poor folk at Westminster at the doles, of whom, as far as I have ever heard, the monks are not wont to send many away unserved, that I have myself for the press of them been fain to ride another way."

" But to this, some one once answered me and said ; 'that it was no thanks to them, for it (came from) lands that good princes have given them.' But, as I then told him, it was then much less thanks to them that would now give good princes evil counsel to take it from them. And also if we are to call it not giving of alms by them, because other good men have given them the lands from which they give it, from what will you have them give alms ? They have no other. . . ."

Further replying to the insinuation of Saint-German that the religious keep retainers and servants out of pride and for " proud worldly countenance," Sir Thomas More says : " If men were as ready in regard to a deed of their own, by nature indifferent, to construe the mind and intent of the doer to the better part, as they are, of their own inward goodness, to construe and report it to the worst, then might I say, that the very thing which they call 'the proud worldly countenance' they might and should call charitable alms. That is to say, (when they furnish) the right honest keep and good bringing up of so many temporal men in their service, who though not beggars yet perhaps the greater part of them might have to beg if they did not support them but sent them out to look for some service for themselves," (they are giving charitable alms).

" And just as if you would give a poor man some money because he was in need and yet would make him go and work for it in your garden, lest by your alms he should live idle and become a loiterer, the labour he does, does not take away the nature nor merit of alms : so neither is the keeping of servants no alms, though they may wait on the finder and serve him in his house. And of all alms the chief is, to see people well brought up and well and honestly guided. In which point, though neither part do fully their duty, yet I believe in good faith that in this matter, which is no small alms, the spirituality is rather somewhat before us than in any way drags behind." [1]

With regard to the charge brought against the clergy of great laxity in fasting and mortification, More thinks this is really a point on which he justly can make merry. Fasting, he says, must be regulated according to custom and the circumstances of time and place. If there were to be a cast-iron rule for fasting, then, when compared with primitive times, people in his day, since they dined at noon, could not be held to fast at all. And yet "the Church to condescend to our infirmity" has allowed men "to say their evensong in Lent before noon," in order that they might not break their fast before the vesper hour. The fact is that, in More's opinion, a great deal of the outcry about the unmortified lives of the religious and clergy had "been made in Germany" by those who desired to throw off all such regulations for themselves. As a Teuton had said to him in "Almaine" colloquial English—"when I blamed him," More says, "for not fasting on a certain day: 'Fare to sould te laye men fasten? let te prester fasten.' So we, God knows, begin to fast very little ourselves, but bid the 'prester to fasten.'" [2]

"And as to such mortifications as the wearing of hair shirts, it would indeed be hard to bind men, even priests, to do this, . . . though among them many do so already, and some whole religious bodies too." If he says, as he does, that this "does not appear," what would he have? Would he wish them

<hr />

[1] Ibid., p. 895.   [2] Ibid.

to publish to the world these penances? If they take his, Saint-German's, advice, " they will come out of their cloisters every man into the market-place, and there kneel down in the gutters, and make their prayers in the open streets, and wear their hair shirts over their cowls, and then it shall appear and men shall see it. And truly in this way there will be no hypocrisy for their shirts of hair, and yet moreover it will be a good policy, for then they will not prick them." [1]

In the same way More points out that people in talking against the wealth of the clergy are not less unreasonable than they are when criticising what they call their idle, easy lives. " Not indeed that we might not be able always to find plenty content to enter into their possessions, though we could not always find men enough content to enter their religions ; " but when the matter is probed to the bottom, and it is a question how their wealth " would be better bestowed," then " such ways as at the first face seemed very good and very charitable for the comfort and help of poor folk, appeared after reasoning more likely in a short while to make many more beggars than to relieve those that are so already. And some other ways that at first appeared for the greater advantage of the realm, and likely to increase the king's honour and be a great strength for the country, and a great security for the prince as well as a great relief of the people's charges, appeared clearly after further discussion to be 'clean contrary, and of all other ways the worst.'"

" And to say the truth," he continues, " I much

[1] Ibid., p. 896.

marvel to see some folk now speak so much and
boldly about taking away any possessions of the
clergy." For though once in the reign of Henry
IV., "about the time of a great rumble that the
heretics made, when they would have destroyed not
only the clergy but the king and his nobility also,
there was a foolish and false bill or two put into
Parliament and dismissed as they deserved; yet in
all my time, when I was conversant with the court,
I had never found of all the nobility of this land
more than seven (of which seven there are now three
dead) who thought that it was either right or reasonable, or could be any way profitable to the realm,
without lawful cause to take away from the clergy
any of the possessions which good and holy princes,
and other devout, virtuous people, of whom many
now are blessed saints in heaven, have of devotion
towards God given to the clergy to serve God and
pray for all Christian souls." [1]

In his *Confutation of Tyndale's Answer*, made in
1532, when Sir Thomas More was still Lord Chancellor of England, he protests against imputations
made by his adversary and his follower Barnes, that
the clergy were as a body corrupt. "Friar Barnes
lasheth out against them, against their pride and
pomp, and all their lives spent in" vicious living,
"as if there were not a good priest in all the Catholic
Church. . . . He jesteth on them because they wear
crowns and long gowns, and the bishops wear rochets.
And he hath likened them to bulls, asses, and apes,
and the rochets to smocks." "But he forgets how
many good virtuous priests and religious people be

[1] Ibid., p. 885.

put out of their places (in Germany) and spoiled of their living, and beaten, and sent out a-begging, while heretics and apostates, with their women, keep their shameless lives with the living that holy folks have dedicated unto God for the support of such as would serve God in spiritual cleanness and vowed chastity. He knows well enough, I warrant you, that the clergy can never lack persecution where heretics may grow; nor soon after the temporality either, as it has hitherto been proved in every such country yet." [1]

He will not repeat all his " ribald railing upon all the clergy of Christendom who will not be heretics " when he calls " them bulls, apes, asses, and abominable harlots and devils." . . . " No good man doubts, although among the clergy there are many full bad (as, indeed, it were hard to have it otherwise among so great a multitude, whilst Christ's own twelve were not without a traitor), that there are again among them many right virtuous folk, and such that the whole world beside fares the better for their holy living and their devout prayer." [2]

[1] Bishop Fisher gives much the same testimony to the moral character of the religious generally in his sermon against Luther. After praising the state of virginity, he continues : " And it is not to be doubted but that there is in Christendom at this day many thousands of religious men and women that full truly keep their religion and their chastity unto Christ. . . . If Almighty God did reserve in that little portion of Jewry so great a multitude beyond the estimation of the prophet, what number suppose ye doth yet remain in Christendom of religious men and women, notwithstanding this great persecution of religious monasteries, both of men and women, done by these heretics by this most execrable doctrine? It is not to be doubted but in all Christendom be left many thousands who at this hour live chaste, and truly keep their virginity unto Christ." (*A Sermon had at Paulis*, Berthelet, f. g. ii.)

[2] *Ibid.*, p. 735. Sir Thomas More, in his *Dyalogue*, thinks that the number of priests without very definite work had tended to diminish the respect paid to them by the laity. "But were I Pope," he says, . . . " I could not well devise better provisions than by the laws of the Church are provided already, if they were as well kept as they are well made. But as for

Beyond the above supposed causes for the growth of the dislike of the clergy which Sir Thomas More weighs and considers in the above extracts, Saint-German gives others which are instructive as to the actual status of the clergy ; but with which, as they do not reflect upon their moral character, Sir Thomas More was not immediately concerned in his reply. One occasion of the present difficulties and division, writes Saint-German, " has partly arisen by temporal men who have desired much the familiarity of priests in their games and sports, and who were wont to make much more of those who were companionable than of those that were not so, and have called them good fellows and good companions. And many also would have chaplains which they would not only suffer, but also command, to go hunting, hawking, and such other vain disports ; and some would let them lie among other lay servants, where they could neither use prayer nor contemplation."

Some even go so far as to insist on their chaplains wearing " liveries," which " are not convenient in colour for a priest to wear." Others give them worldly businesses to attend to in the way of stewardships, &c., " so that in this way their inward devotion of heart has become as cold and as weak, in a manner, as it is in lay men." Nevertheless, in spite of the evil effect to

the number, I would surely see such a way therein that we should not have such a rabble that every mean man must have a priest in his house to wait upon his wife. This no mean man lacketh now, to the contempt of the priesthood, (placed) in as vile an office as his horsekeeper. That is truth indeed, quod he, and in worse, too, for they keep hawks and dogs." If the laws of the Church were kept, there would not be the excessive number of priests for fit and proper positions, so that "the whole order is rebuked by the priests' begging and lewd living who are either obliged to walk as rovers, and live upon trentals or worse, or serve in a secular man's house" (*English Works*, p. 223).

be feared from this training, they do not hesitate to put them into the first benefice they have to dispose of ; " and when they have done so, they will anon speak evil of priests, and report great lightness in them, and lightly compare the faults of one priest with another." This they do " even when they themselves have been partly the occasion of their offences."

Moreover, " where by the law all priests ought to be at the (parish) church on Sundays and holidays, and help the service of God in the choir, and also, when there, to be under the orders of the curate (or parish priest of the place), yet nevertheless many men who have chaplains will not allow them to come to the parish church ; and when they are there, will not suffer them to receive their orders from the curate, but only from themselves ; nor will they tolerate seeing them in the choir ; " and what is the case with " chaplains and serving priests is also (true) of chantry priests and brotherhood priests in many places."

To remedy these evils, Saint-German thinks, as indeed every one would be disposed to agree with him, that priests should be prohibited from hunting and all such games as are unsuitable to the priestly character, " though perchance he may, as for recreation, use honest disportes for a time." Moreover, he should not " frequent the ale house or tavern," and, if in his recreations the people are offended, he should be warned by " an abbot and a justice of the peace of the shire." If, after this, he does not change, he ought to be suspended. Further than this, no one should be permitted to have a chaplain who has not " a standing house," where the priest is able to have his private chamber with a lock and key, so that " he may use himself therein conveniently in reading, prayer, or contemplation, or such other labours and business as it is convenient for a priest to use." [1]

Both in his work on the *Division* and in his previous tract, *A Dyalogue between a Student of Law and a Doctor of Divinity*, Saint-German lays great stress upon the question of mortuaries, as one that gave great offence to lay people at the period when he wrote. As he explained in the *Dyalogue*, the State had already interfered to regulate the exactions made by custom at funerals, but nevertheless " in some places the Church claims to have the taper that stands in the middle of the hearse over the heart of the corpse, and some claim to have all the tapers. Some also claim to have one of the torches that is about the hearse, and others to have all the torches. And if the body be brought in a charette or with coat armour or such other (ornaments), then they claim all the horses and charette and the apparel or part thereof." [2]   Now, in his other book, Saint-German thinks that though these things " are annulled already by statute," there is rising up " a thing concerning mortuaries," that " if it be allowed to continue " will cause great difficulties in the near future. It is this : " Many curates not regarding the king's statute in that behalf, persuade their parishioners when they are sick to believe that they cannot be saved unless they restore them as much as the old mortuary would have amounted to." All those who act in such a way are, he thinks, " bound in conscience to restitution, since they have obtained money under false information." [3]

[1] *A treatise concerning the division*, ff. 14–16.

[2] *Dyalogue*, &c., f. 2.

[3] *A treatise concerning the division*, f. 23.

After arguing that Parliament has a right to legislate in all matters concerning goods and property, our
author says: "It is certain that all such mortuaries
were temporal goods, though they were claimed by
spiritual men; and the cause why they were taken
away was, because there were few things within this
realm which caused more variance among the people
than they did, when they were allowed.   They were
taken so far against the king's laws and against justice
and right, as shall hereafter appear.   First they were
taken not only after the husband's death, but also after
the death of the wife, who by the law of the realm had
no goods, but what were the husband's.   They were
taken also from servants and children, as well infants
as others; and if a man died on a journey and had a
household, he should pay mortuaries in both places."
Whilst in some places both the parson and the vicar
claimed the mortuary; "and sometime even the curate
(*i.e.* parish priest) would prohibit poor men to sell
their goods, as were likely to come to them as mortuaries, for they would say it was done in 'order to
defraud the Church."   And the mortuaries had to be
handed over at once, or they would not bury the body.
All these things led to the great growth of mortuaries
"by the prescription of the spiritual law, and had they
not been put an end to by Parliament they would have
grown more and more.

"And in many places they were taken in such a
way that it made the people think that their curates
loved their mortuaries better than their lives.   For this
reason there rose in many places great division and
grudge between them, which caused a breach of the
peace, love, and charity that ought to be between the

curate and his parishioners, to the great unquietness of many of the king's subjects, as well spiritual as temporal, and to the great danger and peril of their souls. For these causes the said mortuaries be annulled by Parliament, as well in conscience as in law, and yet it is said that some curates use great extremities concerning the said mortuaries another way ; and that is this : If at the first request the executor pay not the money that is appointed by the statute, they will anon have a citation against him, and in this he shall be so handled that, as it is said, it would have been generally much better for him to have paid the old mortuary, than the costs and expenses he will then have to pay." [1]

Another fertile cause of complaint against the clergy at this time was, in Saint-German's opinion, the way in which tithes were exacted ; in many cases without much consideration for justice and reason.   " In some places, the curates all exact their tenth of everything within the parish that is subject to tithe, although their predecessors from time immemorial have been contented to do without it : and this even though there is sufficient besides for the curates to live upon, and though perchance in old time something else has been assigned in place of it.   In some places there has been asked, it is said, tithe of both chickens and eggs ; in some places of milk and cheese ; and in some others tithe of the ground and also of all that falleth to the ground.   In other places tithes of servants' wages is claimed without any deduction ; and indeed it is in but few places that any servant shall go quite without some payment of tithe, though he may have spent all in sickness, or upon his father and mother, or such necessary expenses."

<hr>

[1] Ibid., f. 25.

Our author, from whom we get so much information as to the relations which existed in pre-Reformation times between the clergy and people, goes on to give additional instances of the possible hardships incidental to the collection of the ecclesiastical dues. These, where they exist, he, no doubt rightly, thinks do not tend to a good understanding between those who have the cure of souls, and who ought to be regarded rather in the light of spiritual fathers, than of worldly tax collectors. He admits, however, that these are the abuses of the few, and must not be considered as universally true of all the clergy. "And though," he concludes, "these abusions are not used universally (God forbid that they should), for there are many good curates and other spiritual men that would not use them to win any earthly thing, yet when people of divers countries meet together, and one tells another of some such extremity used by some curates in his country, and the other in like manner to him, soon they come to think that such covetousness and harsh dealing is common to all curates. And although they do not well in so doing, for the offence of one priest is no offence of any other, if they will so take it: yet spiritual men themselves do nothing to bring the people out of this judgment; but allow these abuses to be used by some without correcting them." [1]

To these objections, and more of the same kind, Sir Thomas More did not make, and apparently did not think it at all necessary to make, any formal reply. Indeed, he probably considered that where such things could be proved it would be both just and politic to correct them. His failing to reply on this score, how-

[1] Ibid., f. 26.

ever, seems to have been interpreted by Saint-German as meaning his rejection of all blame attaching to the clerical profession in these matters. In the *Deballacion of Salem and Byzance*, More protests that this is not his meaning at all. " He says," writes he, " that I, in my mind, prove it to be an intolerable fault in the people to misjudge the clergy, since I think they have no cause so to do, and that there I leave them, as if all the whole cause and principal fault was in the temporality." This, More declares he never dreamed of, for " if he seek these seven years in all my *Apology*, he shall find you no such words " to justify this view. On the contrary, he will find that " I say in those places, ' that the people are too reasonable to take this or that thing' amiss for ' any reasonable cause of division.' "[1] The fact is, " I have never either laid the principal fault to the one or to the other." To much that Saint-German said, More assented ; and his general attitude to the general accusations he states in these words : " Many of them I will pass over untouched, both because most of them are such as every wise man will, I suppose, answer them himself in the reading, and satisfy his own mind without any need of my help therein, and because some things are there also very well said."

Reading the four books referred to above together, one is forced to the conviction that the description of Sir Thomas More really represents the state of the clergy as it then was. That there were bad as well as good may be taken for granted, even without the admissions of More, but that as a body the clergy, secular or religious, were as hopelessly bad as subsequent writers have so often asked their readers to

[1] *English Works*, p. 936.

believe, or even that they were as bad as the reports, started chiefly by Lutheran emissaries, who were striving to plough up the soil in order to implant the new German teachings in the place of the old religious faith of England, would make out, is disproved by the tracts of both Saint-German and Sir Thomas More. In such a discussion it may be taken for granted that the worst would have appeared. Had the former any evidence of general and hopeless corruption he would, when pressed by his adversary, have brought it forward. Had the latter—whose honesty and full knowledge must be admitted by all—any suspicion of what later generations have been asked to believe as the true picture of ecclesiastical life in pre-Reformation England, he would not have dared, even if his irreproachable integrity would have permitted him, to reject as a caricature and a libel even Christopher Saint-German's moderate picture.

In one particular More categorically denies a charge made by Tyndale against the clergy in general, and against the Popes for permitting so deplorable a state of things in regard to clerical morals. As the charge first suggested by Tyndale has been repeated very frequently down to our own time, it is useful to give the evidence of so unexceptional authority as that of the Lord Chancellor of England. Tyndale declared that although marriage was prohibited by ecclesiastical law to the clergy of the Western Church, the Pope granted leave " unto as many as bring money" to keep concubines. And after asserting that this was the case in Germany, Wales, Ireland, &c., he adds, " And in England thereto they be not few who have (this) licence—some of the Pope, and some of their ordinaries." To this More says :

"We have had many pardons come hither, and many dispensations and many licences too, but yet I thank our Lord I never knew none such, nor I trust never shall, nor Tyndale, I trow either ; but that he listeth loud to lie. And as for his licences customably given by the ordinaries, I trust he lies in regard to other countries, for as for England I am sure he lies."[1]

It would of course be untrue to suggest that there were no grounds whatever for objection to the clerical life of the period. At all times the ministers of the Church of God are but human instruments, manifesting now more now less the human infirmities of their nature. A passage in a sermon preached by Bishop Longland of Lincoln in 1538 suggests that the most crying abuse among the clergy of that time was simony. " Yet there is one thing, or ill which the prophet saw not in this city (of Sodom). What is that ? That which specially above other things should have been seen. What is it ? That which most is abused in this world. I pray thee, what is it ? Make no more ado : tell it. That which almost destroyed the Church of Christ. Then, I pray thee, shew it : shew what it is : let it be known, that remedy may be had and the thing holpen. What is it ? Forsooth it is simony, simony : chapping and changing, buying and selling of benefices and of spiritual gifts and promotions. And no better merchandise is nowadays than to procure advowsons of patrons for benefices, for prebends, for other spiritual livelihood, whether it be by suit, request, by letters, by money bargain or otherwise : yea, whether it be to buy them or to sell them, thou shalt have merchants plenty, merchants enough for it.

" These advowsons are abroad here in this city. In

[1] *English Works*, p. 620.

which city ? In most part of all the great cities of this realm. In the shops, in the streets, a common merchandise. And they that do come by their benefices or promotions under such a manner shall never have grace of God to profit the Church."[1]

It is interesting to recall the fact that the late Mr. Brewer, whose intimate knowledge of this period of our national history is admitted on all hands, arrived, after the fullest investigation, at a similar conclusion as to the real state of the Church in pre-Reformation England. Taking first the religious houses, this high authority considers that no doubt many circumstances had contributed at this time to lower the tone of religious discipline ; but taking a broad survey, the following is the historian's verdict: " That in so large a body of men, so widely dispersed, seated for so many centuries in the richest and fairest estates of England, for which they were mainly indebted to their own skill, perseverance, and industry, discreditable members were to be found (and what literary *chiffonnier,* raking in the scandalous annals of any profession, cannot find filth and corruption ?) is likely enough, but that the corruption was either so black or so general as party spirit would have us believe, is contrary to all analogy, and is unsupported by impartial and contemporary evidence." [2]

" It is impossible," he says in another place, " that the clergy can have been universally immoral and the laity have remained sound, temperate, and loyal." This, by the way, is exactly what More, who lived in the period, insisted upon.

" But," continues Brewer, " if these general argu-

[1] *A Sermonde . . . made in* 1538. By John Longlande, Bishop of Lincolne. London : f. 2.
[2] *Henry VIII.,* vol. ii. pp. 50–1.

ments are not sufficient, I refer my readers to a very curious document, dated the 8th of July 1519, when a search was instituted by different commissioners on a Sunday night, in London and its suburbs, for all suspected and disorderly persons. I fear no parish in London, nor any town in the United Kingdom, of the same amount of population, would at this day pass a similar ordeal with equal credit."[1]   And in another place he sums up the question in these words : " Considering the temper of the English people, it is not probable that immorality could have existed among the ancient clergy to the degree which the exaggeration of poets, preachers, and satirists might lead us to suppose. The existence of such corruption is not justified by authentic documents or by any impartial and broad estimate of the character and conduct of the nation before the Reformation.   If these complaints of preachers and moralists are to be accepted as authoritative on this head, there would be no difficulty in producing abundant evidence from the Reformers themselves that the abuses and enormities of their own age, under Edward VI. and Elizabeth, were far greater than in the ages preceding."[2]

It is too often assumed that in the choice and education of the clergy little care and discretion was exercised by the bishops and other responsible officials, and that thus those unfit for the sacred ministry by education and character often found their way into the priesthood.   In the last Convocation held on the eve of the Reformation a serious attempt was evidently made to correct whatever abuses existed in this matter, when it was enacted that no bishop might ordain any subject

---

[1] Ibid., vol. i. p. 600.   [2] Ibid., ii. p. 470.

not born in his diocese or beneficed in it, or without a domicile in it for three months, even with dimissorial letters. Further, that no secular clerk should be ordained without testimonial letters as to character from the parish priest of the place where he was born or had lived for three years, sealed by the archdeacon of the district, or in the case of a university, by the seal of the vice-chancellor. No one whatsoever was to be admitted to the subdiaconate " who was not so versed in the Epistles and Gospels, at least those contained in the Missal, as to be able at once to explain their grammatical meaning to the examiner." He must also show that he understands and knows whatever pertains to his office.[1]

The most important book of this period dealing with the life and education of the clergy is a tract printed by Wynkyn de Worde about the beginning of the sixteenth century. It was written by William de Melton, Chancellor of York, and at the end is the declaration of Colet, that he has read it and highly approves of its contents.[2] The author states that he desires to instruct the " many young men " who every Ember time come up to York for ordination in their duties. No person, he says, ought to present himself to receive the priesthood who is not prepared to lead a life in all things worthy of the sacred ministry. He should remember that he is really to be accounted one of the twelve who sat with our Lord at His last supper. He must be sufficiently versed in the learning of the world not to dishonour the priestly calling, and above all be taught in His school " who has

---

[1] Wilkins, *Concilia*, iii. 717.
[2] *Sermo Exhortatorius*, W. de Worde.

said, 'Learn of Me, for I am meek and humble of heart.'"

"And since I am now on the question of those only partly well learned," continues the author, " I wish all coming for ordination to understand that always and everywhere those who have not yet attained to at least a fair knowledge of good letters are to be rejected as candidates for Holy Orders. They can in no way be considered to have a fair knowledge of letters who, though skilful in grammar, do not possess the science well enough to read promptly and easily Latin books, and above all, the sacred Scriptures, and expound their meaning and the literal signification of the words as they stand in the books ; and this not haltingly, but readily and easily, so as to show that they know the language not merely slightly and slenderly, but that they possess a full and radical knowledge of it and its construction. Therefore, those who read the sacred Scriptures or other Latin work with difficulty, or, whilst reading, often mistake the proper connection of the words, or read them with such pauses as to seem not to be used to the Latin language, are to be refused Sacred Orders until, by diligent study, they have become more skilled in their letters."

In the same way the tract goes on to declare that those who are unable to explain or understand the spiritual signification of Scripture are to be refused ordination to the sacred ministry until they show themselves at least fairly well able to do so. " To be reckoned among even the fairly proficient, we require," says the author, " such a thorough and sure foundation of grammatical knowledge that there may be hopes that alone and without other teachers they may, from books and diligent study, endeavour day by day to improve themselves by reading and study." Then addressing the candidates the author begs them, if they feel they have not this necessary foundation, "not through mere presumption to offer themselves to the examiners." "Seek not a position in the Church of God in which neither now nor during your whole life will you be able to show yourself a fitting minister. For those who before taking Holy Orders have not fitted themselves fairly well in learning rarely if ever are seen to make progress in literature. On the contrary, they ever remain, even to old age, dunces and stupid, and, furthermore, such priests known to the common people for such manifest ignorance are a great scandal which involves the whole sacred ministry."

Great damage is done to the whole Church of God through the ignorance of the clergy. Both in towns and country places there are priests who occupy themselves, some in mean and servile work, some who give themselves to tavern drinking; the former can hardly help mixing themselves up with women, the latter employ their time in games of dice, &c., and some of them pass it in the vanities of hunting and hawking. Thus do they spend their whole lives to extreme old age in idleness and non-religious occupations. Nor could they do otherwise, for as they are quite ignorant of good letters, how can they be expected to work at and take a pleasure in reading and study; rather throwing away these despised and neglected books, they turn to that kind of miserable and unpriestly life described above, hoping to kill time and cure their dulness by such things.

He then goes on to exhort the young to implant in their hearts a strong desire to study deeply in the books of God's Law rather than to be tainted thus by the stains and vanities of the world which they were supposed to have left. "It is," he continues, "impossible that such a holy desire should possess you, unless you have made progress in such studies before taking Holy Orders, and are so advanced in your literary studies that the reading of many books is both easy and pleasant to you, and the construction of the meaning of a passage no longer difficult, but whilst reading you may quickly and easily follow at least the literal sense of the sentence."

This interesting tract then goes on to warn subdeacons not to take upon themselves the perpetual obligations of Sacred Orders unless they are conscious to themselves of no reason or objection, however secret and hidden, which may stand in the way of their faithfully keeping their promises. They must feel that they enter the ranks of the clergy only from the motive of serving God. Then, after warning the clergy against the vices which specially detract from the sacred character of the priesthood, the author continues, "Let us therefore turn to study, reading, and meditation of the Holy Scriptures as the best remedy against unworthy sloth and foolish desires. Let us not consume the time given us uselessly and fruitlessly." A priest should say his Hours and Mass daily. He should spend the morning till mid-day in choir and other works, and even then not think he has fulfilled the whole duty of the priesthood. A priest is bound to serious studies and meditation. "Constant reading and meditation of the books of God's law and the

writings of the holy Fathers and Doctors are the best
remedy for slothful habits," and these have been put
at the disposition of all through the printing-press.
Just as a workman has besides his shop a workroom
where he has to spend hours preparing the wares that
he offers for sale, so the priest, who in the church on
Sunday offers his people the things necessary for salvation, should spend days and nights in holy reading and
study in order to make them his own before he hands
them on to others. "Wherefore, my dearest brethren,
let us think ourselves proper priests only when we find
our delight and joy in the constant study of Holy
Scripture."

So much for the important advice given to priests
or those intending to be priests as to the necessity of
acquiring previous habits of study. Not infrequently
the fact that in 1532 Parliament did actually transfer
the power of ecclesiastical legislation hitherto possessed
by Convocation to the Crown, is adduced as proof that
to the nation at large the powers of the clergy, for a
long time resented, had at length become a yoke not
to be borne. Yet it is clear that the policy of the king
to crush the clergy in this way was by no means heartily
supported by the Commons. There can be no doubt
whatever that the petition of the Commons against the
spirituality really emanated from the Court, and that the
Lower House was compelled by direct royal influence to
take the course indicated by royal will. Four drafts
of the petition existing among the State papers in the
Record Office put this beyond doubt, as they are all
corrected in the well-known hand of Henry's adviser at
this time, Thomas Crumwell. The substance of the
petition states that on account of the diffusion of

heretical books, and the action of the bishops in spiritual courts, "much discord had arisen between the clergy and the laity at large." The answer of the bishops denies all knowledge of this discord, at least on their parts. The ordinaries, they said, exercised spiritual jurisdiction, and no one might interfere in that, as their right to make laws in this sphere was from God, and could be proved by Scripture. The two jurisdictions could not clash as they were derived from the same source, namely, the authority given by God. Finally, they practically refused to consider the possibility of any just royal interference in matters of the purely ecclesiastical domain. Their resistance was, of course, as we know, of no avail ; but the incident shows that up to the very eve of the changes the clergy had no notion of any surrender of their spiritual prerogatives, and that it was the Crown and not the Commons that was hostile to them.[1]

[1] Gairdner, *Calendar of Papers Foreign and Domestic*, v., preface, ix.

CHAPTER VI

ERASMUS

DURING the first portion of the sixteenth century Erasmus occupied a unique position in Europe. He was beyond question the most remarkable outcome of the renaissance in its literary aspect; and he may fairly be taken as a type of the critical attitude of mind in which many even of the best and the most loyal Catholics of the day approached the consideration of the serious religious problems which were, at that time, forcing themselves upon the notice of the ecclesiastical authorities. Such men held that the best service a true son of the Church could give to religion was the service of a trained mind, ready to face facts as they were, convinced that the Christian faith had nothing to lose by the fullest light and the freest investigation, but at the same time protesting that they would suffer no suspicion to rest on their entire loyalty of heart to the authority of the teaching Church.

Keenly alive to the spiritual wants of the age, and to what he, in common with many others of the time, considered crying abuses in the government of the Church, resulting from the excessive temporal grandeur of ecclesiastics engaged in secular sovereignty and government, Erasmus, like many of his contemporaries, is often perhaps injudicious in the manner in which he advocated reforms. But when the matter is sifted to the bottom, it will commonly be found that his ideas are just.   He clamoured loudly and fearlessly for the proper enforcing of ecclesiastical discipline, and for a complete change in the stereotyped modes of teaching ; and he proclaimed the need of a thorough literary education for Churchmen as the best corrective of what he held to be the narrowing formalism of mediæval scholastic training.   It is, perhaps, hardly wonderful that his general attitude in these matters should have been misunderstood and exaggerated.   By many of his Catholic contemporaries he was looked upon as a secret rebel against received authority, and in truth as the real intellectual force of the whole Lutheran movement.   By the Reformers themselves, regarded as at heart belonging to them, he was upbraided as a coward, and spoken of as one who had not the courage of his convictions.   Posterity has represented him now in the one aspect, now in the other, now as at best a lukewarm Catholic, now as a secret and dangerous heretic.   By most Catholics probably he has been regarded as a Reformer, as pronounced even as Luther himself ; or to use the familiar phrase founded upon an expression of his own, they considered that "his was the egg which Luther hatched."   Few writers have endeavoured to read any meaning into his seemingly paradoxical position by reference to his own explanations, or by viewing it in the light of the peculiar circumstances of the times in which he lived, and which are, to some extent at least, responsible for it.

Desiderius Erasmus was born at Rotterdam, in the year 1467.   His father's Christian name was Gerhard, of which Desiderius was intended for the Latin, and Erasmus for the Greek, equivalent.   Other surname he had none, as he was born out of wedlock; but his father adopted the responsibility of his education, for which he provided by placing him first as a chorister in the cathedral of Utrecht, and subsequently by sending him to Deventer, then one of the best schools in Northern Europe. Deventer was at that time presided over by the learned scholar and teacher Alexander Hegius, and amongst his fellow-students there, Erasmus found several youths who subsequently, as men, won for themselves renown in the learned world. One of them, under the title of Adrian VI., subsequently occupied the Papal chair.

His father and mother both died of the plague whilst Erasmus was still young. At the age of thirteen he was taken from Deventer by the three guardians to whose charge he had been committed, and sent to a purely ecclesiastical school, meant to prepare those intended only for a life in the cloister. Here he remained for three years, and after having for a considerable time resisted the suggestions of his masters that he should join their Order, he finally entered the novitiate of the Canons Regular of St. Augustine at Stein, near Gouda. Here he was professed at the age of nineteen, and after the usual interval was ordained priest.

Much obscurity and many apparent contradictions prevent us fully understanding Erasmus's early life, and in particular the portion spent by him in the cloister. One thing, however, would seem to be quite clear ; he could never have had any vocation for the religious life. His whole subsequent history shows this unmistakeably ; and the ill-judged zeal of those who practically forced him into a state for which he was constitutionally unfitted, and for which he had no aptitude or inclination, must, if we take his account of the facts as correct, be as strongly condemned by all right-thinking people as by himself. He, however, appears not to have understood that this may have been a special case, and not the usual lot of youths entering religion. One evident result of his experience is the bitter feeling created in his heart towards the religious Orders and the uncompromising hostility he ever after displayed towards them. In the celebrated letter he wrote to the papal secretary, Lambert Grunnius, which was intended for the information of the Pope himself, and which is supposed to describe his own case, Erasmus justly condemns in the strongest language the practice of enticing youths into the cloister before they were fully aware of what they were doing. If we are to believe the statements made in that letter, Erasmus did not think that his was by any means a singular case. Agents of the religious Orders, he declared, were ever hanging about the schools and colleges, endeavouring to entice the youthful students into their ranks by any and every method. But he is careful to add, " I do not condemn the religious Orders as such. I do not approve of those who make the plunge and then fly back to liberty as a licence for loose living, and desert improperly what they undertook foolishly. But dispositions vary ; all things do not suit all characters, and no worse misfortune can befall a youth of intellect than to be buried under conditions from which he can never after extricate himself. The world thought well of my schoolmaster guardian because he was neither a liar nor a scamp nor a gambler, but he was coarse, avaricious, and ignorant, he knew nothing beyond the confused lessons he taught to his classes. He imagined that in forcing a youth to become a monk he would be offering a sacrifice acceptable to God. He used to boast of the many victims which he destined to Dominic and Francis and Benedict." [1]

Without any taste for the routine of conventual life, and with his mind filled by an ardent love-of letters, which there seemed in the narrow circle of his cloister no prospect of ever being able to gratify, the short period of Erasmus's stay at Stein must have been to him in the last degree uncongenial and irksome. Fortunately, however, for his own peace of mind and for the cause of general learning, a means was quickly found by which he was practically emancipated from the restraints he ought never to have undertaken. The Bishop of Cambray obtained permission to have him as secretary, and after keeping him a short time in this position he enabled him to proceed to the University of Paris. From this time Erasmus was practically released from the obligations of conventual life; and in 1514, when some question had been raised about his return to the cloister, he readily obtained from the Pope a final release from a form of life for which obviously he was constitutionally unfitted, and the dress of which he had been permitted to lay aside seven years previously.

The generosity of his episcopal patron did not suffice to meet all Erasmus's wants. To add to his income he took pupils, and with one of them, Lord Mountjoy, he came to England in 1497. He spent, apparently, the next three years at Oxford, living in

---

[1] Froude's translation.

the house which his Order had at that University ; whilst there he made the acquaintance of the most learned Englishmen of that time, and amongst others of Grocyn, Linacre, and Colet. He also at this time took up the study of the Greek language, with which previously he had but a slender acquaintance, and his ardour was so great that the following year, 1498, whilst at work on the *Adagia,* he could write, " I am giving my whole soul to the study of Greek ; directly I get some money I shall buy Greek authors first, and then some clothes." From 1499 to 1506 he was continually moving about in various learned centres of France and Holland, his longest stay being at the University of Louvain.

In the April of 1506 he was again in England, first with Archbishop Warham and Sir Thomas More in London, and subsequently at Cambridge ; but in a few months he was enabled to carry out the plan of visiting Italy which he had long contemplated. He engaged to escort the two sons of Sebastian Boyer, the English court physician, as far as Bologna, and by September he was already in Turin, where he took his doctor's degree in divinity. The winter of the same year he passed at Bologna, and reached Venice in the spring of 1507.

His main object in directing his steps to this last-named city was to pass the second and enlarged edition of his *Adagia* through the celebrated Aldine printing-press. Here he found gathered together, within reach of the press, a circle of illustrious scholars. Aldus himself, a man, as Erasmus recalled in a letter written in 1524, " approaching the age of seventy years, but in all matters relating to letters still in the prime of his youth," was his host. In 1508 Erasmus removed to Padua, and the following year passed on to Rome, where he was well received. His stay in the eternal city at this time was not prolonged, for a letter received from Lord Mountjoy announcing the death of Henry VII., and the good affection of his youthful successor to learning, determined him to turn his face once more towards England. He had left the country with keen regret, for, as he wrote to Dean Colet, "I can truly say that no place in the world has given me so many friends—true, learned, helpful, and illustrious friends—as the single city of London," and he looked forward to his return with pleasurable expectation.

For a brief period on his arrival again in this country Erasmus stayed in London at the house of Sir Thomas More, where, at his suggestion, he wrote the *Enconium Moriæ*, one of the works by which he is best known to the general reader, and the one, perhaps, the spirit of which has the most given rise to many mistaken notions as to the author's religious convictions.

From London, in 1510, he was invited by Bishop Fisher to come and teach at Cambridge, where by his influence he had been appointed Lady Margaret Professor of Divinity and Regius Reader of Greek. "Unless I am much mistaken," Erasmus writes, "the Bishop of Rochester is a man without an equal at this time, both as to integrity of life, learning, or broad-minded sympathies. One only do I except, as a very Achilles, the Archbishop of Canterbury (Warham), who alone keeps me in London, though I confess not very unwillingly."[1]

In estimating the spirit which dictated the composition of the *Moriæ*, it is well to remember not only that

---

[1] *Opera*, ed. Leclerc, iii. col. 102.

it represented almost as much the thought and genius
of Sir Thomas More as of Erasmus himself, but that,
at the very time it was taking definite shape in More's
house at Chelsea, the author's two best friends were the
two great and devout churchmen, Archbishop Warham
and the saintly Bishop Fisher.   Moreover, Sir Thomas
More himself denies that to this work of Erasmus there
can justly be affixed the note of irreverence or irreligion ;
he answers for the good intention of the author, and
accepts his own share of responsibility for the publication
of the book.

The period of Erasmus's stay at Cambridge did not
extend beyond three years.   The stipend attached to
his professorships was not large, and Erasmus was still,
apparently, in constant want of money.   Archbishop
Warham continued his friend, and by every means
tried continually to interest others directly in the cause
of learning and indirectly in the support of Erasmus,
who is ever complaining that his means are wholly
inadequate to supply his wants.   The scholar, however,
remained on the best of terms with all the chief English
churchmen of the day, until, as he wrote to the Abbot
of St. Bertin, "Erasmus has been almost transformed
into an Englishman, with such overwhelming kindness
do so many treat me, and above all, my special Mæcenas,
the Archbishop of Canterbury.   He indeed is not only
my patron, but that of all the learned, amongst whom I
but hold a low place.   Immortal gods ! how pleasant,
how ready, how fertile is the wit of that man !   What
dexterity does he not show in managing the most complicated business !   What exceptional learning !   What
singular courtesy does he not extend to all !   What
gaiety and geniality at interviews ! so that he never

sends people away from him sad. Added to this, how
great and how prompt is his liberality! He alone
seems to be ignorant of his own great qualities and the
height of his dignity and fortune. No one can be more
true and faithful to his friends; and, in a word, he is
truly a Primate, not only in dignity, but in everything
worthy of praise." [1]

Erasmus returns to this same subject in writing to
a Roman Cardinal about this time. When I think, he
says, of the Italian sky, the rich libraries, and the
society of the learned men in Rome, I am tempted to
look back to the eternal city with regret. " But the
wonderful kindness of William Warham, Archbishop
of Canterbury, to me mitigates my desire to return.
Had he been my father or brother he could not have
been more kind and loving. I have been accorded,
too, the same reception by many other bishops of
England. Amongst these stands pre-eminent the
Bishop of Rochester, a man who, in addition to
his uprightness of life, is possessed of deep and varied
learning, and of a soul above all meanness, for which
gifts he is held here in England in the highest estimation." [2]

[1] Ibid., Ep. 144.

[2] In one of his works Erasmus gives the highest praise to English
ecclesiastics for their single-minded devotion to their clerical duties. He
contrasts them with clerics of other nations in regard to worldly ambitions,
&c. "Those who are nearest to Christ," he writes, " should keep themselves
free from the baser things of this world. How ill the word ' general ' sounds
when connected with that of ' Cardinal,' or ' duke ' with that of ' bishop,'
' earl ' with that of ' abbot,' or ' commander ' with that of ' priest.' In
England the ecclesiastical dignity is the highest, and the revenues of churchmen
abundant. In that country, however, no one who is a bishop or abbot has
even a semblance of temporal dominion, or possesses castles or musicians or
bands of retainers, nor does any of them coin his own money, excepting only
the Archbishop of Canterbury, as a mark of dignity and honour, which has
been conferred on him on account of the death of Saint Thomas; he is, how-

Erasmus certainly had reason to be grateful to
Warham and his other English friends for their ready
attention to his, at times importunate, requests.   Warham, he writes at one time, " has given me a living
worth a hundred nobles and changed it at my request
into a pension of one hundred crowns.   Within these
few years he has given me more than four hundred
nobles without my asking.   One day he gave me one
hundred and fifty.   From other bishops I have received more than one hundred, and Lord Mountjoy
has secured me a pension of one hundred crowns."   In
fact, in the *Compendium Vitæ*, a few years later, he says
that he would have remained for the rest of his life
in England had the promises made to him been always
fulfilled.   This constant and importunate begging on
the part of the great scholar forms certainly an unpleasant feature in his life.   He gets from Dean Colet
fifteen angels for a dedication, and in reference to
his translation of St. Basil on the Prophet Isaias,
begs Colet to find out whether Bishop Fisher will
be inclined " to ease his labours with a little reward,"
adding himself, " O this begging!   I know well
enough that you will be laughing at me." [1]   Again,
whilst lamenting his poverty and his being compelled
to beg continually in this way, he adds that Linacre
has been lecturing him for thus pestering his friends,
and has warned him to spare Archbishop Warham and
his friend Mountjoy a little.   In this same letter,
written in October 1513, there are signs of friction
with some of the Cambridge teachers of theology,

ever, never concerned in matters of war, but is occupied only in the care of
the churches." (*Consultatio de Bello Turcico. Opera*, ed. Leclerc, tom. v.
p. 363.)

[1] *Opera*, &c., *ut sup.*, Ep. 149.

which may have helped Erasmus in his determination once more to leave England. Not that he professed to care what people thought, for he tells Colet he does not worry about those whom he calls in derision "the Scotists," but would treat them as he would a wasp. Nevertheless, he is still half inclined by the opposition to stop the work he is engaged on ; confessing, also, that he is almost turned away from the design of thus translating St. Basil, as the Bishop of Rochester is not anxious for him to do it, and—at least so a friend has told him—rather suspects that he is translating, not from the original Greek, but is making use of a Latin version.

Almost immediately after writing this letter Erasmus again bade farewell to England, and passed up the Rhine to Strasburg, where he made the acquaintance of Wimpheling, Sebastian Brant, and others. The following year, 1515, he went on to Basle, attracted by the great reputation of the printing-press set up in that city by Froben. He was there eagerly welcomed by the bishop of the city, who had gathered round him many men imbued with the true spirit of learning ; and Erasmus soon became the centre of this brilliant group of scholars. From this time Basle became Erasmus's home, although, especially in the early years, he was always on the move. He paid a flying visit once more, in 1517, to England, but he had learnt to love his independence too much to entertain any proposals for again undertaking duties that would tie him to any definite work in any definite place. Even the suggestions of friends that he would find congenial and profitable pursuits in England were unheeded, and he remained unmoved even when his friend Andrew

Ammonius wrote to say the king himself was looking for his return. " What about Erasmus ? " Henry had asked. " When is he coming back to us ?   He is the light of our age.   Oh that he would return to us ! " [1]

From England, however, he continued to receive supplies of money ; although his circumstances improved so much with the steady circulation of his books, that he was not at this second period of his life so dependent upon the charity of his friends. About the year 1520 Erasmus settled permanently at Basle as literary superintendent of Froben's press.   What, no doubt, induced him to do so, even more than the offer of this position, was the fact that Basle had then become, by the establishment of printing-presses by Amberbach and Froben, the centre of the German book-trade. Froben died in 1527, and that circumstance, as well as the religious troubles which, separating Basle from the empire and making it the focus of civil strife, ended in wrecking learning there altogether, put an end to Erasmus's connection with the press which for eight years had taken the lead of all the presses of Europe. Not only was the literary superintendence of the work completely in the hands of Erasmus during this period which he described as his " mill," but all the dedications and prefaces to Froben's editions of the Fathers were the distinct work of his own pen.   His literary activity at this period was enormous, and only the power he had acquired of working with the greatest rapidity could have enabled him to cope with the multiplicity of demands made upon him. Scaliger relates that Aldus informed him Erasmus

[1] Ibid., Ep. 175.

could do twice as much work in a given time as any other man he had ever met. This untiring energy enabled him to cope with the immense correspondence which, as he says, came pouring in " daily from almost all parts, from kings, princes, prelates, men of learning, and even from persons of whose existence I was, till then, ignorant," and caused him not infrequently to write as many as forty letters a day.

On Froben's death in 1527, the fanatical religious contentions forced him to remove to Freiburg, in Breisgau, where he resided from 1529 to 1535. The need for seeing his *Ecclesiastes* through the press, as well as a desire to revisit the scenes of his former activity, took him back to Basle ; but his health had been giving way for some years, and, at the age of sixty-nine, he expired at Basle on July 12, 1536.

Such is a brief outline of the life of the most remarkable among the leaders of the movement known as the renaissance of letters. Without some general knowledge of the main facts of his life and work, it would be still more difficult than it is to understand the position he took in regard to the great religious revolution during the later half of his life. With these main facts before us we may turn to a consideration of his mental attitude towards some of the many momentous questions which were then searching men's hearts and troubling their souls.

In the first place, of course, comes the important problem of Erasmus's real position as regards the Church itself and its authority. That he was outspoken on many points, even on points which we now regard as well within the border-line of settled matters of faith and practice, may be at once admitted, but he never appears to have wavered in his determination at all costs to remain true and loyal to the Pope and the other constituted ecclesiastical authorities. The open criticism of time-worn institutions in which he indulged, and the sweeping condemnation of the ordinary teachings of the theological schools, which he never sought to disguise, brought him early in his public life into fierce antagonism with many devoted believers in the system then in vogue.

The publication of his translation of the New Testament from the Greek brought matters to an issue. The general feeling in England and amongst those best able to judge had been favourable to the undertaking, and on its first appearance Erasmus was assured of the approval of the learned world at the English universities.[1]   More wrote Latin verses addressed to the reader of the new translation, calling it " the holy work and labour of the learned and immortal Erasmus," to purify the text of God's Word. Colet was warm in its praises. Copies, he writes to Erasmus, are being readily bought and read. Many approved, although, of course, as was to be expected, some spoke against the undertaking. In England, as elsewhere, says Colet, " we have theologians such as you describe in your *Moriæ*, by whom to be praised is dishonour, to be blamed is the highest praise." For his part, Colet has, he says, only one regret that he did not himself know Greek sufficiently well to be able fully to appreciate what Erasmus had done, though " he is only too thankful for the light that has been thrown upon the true meaning of the Holy Scripture." Archbishop Warham writes what is almost an official letter, to tell Erasmus

[1] Ibid., Ep. 216.

that his edition of the New Testament has been welcomed by all his brother bishops in England to whom he has shown it. Bishop Tunstall was away in Holland, where, amidst the insanitary condition of the islands of Zeeland, which he so graphically describes, he finds consolation in the study of the work. He cannot too highly praise it—not merely as the opening up of Greek sources of information upon the meaning of the Bible, but as affording the fullest commentary on the sacred text.[1] Bishop Fisher was equally clear as to the service rendered to religion by Erasmus in this version of the Testament ; and when, in 1519, Froben had agreed to bring out a second edition, Erasmus turned to Fisher and More to assist in making the necessary corrections.[2]

More defended his friend most strenuously. Writing to Marten Dorpius in 1515, he upbraided him with suggesting that theologians would never welcome the help afforded to biblical studies by Erasmus's work on the Greek text of the Bible. He ridicules as a joke not meriting a serious reply the report that Erasmus and his friends had declared there was no need of the theologians and philosophers, but that grammar would suffice. Erasmus, who has studied in the universities of Paris, Padua, Bologna, and Rome, and taught with distinction in some of them, is not likely to hold such absurd ideas. At the same time, More does not hesitate to say that in many things he thinks some theologians are to be blamed, especially those who, rejecting all positive science, hold that man is born to dispute about questions of all kinds which have not the least practical

[1] Ibid., Ep. 272.　　　　[2] Ibid., Ep. 474.

utility "even as regards the *pietas fidei* or the cultivation of sound morals."

At great length More defends the translation against the insinuations made by Dorpius, who evidently regarded it as a sacrilege to suggest that the old Latin editions in use in the Church were incorrect. St. Jerome, says More, did not hesitate to change when he believed the Latin to be wrong, and Dorpius's suggestion that Erasmus should have only noted the errors and not actually made any change would, had the same principle been applied, have prevented St. Jerome's work altogether. If it was thought proper that the Latin codices should be corrected at that time by Greek manuscripts, why not now? The Church had then an equally recognised version before the corrections of St. Jerome.[1]

There were, indeed, as might be expected, some discordant notes in the general chorus of English praise. For the time, however, they remained unheeded, and, in fact, were hardly heard amid the general verdict of approval, in which the Pope, cardinals, and other highly-placed ecclesiastics joined. Erasmus, however, was fully prepared for opposition of a serious character. Writing to Cambridge at the time, he says that he knows what numbers of people prefer "their old *mumpsimus* to the new *sumpsimus*," and condemn the undertaking on the plea that no such work as the correction of the text of Holy Scripture ought to be undertaken without the authority of a general Council.[2]

It is easy to understand the grounds upon which

[1] Thomas More, *Epigrammata* (ed. Frankfort, 1689), p. 284 *seqq*.
[2] Ibid., Ep. 148.

men who had been trained on old methods looked
with anxiety, and even horror, at this new departure.
Scholarship and literary criticism, when applied to the
pagan classics, might be tolerable enough ; but what
would be the result were the same methods to be
used in the examination of the works of the Fathers,
and more especially in criticism of the text of the Holy
Scripture itself ? Overmuch study of the writings of
ancient Greece and Rome had, it appeared to many,
in those days, hardly tended to make the world much
better : even in high places pagan models had been
allowed to displace ideals and sentiments, which, if barbarous and homely, were yet Christian. Theologians
had long been accustomed to look upon the Latin Vulgate text as almost sacrosanct, and after the failure of the
attempt in the thirteenth century to improve and correct
the received version, no critical revision had been dreamt
of as possible, or indeed considered advisable. Those
best able to judge, such as Warham and More and
Fisher, were not more eager to welcome, than others
to condemn and ban, this attempt on the part of
Erasmus to apply the now established methods of
criticism to the sacred text. Not that the edition
itself was in reality a work of either sound learning
or thorough scholarship. As an edition of the Greek
Testament it is now allowed on all hands to have no
value whatever ; but the truth is, that the Greek played
only a subordinate part in Erasmus's scheme. His
principal object was to produce a new Latin version,
and to justify this he printed the Greek text along
with it. And this, though in itself possessing little
critical value, was, in reality, the starting-point for all
modern Biblical criticism. As a modern writer has

said, "Erasmus did nothing to solve the problem, but to him belongs the honour of having first propounded it."

It must, however, be borne in mind that the publication of Erasmus's New Testament was not, as is claimed for it by some modern writers, a new revelation of the Gospel to the world at large, nor is it true that the sacred text had become so obscured by scholastic theological disquisitions on side issues as almost to be forgotten. According to Mr. Froude, "the New Testament to the mass of Christians was an unknown book," when Erasmus's edition, which was multiplied and spread all over Europe, changed all this. Pious and ignorant men had come to look on the text of the Vulgate as inspired. "Read it intelligently they could not, but they had made the language into an idol, and they were filled with horrified amazement when they found in page after page that Erasmus had anticipated modern critical corrections of the text, introduced various readings, and re-translated passages from the Greek into a new version."[1]   The truth is that the publication of the New Testament was in no sense an appeal *ad populum*, but to the cultivated few. A writer in the *Quarterly Review*, commenting upon Mr. Froude's picture of the effect of the new edition on the people generally, is by no means unjust when he says, "Erasmus beyond all question would have been very much astonished by this account of the matter. Certain it is that during the Middle Ages the minds of the most popular preachers and teachers (and we might add of the laity too) were saturated with the sacred Scriptures."[2]

[1] *Erasmus*, p. 63.   [2] *Quarterly Review*, January 1895, p. 23.

Loud, however, was the outcry in many quarters against the rash author. His translations were glibly condemned, and it was pointed out as conclusive evidence of his heterodoxy that he had actually changed some words in the Our Father, and substituted the word *congregatio* for *ecclesia*.[1]

The year 1519 witnessed the most virulent and persistent attacks upon the good name of Erasmus. Of these, and the malicious reports being spread about him, he complains in numerous letters at this period. One Englishman in particular at this time, and subsequently, devoted all his energies to prove not only that Erasmus had falsified many of his translations, but that his whole spirit in undertaking the work was manifestly uncatholic. This was Edward Lee, then a comparatively unknown youth, but who was subsequently created Archbishop of York. In February 1519, Erasmus wrote to Cardinal Wolsey, complaining of these continued attacks upon his work, although so many learned men, including bishops, cardinals, and even the Pope Leo X. himself, had given their cordial approval to the undertaking. Those who were at the bottom of the movement against the work, he considered, were those who had not read it, though they

---

[1] The question about Erasmus's translation of this word came up in the discussion between Sir Thomas More and Tyndale about the use made by the latter of the word *congregation* for Church in his version of the New Testament. More writes: "Then he asketh me why I have not contended with Erasmus, whom he calls my darling, all this long time, for translating this word *ecclesia* into this word *congregatio*, and then he cometh forth with his proper taunt, that I favour him of likelihood for making of his book of *Moriæ* in my house. . . . Now for his translation of *ecclesia* by *congregatio* his deed is nothing like Tyndale's. For the Latin tongue had no Latin word used before for the Church but the Greek work *ecclesia*, therefore Erasmus in his new translation gave it a Latin word. . . . Erasmus also meant no heresy therein, as appears by his writings against the heretics." (*English Works*, pp. 421, 422.)

still had no shame in crying out against it and its author. He was told that in some public discourses in England he had been blamed for translating the word *verbum* in St. John's Gospel by *sermo*, and about this matter he addressed a letter to the Pope defending himself.[1]   To the Bishop of Winchester he wrote more explicitly about his chief opponent.   "By your love for me," he says, "I beg you will not too readily credit those sycophants about me, for by their action all things seem to me at present infected by a deadly plague.   If Edward Lee can prove that he knows better than I do, he will never offend me. But when he, by writing and speech, and by means of his followers, spreads rumours hurtful to my reputation, he is not even rightly consulting his own reputation. He has openly shown a hostile spirit against me, who never, either in word or deed, have done him harm. He is young, and lusts for fame. . . . Time will bring all to light.   Truth may be obscured ; overcome it cannot be."[2]   To the English king he writes that in all he had published he had been actuated by the sole desire to glorify Christ, and in this particular work had obtained the highest approval, even that of the Pope himself.   Some people, indeed, have conspired to destroy his good name.   They are so pleased with their " old wine," that " Erasmus's new " does not satisfy them.   Edward Lee had been instigated to become their champion, and Erasmus only wished that Lee were not an Englishman, since he owed more to England than to any other nation, and did not like to think ill even of an individual.[3]

---

[1] Ep. 384.   [2] Ep. 423.

[3] Ep. 531.   Lee's account of his quarrel with Erasmus is given in his *Apologia*, which he addressed to the University of Louvain.   He states that

When men are thoroughly alarmed, they do not
stop to reason or count the cost ; and so those, who
saw in the work of Erasmus nothing but danger to
the Church, at once jumped to the conclusion that the

Erasmus had come to his house at that place, and had asked him to aid in
the corrected version of his New Testament which he was then projecting.
At first Lee refused, but finally, on being pressed by Erasmus, he consented,
and began the work of revision, but Erasmus quickly became angry at so
many suggested changes. Reports about the annotations and corrections
proposed by Lee began to be spread abroad, and Erasmus hearing of them,
suspected some secret design, and came from Basle to try and get a copy
of the proposed criticism. Lee wished that it should be considered rather
a matter of *theology* than of *letters*. Bishop Fisher wrote, on hearing
rumours of the quarrel, urging Lee to try and make his peace with Erasmus,
and in deference to this, Lee informed Erasmus that he would leave the
matter entirely in the hands of the bishop, and had forwarded to him the
book of his proposed criticisms. Erasmus, however, did not wait, but published the *Dialogus Domini Jacobi Latomi*, which all regarded as an attack
upon Lee. The latter would have published a reply had he not received
letters from England from Fisher, Colet, Pace, and More, begging him to keep
his temper. Lee agreed to stop, and only asked Fisher to decide the matter
quickly. On returning to Louvain, Lee found that Erasmus had published
his *Dialogus bilingium et trilingium*, in which Lee was plainly indicated as
a man hostile to the study of letters in general. This Lee denied altogether,
and in brief, he does not, he says, condemn Erasmus's notes on the New
Testament so much as the copy he had taken as the basis for his corrections
of the later text. " Politian," says Lee, at the end of his *Apologia*, " Politian
declares that there are two great pests of literature—ignorance and envy. To
these I will add a third—'adulation'—for I have no belief in any one who,
having made a mistake, is not willing to acknowledge it."

Lee's criticism of Erasmus's translation appeared at Louvain in January
1520. It produced an immediate reply from Erasmus, published at Antwerp
in May 1520—a reply "all nose, teeth, nails, and stomach." In this Erasmus
says that 1200 copies of the New Testament had been printed by Froben. In
the collation he had been much assisted by Bishop Tunstall, who had, in fact,
supplied the exemplar on which he had worked. Erasmus then gives what he
thinks is the correct version of the differences between Lee and himself. Lee,
he says, was only just beginning Greek, and Erasmus, who had been working
at the correction of his version of the Testament, showed him what he was
doing. The margins of the book were then full of notes, and here and
there whole pages of paper were added. Lee said that he had a few notes
that might be useful, and Erasmus expressed his pleasure at receiving help and
asked for them. Lee thereupon gave him some miscellaneous jottings, and of
these, according to Erasmus's version of the facts, he made use of hardly anything. Soon, however, reports were spread about that out of some three
hundred places in which Lee had corrected the first edition of the translation,

root of the danger really lay in the classical revival itself, of which he was regarded as the chief exponent and apostle. The evil must be attacked in its cause, and the spread of the canker, which threatened to eat into the body of the Christian Church, stayed before it was too late. From the theologians of Louvain, with which university Erasmus was then connected, he experienced the earliest and most uncompromising opposition. He was " daily," to use his own words, " pounded with stones," and proclaimed a traitor to the Church.[1] His opponents did not stop to inquire into the truth of their charges too strictly, and Erasmus bitterly complains of the damaging reports that are being spread all over Europe concerning his good name and his loyalty to religion. To him all opposition came from " the monks," who were, in his eyes, typical of antiquated ecclesiastical narrowness and bigotry. In a letter written in 1519, at the height of " the battle of the languages," as it was called, he gives several instances of this attitude towards himself at Louvain when he suggested some alteration in a text of Holy Scripture. A preacher told the people that he had declared the Gospel " to be merely a collection of stupid fables," and at Antwerp, a Carmelite attacked him in a sermon, at which he happened to be present, and denounced the appearance of his New Testament as a sign of the coming of Antichrist. On being asked afterwards for his reasons, he confessed that he had

Erasmus had adopted two hundred.   Bishop Fisher tried to make peace, and to prevent two men who both meant well to the cause of religion from quarrelling in public.   His intervention was, however, too late, as already the letter of Erasmus to Thomas Lupset had appeared and thus rendered reconciliation impossible.

[1] Ep. 231.

never even read the book himself. "This," says Erasmus sadly, "I generally find to be the case : that none are more bitter in their outcry than they who do not read what I write." In this same letter, Erasmus describes the ferment raised in England against the study of languages. At Cambridge, Greek was making progress in peace, "because the university was presided over by John Fisher, Bishop of Rochester, a theologian of learning and uprightness of life." At Oxford, however, fierce public attacks were made in sermons on Greek studies ; "but the king," continues Erasmus, "as one not unlearned himself, and most favourable to the cause of letters, happened to be in the neighbourhood, and hearing of the matter from More and Pace, ordered that all wishing to study Greek literature should be encouraged, and so put a stop to the business."

The contest was not confined to the schools. "A theologian preaching in the royal palace before the king took this opportunity to inveigh boldly and uncompromisingly against Greek studies and the new methods of interpretation. Pace, who was present, glanced at the king to see how he took it, and Henry smiled at Pace. After the sermon the theologian was bidden to the king, and to More was assigned the task of defending Greek learning against him, the king himself desiring to be present at the discussion. After More had spoken for some time most happily, he paused to hear the theologian's reply ; but he, on bended knees, asked pardon for what he had said, asserting that whilst talking he was moved by some spirit to speak about Greek as he had done. Thereupon the king said, 'And that spirit was not that of

Christ, but of folly!'   Then Henry asked him whether
he had read Erasmus's works—he admitted that he had
not.   Then said the king, 'By this you prove your
folly, in condemning what you have not read.'   Finally
the king dismissed him, and ordered that he should
never be allowed to preach in the royal presence
again."

Those who desired to carry on the campaign to
extremities, endeavoured, and even with temporary
success, to influence Queen Katherine against Erasmus
and the party for the revival of letters which he represented.   Her confessor, a Dominican bishop, persuaded
her that in correcting St. Jerome, Erasmus had perpe-
trated a crime which admitted of no excuse.[1]   It was
but another step to connect the renaissance of letters
generally with the revolt now associated with the name
of Luther.   In England, however, it was not so easy
to persuade people of this, since, among the chief
supporters of the movement were to be numbered the
best and wisest of churchmen and laymen whose entire
orthodoxy was not open to suspicion.   Abroad, however, the cry once started, was quickly taken up.   A
theologian at Louvain, writes Erasmus, who up to this
time had been noted for his sober judgment, before
a large audience, after having spoken of Lutheranism,
attacked "the teaching of languages and polite letters,
joining the two together, and asserting that heresy
came from these springs, as if experience had shown
eloquence to be a mark rather of the heretics than
of the orthodox, or that the Latin authors of heresy
were not mere children so far as languages went, or

[1] Ep. 380.   This bishop must have been the Spaniard, George de Athegua,
who was appointed to the see of Llandaff in 1517, and held it for twenty years.

that Luther had been schooled by those masters and not rather by the scholastics, according to scholastic methods."[1]

Erasmus puts the position even more clearly in a letter to Pope Leo X. on the publication of the revised version of his New Testament in August 1519. The book is now in people's hands, he says, and as it has appeared under the direct auspices of the Holy Father himself, it may be regarded as his work. Some foolish people, he understands, have been trying to get the Pope to believe that a knowledge of languages is detrimental to the true study of theology, whereas, in reality, the very contrary is obviously the case. Such people will not reason, they cry out and will not listen. They suggest damning words, such words for example as " heretics," " antichrists," &c., as appropriate to their opponents. They call out that even the Christian religion is imperilled, and beg the Pope to come forward and save it. On his part Erasmus hopes that the Pope will believe that all his work is for Christ alone, and His Church. " This only reward do I desire, that I may ever seek the glory of Christ rather than my own. From boyhood I have ever endeavoured to write nothing that savoured of impiety or disloyalty. No one has ever yet been made blacker by my writings ; no one less pious, no one stirred up to tumult."[2] Again, writing to Cardinal Campeggio, when sending him a copy of the New Testament " which Pope Leo had approved by his Brief," Erasmus tells him that, to his great regret, many at Louvain were doing their best not to allow good letters to flourish. As for himself, his only real desire was to serve Christ and increase

[1] Ep. 380.　　　　　　　　　　[2] Ep. 453.

the glory of His Church ; though, he adds, " I am a man, and as such liable to err." No one has ever succeeded in pleasing every one, and he, Erasmus, will not try to do the impossible. Still he wishes to be judged by what he really has said and written ; whereas all kinds of things, letters, books, &c., are attributed to him, about which he knows nothing : " even Martin Luther's work, amongst the rest," whilst the truth is, he does not know Luther, and certainly has never read his book.[1]

At the end of the following year, 1520, Erasmus again writes to Cardinal Campeggio at great length. After telling him that he had hoped to have passed the winter in Rome to search in the libraries for Greek manuscripts, he informs him that in Louvain those who prefer the old barbarism are now rampant. Some think to please the people by opposition to learning, and amongst the aiders and abettors of the Lutheran movement they place Erasmus in the forefront. The Dominicans and Carmelites, he says, will regard him only as their enemy. Why, he does not know, for in reality he reverences true religion under " any coloured coat." If on occasion he has said something about the vices of the monks, he does not think it were more right for the religious, as a body, to turn against him, than it would be for priests as a body, when their vices were spoken against. He does not in the least wish to be thought opposed to the religious life, as such. The condemnation of Luther had been interpreted by many as a condemnation of learning, and had been turned against Reuchlin and Erasmus. As for himself, he has never, he declares, even seen Luther, who has certainly

[1] Ep. 416.

never been famous for good letters or for any knowledge of ancient tongues, and hence the revival of letters has no connection whatever with the Lutheran movement. The prefaces of some of Luther's books, because written in good Latin, are considered sufficient proof of his (Erasmus's) connection with the matter, and it is asserted openly that he was working cordially with the Reformer ; whereas, as a fact, he had not suggested even so much as a full stop or comma for his writings. He had, he admitted, written to Luther, and this and another letter to the Cardinal of Mentz were pointed to as proof positive of his Lutheran leanings. For these he has been denounced to bishops as a heretic and delated to the Pope himself, while all the time, in truth, he has never read two pages of Luther's writings. Certainly, indeed, he recognised in Luther considerable power, but he was not by any means alone in doing so. Men of undoubted faith and uprightness had congratulated themselves on having fallen in with Luther's works. For himself, he adds, " I have always preferred to look for the good rather than to search for the evil, and I have long thought that the world needed many changes." Finally, before passing from the subject, he begs Cardinal Campeggio to look at the letter in question himself, and see whether it could justly be said to favour Luther in any way.[1]

To Pope Leo X. Erasmus also wrote, protesting against the cause of letters generally being made the same as that of Reuchlin and Luther. With the former movement he was identified heart and soul ; with Luther and his revolt he had, he declared, no part nor sympathy. " I have not known Luther," he says, " nor

[1] Ep. 547.

have I ever read his books, except perhaps ten or a dozen pages in various places. It was really I who first scented the danger of the business issuing in tumults, which I have always detested." Moreover, he declares that he had induced the Basle printer, Johann Froben, to refuse to print Luther's works, and that by means of friends he had tried to induce Luther to think only of the peace of the Church. Two years previously, he says, Luther had written to him, and he had replied in a kindly spirit in order to get him, if possible, to follow his advice. Now, he hears, that this letter has been delated to the Pope in order to prejudice him in the Pontiff's eyes ; but he is quite prepared to defend its form and expression. "If any one," he says, "can say he has ever heard me, even at the table, maintain the teaching of Luther, I will not refuse to be called a Lutheran." Finally, he expresses the hope that, if the opponents of letters have been trying to calumniate him, he may rely on the Pope's prudence and the knowledge of his own complete innocence. "I, who do not wish to oppose even my own bishop, am not," he writes, "so mad as to act in any way against the supreme Vicar of Christ." [1]

---

[1] Ep. 529. Erasmus wrote strongly against anything that seemed to favour the idea of national churches. After declaring that national dislikes and enmities were unmeaning and unchristian, he continues : "As an Englishman you wish evil fortune to a Frenchman. Why not rather do your wishes come as a man to a fellow-man ? Why not as a Christian to a Christian ? Why do these frivolous things have greater weight than such natural ties, such bonds of Christ ? Places separate bodies, not souls. In old days the Rhine divided a Frenchman from a German, but the Rhine cannot divide one Christian from another. The Pyrenees cut off Spain from France, but these mountains do not destroy the communion of the Church. The sea divides the English and French peoples, but it cannot cut off the society of religion. . . ." The world is the fatherland of all people ; all men are sprung from a common stock. "The Church is but one family, common to all." (*Opera.*, tom. iv. col. 638.)

As time went on, the position of Erasmus did not become more comfortable. Whilst the Lutherans were hoping that sooner or later something would happen to compromise the outspoken scholar and force him to transfer the weight of his learning to their side, the champions of Catholicity were ill satisfied that he did not boldly strike out in defence of the Church. To this latter course many of his English friends had strongly urged him, and both the king, Fisher, and others had set him an example by publishing works against Luther's position, which they invited him to follow. The Pope, too, had on more than one occasion personally appealed to him to throw off his reserve and come to the aid of orthodoxy. They could not understand how he was able to talk of peace and kindness amidst the din of strife, and plead for less harsh measures and less bitter words against Luther and his adherents, when the battle was raging, and cities and peoples and even countries were being seduced by the German Reformer's plausible plea for freedom and liberty. Those who believed in Erasmus's orthodoxy, as did the Pope and his English friends, considered that no voice was more calculated to calm the storm and compel the German people to listen to reason than was his. Whilst the Reforming party, on the other hand, were doing their best to compromise him in the eyes of their opponents, Erasmus was most unwilling to be forced into action. "Why," he writes, "do people wish to associate me with Luther? What Luther thinks of me, where it is a question of matters of faith, I care very little. That he doesn't think much of me he shows in many letters to his friends. In his opinion I am 'blind,' 'miserable,' 'ignorant of Christ and Christianity,' 'thinking of nothing but letters.' This is just what I should expect," he says, "for Luther has always despised the ancients." As for himself, he (Erasmus) has always tried his best to inculcate true piety along with learning.[1]

To Œcolampadius, in February 1525, he wrote a letter of protest against the way some of Luther's followers were doing all they could to associate his name with their movement. He does not wish, he says, to give his own opinion on the questions at issue ; but he can tell his correspondent what the King of England, Bishop Fisher, and Cardinal Wolsey think on these grave matters. He objects to Œcolampadius putting *Magnus Erasmus noster*—"our great Erasmus"— in a preface he wrote, without any justification. "This naturally makes people suppose," he adds, "that I am really on your side in these controversies," and he begs that he will strike out the expression.[2]

This was no new position that Erasmus had taken up in view of the ever-increasing difficulties of the situation. Six years before (in 1519) he had written fully on the subject to the Cardinal Archbishop of Mentz. It was this letter which had been much misunderstood, and even denounced to the Pope as the work of a disloyal son of the Church. He, on the other hand, declared that he was not committed in any way to the cause of Reuchlin or Luther. " Luther is perfectly unknown to me, and his books I have not read, except here and there. If he had written well it would not have been to my credit; if then the opposite, no blame should attach to me. I regretted his public action, and when the first tract, I forget

<hr>

[1] Ep. 715.   [2] Ep. 723.

which, was talked about, I did all I could to prevent its being issued, especially as I feared that tumults would come out of all this. Luther had written me what appeared to my mind to be a very Christian letter, and, in replying, I, by the way, warned him not to write anything seditious, nor to abuse the Roman Pontiff, &c., but to preach the Gospel truly and humbly." He adds that he was kind in his reply purposely, as he did not wish to be Luther's judge. And, as he thought that there was much good in the man, he would willingly do all he could to keep him in the right way. People are too fond, he says, of crying out "heretic," &c., and "the cry generally comes from those who have not read the works they exclaim against." [1]

"I greatly fear," he writes shortly after, "for this miserable Luther ; so angry are his opponents on all sides, and so irritated against him are princes, and, above all, Pope Leo. Would that he had taken my advice and abstained from these hateful and seditious publications. There would have been more fruit and less rancour." [2]

Testimonies might be multiplied almost indefinitely from Erasmus's writings to show that with Lutheranism as such he had no connection nor sympathy. Yet his best friends seem to have doubted him, and some, in England, suspected that Erasmus's hand and spirit were to be detected in the reply that Luther made to King Henry's book against him. Bishop Tunstall confesses that he is relieved to hear by the letter Erasmus had addressed to the king and the legate that he had had nothing to do with this violent composition, and, moreover, that he was op-

[1] Ep. 477.   [2] Ep. 528.

posed to Lutheran principles.   In his letter on this subject, the bishop laments the rapid spread of these dangerous opinions which threaten disturbances everywhere.   When the sacred ceremonies of the Church and all pious customs are attacked as they are, he says, civil tumults are sure to follow.   After Luther's book *De abroganda Missa*, the Reformer will quickly go further, and so Tunstall begs and beseeches Erasmus, by " Christ's Passion and glory " and " by the reward " he expects ; " yea, and the Church itself prays and desires you," he adds, " to engage in combat with this hydra." [1]

At length, urged by so many of his best friends, Erasmus took up his pen against Luther and produced his book *De libero Arbitrio*, to which Luther, a past master in invective, replied in his contemptuous *De servo Arbitrio*, Erasmus rejoining in the *Hyperaspistes*.   Sir Thomas More wrote that this last book delighted him, and urged Erasmus to further attacks.   " I cannot say how foolish and inflated I think Luther's letter to you," he writes.   " He knows well how the wretched glosses into which he has darkened Scripture turn to ice at your touch.   They were, it is true, cold enough already." [2]

Erasmus's volume on *Free-will* drew down on him, as might be expected, the anger of the advanced Lutherans.   Ulrich von Hutten, formerly a brilliant follower of Erasmus and Reuchlin in their attempts to secure a revival of letters, was now the leader of the most reckless and forward of the young German Lutherans, who assisted the Reformer by their violence and their readiness to promote any and all of his doctrinal changes by stirring up civil dissensions.   Von

[1] Ep. 656.   [2] Ep. 334 (second series.)

Hutten endeavoured to throw discredit upon Erasmus by a brilliant and sarcastic attack upon it. In 1523, Erasmus published what he called the *Spongia*, or reply to the assertions of von Hutten on his honour and character. The tract is really an apology or explanation of his own position as regards the Lutherans, and an assertion of his complete loyalty to the Church. The book was in Froben's hands for press in June 1523, but before it could appear in September von Hutten had died. Erasmus, however, determined to publish the work on account of the gravity of the issues. It is necessary, if we would understand Erasmus's position fully, to refer to this work at some considerable length. After complaining most bitterly that many people had tried to defame him to the Pope and to his English friends, and to make him a Lutheran whether he would or no ; and after defending his attitude towards Reuchlin as consistent throughout, he meets directly von Hutten's assertion that he had condemned the whole Dominican body. " I have never," he says, " been ill disposed to that Order. I have never been so foolish as to wish ill to any Order. If it were necessary to hate all Dominicans because, in the Order, there were some bad members, on the same ground it would be needful to detest all Orders, since in every one there are many black sheep." On the same principle Christianity itself would be worthy of hatred.[1] The fact really is that the Dominicans have many members who are friendly to Erasmus, and who are favourable to learning in general, and Scripture study and criticism in particular.

In the same way, von Hutten had mistaken Erasmus's

[1] *Spongia* (Basle, Froben, 1523), c. 5.

whole attitude towards the Roman Church. He had charged him with being inconsistent, in now praising, now blaming the authorities. Erasmus characterises this as the height of impudence. "Who," he asks, "has ever approved of the vices of the Roman authorities? But, on the other hand, who has ever condemned the Roman Church?"

Continuing, he declares that he has never been the occasion of discord or tumult in any way, and appeals with confidence to his numerous letters and works as sufficient evidence of his love of peace. "I love liberty," he writes ; "I neither can aid, nor desire to aid, any faction." Already many confess that they were wrong in taking a part ; and he sees many, who had thrown in their lot with Luther, now drawing back, and regretting that they had ever given any countenance to him.[1] His (Erasmus's) sole object has been to promote good letters, and to restore Theology to its simple and true basis, the Holy Scripture. This he will endeavour to do as long as he has life. "Luther," he says, "I hold to be a man liable to err, and one who has erred. Luther, with the rest of his followers will pass away ; Christ alone remains for ever."

In more than one place of this *Spongia*, Erasmus complains bitterly that what he had said in joke, and as mere pleasantry at the table, had been taken seriously. "What is said over a glass of wine," he writes, "ought not to be remembered and written down as a serious statement of belief. Often at a feast, for example, we have transferred the worldly sovereignty to Pope Julius, and made Maximilian, the emperor, into the supreme Pontiff. Thus, too, we have married monasteries of

[1] Ibid., sig. d. 4.

monks to convents of nuns ; we have sent armies of them against the Turks, and colonised new islands with them. In a word, we turn the universe topsy-turvy. But, such whims are never meant to be taken seriously, as our own true convictions."

Von Hutten had complained that Erasmus had spoken harshly about Luther, and hinted that he was really actuated by a spirit of envy, on seeing Luther's books more read than his own. Erasmus denies that he has ever called Luther by any harsh names, and particularly that he has ever called him "heretic." He admits, however, that he had frequently spoken of the movement as a "tragedy," and he points to the public discords and tumults then distracting Germany as the best justification of this verdict.[1]

Von Hutten having said that children were being taught by their nurses to lisp the name Luther, Erasmus declares that he cannot imagine whose children these can be ; for, he says, " I daily see how many influential, learned, grave, and good men have come to curse his very name."

The most interesting portion, however, of the *Spongia* is that in which, at considerable length, Erasmus explains his real attitude to Rome and the Pope. "Not even about the Roman See," he says, " will I admit that I have ever spoken inconsistently. I have never approved of its tyranny, rapacity, and other vices about which of old common complaints were heard from good men. Neither do I sweepingly condemn 'Indulgences,' though I have always disliked any barefaced traffic in them. What I think about ceremonies, many places in my works plainly show. . . .

[1] Ibid., sig. e. 2.

What it may mean 'to reduce the Pope to order' I do not rightly understand. First, I think it must be allowed that Rome is *a* Church, for no number of evils can make it cease to be a Church, otherwise we should have no Churches whatever. Moreover, I hold it to be an orthodox Church; and this Church, it must be admitted, has a Bishop. Let him be allowed also to be Metropolitan, seeing there are very many archbishops in countries where there has been no apostle, and Rome, without controversy, had certainly SS. Peter and Paul, the two chief apostles. Then how is it absurd that among Metropolitans the chief place be granted to the Roman Pontiff?"[1]

As to the rest, Erasmus had never, he declares, defended the excessive powers which for many years the popes have usurped, and, like all men, he wishes for a thorough apostolic man for Pope. For his part, if the Pope were not above all things else an apostle, he would have him deposed as well as any other bishop, who did not fulfil the office of his state. For many years, no doubt, the chief evils of the world have come from Rome, but now, as he believes, the world has a Pope who will try at all costs to purify the See and Curia of Rome. This, however, Erasmus fancies is not quite what von Hutten desires. He would declare war

---

[1] *Ibid.*, sig. e. 2. The supreme authority of the Pope is asserted by Erasmus in numberless places in his works. For example, in the tract *Pacis Querimonia*, after saying that he cannot understand how Christians, who understand Christ's teaching and say their *Pater noster* with intelligence, can always be at strife, he proceeds: "The authority of the Roman Pontiff is supreme. But when peoples and princes wage impious wars, and that for years, where then is the authority of the Pontiffs, where then is the power next to Christ's power?" &c. (*Opera.*, tom iv. p. 635). So too in his *Precatio pro Pace Ecclesiæ*, after praying that God would turn the eyes of His mercy upon the Church, over which "Peter was made Supreme Pastor," he declares that there is but "one Church, out of which there is no salvation."

against the Pope and his adherents, even were the Pope a good Pope, and his followers good Christians. War is what von Hutten wants, and he cares not whether it brings destruction to cities and peoples and countries.

Erasmus admits that he knows many people who are ready to go some way in the Lutheran direction; but who would strongly object to the overthrow of papal authority. Many would rather feel that they have a father than a tyrant: who would like to see the tables of the money-changers in the temple overthrown, and the barefaced granting of indulgences and trafficking in dispensations and papal bulls repressed: who would not object to have ceremonies simplified, and solid piety inculcated: who would like to insist on the sacred Scriptures as the true and only basis of authoritative teaching, and would not give to scholastic conclusions and the mere opinions of schools the force of an infallible oracle. With those who think thus, says Erasmus, "if (as is the case) there is no compact on my part, certainly my old friendly feeling for them remains cemented by the bond of learning, even if I do not agree with them in all these things."

But, he continues, it is not among these well-wishers of reform that von Hutten and Luther will find their support. This is to be found among the "unlettered people without any judgment; among those who are impure in their own lives, and detractors of men; amongst those who are headstrong and ungovernable. These are they who are so favourable to Luther's cause that they neither know nor care to examine what Luther teaches. They only have the Gospel on their lips; they neglect prayer and the Sacraments; they eat what they like; and they live

to curse the Roman Pontiff.   These are the Lutherans."
From such material spring forth tumults that cannot
be put down.   "It is generally in their cups," adds
Erasmus, "that the Evangelical league is recruited."
They are too stupid to see whither they are drifting,
and "with such a type of mankind I have no wish
to have anything to do."   Some make the Gospel but
the pretext for theft and rapine ; and "there are some
who, having squandered or lost all their own property,
pretend to be Lutherans in order to be able to help
themselves to the wealth of others."   Von Hutten
wants me, says Erasmus, to come to them.   "To
whom ?   To those who are good and actuated by the
true Gospel teaching ?   I would willingly fly to them
if any one will point them out.   If he knew of any
Lutherans, who in place of wine, prostitutes, and dice,
have at any time delighted in holy reading and conversation ; of any who never cheat or neglect to pay
their debts, but are ready to give to the needy ; of any
who look on injuries done to them as favours, who
bless those who curse them—if he can show me such
people, he may count on me as an associate.   Lutherans,
I see ; but followers of the Gospel, I can discover few
or none."

Von Hutten had, in his attack, with much bitter-
ness condemned Erasmus for not renouncing connection with those who had written strongly against
Luther.   Erasmus refused to entertain the notion.
"There is," he says, "the reverend Father John,
Bishop of Rochester.   He has written a big volume
against Luther.   For a long period that man has been
my very special friend and most constant patron.
Does von Hutten seriously want me to break with

him, because he has sharpened his pen in writing
against Luther ?   Long before Luther was thought
of," he says, " I enjoyed the friendship of many
learned men.   Of these, some in later years took
Luther's side, but on that account I have not re-
nounced outwardly my friendship for them.   Some
of these have changed their views and now do not
think much of Luther, still I do not cease to regard
them as my friends."

Towards the close of his reply, Erasmus returns
to the question of the Pope.   Von Hutten had charged
him with inconsistency in his views, and Erasmus replies, " He who most desires to see the apostolic
character manifested in the Pope is most in his
favour."   It may be that one can hate the individual
and approve of the office.   Whoever is favourable to,
and defends, bad Popes does not honour the office.
He (Erasmus) has been found fault with for saying
that the authority of the Pope has been followed by
the Christian world for very many ages.   What he
wrote is true, and as long as the work of Christ is
done may it be followed for ever.   Luther wants
people to take his *ipse dixit* and authority, but he
(Erasmus) would prefer to take that of the Pope.
" Even if the supremacy of the Pope was not established by Christ, still it would be expedient that there
should be one ruler possessing full authority over
others, but which authority no doubt should be free
from all idea of tyranny. . . . Because I have criti-
cised certain points in the See of Rome, I have not
for that reason ever departed from it.   Who would
not uphold the dignity of one who, by manifesting the
virtues of the Gospel, represents Christ to us ? "   The

paradoxes of Luther are not worth dying for. " There is no question of articles of faith, but of such matters as 'Whether the supremacy of the Roman Pontiff was established by Christ:' 'whether cardinals are necessary to the Christian Church:' 'whether confession is *de jure divino:*' 'whether bishops can make their laws binding under pain of mortal sin:' 'whether free will is necessary for salvation:' 'whether faith alone assures salvation,' &c. If Christ gave him grace," Erasmus hopes that " he would be a martyr for His truth, but he has no desire whatever to be one for Luther."

This last point was immediately taken up by the Lutherans. Von Hutten, as it has already been said, had died before the publication of the *Spongia,* and the reply to Erasmus was undertaken by Otto Brunfels. He rejected Erasmus's suggestion that nearly all that the Lutherans were fighting for were matters of opinion. They were matters of faith, he says, and no uncertainty could be admitted on this point. In order to make the matter clear, he enumerates a great number of tenets of Lutheranism which they hold to as matters of revealed certainty. For instance: that Christ is the only head of the Church; that the Church has no corporate existence; that the mass is no sacrifice; that justification comes by faith alone; that our works are sins and cannot justify; that good men cannot sin; that there are only two Sacraments; that the Pope's traditions are heretical and against Scripture; that the religious state is from the devil; and several score more of similar points more or less important.

That Erasmus's views upon the necessity of the Papacy expressed in the *Spongia* were not inconsistent with his previous position there is ample evidence in his letters, to which he himself appeals.   Replying, for example, to one who had written to him deploring the religious differences in Bohemia, Erasmus declares that, in his opinion, it is needful for unity that there should be one head.   If the prince is tyrannical, he should be reduced to order by the teaching and authority of the Roman Pontiff.   If the bishop play the tyrant, there is still the authority of the Roman Pontiff, who is the dispenser of the authority and the Vicar of Christ.   He may not please all, but who that really rules can expect to do that ?   "In my opinion," he adds, "those who reject the Pope are more in error than they who demand the Eucharist under two kinds."   Personally, he would have allowed this, although he thinks that, as most Christians have now the other custom, those who demand it as a necessity are unreasonable and to be greatly blamed.   Above all others, he reprobates the position of those who refuse to obey, speak of the Pope as Antichrist, and the Roman Church as a "harlot" because there have been bad Popes.   There have been bad cardinals and bishops, bad priests and princes, and on this ground we ought not to obey bishop or pastor or king or ruler.[1]   In the same letter he rebukes those who desire to sweep away vestments and ceremonies on the plea that they may not have been used in apostolic times.

Later on, in another letter, he complained that people call him a favourer of Luther.   This is quite untrue. "I would prefer," he says, "to have Luther corrected rather than destroyed ; then I should prefer that it should be done without any great social tumults. Christ I acknowledge ; Luther I know not.   I ac-

[1] Ep. 478.

knowledge the Roman Church, which, in my opinion, is Catholic. I praise those who are on the side of the Roman Pontiff, who is supported by every good man." [1]

Again, the following year, writing on the subject of the invocation of Papal authority against Luther, he says : " I do not question the origin of that authority, which is most certainly just, as in ancient times from among many priests equal in office one was chosen as the bishop ; so now from the bishops it is necessary to make choice of one Pontiff, not merely to prevent discords, but to temper the tyrannical exercise of authority on the part of the other bishops and secular princes." [2]

The publication of Erasmus's book against Luther and of his reply to von Hutten made little change, however, in the adverse feeling manifested against him by those who were most busily engaged in combating the spread of Lutheran opinions. As he wrote to King Henry VIII., the noisy tumults and discords made him long for the end of life, when he might hope at least to find peace.[3] Luckily for him, he still retained the confidence of the Pope and some of the best churchmen in Europe. Had he not done so, the very violence of the attack against his good name might have driven him out of the Church in spite of himself. Kind words, he more than once said, would have done more for the cause of peace in the Church than all the biting sarcasm and unmeasured invective that was launched against Luther, and those who, like Erasmus, either were, or were supposed to be, associated with his cause. Luther was not delicate about the choice of his language when he had an enemy to pelt, but some of the

[1] Ep. 501.   [2] Ep. 563.

[3] Ep. 600.

preachers and pamphlet writers on the orthodox side were his match in this respect. In this way Erasmus puts the responsibility for "the tragedy" of Lutheranism upon the theologians, and in part especially upon the Dominicans and Carmelites. "Ass," "pig," "sow," "heretic," "antichrist," and "pest of the world," are terms named by Erasmus as samples of the epithets launched from the pulpit, or more deliberately set up in type, as arguments against Luther and himself.[1]

In writing to one of the cardinals after the publication of his *Spongia*, there is a touch of sadness in his complaints, that having been forced to do battle with the "Lutherans as against a hydra of many heads," Catholics should still try and make the world believe that he was really a Lutheran at heart. "I have never," he declares, "doubted about the sovereignty of the Pope, but whether this supremacy was recognised in the time of St. Jerome, I have my doubts, on account of certain passages I have noted in my edition of St. Jerome. In the same place, however, I have marked what would appear to make for the contrary opinion; and in numerous other places I call Peter 'Prince of the apostolic order,' and the Roman Pontiff, Christ's Vicar and the Head of His Church, giving him the highest power according to Christ."[2]

Probably a more correct view of Erasmus's real mind can hardly be obtained than in part of a letter already quoted (Ep. 501) addressed to Bishop Marlianus of Tuy in Galicia, on March 25, 1520. "I would have the Church," he writes, "purified, lest the good in it suffer by conjunction with the evil. In avoiding the Scylla of Luther, however, I would have care taken to

---

[1] Ep. 563.　　　　　[2] Ep. 667.

avoid Charybdis. If this be sin, then I own my guilt. I have sought to save the dignity of the Roman Pontiff, the honour of Catholic theology, and to look to the welfare of Christendom. I have, as yet, read no whole work of Luther, however short, and I have never even in jest defended his paradoxes. Be assured that if any movement is set on foot which is injurious to the Christian religion and dangerous to the public peace or the supremacy of the Holy See, it does not proceed from Erasmus. . . . In all I have written, I have not deviated one hair's-breadth from the teaching of the Church. But every wise man knows that practices and teachings have been introduced into the Church partly by custom, partly by the canonists, partly by means of scholastic definitions, partly by the tricks and arts of secular sovereigns, which have no sound sanction. Many great people have begged me to support Luther, but I have ever replied that I would be ready to take his part when he was on the Catholic side. They have asked me to draw up a formula of faith ; I have said that I know of none save the creed of the Catholic Church, and every one who consults me I urge to submit to the authority of the Pope." [1]

In many ways Erasmus regarded the rise of Lutheranism as the greatest misfortune. Not only did it tend to make good men suspicious of the general revival of letters, with which without reason they associated it, but the necessity of defending the Catholic position against the assaults of the new sectaries naturally obscured the need of reform within the Church itself, for which farseeing and good men had long been looking. To Bishop

---

[1] Ep. 501 (Mr. Froude's translation).

Tunstall he expressed his fears lest in pulling up the tares, some, and perchance much, of the precious wheat might perish. Whilst, undoubtedly, there was in Luther's work a great deal that he cordially detested, there was also much that would never have been condemned, had the points been calmly considered by learned men, apart from the ferment of revolt. "This, however, I promise you," he adds, "that for my part I will never forsake the Church."[1]

This same sentiment he repeats the following year, 1526: "From the judgment of the Church I am not able to dissent, nor have I ever dissented."[2] Had this tempest not risen up, he said, in another letter from Basle, he had hoped to have lived long enough to have seen a general revival of letters and theology returning more and more to the foundation of all true divinity, Holy Scripture. For his part, he cordially disliked controversy, and especially the discussion of such questions as "whether the Council was above the Pope," and such like. He held that he was himself in all things a sound Catholic, and at peace with the Pope and his bishop, whilst no name was more hated by the Lutherans than that of Erasmus.[3]

So much with regard to the attitude of mind manifested by Erasmus towards the authority of the teaching Church, which is the main point of interest in the present inquiry. His disposition will probably be construed by some into a critical opposition to much that was taught and practised; but it seems certain that Erasmus did not so regard his own position. He was a reformer in the best sense, as so many far-seeing and

---

[1] Ep. 793.   [2] Ep. 823.
[3] Ep. 751.

spiritual-minded churchmen of those days were. He desired to better and beautify and perfect the system he found in vogue, and he had the courage of his convictions to point out what he thought stood in need of change and improvement, but he was no iconoclast ; he had no desire to pull down or root up or destroy under the plea of improvement. That he remained to the last the friend of Popes and bishops and other orthodox churchmen, is the best evidence, over and above his own words, that his real sentiments were not misunderstood by men who had the interests of the Church at heart, and who looked upon him as true and loyal, if perhaps a somewhat eccentric and caustic son of Holy Church. Even in his last sickness he received from the Pope proof of his esteem, for he was given a benefice of considerable value, and it was hinted to him that another honour, as was commonly supposed at the time nothing less than the sacred purple, was in store for him.

Most people are of course chiefly interested in the determination of Erasmus's general attitude to the great religious movement of the age. In this place, however, one or two minor points in his literary history can hardly be passed over in silence. His attitude to the monks and the religious Orders generally, was one of acknowledged hostility, although there are passages in his writings, some of which have been already quoted, which seem to show that this hostility was neither so sweeping nor so deeply rooted as is generally thought. Still, it may be admitted that he has few good words for the religious Orders, and he certainly brings many and even grave accusations against their good name. There is little doubt, however, that much he had to say on the subject was, as he himself tells us, said to emphasise abuses that existed, and was not intended to be taken as any wholesale sweeping condemnation of the system of regular life. Very frequently the *Enconium Moriæ* has been named as the work in which Erasmus hits the monks the hardest. Those who so regard it can hardly have read it with attention, and most certainly they fail to appreciate its spirit. It was composed, as we have seen, at Sir Thomas More's suggestion, and in his house at Chelsea in 1512, on Erasmus's return from Italy. It is a satire on the ecclesiastical manners and customs in which all abuses in turn come in for their share of sarcastic condemnation ; superstitions of people as to particular days and images, superstitions about " magic prayers and charmlike rosaries," as to saints set to this or that office, to cure the toothache, to discover stolen goods, &c., in the first place came under the lash of Erasmus's sarcasm. Then come, in turn, doctors of divinity and theologians, " a nest of men so crabbed and morose " that he has half a mind, he says, to leave them severely alone, " lest perchance they should all at once fall upon me with six hundred conclusions, driving me to recant." They are high and mighty and look down on other men, thinking of common individuals as " silly men like worms creeping on the ground," and startling ordinary folk by the variety of their unpractical discussions and questions. " Nowadays," he says, " not baptism, nor the Gospel, nor Paul, nor Peter, nor Jerome, nor Augustine, nor yet Thomas Aquinas, are able to make men Christians, unless those Father Bachelors in divinity are pleased to subscribe to the same. They require us to address them as *Magister noster* in the biggest of letters."

Following upon this treatment of the scholastic theologians come the few pages devoted to monks, those "whose trade and observance were surely most miserable and abject, unless I (Folly) did many ways assist them." They are so ignorant (at least so says Folly), that they can hardly read their own names. Erasmus makes merry over the office they chant, and the begging practised by the friars, and jeers amusingly at their style of dressing, at their mode of cutting their hair, and at their sleeping and working by *rule*. " Yea," he says, " some of them being of a straightened rule are such sore punishers of their flesh, as outwardly they wear nought but sackcloth and inwardly no better. than fine holland." In a word, he laughs at the general observance of regular life, and in one place only passes a hint that some of their lives are not so saintly as they pretend. As a whole, however, the sarcasm is not so bitter as that addressed to other ecclesiastics, and even to the Pope himself. In view of Sir Thomas More's subsequent explanation about the spirit of the *Enconium Moriæ*, there can be no doubt that it was intended mainly as a playful, if somewhat ill-judged and severe, lampoon on some patent abuses, and in no sense an attack upon the ecclesiastical system of the Catholic Church." [1]

[1] The Pope himself read the *Enconium Moriæ* and understood the spirit of the author; at least so Erasmus was told. He wrote at the time "the Supreme Pontiff has read through *Moriæ* and laughed ; all he said was, ' I am glad to see that friend Erasmus is in the *Moriæ*,' and this though I have touched no others so sharply as the Pontiffs " (Ep. p. 1667). What Sir Thomas More thought about it may be given in his own words, written some years later. " As touching *Moriæ*, in which Erasmus, under the name and person of *Moria*, which word in Greek signifies 'folly,' merely touches and reproves such faults and follies as he found in any kind of people pursuing every state and condition, spiritual and temporal, leaving almost none untouched. By this book, says Tyndale, if it were in English, every man should

One other misunderstanding about Erasmus's position in regard to the revival of letters may be here
noticed. The great scholar has been regarded as the
incarnation of the spirit of practical paganism, which,
unfortunately, was quickly the outcome of the movement in Italy, and which at this time gave so much
colour and point to the denunciations of those of the
opposite school.   No view can be more unjust to Erasmus. Though he longed anxiously for the clergy to
awake to a sense of the importance of studies in general,
of classical and scriptural studies in particular, there
was no one who saw more clearly the danger and
absurdity of carrying the classical revivalist spirit to
extremes.   In fact, in his *Ciceroniana,* he expressly ridicules what he has seen in Rome of the classical spirit
run mad.   Those afflicted by it, he says, try to think
that old Rome has returned.   They speak of the
" Senate," the " conscript fathers," the " plebs," the
" chief auger," and the " college of soothsayers," " Pon-
tifices Maximi," " Vestals," " triumphs," &c.   Nothing
can be more unlike the true Ciceronian spirit.   Am I,
he asks, as a Christian speaking to Christians about the

---

then well see that I was then far otherwise minded than I now write.   If this
be true, then the more cause have I to thank God for the amendment.   God
be thanked I never had that mind in my life to have holy saints' images or
their holy relics out of reverence.   Nor if there were any such thing in *Moriæ*
this could not make any man see that I were myself of that mind, the book
being made by another man though he were my darling never so dear.   How-
beit, that book of *Moriæ* doth indeed but jest upon abuses of such things. . . .
But in these days, in which men by their own default misconstrue and take
harm from the very Scripture of God, until men better amend, if any man
would now translate *Moriæ* into English, or some work either that I have
myself written ere this, albeit there be no harm therein, folks being (as they
be) given to take harm of what is good, I would not only my darling's books,
but my own also, help to burn them both with my own hands, rather than
folk should (though through their own fault) take any harm of them." (*English
Works,* pp. 422–3.)

Christian religion to try and suppose I am living in the age of Cicero, and speak as if I were addressing a meeting of the conscript fathers on the Capitol? Am I to pick my words, choose my figures and illustrations from Cicero's speeches to the Senate? How can Cicero's eloquence help me to speak to a mixed audience of virgins, wives, and widows in praise of fasting, penance, prayer, almsgiving, the sanctity of marriage, the contempt of the fleeting pleasures of this world, or of the study of Holy Scripture. No, a Christian orator dressed in Cicero's clothes is ridiculous.[1]

As an illustration of the height of absurdity to which the madness of the classical craze had brought people in Rome in his day, Erasmus relates the story of a sermon he himself once heard in the Eternal City during the pontificate of Pope Julius II. "I had been invited," he says, "a few days before, by some learned men to be present at this sermon (to be preached on Good Friday). 'Take care not to miss it,' they said, 'for you will at last be enabled to appreciate the tone of the Roman language, spoken by a Roman mouth.' Hence, with great curiosity, I went to the church, procuring a place near the orator so as not to miss even one word. Julius II. was himself present, a very unusual thing, probably on account of his health. And there were also there many cardinals and bishops, and in the crowd most of the men of letters who were then in Rome.

"The exordium and peroration were nearly as long as the rest of the discourse, and they all rang the changes of praise of Julius II. He called him the almighty Jove, and pictured him as brandishing the

---

[1] *Opera Omnia* (Froben's ed., 1540), i. p. 831.

trident, casting his thunderbolts with his right hand, and accomplishing all he willed by the mere nod of his head. All that had taken place of late years in Gaul, Germany, Spain, &c., were but the efforts of his simple will. Then came a hundred times repeated, such words as ' Rome,' ' Romans,' ' Roman mouth,' ' Roman eloquence,' &c." But what, asks Erasmus, were all these to Julius, bishop of the Christian religion, Christ's vicegerent, successor of Peter and Paul ? What are these to cardinals and bishops who are in the places of the other apostles ?

" The orator's design," he continues, " was to represent to us Jesus Christ, at first in the agony of His Passion, and then in the glory of His triumph. To do this, he recalled the memory of Curtius and Decius, who had given themselves to the gods for the salvation of the Republic. He reminded us of Cecrops, of Menelaus, of Iphigenia, and of other noble victims who had valued their lives less than the honour and welfare of their country. Public gratitude (he continued, in tears and in most lugubrious tones) had always surrounded these noble and generous characters with its homage, sometimes raising gilded statues to their memory in the forum ; sometimes decreeing them even divine honours, whilst Jesus Christ, for all His benefits, had received no other reward but death. The orator then went on to compare our Saviour, who had deserved so well of His country, to Phocion and to Socrates, who were compelled to drink hemlock though accused of no crime; to Epaminondas, driven to defend himself against envy roused by his noble deeds ; to Scipio and to Aristides, whom the Athenians were tired of hearing called the ' Just one,' &c.

"I ask, can anything be imagined colder and more inept? Yet, over all his efforts, the preacher sweated blood and water to rival Cicero. In brief, my Roman preacher spoke Roman so well that I heard nothing about the death of Christ.[1] If Cicero had lived in our days," asks Erasmus, "would he not think the name of God the Father as elegant as Jupiter the almighty? Would he think it less elegant to speak of Jesus Christ than of Romulus, or of Scipio Africanus, of Quintus Curtius, or of Marcus Decius? Would he think the name of the Catholic Church less illustrious than that of 'Conscript Fathers,' 'Quirites,' or 'Senate and people of Rome'? He would speak to us of faith in Christ, of the Holy Ghost, or the Holy Trinity?" &c.[2]

At considerable length Erasmus pours out the vials of his scorn upon those who act so foolishly under the influence of the false classical spirit. He points out the danger to be avoided. People, he says, go into raptures over pagan antiquities, and laugh at others who are enthusiastic about Christian archæology. "We kiss, venerate, almost adore a piece of antiquity," he says, "and mock at relics of the Apostles. If any one finds something from the twelve tables, who does not consider it worthy of the most holy place? And the laws written by the finger of God, who venerates, who kisses them? How delighted we are with a medal stamped with the head of Hercules, or of Mercury, or of Fortune, or of Victory, or of Alexander the Great, or one of the Cæsars,[3] and we deride those who treasure

---

[1] Pp. 832–33.   [2] P. 837.

[3] A case in point was the finding of the celebrated statue of the Laocöon on January 14, 1506. This discovery was accidentally made in a vineyard, near Santa Maria Maggiore, and no statue ever produced so general and so profound an emotion as the uncovering of this work of art did upon

the wood of the cross or images of the Virgin and saints as superstitious.[1] If in dealing with his subject Erasmus may appear to exaggerate the evil he condemns, this much is clear, that his advocacy of letters and learning, however strenuous and enthusiastic, was tempered by a sense of the paramount importance of the Christian spirit in the pursuit of science.

the learned world of Rome. The whole city flocked out to see it, and the road to the vineyard was blocked day and night by the crowds of cardinals and people waiting to look at it. "One would have said," writes a contemporary, "that it was a Jubilee." And even to-day the visitor to the Ara Cœli may read on the tomb of Felice de Fredis, the happy owner of the vineyard, the promise of "immortality," *ob proprias virtutes et repertum Laocohontis divinum simulachrum* (I. Klaczki, *Jules II.*, p. 115). It is not at all improbable that in the above passage Erasmus was actually thinking of the delirium caused by the finding of this statue.

[1] Ibid., p. 838.

CHAPTER VII

THE LUTHERAN INVASION

IT is not uncommonly asserted that the religious changes in England, although for convenience' sake dated from the rejection of Papal supremacy, were in reality the outcome of long-continued and ever-increasing dissatisfaction with the then existing ecclesiastical system. The Pope's refusal to grant Henry his wished-for divorce from Katherine, we are told, was a mere incident, which at most, precipitated by a short while what had long been inevitable.[1] Those

[1] For example, the Rev. W. H. Hutton states in the *Guardian*, January 25, 1899, as the result of his mature studies upon the Reformation period, that "the so-called divorce question had very little indeed to do with the Reformation." Mr. James Gairdner, who speaks with all the authority of a full and complete knowledge of the State papers of this period, in a letter to a subsequent number of the *Guardian*, says, "When a gentleman of Mr. Hutton's attainments is able seriously to tell us this, I think it is really time to ask people to put two and two together, and say whether the sum can be anything but four. It may be disagreeable to trace the Reformation to such a very ignoble origin, but facts, as the Scottish poet says, are fellows you can't coerce. . . . and won't bear to be disputed." What "we call *the* Reformation in England . . . was the result of Henry VIII.'s quarrel with the Court of Rome on the subject of his divorce, and *the same* results could not possibly have come about in any other way." When "Henry VIII. found himself disappointed in the expectation, which he had ardently cherished for a while, that he could manage, by hook or by crook, to obtain from the See of Rome something like an ecclesiastical licence for bigamy," he took matters into his own hands, "and self-willed as he was, never did self-will lead him into such a tremendous and dangerous undertaking as in throwing off the Pope. How much this was resented among the people, what secret communications there were between leading noblemen with the imperial ambassador, strongly urging the emperor to invade England, and deliver the people from a tyranny from which they were unable to free themselves, we know in these days as we did not know before."

who take this view are bound to believe that the
Church in England in the early sixteenth century was
honeycombed by disbelief in the traditional teachings,
and that men were only too ready to welcome emancipation. What then is the evidence for this picture of
the religious state of men's minds in England on the
eve of the Reformation ?

It is, indeed, not improbable that up and down
the country there were, at this period, some dissatisfied
spirits ; some who would eagerly seize any opportunity
to free themselves from the restraints which no longer
appealed to their consciences, and from teachings they
had come to consider as mere ecclesiastical formalism.
A Venetian traveller of intelligence and observation,
who visited the country at the beginning of the century,
whilst struck with the Catholic practices and with the
general manifestations of English piety he witnessed,
understood that there were " many who have various
opinions concerning religion." [1] But so far as there
is evidence at all, it points to the fact, that of religious
unrest, in any real sense, there could have been very
little in the country generally. It is, of course, impossible to suppose that any measurable proportion of
the people could have openly rejected the teaching of
the Church or have been even crypto-Lollards, without
there being satisfactory evidence of the fact forthcoming
at the present day.

The similarity of the doctrines held by the English
Reformers of the sixteenth century with many of those
taught by the followers of Wycliffe has, indeed, led some
writers to assume a direct connection between them
which certainly did not exist in fact. So far as Eng-

[1] Camden Society, p. 163.

land at least is concerned, there is no justification for
assuming for the Reformation a line of descent from any
form of English Lollardism. It is impossible to study
the century which preceded the overthrow of the old
religious system in England without coming to the
conclusion that as a body the Lollards had been long
extinct, and that as individuals, scattered over the
length and breadth of the land, without any practical
principle of cohesion, the few who clung to the tenets
of Wycliffe were powerless to effect any change of
opinion in the overwhelming mass of the population
at large. Lollardry, to the Englishman of the day, was
"heresy," and any attempt to teach it was firmly
repressed by the ecclesiastical authority, supported by
the strong arm of the State ; but it was also an offence
against the common feeling of the people, and there can
be no manner of doubt that its repression was popular.
The genius of Milton enabled him to see the fact that
"Wycliffe's preaching was soon damped and stifled by
the Pope and prelates for six or seven kings' reigns,"
and Mr. James Gairdner, whose studies in this period
of our national history enable him to speak with
authority, comes to the same conclusion. "Notwithstanding the darkness that surrounds all subjects connected with the history of the fifteenth century," he
writes, "we may venture pretty safely to affirm that
Lollardry was *not* the beginning of modern Protestantism. Plausible as it seems to regard Wycliffe as 'the
morning star of the Reformation,' the figure conveys
an impression which is altogether erroneous. Wycliffe's
real influence did not long survive his own day, and
so far from Lollardry having taken any deep root among
the English people, the traces of it had wholly dis-

appeared long before the great revolution of which it is thought to be the forerunner. At all events, in the rich historical material for the beginning of Henry VIII.'s reign, supplied by the correspondence of the time, we look in vain for a single indication that any such thing as a Lollard sect existed. The movement had died a natural death ; from the time of Oldcastle it sank into insignificance. Though still for a while considerable in point of numbers, it no longer counted among its adherents any men of note ; and when another generation had passed away the serious action of civil war left no place for the crotchets of fanaticism." [1]

On the only evidence available, the student of the reign of Henry VII. and of that of Henry VIII. up to the breach with Rome is bound to come to the same conclusion as to the state of the English Church. If we except manifestations of impatience with the Pope and Curia, which could be paralleled in any age and country, and which were rather on the secular side than on the religious, there is nothing that would make us think that England was not fully loyal in mind and heart to the established ecclesiastical system. In fact, as Mr. Brewer

[1] The same high authority, in a letter to the *Guardian*, March 1, 1899, says, " People will tell you, of course, that the seeds of the Reformation were sown before Henry VIII.'s days, and particularly that it was Wycliffe who brought the great movement on. I should be sorry to depreciate Wycliffe, who did undoubtedly bring about a great movement in his day, though a careful estimate of that movement is still a *desideratum*. Even in theology the cardinal doctrine of the Reformation—justification by faith—is in Wycliffe, I should say, conspicuous by its absence. But, whatever may be the theological debt of England to Wycliffe at the present day, twenty Wycliffes, all highly popular, in the fifteenth and sixteenth centuries would not have brought about a Reformation like that under which we have lived during the last centuries. That was a thing which could only have been effected by royal power—as in England, or by a subversion of royal authority through the medium of successful rebellion—as in Scotland."

says, everything proves that "the general body of the people had not as yet learned to question the established doctrines of the Church. For the most part, they paid their Peter pence and heard mass, and did as their fathers had done before them."[1]

It may be taken, therefore, for granted that the seeds of religious discord were not the product of the country itself, nor, so far as we have evidence on the subject at all, does it appear that the soil of the country was in any way specially adapted for its fructification. The work, both of raising the seed and of scattering it over the soil of England, must be attributed, if the plain facts of history are to be believed, to Germans and the handful of English followers of the German Reformers. If we would rightly understand the religious situation in England at the commencement of the Reformation, it is of importance to inquire into the methods of attack adopted in the Lutheran invasion, and to note the chief doctrinal points which were first assailed.

Very shortly after the religious revolt had established itself in Germany, the first indications of a serious attempt to undermine the traditional faith of the English Church became manifest in England. Roger Edgworth, a preacher during the reigns of Henry and Queen Mary, says that his "long labours have been cast in most troublesome times and most encumbered with errors and heresies, change of minds and schisms that ever was in the realm. . . . Whilst I was a young student in divinity," he continues, "Luther's heresies rose and were scattered here in this realm, which, in less space than a man would think, had so sore infected the Christian folk, first the youth and then the elders, where the children

---

[1] *Henry VIII.*, i. p. 51.

could set their fathers to school, that the king's Majesty and all Christian clerks in the realm had much ado to extinguish them. This they could not so perfectly quench, but that ever since, when they might have any maintenance by man or woman of great power, they burst forth afresh, even like fire hid under chaff." [1]

Sir Thomas More, when Chancellor in 1532, attributed the rapid spread of what to him and most people of his day in England was heresy, to the flood of literature which was poured forth over the country by the help of printing. " We have had," he writes, " some years of late, plenteous of evil books. For they have grown up so fast and sprung up so thick, full of pestilent errors and pernicious heresies, that they have infected and killed, I fear me, more simple souls than the famine of the dear years have destroyed bodies." [2]

We are not left in ignorance as to the books here referred to, as some few years previously the bishops of England had issued a list of the prohibited volumes. Thus, in October 1526, Bishop Tunstall ordered that in London people should be warned not to read the works in question, but that all who possessed them should deliver them over to the bishop's officials in order that they might be destroyed as pernicious literature. The list included several works of Luther, three or four of Tyndale, a couple of Zwingle, and several isolated works, such as the *Supplication of Beggars*, and the *Dyalogue between the Father and the Son*.[3]

---

[1] Roger Edgworth, *Sermons* (London : Robert Caly, 1557), preface.
[2] *English Works*, p. 339.
[3] Strype, *Eccl. Mem.* (ed. 1822), I. i. p. 254.

In 1530 the king by proclamation forbade the reading or possession of some eighty-five works of Wycliffe, Luther, Œcolampadius, Zwingle, Pomeranus, Bucer, Wesselius, and indeed the German divines generally, under the heading of "books of the Lutheran sect or faction conveyed into the city of London." Besides these Latin treatises, the prohibition included many English tracts, such as *A book of the old God and the new*, the *Burying of the Mass*, Frith's *Disputation concerning Purgatory*, and several prayer-books intended to propagate the new doctrines, such as *Godly prayers; Matins and Evensong with the seven Psalms and other heavenly psalms with commendations;* the *Hortulus Animæ* in English,[1] and the *Primer* in English.

In his proclamation Henry VIII. speaks of the determination of the English nation in times past to be true to the Catholic faith and to defend the country against "wicked sects of heretics and Lollards, who, by perversion of Holy Scripture, do induce erroneous opinions, sow sedition amongst Christian people, and disturb the peace and tranquillity of Christian realms, as lately happened in some parts of Germany, where, by the procurement and sedition of Martin Luther and other heretics, were slain an infinite number of Christian people." To prevent like misfortunes happening in England, he orders prompt measures to be taken to put a stop to the circulation of books in English and

---

[1] This book was apparently condemned for reflecting on the king's divorce rather than for its Lutheran tendencies. "The Soul's Garden," as Bishop Tunstall calls it, was printed abroad, and "very many lately brought into the realm, chiefly into London and into other haven towns." The objectionable portion was contained in "a declaration made in the kalendar of the said book, about the end of the month of August, upon the day of the decollation of St. John Baptist, to show the cause of why he was beheaded." (Strype, *ut supra*, ii. p. 274.)

other languages, which teach things "intolerable to the clean ears of any good Christian man."[1]

By the king's command, the convocation of Canterbury drew up a list of prohibited heretical books. In the first catalogue of fifty-three tracts and volumes, there is no mention of any work of Wycliffe, and besides some volumes which had come from the pens of Tyndale, Frith, and Roy, who were acknowledged disciples of Luther, the rest are all the compositions of the German Reformers. The same may be said of a supplementary list of tracts, the authors of which were unknown. All these are condemned as containing false teaching, plainly contrary to the Catholic faith, and the bishops add : " Moreover, following closely in the footsteps of our fathers, we prohibit all from selling, giving, reading, distributing, or publishing any tract, booklet, pamphlet, or book, which translates or interprets the Holy Scripture in the vernacular. . . . or even knowingly to keep such volumes without the licence of their diocesan in writing."[2]

About the same time a committee of bishops, including Archbishop Warham and Bishop Tunstall was appointed to draw up a list of some of the principal errors contained in the prohibited works of English heretics beyond the sea. The king had heard that " many books in the English tongue containing many detestable errors and damnable opinions, printed in parts beyond the sea," were being brought into England and spread abroad. He was unwilling that " such evil seed sown amongst his people (should) so take root that it might overgrow the corn of the Catholic doctrine

---

[1] Wilkins, *Concilia*, iii. p. 737.
[2] Ibid., 720.

before sprung up in the souls of his subjects," and he consequently ordered this examination. This has been done and the errors noted, " albeit many more there be in those books ; which books totally do swarm full of heresies and detestable opinions." The books thus examined and noted were eight in number : The *Wicked Mammon ;* the *Obedience of Christian man ;* the *Revelation of Antichrist ;* the *Sum of Scripture ;* the *Book of Beggars ;* the *Kalendar of the Prymer ;* the *Prymer,* and an *Exposition unto the Seventh Chapter of I Corinthians.* From these some hundreds of propositions were culled which contradicted the plain teaching of the Church in matters of faith and morality. In this condemnation, as the king states in his directions to preachers to publish the same, the commission were unanimous.[1]

The attack on the traditional teachings of the Church, moreover, was not confined to unimportant points. From the first, high and fundamental doctrines, as it seemed to men in those days, were put in peril. The works sent forth by the advocates of the change speak for themselves, and, when contrasted with those of Luther, leave no room for doubt that they were founded on them, and inspired by the spirit of the leader of the revolt, although, as was inevitable in such circumstances, in particulars the disciples proved themselves in advance of their master. Writing in 1546, Dr. Richard Smythe contrasts the old times, when the faith was respected, with the then state of mental unrest in religious matters. " In our days," he writes, " not a few things, nor of small importance, but (alack the more is the pity) even the chiefest and most weighty matters of our religion and faith are

---

[1] Wilkins, *Concilia,* iii. p. 727.

called in question, babbled, talked, and jangled upon (reasoned I cannot nor ought not to call it). These matters in time past (when reason had place and virtue with learning was duly regarded, yea, and vice with insolency was generally detested and abhorred) were held in such reverence and honour, in such esteem and dignity, yea, so received and embraced by all estates, that it was not in any wise sufferable that tag and rag, learned and unlearned, old and young, wise and foolish, boys and wenches, master and man, tinkers and tilers, colliers and coblers, with other such raskabilia might at their pleasure rail and jest (for what is it else they now do ?) against everything that is good and virtuous, against all things that are expedient and profitable, not sparing any Sacrament of the Church or ordinance of the same, no matter how laudable, decent, or fitting it has been regarded in times past, or how much it be now accepted by good and Catholic men. In this way, both by preaching and teaching (if it so ought to be called), playing, writing, printing, singing, and (Oh, good Lord !) in how many other ways besides, divers of our age, being their own schoolmasters, or rather scholars of the devil, have not forborne or feared to speak and write against the most excellent and most blessed Sacrament of the Altar, affirming that the said Sacrament is nothing more than a bare figure, and that there is not in the same Sacrament the very body and blood of our blessed Saviour and Redeemer, Jesus Christ, but only a naked sign, a token, a memorial and a remembrance only of the same, if they take it for so much even and do not call it (as they are wont to do) an idol and very plain idolatry." [1]

[1] Richard Smythe, D.D., *The assertion and defence of the Sacrament of the Altar*, 1546, f. 3.

As to the date of the introduction of these heretical views into England, Sir Thomas More entirely agreed with Dr. Smythe, the writer just quoted. He places the growth of these ideas in the circulation of books by Tyndale, Frith, and Barnes, and even as late as 1533, declares that the number of those who had accepted the new teaching was grossly exaggerated. He states his belief that " the realm is not full of heretics, and it has in it but a few, though that few be indeed over many and grown more also by negligence in some part than there has been in some late years past."[1]   It was, indeed, part of the strategy pursued by the innovators in religion to endeavour to make the movement appear more important than it had any claim to be.   It is, writes More, the " policy " of " these heretics who call themselves 'evangelical brethren,'" to make their number appear larger than it is.   " Some pot-headed apostles they have that wander about the realm into sundry shires, for whom every one has a different name in every shire, and some, peradventure, in corners here and there they bring into the brotherhood.   But whether they get any or none they do not hesitate to lie when they come home, and say that more than half of every shire is of their own sect.   Boast and brag these blessed brethren never so fast, they feel full well themselves that they be too feeble in what country so ever they be strongest.   For if they thought themselves able to meet and match the Catholics they would not, I ween, lie still at rest for three days."

" For in all places where heresies have sprung up hitherto so hath it proved yet.   And so negligently might these things be handled, that at length it might

[1] *English Works*, p. 940.

happen so here. And verily they look (far as they be yet from the power) for it, and some of them have not hesitated to say this, and some to write it, too. For I read the letter myself which was cast into the palace of the Right Reverend Father in God, Cuthbert, now Bishop of Durham, but then Bishop of London, in which among other bragging word . . . were these words contained : ' There will once come a day.' And out of question that day they long for but also daily look for, and would, if they were not too weak, not fail to find it. And they have the greater hope because . . . they see that it begins to grow into a custom that among good Catholic folk they are suffered to talk unchecked." For good men in their own minds indeed think the Catholic faith so strong that heretics with all their babbling will never be able to vanquish it, " and in this undoubtedly their mind is not only good, but also very true. But they do not look far enough. For as the sea will never surround and overwhelm all the land, and yet has eaten it in many places, and swallowed whole countries up and made many places sea, which sometime were well-inhabited lands, and has lost part of its own possession again in other places, so, though the faith of Christ shall never be overwhelmed with heresy, nor the gate of hell prevail against Christ's Church, yet as in some places it winneth in new peoples, so by negligence in some places the old may be lost." [1]

Sir Thomas More is all for vigilance on the part of the authorities. He likens those who are in power and office to the guardians of a fertile field who are bound to prevent the sowing of tares on their master's land ; and the multiplication of evil books and their circula-

[1] *English Works*, p. 921.

tion among the people, cannot, in his opinion, have any
other effect than to prevent the fertilisation of the good
seed of God's word in the hearts of many. "These new
teachers," he says, "despise Christ's Sacraments, which
are His holy ordinances and a great part of Christ's New
Law and Testament. Who can place less value on His
commandments than they who, upon the boldness of
faith only, set all good works at naught, and little consider the danger of their evil deeds upon the boldness
that a bare faith and slight repentance, without shrift or
penance, suffices, and that no vow made to God can
bind a man to live chastely or hinder a monk from
marriage. All these things, with many pestilent errors
besides, these abominable books of Tyndale and his
fellows teach us. Of these books of heresies there are
so many made within these few years, what by Luther
himself and by his fellows, and afterwards by the new
sects sprung out of his, which, like the children of
Vippara, would now gnaw out their mother's belly, that
the bare names of those books were almost enough to
make a book. Some of every sort of those books are
brought into this realm and kept in 'hucker mucker'
by some shrewd masters who keep them for no good.
Besides the Latin, French, and German books of which
these evil sects have put forth an innumerable number,
there are some made in the English tongue. First,
Tyndale's *English Testament*, father of them all by reason
of his false translating, and after that, the *Five Books of
Moses* translated by the same man ; we need not doubt
in what manner and for what purpose. Then you have
his *Introduction to Saint Paul's Epistle*, with which he in-
troduces his readers to a false understanding of Saint
Paul, making them believe, among many other heresies,

that Saint Paul held that faith only was always sufficient
for salvation, and that men's good works were worth
nothing and could not deserve thanks or reward in
heaven, although they were done in grace. . . . Then
we have from Tyndale *The Wicked Mammona*, by which
many a man has been beguiled and brought into many
wicked heresies, which in good faith would be to me a
matter of no little wonder, for there was never a more
foolish frantic book, were it not that the devil is ever
ready to put out the eyes of those who are content to
become blind.   Then we have Tyndale's *Book of Obedience*, by which we are taught to disobey the teaching of
Christ's Catholic Church and set His holy Sacraments
at naught.   Then we have from Tyndale the *First
Epistle of Saint John*, expounded in such wise that I dare
say that blessed Apostle had rather his Epistle had
never been put in writing than that his holy words
should be believed by all Christian people in such a
sense.   Then we have the *Supplication of Beggars*, a
piteous beggarly book, in which he would have all the
souls in Purgatory beg all about for nothing.   Then we
have from George Joye, otherwise called Clarke, a
Goodly Godly Epistle, wherein he teaches divers other
heresies, but specially that men's vows and promises of
chastity are not lawful, and can bind no man in conscience not to wed when he will.   And this man, considering that when a man teaches one thing and does
another himself, the people set less value by his preaching, determined therefore with himself, that he would
show himself an example of his preaching.   Therefore,
being a priest, he has beguiled a woman and wedded
her ; the poor woman, I ween, being unaware that he is
a priest.   Then you have also an *Exposition on the Seventh*

Chapter of Saint Paul's Epistle to the Corinthians, by which exposition also priests, friars, monks, and nuns are taught the evangelical liberty that they may run out a-caterwauling and wed. That work has no name of the maker, but some think it was Friar Roy who, when he had fallen into heresy, then found it unlawful to live in chastity and ran out of his Order. Then have we the *Examinations of Thorpe* put forth as it is said by George Constantine (by whom I know well there has been a great many books of that sort sent into this realm). In that book, the heretic that made it as (if it were) a communication between the bishop and his chaplains and himself, makes all the parties speak as he himself likes, and sets down nothing as spoken against his heresies, but what he himself would seem solemnly to answer. When any good Christian man who has either learning or any natural wit reads this book, he shall be able not only to perceive him for a foolish heretic and his arguments easy to answer, but shall also see that he shows himself a false liar in his rehearsal of the matter in which he makes the other part sometimes speak for his own convenience such manner of things as no man who was not a very wild goose would have done.

" Then have we *Jonas* made out by Tyndale, a book that whosoever delight therein shall stand in such peril, that Jonas was never so swallowed up by the whale, as by the delight of that book a man's soul may be so swallowed by the devil that he shall never have the grace to get out again. Then, we have from Tyndale the answer to my *Dyalogue*. Then, the book of Frith against *Purgatory*. Then, the book of Luther translated into English in the name of Brightwell, but, as

I am informed, it was translated by Frith ; a book, such as Tyndale never made one more foolish nor one more full of lies. . . . Then, we have the *Practice of Prelates*, wherein Tyndale intended to have made a special show of his high worldly wit, so that men should have seen therein that there was nothing done among princes that he was not fully advertised of the secrets. Then, we have now the book of Friar Barnes, sometime a doctor of Cambridge, who was abjured before this time for heresy, and is at this day come under a safe conduct to the realm. Surely, of all their books that yet came abroad in English (of all which there was never one wise nor good) there was none so bad, so foolish, so false as his. This, since his coming, has been plainly proved to his face, and that in such wise that, when the books that he cites and alleges in his book were brought forth before him, and his ignorance showed him, he himself did in divers things confess his oversight, and clearly acknowledged that he had been mistaken and wrongly understood the passages.

"Then, we have besides Barnes's book, the *A B C for children*.. And because there is no grace therein, lest we should lack prayers, we have the *Primer* and the *Ploughman's Prayer* and a book of other small devotions, and then the whole *Psalter* too. After the *Psalter*, children were wont to go straight to their *Donat* and their Accidence, but now they go straight to Scripture. And for this end we have as a Donat, the book of the *Pathway to Scripture*, and for an Accidence, the *Whole sum of Scripture* in a little book, so that after these books are learned well, we are ready for Tyndale's *Pentateuchs* and Tyndale's *Testament*, and all the other

high heresies that he and Joye and Frith and Friar
Barnes teach in all their books. Of all these heresies
the seed is sown, and prettily sprung up in these little
books before. For the *Primer* and *Psalter*, prayers and
all, were translated and made in this manner by heretics
only. The *Psalter* was translated by George Joye, the
priest that is wedded now, and I hear say the *Primer*
too, in which the seven Psalms are printed without the
Litany, lest folks should pray to the saints ; and the
Dirge is left out altogether, lest a man might happen
to pray with it for his father's soul. In their Calendar,
before their devout prayers, they have given us a new
saint, Sir Thomas Hytton, the heretic who was burned
in Kent. They have put him in on St. Matthew's Eve,
by the name of St. Thomas the Martyr.

"It would be a long work to rehearse all their
books, for there are yet more than I have known.
Against all these the king's high wisdom politically
provided, in that his proclamation forbade any manner
of English books printed beyond the sea to be brought
into this realm, or any printed within this realm to be
sold unless the name of the printer and his dwelling-
place were set upon the book. But still, as I said
before, a few malicious, mischievous persons have
now brought into this realm these ungracious books
full of pestilent, poisoned heresies that have already in
other realms killed, by schisms and war, many thousand
bodies, and by sinful errors and abominable heresies
many more thousand souls.

"Although these books cannot either be there
printed without great cost, nor here sold without
great adventure and peril, yet, with money sent hence,
they cease not to print them there, and send them

hither by the whole sacks full at once ; and in some places, looking for no lucre, cast them abroad at night, so great a pestilent pleasure have some devilish people caught with the labour, travail, cast, charge, peril, harm, and hurt of themselves to seek the destruction of others." [1]

In his introduction to the *Confutation* of Tyndale's answer, from which the foregoing extracts are taken, Sir Thomas More gives ample evidence that the teaching of "the New Learning" was founded entirely upon that of the German Reformer Luther, although on certain points his English followers had gone beyond their master. He takes for example what Hytton, "whom Tyndale has canonized," had been teaching "his holy congregations, in divers corners and luskes lanes." Baptism, he had allowed to be "a sacrament necessary for salvation," though he declared that there was no need for a priest to administer it. Matrimony, he thought a good thing for Christians, but would be sorry to say it was a sacrament. Extreme Unction and Confirmation, together with Holy Orders, he altogether rejected as sacraments, declaring them to be mere ceremonies of man's invention. "The mass," he declared, "should never be said," since to do so was rather an act of sin than virtue. Confession to a priest was unnecessary, and the penance enjoined was "without profit to the soul." Purgatory he denied, "and said further, that neither prayer nor fasting for the souls departed can do them any good." Religious vows were wrong, and those who entered religion "sinned in so doing." He held further, that "no man had any free-will after he had once sinned;" that "all the images of Christ and His saints should be thrown out of the Church," and that whatsoever laws "the Pope or a General Council might make beyond what is expressly commanded in Scripture" need not be obeyed. "As touching the Sacrament of the Altar, he said that it was a necessary sacrament, but held that after the consecration, there was nothing whatever therein, but only the very substance of material bread and wine." [1]

Now, it was to defend these points of Catholic faith, as More, in common with the most learned in the land, believed them to be, that he took up his pen against Tyndale and others. I wish, he says, to second "the king's gracious purpose, as being his most unworthy chancellor," since "I know well that the king's highness, for his faithful mind to God, desires nothing more effectually than the maintenance of the true Catholic faith, whereof is his no more honourable than well-deserved title, 'defensor.' He detests nothing more than these pestilent books which Tyndale and others send over into the realm in order to set forth their abominable heresies. For this purpose he has not only by his most erudite famous books, both in English and Latin, declared his most Catholic purpose and intent, but also by his open proclamations divers times renewed, and finally in his own most royal person in the Star Chamber most eloquently by his mouth, in the presence of his lords spiritual and temporal, has given monition and warning to all the justices of peace of every quarter of his realm then assembled before his Highness, to be declared by them to all his people, and did prohibit and forbid under

[1] Ibid., p. 346.

great penalties, the bringing in, reading, and keep of those pernicious poisoned books." [1]

The other writers of the time, moreover, had no doubt whatever as to the place whence the novel opinions had sprung, and they feared that social disturbances would follow in the wake of the religious teaching of the sectaries as they had done in the country of their birth. Thus Germen Gardynare, writing to a friend about the execution of John Frith for heresy, says that he was " amongst others found busy at Oxford in setting abroad these heresies which lately sprang up in Germany, and by the help of such folk are spread abroad into sundry places of Christendom, tending to nothing else but to the division and rending asunder of Christ's mystical body, His Church ; and to the pulling down of all power and the utter subversion of all commonwealths." [2]

Sir Thomas More, too, saw danger to the ship of State from the storms which threatened the nation in the rise of the religious novelties imported from abroad. As a warning anticipation of what might come to pass in England if the flood was allowed to gain head, he describes what was known of the state of Germany when he wrote in 1528. What helped Luther to successfully spread his poison was, he says, " that liberty which he so highly commended unto the people, inducing them to believe that having faith they needed nothing else. For he taught them to neglect fasting, prayer, and such other things as vain and unfruitful ceremonies, teaching them also that being faith-

[1] Ibid., p. 351.
[2] Germen Gardynare, *A letter of a yonge gentylman*, &c.   London : W. Rastell, 1534.

ful Christians they were so near cousins to Christ that they were, in a full freedom and liberty, discharged of all governors and all manner of laws spiritual and temporal, except only the Gospel.   And though he said that, as a point of special perfection, it would be good to suffer and bear the rule and authority of Popes and princes and other governors, whose rule and authority he calls mere tyranny, yet he says the people are so free by faith that they are no more bound thereto than they are to suffer wrong.   And this doctrine Tyndale also teaches as the special matter of his holy book of disobedience.   Now, this doctrine was heard so pleasantly in Germany by the common people that it blinded them in looking on the remnant, and would not allow them to consider and see what end the same would come to.   The temporal lords also were glad to hear this talk against the clergy, and the people were as glad to hear it against the clergy and against the lords too, and against all the governors of every good town and city.   Finally, it went so far that it began to burst out and fall to open force and violence.   For intending to begin at the most feeble, a boisterous company of the unhappy sect gathered together and first rebelled against an abbot, and afterwards against a bishop, wherewith the temporal lords had good game and sport and dissembled the matter, gaping after the lands of the spirituality, till they had almost played as Æsop tells of the dog, which, in order to snatch at the shadow of the cheese in the water, let the cheese he had in his mouth fall, and lost it.   For so it was shortly after that those uplandish Lutherans took so great boldness and began to grow so strong that they set also upon the temporal lords.   These . . . so acquitted themselves that they slew in one summer 70,000 Lutherans and subdued the rest in that part of Germany to a most miserable servitude. . . . And in divers other parts of Germany and Switzerland this ungracious sect is so grown, by the negligence of governors in great cities, that in the end the common people have compelled the rulers to follow them. . . .

"And now it is too piteous a sight to see the ' dispiteous dispyghts ' done in many places to God and all good men, with the marvellous change from the face and fashion of Christendom into a very tyrannous persecution, not only of all good Christians living and dead, but also of Christ Himself. For there you will see now goodly monasteries destroyed, the places burnt up, and the religious people put out and sent to seek their living ; or, in many cities, the places (the buildings) yet standing with more despite to God than if they were burned to ashes. For the religious people, monks, friars, and nuns, are wholly driven or drawn out, except such as would agree to forsake their vows of chastity and be wedded ; and places dedicated to cleanliness and chastity, left only to these apostates as brothels to live there in lechery. Now are the parish churches in many places not only defaced, all the ornaments taken away, the holy images pulled down, and either broken or burned, but also the Holy Sacrament cast out. And the abominable beasts (which I abhor to think about) did not abhor in despite to defile the pixes and in many places use the churches continually for a common siege. And that they have done in so despiteful a wise that when a stranger from other places where Christ is worshipped resorts to these cities, some of those unhappy wretched citizens do not fail, as it were, for courtesy and kindness, to accompany them in their walking abroad to show them the pleasures and commodities of the town, and then bring them to the church, only to show them in derision what uses the churches serve for !" Then, after pointing out that " of this sect were the greater part of those ungracious people who lately entered into Rome with the Duke of Bourbon," Sir Thomas More details at considerable length the horrors committed during that sack of the Eternal City ; adding : " For this purpose I rehearse to you these their heavy mischievous dealings, that you may perceive by their deeds what good comes of their sect.   For as our Saviour says : ' ye shall know the tree by the fruit.' " [1]

The activity of the teachers of the new doctrine was everywhere remarkable.   More only wished that the maintainers of the traditional Catholic faith were half so zealous " as those that are fallen into false heresies and have forsaken the faith." These seem, he says, indeed to " have a hot fire of hell in their hearts that can never suffer them to rest or cease, but forces them night and day to labour and work busily to subvert and destroy the Catholic Christian faith by every means they can devise." [2]   The time was, " and even until now very late," when no man would allow any heresy to be spoken at his table ; for this " has been till of late the common Christian zeal towards the Catholic faith."   But now (1533) "though, God be thanked, the faith is itself as fast rooted in this realm as ever it was before (except in some very few places, and yet even in those few the very faithful folk

[1] *English Works*, pp. 257–259.
[2] Ibid., p. 1035.

are many more than the faithless), even good men are beginning to tolerate the discussion of heretical views, and to take part in ‘the evil talk.’ ”

To understand the Reformation in England, it is important to note the progress of its growth, and to note that the lines upon which it developed were to all intents and purposes those which had been laid down by Luther for the German religious revolution, although, in many ways, England was carried along the path of reformed doctrines, even further than the original leader had been prepared to go. The special points of the traditional faith of the English people, which the reforming party successfully attacked, were precisely those which had been the battle-ground in Germany, and Sir Thomas More's description of the result there might somewhat later have been written of this country. Tyndale was described by More as " the captain of the English heretics," and the influence of his works no doubt greatly helped to the overthrow of the traditional teaching. The key of the position taken up by the English Reformers, as well as by their German predecessors, was the claim that all belief must be determined by the plain word of Holy Scripture, and by that alone. Tradition they rejected, although Sir Thomas More pointed out forcibly that the Church had always acknowledged the twofold authority of the written and unwritten word.[1] Upon this ground Tyndale and his successors rejected all the sacraments but two, attacked popular devotion to sacred images and prayers to our Lady and the saints, and rejected the old teaching about Purgatory and the help the souls of the departed faithful could derive from the

[1] Ibid., p. 409.

suffrages and penances of the living. Confirmation
and the anointing of priests at ordination they con-
temptuously called " butter smearing," and with their
denial of the priesthood quickly came their rejection
of the doctrine of the Sacrifice in the Mass, and their
teaching that the Holy Eucharist is a "token and
sign" rather than the actual Body and Blood of our
Lord.

No means were left untried to further the spread
of the new views. Books of prayer were drawn up, in
which, under the guise of familiar devotions, the poison
of the reformed doctrine was unsuspectedly imbibed.
Richard Whitford complains that his works, which just
on the eve of the Reformation were deservedly popular,
had been made use of for the purpose of interpolating
tracts against points of Catholic faith, which people were
induced to buy under the supposition that they were
from the pen of the celebrated monk of Sion. John
Waylande, the printer of some Whitford books, in 1537
prefixed the following notice to the new edition of
the *Werke for Householders*. " The said author required
me instantly that I should not print nor join any other
works with his, specially of uncertain authors. For
of late he found a work joined in the same volume
with his works, and bought and taken for his work.
This was not his, but was put there instead of his work
that before was named among the contents of his book,
and yet his (real) work was left out, as is complained in
this preface here unto the Reader."

In his preface Whitford says that the substituted
work was obviously by one of the Reformers, and " not
only puts me into infamy and slander, but also puts
all readers in jeopardy of conscience to be infected

(by heresy) and in danger of the king's laws, for the manifold erroneous opinions that are contained in the same book." He consequently adds a warning to his readers: "By my poor advice," he says, "read not those books that go forth without named authors. For, doubtless, many of them that seem very devout and good works, are full of heresies, and your old English poet says, 'There is no poison so perilous of sharpness as that is that hath of sugar a sweetness.'"[1]

In a subsequent volume, published in 1541, called *Dyvers holy instructions and teachings*, Whitford again complains of this device of the teachers of the new doctrines. In the preface he gives the exact titles of the four little tracts which go to make up the volume, in order, as he says, "to give you warning to search well and surely that no other works are put amongst them that might deceive you. For, of a certainty, I found now but very lately a work joined and bound with my poor labours and under the contents of the same volume, and one of my works which was named in the same contents left out. Instead of this, was put this other work that was not mine. For the title of mine was this, 'A daily exercise and experience of death,' and the other work has no name of any author. And all such works in this time are ever to be suspected, for so the heretics are used to send forth their poison among the people covered with sugar. For they seem to be good and devout workers, and are in very deed stark heresies."[2]

[1] *The Werke for Householders.* London: John Waylande, 1537.
[2] Richard Whitford, *Dyvers holy instructions.* London: W. Mydylton, 1541.

Even the smallest points were not deemed too in-significant for the teaching of novel doctrines destructive of the old Catholic spirit. To take an example: John Standish, writing in Mary's reign about the vernacular Scripture, complains of the translation which had been made in the time of Henry VIII. "Who is able," he writes, "to tell at first sight how many hundred faults are even in their best translation (if there is any good). Shall they be suffered still to continue? Shall they still poison more like as they do in a thousand damnable English books set forth within the last twenty-two years? Lord deliver us from them all, and that with all speed! I take God to record (if I may speak only of one fault in the translation and touch no more) my heart did ever abhor to hear this word *Dominus* . . . translated *the* Lord, whereas it ought to be translated *our* Lord, the very Latin phrase so declaring. Is not St. John saying to Peter (John, xxi.), *Dominus est*, 'it is our Lord'? whereas they have falsely translated it as in many other places '*the* Lord.' And likewise in the salutation of our Lady, 'Hail, Mary, full of grace, *dominus tecum*,' does not this word *dominus* here include *noster*, and so ought to be translated 'our Lord is with thee'? Would you make the Archangel like a devil call him *the* Lord? He is the Lord to every evil spirit, but to us He is our most merciful Lord and ought to be called so. If, perchance, you ask of a husbandman whose ground that is, he will answer, 'the lord's,' who is perhaps no better than a collier. Well, I speak this, not now so much for the translation, seeing that it swarms as full of faults as leaves (I will not say lines) as I do, because I wish that the common speech

among people sprung from this fond translation, ' I
thank the Lord '; ' the Lord be praised '; ' the Lord
knoweth '; with all such-like phrases might be given
up, and that the people might be taught to call Him
' our Lord,' saying, ' I thank our Lord '; ' our Lord
be praised,' [1] &c., &c."

[1] *Sermons*, sig. h. vij.

CHAPTER VIII

THE PRINTED ENGLISH BIBLE

It is very commonly believed that until the influence of Cranmer had made itself felt, the ecclesiastical authorities continued to maintain the traditionally hostile attitude of the English Church towards the English Bible. In proof of this, writers point to the condemnation of the translations issued by Tyndale, and the wholesale destruction of all copies of this, the first printed edition of the English New Testament. It is consequently of importance to examine into the extent of the supposed clerical hostility to the vernacular Scriptures, and into the reasons assigned by those having the conduct of ecclesiastical affairs at that period for the prohibition of Tyndale's Testament.

It may not be without utility to point out that the existence of any determination on the part of the Church to prevent the circulation of vernacular Bibles in the fifteenth century has been hitherto too hastily assumed. Those who were living during that period may be fairly considered the most fitting interpreters of the prohibition of Archbishop Arundel, which has been so frequently adduced as sufficient evidence of this supposed uncompromising hostility to what is now called "the open Bible." The terms of the archbishop's monition do not, on examination, bear the meaning usually put upon it ; and should the language be considered by some obscure, there is absolute evidence of the possession of vernacular Bibles by Catholics of undoubted orthodoxy with, at the very least, the tacit consent of the ecclesiastical authorities.   When to this is added the fact that texts from the then known English Scriptures were painted on the walls of churches, and portions of the various books were used in authorised manuals of prayer, it is impossible to doubt that the hostility of the English Church to the vernacular Bible has been greatly exaggerated, if indeed its attitude has not altogether been misunderstood.   This much may, and indeed must, be conceded, wholly apart from the further question whether the particular version now known as the Wycliffite Scriptures is, or is not, the version used in the fifteenth and early sixteenth century by Catholic Englishmen.   That a Catholic version, or some version viewed as Catholic and orthodox by those who lived in the sixteenth century, really existed does not admit of any doubt at all on the distinct testimony of Sir Thomas More.   It will be readily admitted that he was no ordinary witness.   As one eminent in legal matters, he must be supposed to know the value of evidence, and his uncompromising attitude towards all innovators in matters of religion is a sufficient guarantee that he would be no party to the propagation of any unorthodox or unauthorised translations.

Some quotations from Sir Thomas More's works will illustrate his belief better than any lengthy exposition.   It is unnecessary, he says, to defend the law prohibiting any English version of the Bible, " for there is none such, indeed.   There is of truth a Constitution which speaks of this matter, but nothing of such fashion. For you shall understand that the great arch-heretic

Wycliffe, whereas the whole Bible was long before his days by virtuous and well-learned men translated into the English tongue, and by good and godly people and with devotion and soberness well and reverently read, took upon himself to translate it anew. In this translation he purposely corrupted the holy text, maliciously planting in it such words, as might in the readers' ears serve to prove such heresies as he 'went about' to sow. These he not only set forth with his own translation of the Bible, but also with certain prologues and glosses he made upon it, and he so managed this matter, assigning probable and likely reasons suitable for lay and unlearned people, that he corrupted in his time many folk in this realm. . . .

"After it was seen what harm the people took from the translation, prologues, and glosses of Wycliffe and also of some others, who after him helped to set forth his sect for that cause, and also for as much as it is dangerous to translate the text of Scripture out of one tongue into another, as St. Jerome testifieth, since in translating it is hard to keep the same sentence whole (*i.e.* the exact meaning): it was, I say, for these causes at a Council held at Oxford, ordered under great penalties that no one might thenceforth translate (the Scripture) into English, or any other language, on his own authority, in a book, booklet, or tract, and that no one might read openly or secretly any such book, booklet, or treatise newly made in the time of the said John Wycliffe, or since, or should be made any time after, till the same translation had been approved by the diocesan, or, if need should require, by a Provincial Council.

"This is the law that so many have so long spoken about, and so few have all this time sought to look whether they say the truth or not. For I hope you see in this law nothing unreasonable, since it neither forbids good translations to be read that were already made of old before Wycliffe's time, nor condemns his because it was new, but because it was 'naught.' Neither does it prohibit new translations to be made, but provides that if they are badly made they shall not be read till they are thoroughly examined and corrected, unless indeed they are such translations as Wycliffe and Tyndale made, which the malicious mind of the translator has handled in such a way that it were labour lost to try and correct them."

The "objector," whom Sir Thomas More was engaged in instructing in the *Dialogue*, could hardly believe that the formal Provincial Constitution meant nothing more than this, and thereupon, as Sir Thomas says: "I set before him the Constitutions Provincial, with Lyndwood upon it, and directed him to the place under the title *De magistris*. When he himself had read this, he said he marvelled greatly how it happened that in so plain a matter men were so deceived." But he thought that even if the law was not as he had supposed, nevertheless the clergy acted as if it were, and always "took all translations out of every man's hand whether the translation was good or bad, old or new." To this More replied that to his knowledge this was not correct. "I myself," he says, "have seen and can show you Bibles, fair and old, written in English, which have been known and seen by the bishop of the diocese, and left in the hands of laymen and women, whom he knew to be good and Catholic people who used the books with devotion and soberness." He admitted indeed that all Bibles found in the hands of heretics were taken away from them, but none of these, so far as he had ever heard, were burnt, except such as were found to be garbled and false. Such were the Bibles issued with evil prologues or glosses, maliciously made by Wycliffe and other heretics. "Further," he declared, "no good man would be so mad as to burn a Bible in which they found no fault." Nor was there any law whatever that prohibited the possession, examination, or reading of the Holy Scripture in English.[1]

In reply to the case of Richard Hunn, who, according to the story set about by the religious innovators, had been condemned and his dead body burnt "only because they found English Bibles in his house, in which they never found other fault than because they

---

[1] *English Works* (ed. 1557), pp. 233–4. This positive declaration of Sir Thomas More is generally ignored by modern writers. In a recently published work, for example (*England in the Age of Wycliffe*, by George Macaulay Trevelyan), it is stated that "we have positive proof that the bishops denounced the dissemination of the English Bible among classes and persons prone to heresy, burnt copies of it, and cruelly persecuted Lollards on the charge of reading it" (p. 131). In proof of this statement the author refers his readers to a later page (p. 342) of his volume. Here he culls from Foxe (*Acts and Monuments*) the depositions of certain witnesses against people suspected of teaching heresy. Amongst these depositions it is said by a few of the witnesses that some of these teachers were possessed of portions of the Scriptures in English. Mr. Trevelyan assumes, because witnesses speak to this fact, that it was for this they were condemned, or, as he puts it, "cruelly persecuted," by the ecclesiastical authorities. Had he examined his authority, Foxe, more carefully, he would have found the actual list of *articles* formulated against these teachers of heresy. These alone are, of course, the *charges* actually made against them ; and the mere deposition of witnesses in those days were, no more than they are in ours, the charges upon which the accused were condemned. In the *articles* or charges we find no mention whatever of the English Bible, and, according to the ordinary rules of interpretation of documents, this absence of any mention of Bible-reading in the indictment, formulated after the hearing of the evidence, and when witnesses had testified to the fact, should be taken to show that the mere possession of the vernacular Scriptures, &c., was not accounted an offence by the Church authorities. The real charge in these cases, as in others, was of teaching what was then held to be false and heretical, teaching founded upon false interpretations of the Scripture text, or upon false translations.

were in English," Sir Thomas More, professedly, and with full knowledge of the circumstances, absolutely denies, as he says, "from top to toe," the truth of this story.[1] He shows at great length that the whole tale of Hunn's death was carefully examined into by the king's officials, and declares that at many of the examinations he himself had been present and heard the witnesses, and that in the end it had been fully shown that Hunn was in reality a heretic and a teacher of heresy. " But," urged his objector, " though Hunn were himself a heretic, yet might the book (of the English Bible) be good enough ; and there is no good reason why a good book should be burnt." The copy of this Bible, replied More, was of great use in showing the kind of man Hunn really was, " for at the time he was denounced as a heretic, there lay his English Bible open, and some other English books of his, so that every one could see the places noted with his own hand, such words and in such a way that no wise and good man could, after seeing them, doubt what ' naughty minds ' the men had, both he that so noted them and he that so made them. I do not remember the particulars," he continued, " nor the formal words as they were written, but this I do remember well, that besides other things found to support divers other heresies, there were in the prologue of that Bible such words touching the Blessed Sacrament as good Christian men did much abhor to hear, and which gave the readers undoubted occasion to think that the book was written after Wycliffe's copy, and by him translated into our tongue." [2]

More then goes on to state his own mind as to the

---

[1] Ibid., p. 235.   [2] Ibid., p. 240.

utility of vernacular Scriptures. And, in the first place, he utterly denies again that the Church, or any ecclesiastical authority, ever kept the Bible in English from the people, except " such translations as were either not approved as good translations, or such as had already been condemned as false, such as Wycliffe's and Tyndale's were. For, as for other old ones that were before Wycliffe's days, they remain lawful, and are in the possession of some people, and are read." To this assertion of a plain fact Sir Thomas More's opponent did not dissent, but frankly admitted that this was certainly the case,[1] although he still thought that the English Bible might be in greater circulation than it was.[2] Sir Thomas More considered that the clergy really had good grounds not to encourage the spread of the vernacular Scriptures at that time, inasmuch as those who were most urgent in the matter were precisely those whose orthodoxy was reasonably suspected. It made men fear, he says, "that seditious people would do more harm with it than good and honest folk would derive benefit." This, however, he declared was not his own personal view.[3] " I would not," he writes, " for my part, withhold the profit that one good, devout, unlearned man might get by the reading, for fear of the harm a hundred heretics might take by their own wilful abuse. . . . Finally, I think that the Provincial Constitution (already spoken of) has long ago determined the question. For when the clergy in that synod agreed that the English Bibles should remain which were translated before Wycliffe's days, they, as a necessary consequence, agreed that it was no harm to have the Bible

---

[1] Ibid., p. 241.   [2] Ibid., p. 240.
[3] Ibid., p. 241.

in English. And when they forbade any new translation to be read till it were approved by the bishops, it
appears clearly that they intended that the bishop should
approve it, if he found it to be faultless, and also to
amend it where it was found faulty, unless the man
who made it was a heretic, or the faults were so many
and of such a character that it would be easier to re-
translate it than to mend it." [1]

This absolute denial of any attitude of hostility on
the part of the Church to the translated Bible is reiterated in many parts of Sir Thomas More's English
works. When, upon the condemnation of Tyndale's
Testament, the author pointed to this fact as proof of
the determination of the clergy to keep the Word of God
from the people, More replied at considerable length.
He showed how the ground of the condemnation had
nothing whatever to do with any anxiety upon the part of
ecclesiastics to keep the Scriptures from lay people, but
was entirely based upon the complete falsity of Tyndale's translation itself. " He pretends," says Sir Thomas
More, "that the Church makes some (statutes) openly
and directly against the Word of God, as in that statute
whereby they have condemned the New Testament.
Now, in truth, there is no such statute made. For
as for the New Testament, if he mean the Testament of Christ, it is not condemned nor forbidden. But there is forbidden a false English
translation of the New Testament newly forged by
Tyndale, altered and changed in matters of great weight,
in order maliciously to set forth against Christ's true
doctrine Tyndale's anti-Christian heresies. Therefore
that book is condemned, as it is well worthy to be, and

[1] Ibid., p. 245.

the condemnation thereof is neither openly nor privily, directly nor indirectly, against the word of God." [1]

Again, in another place, More replies to what he calls Tyndale's "railing" against the clergy, and in particular his saying that they keep the Scripture from lay people in order that they may not see how they "juggle with it." "I have," he says, "in the book of my *Dyalogue* proved already that Tyndale in this point falsely belies the clergy, and that in truth Wycliffe, and Tyndale, and Friar Barnes, and such others, have been the original cause why the Scripture has been of necessity kept out of lay people's hands. And of late, specially, by the politic provision and ordinance of our most excellent sovereign the king's noble grace, not without great and urgent causes manifestly rising from the false malicious means of Wycliffe and Tyndale," this has been prevented. "For this (attempt of Tyndale) all the lay people of this realm, both the evil folk who take harm from him, and the good folk that lose their profit by him, have great cause to lament that ever the man was born." [2]

The same view is taken by Roger Edgworth, a popular preacher in the reign of Henry VIII. After describing what he considered to be the evils which had resulted from the spread of Lutheran literature in England, he says : " By this effect you may judge the cause. The effect was evil, therefore there must needs be some fault in the cause. But what sayest thou ? Is not the study of Scripture good ? Is not the knowledge of the Gospels and of the New Testament godly, good, and profitable for a Christian man or woman ? I shall tell you what I think in this matter. I have

[1] Ibid., p. 510.   [2] Ibid., p. 678.

ever been in this mind, that I have thought it no harm, but rather good and profitable, that Holy Scripture should be had in the mother tongue, and withheld from no man that was apt and meet to take it in hand, specially if we could get it well and truly translated, which will be very hard to be had."[1]

There is, it is true, no doubt, that the destruction of Tyndale's Testaments and the increasing number of those who favoured the new religious opinions, caused people to spread all manner of stories abroad as to the attitude of the Church authorities in England towards the vernacular Scriptures.   Probably the declaration of the friend, against whom Sir Thomas More, then Chancellor, in 1530, wrote his *Dyalogue*, "that great murmurs were heard against the clergy on this score," is not far from the truth.   Ecclesiastics, he said, in the opinion of the common people, would not tolerate criticism of their lives or words, and desired to keep laymen ignorant.   " And they " (the people) " think," he adds, " that for no other cause was there burned at St. Paul's Cross the New Testament, late translated by Master William Huchin, otherwise called Tyndale, who was (as men say) well known, before he went over the sea, as a man of right good life, studious and well learned in the Scriptures.   And men mutter among themselves that the book was not only faultless, but also very well translated, and was ordered to be burned, because men should not be able to prove that such faults (as were at Paul's Cross declared to have been found in it) were never in fact found there at all ; but untruly surmised, in order to have some just cause to burn it, and that for no other reason than to keep

[1] Roger Edgworth, *Sermons*, London, Caly, 1557, f. 31.

out of the people's hands all knowledge of Christ's Gospel and of God's law, except so much as the clergy themselves please now and then to tell them. Further, that little as this is, it is seldom expounded. And, as it is feared, even this is not well and truly told ; but watered with false glosses and altered from the truth of the words and meaning of Scripture, only to maintain the clerical authority. And the fear lest this should appear evident to the people, if they were suffered to read the Scripture themselves in their own tongue, was (it is thought) the very cause, not only for which the New Testament translated by Tyndale was burned, but also why the clergy of this realm have before this time, by a Constitution Provincial, prohibited any book of Scripture to be translated into the English tongue, and threaten with fire men who should presume to keep them, as heretics ; as though it were heresy for a Christian man to read Christ's Gospel." [1]

It has been already pointed out how Sir Thomas More completely disposed of this assertion as to the hostility of the clergy to "the open Bible." In his position of Chancellor of England, More could hardly have been able to speak with so much certainty about the real attitude of the Church, had not the true facts been at the same time well understood and commonly acknowledged. The words of the " objector," however, not only express the murmurs of those who were at that period discontented with the ecclesiastical system ; but they voice the accusations which have been so frequently made from that day to this, by those who do not as a fact look at the other side. Sir Thomas More's testimony proves absolutely that no such hostility to the

---

[1] Sir Thomas More, *English Works*, p. 108.

English Bible as is so generally assumed of the pre-Reformation Church did, in fact, exist. Most certainly there never was any ecclesiastical prohibition against vernacular versions as such, and the most orthodox sons of the Church did in fact possess copies of the English Scriptures, which they read openly and devoutly. This much seems certain.

Moreover, Sir Thomas More's contention that there was no prohibition is borne out by other evidence. The great canonist Lyndwood undoubtedly understood the Constitution of Oxford on the Scriptures in the same sense as Sir Thomas More. In fact, as it has been pointed out already, to his explanation Sir Thomas More successfully appealed in proof of his assertion that there was no such condemnation of the English Scriptures, as had been, and is still, asserted by some. It has, of course, been often said that Sir Thomas More, and of course Lyndwood, were wrong in supposing that there were any translations previous to that of the version now known as Wycliffite. This is by no means so clear; and even supposing they were in error as to the date of the version, it is impossible that they could have been wrong as to the meaning and interpretation of the law itself, and as to the fact that versions were certainly in circulation which were presumed by those who used them to be Catholic and orthodox. Archbishop Cranmer himself may also be cited as a witness to the free circulation of manuscript copies of the English Scriptures in pre-Reformation times, since the whole of his argument for allowing a new version, in the preface to the Bishops' Bible, rests on the well-known custom of the Church to allow vernacular versions, and on the fact that copies of the English Scriptures had previously been in daily use with ecclesiastical sanction.

The same conclusion must be deduced from books printed by men of authority and unquestionable piety. In them we find the reading of the Scriptures strongly recommended. To take an example : Thomas Lupset, the friend and protégé of Colet and Lilly, gives the following advice to his sisters, two of whom were nuns : " Give thee much to reading ; take heed in meditation of the Scripture, busy thee in the law of God ; have a customable use in divine books." [1] The same pious scholar has much the same advice for a youth in the world who had been his pupil. After urging him to avoid " meddling in any point of faith otherwise than as the Church shall instruct and teach," he adds, " more particularly in writings you shall learn this lesson, if you would sometimes take in your hand the New Testament and read it with a due reverence " ; and again : " in reading the Gospels, I would you had at hand Chrysostom and Jerome, by whom you might surely be brought to a perfect understanding of the text." [2]

Moreover, the testimony of Sir Thomas More that translations were allowed by the Church, and that these, men considered rightly or wrongly, had been made prior to the time of Wycliffe, is confirmed by Archdeacon John Standish in Queen Mary's reign. When the question of the advisability of a vernacular translation was then seriously debated, he says : " To the intent that none should have occasion to misconstrue the true meaning thereof, it is to be thought that, if all men

---

[1] Thomas Lupset, *Collected Works*, 1546. *Gathered Counsails*, f. 202.

[2] Ibid. *An Exhortation to young men*, written 1529. He insists much on the obligation of following the teaching of the Church.

were good and Catholic, then were it lawful, yea, and very profitable also, that the Scripture should be in English, as long as the translations were true and faithful. . . . And that is the cause that the clergy did agree (as it is in the Constitution Provincial) that the Bibles that were translated into English before Wycliffe's days might be suffered ; so that only such as had them in handling were allowed by the ordinary and approved as proper to read them, and so that their reading should be only for the setting forth of God's glory." [1]

Sir Thomas More, in his *Apology*, points out that although, in his opinion, it would be a good thing to have a proper English translation, still it was obviously not necessary for the salvation of man's soul. " If the having of the Scripture in English," he writes, " be a thing so requisite of precise necessity, that the people's souls must needs perish unless they have it translated into their own tongue, then the greater part of them must indeed perish, unless the preacher further provide that all people shall be able to read it when they have it. For of the whole people, far more than four-tenths could never read English yet, and many are now too old to begin to go to school. . . . Many, indeed, have thought it a good and profitable thing to have the Scripture well and truly translated into English, and although many equally wise and learned and also very virtuous folk have been and are of a very different mind ; yet, for my own part, I have been and am still of the same opinion as I expressed in my *Dyalogue*,

---

[1] John Standish, *A discourse wherein is debated whether it be expedient that the Scripture should be in English for all men to read that wyll* (1555), A. iij.

if the people were amended, and the time meet for it." [1]

The truth is, that there was then no such clamour for the translated Bible as it has suited the purposes of some writers to represent.   In view of all that is known about the circumstances of those times, it does not appear at all likely that the popular mind would be really stirred by any desire for Bible reading.   The late Mr. Brewer may be allowed to speak with authority on this matter when he writes : " Nor, indeed, is it possible that Tyndale's writings and translations could at this early period have produced any such impressions as is generally surmised, or have fallen into the hands of many readers.   His works were printed abroad ; their circulation was strictly forbidden ; the price of them was beyond the means of the poorer classes, even supposing that the knowledge of letters at that time was more generally diffused than it was for centuries afterwards. To imagine that ploughmen and shepherds in the country read the New Testament in English by stealth, or that smiths and carpenters in towns pored over its pages in the corners of their masters' workshops, is to mistake the character and acquirements of the age." [2]

" So far from England then being a ' Bible-thirsty land,' " says a well-informed writer, " there was no anxiety whatever for an English version at that time, excepting among a small minority of the people," [3] and these desired it not for the thing in itself so much as a means of bringing about the changes in doctrine and practice which they desired.   " Who is there

---

[1] *English Works*, p. 850.
[2] J. S. Brewer, *Henry VIII.*, vol. ii. p. 468.
[3] Dore, *Old Bibles*, p. 13.

among us," says one preacher of the period, "that will have a Bible, but he must be compelled thereto." And the single fact that the same edition of the Bible was often reissued with new titles, &c., is sufficient proof that there was no such general demand for Bibles as is pretended by Foxe when he writes: "It was wonderful to see with what joy this book of God was received, not only among the learneder sort, and those that were noted for lovers of the Reformation, but generally all England over among all the vulgar common people." "For," says the writer above quoted, "if the people all England over were so anxious to possess the new translation, what need was there of so many penal enactments to force it into circulation, and of royal proclamations threatening with the king's displeasure those who neglected to purchase copies." [1]

There can be little doubt that the condemnation of the first printed English Testament, and the destruction, by order of the ecclesiastical authority, of all copies which Tyndale had sent over to England for sale, have tended, more than anything else, to confirm in their opinion those who held that the Church in pre-Reformation England would not tolerate the vernacular Scriptures at all. It is of interest, therefore, and importance, if we would determine the real attitude of churchmen in the sixteenth century to the English Bible, to understand the grounds of this condemnation. As the question was keenly debated at the time, there is little need to seek for information beyond the pages of Sir Thomas More's works.

The history of Tyndale's translation is not of such

[1] P. 15.

importance in this respect, as a knowledge of the chief points objected against it. Some brief account of this history, however, is almost necessary if we would fully understand the character and purpose of the translation. William Tyndale was born about the year 1484, and was in turn at Oxford and Cambridge Universities, and professed among the Friars Observant at Greenwich. In 1524 he passed over to Hamburg, and then, about the middle of the year, to Wittenberg, where he attached himself to Luther. Under the direction at least, of the German reformer, and very possibly also with his actual assistance, he commenced his translation of the New Testament. The royal almoner, Edward Lee, afterwards Archbishop of York, being on a journey to Spain, wrote on December 2, 1525, from Bordeaux, warning Henry VIII. of the preparation of this book. " I am certainly informed," he says, " that an Englishman, your subject, at the solicitation and instance of Luther, with whom he is, hath translated the New Testament into English ; and within a few days intendeth to return with the same imprinted into England. I need not to advertise your Grace what infection and danger may ensue hereby if it be not withstanded. This is the way to fill your realm with Lutherans. For all Luther's perverse opinions be grounded upon bare words of Scripture not well taken nor understood, which your Grace hath opened (*i.e.* pointed out) in sundry places of your royal book." [1]

Luther's direct influence may be detected on almost every page of the printed edition issued by Tyndale, and there can be no doubt that it was prepared with Luther's version of 1522 as a guide. From the general

[1] Ellis, *Historical Letters*, 3rd Series, ii. p. 71.

introduction of this German Bible, nearly half, or some sixty lines, are transferred by Tyndale almost bodily to his prologue, whilst he adopted and printed over against the same chapters and verses, placing them in the same position in the inner margins, some 190 of the German reformer's marginal references.   Besides this, the marginal notes on the outer margin of the English Testament are all Luther's glosses, translated from the German.   In view of this, it can hardly be a matter of surprise that Tyndale's Testament was very commonly known at the time as " Luther's Testament in English."

In this work of translation or adaptation, Tyndale was assisted by another ex-friar, named Joye, with whom, however, he subsequently quarrelled, and about whom he then spoke in abusive and violent terms.   At first it was intended to print the edition at Cologne, but being disturbed by the authorities there, Tyndale fled to Worms, and at once commenced printing at the press of Peter Schœffer, the octavo volume which is known as the first edition of Tyndale's New Testament. Although the author is supposed to have been a good Greek scholar, there is evidence to show that the copy he used for the work of translation was the Latin version of Erasmus, printed by Fisher in 1519, with some alterations taken from the edition of 1522, and some other corrections from the Vulgate.

John Cochlæus, who had a full and personal knowledge of all the Lutheran movements at the time, writing in 1533, says: " Eight years previously, two apostates from England, knowing the German language, came to Wittenberg, and translated Luther's New Testament into English.   They then came to Cologne, as to a city nearer to England, with a more established trade, and more adapted for the despatch of merchandise. Here . . . they secretly agreed with printers to print at first three thousand copies, and printers and publishers pushed on the work with the firm expectation of success, boasting that whether the king and cardinal liked it or not, England would shortly ‘ be Lutheran.’ ” [1]

It was this scheme that Cochlæus was instrumental in frustrating, his representations forcing Tyndale to remove the centre of his operations to Worms. For the benefit of the Scotch king, to whom his account was addressed, Cochlæus adds, that Luther's German translation of the New Testament was intended of set purpose to spread his errors ; that the people had bought up thousands, and that thereby “ they have not been made better but rather the worse, artificers who were able to read neglecting their shops and the work by which they ought to gain the bread of their wives and children.” For this reason, he says, magistrates in Germany have had 'to forbid the reading of Luther's Testament, and many have been put in prison for reading it. In his opinion the translation of the Testament into the vernacular had become an idol and a fetish to the German Lutherans, although in Germany there were many vernacular translations of both the Old and the New Testaments, before the rise of Lutheranism.[2]

---

[1] Johannes Cochlæus, *An expediat laicis legere Novi Testamenti libros lingua vernacula*, 1533, A. i. The warning of Cochlæus was addressed to the Scotch king, and as a result of this letter, pointing out the Lutheran character of the English version of Tyndale, the Scotch bishops in the Synod of St. Andrews in 1529 forbade the importation of Bibles into Scotland.

[2] Ibid., L. iij.

With a full understanding of the purpose and tendency of Tyndale's translation and of the evils which at least some hard-headed men had attributed to the spread of Luther's German version, upon which almost admittedly the English was modelled, the ecclesiastical authorities of England approached the practical question—what was to be done in the matter ?   Copies of the printed edition must have reached England some time in 1526, for in October of that year Bishop Tunstall of London addressed a monition to the archdeacons on the subject.   " Many children of iniquity," he says, " maintainers of Luther's sect, blinded through extreme wickedness, wandering from the way of truth and the Catholic faith, have craftily translated the New Testament into our English tongue, intermeddling therewith many heretical articles and erroneous opinions, pernicious and offensive, seducing the simple people ; attempting by their wicked and perverse interpretations to profane the majesty of Scripture, which hitherto hath remained undefiled, and craftily to abuse the most holy Word of God, and the true sense of the same.   Of this translation there are many books printed, some with glosses and some without, containing in the English tongue that pestiferous and pernicious poison, (and these are) dispersed in our diocese of London."   He consequently orders all such copies of the New Testament to be delivered up to his offices within thirty days.[1]

This was the first action of the English ecclesiastical authorities, and it was clearly taken not from distrust of what the same bishop calls "the most holy Word of God," but because they looked on the version sent

[1] Wilkins, *Concilia*, iii. p. 727.

forth by Tyndale as a profanation of the Bible, and as intended to disseminate the errors of Lutheranism.

Of the Lutheran character of the translation the authorities, whether in Church or State, do not seem to have had from the first the least doubt. The king himself, in a rejoinder to Luther's letter of apology, says that the German reformer " fell in device with one or two lewd persons, born in this our realm, for the translating of the New Testament into English, as well with many corruptions of that holy text, as certain prefaces and other pestilent glosses in the margins, for the advancement and setting forth of his abominable heresies, intending to abuse the good minds and devotion that you, our dearly beloved people, bear toward the Holy Scripture and infect you with the deadly corruption and contagious odour of his pestilent errors." [1]

Bishop Tunstall, in 1529, whilst returning from an embassy abroad, purchased at Antwerp through one Packington, all copies of the English printed New Testament that were for sale, and, according to the chronicler Hall, burned them publicly at St. Paul's in May 1530. For the same reason the confiscated volumes of the edition first sent over were committed to the flames some time in 1527,[2] and Bishop Tunstall explained to the people at Paul's Cross that the book was destroyed because in more than two thousand places wrong translations and corruptions had been detected. Tyndale made a great outcry at the iniquity of burning the Word of God ; but in *The Wicked*

---

[1] *Cf.* Parker Soc. Tyndale's *Doctrinal treatises*, &c., preface xxx.

[2] Probably on Sunday, February 11, when Cardinal Wolsey, with six and thirty bishops and other ecclesiastics, were present at the burning of Lutheran books before the great crucifix at the north gate. Amongst the books, according to Tyndale, were copies of his translated Testament.

Mammon he declares that, "in burning the New Testament they did none other thynge than I looked for." Moreover, as he sold the books knowing the purpose for which they were purchased, he may be said to have been a participator in the act he blames. "The fact is," says a modern authority, "the books were full of errors and unsaleable, and Tyndale wanted money to pay the expense of a revised version and to purchase Vastermann's old Dutch blocks to illustrate his Pentateuch, and was glad to make capital in more ways than one by the translation. 'I am glad,' said he, 'for these two benefits shall come thereof : I shall get money to bring myself out of debt, and the whole world will cry out against the burning of God's Word, and the overplus of the money that shall remain to me shall make me more studious to correct the said New Testament, and so newly to imprint the same once again, and I trust the second you will much better like than you ever did the first.'" [1]

Tyndale allowed nine years to elapse before issuing a second edition of his Testament. Meantime, as his former assistant, Joye, says, foreigners looking upon the English Testament as a good commercial speculation, and seeing that the ecclesiastical authorities in England had given orders to purchase the entire first issue of Tyndale's print, set to work to produce other reprints. Through ignorance of the language, the various editions they issued were naturally full of typographical errors, and, as Joye declared, "England hath enough and too many false Testaments, and is now likely to have many more." He consequently set to work himself to see an edition through the press, in which, without Tyndale's

[1] Dore, *Old Bibles*, p. 26.

leave, he made substantial alterations in his translation. Joye's version appeared in 1534, and immediately Tyndale attacked its editor in the most bitter, reproachful terms. In George Joye's *Apology*, which appeared in 1535, he tried, as he says, " to defend himself against so many slanderous lies upon him in Tyndale's uncharitable and unsober epistle." In the course of the tract, Joye charges Tyndale with claiming as his own what in reality was Luther's. " I have never," he says, " heard a sober, wise man praise his own works as I have heard him praise his exposition of the fifth, sixth, and seventh chapters of St. Matthew, insomuch that mine ears glowed for shame to hear him ; and yet it was Luther that made it, Tyndale only translating it and powdering it here and there with his own fantasies."

In a second publication Joye declares Tyndale's incompetence to judge of the original Greek. " I wonder," he says, " how he could compare it with the Greek, since he himself is not so exquisitely seen therein. . . . I know well (he) was not able to do it without such a helper as he hath ever had hitherto." [1] Tyndale, however, continued his work of revision in spite of opposition, and further, with the aid of Miles Coverdale, issued translations of various portions of the Old Testament.

Shortly after the public burning of the copies of the translated Testament by Bishop Tunstall, on May 24, 1530, an assembly was called together by Archbishop Warham to formally condemn these and other books then being circulated with the intention of undermining the religion of the country. The king was present in person, and a list of errors was drawn up

[1] Dore, *ut sup.*, 32.

and condemned "with all the books containing the same, with the translation also of Scripture corrupted by William Tyndale, as well in the Old Testament as in the New." After this meeting, a document was issued with the king's authority, which preachers were required to read to their people. After speaking of the books condemned for teaching error, the paper takes notice of an opinion "in some of his subjects" that the Scripture should be allowed in English. The king declares that it is a good thing the Scriptures should be circulated at certain times, but that there are others when they should not be generally allowed, and taking into consideration all the then existing circumstances, he "thinketh in his conscience that the divulging of the Scripture at this time in the English tongue to be committed to the people . . . would rather be to their further confusion and destruction than for the edification of their souls."

In this opinion, we are told, all in the assembly concurred. At the same time, however, the king promised that he would have the New Testament "faithfully and purely translated by the most learned men," ready to be distributed when circumstances might allow.

Sir Thomas More plainly states the reason for this prohibition. "In these days, in which Tyndale (God amend him) has so sore poisoned malicious and newfangled folk with the infectious contagion of his heresies, the king's highness, and not without the counsel and advice, not only of his nobles with his other counsellors attending upon his Grace's person, but also of the most virtuous and learned men of both universities and other parts of the realm, specially called thereto, has been obliged for the time to prohibit the Scriptures of God to be allowed in the English tongue in the hands of the people, lest evil folk . . . may turn all the honey into poison, and do hurt unto themselves, and spread also the infection further abroad . . . and by their own fault misconstrue and take harm from the very Scripture of God." [1]

Early in 1534 Tyndale took up his abode once more in Antwerp at the house of an English merchant, and busied himself in passing his revised New Testament through the press. This was published in the following November. To it he prefixed a second prologue dealing with the edition just published by George Joye. This he declares was no true translation, and charges his former assistant with deliberate falsification of the text of Holy Scripture in order to support his errors and false opinions. The edition itself manifests many changes in the text caused by the criticism to which the former impression had been subjected, whilst many of the marginal notes " exhibit the great change that had taken place in Tyndale's religious opinions, and show that he had ceased to be an Episcopalian." [2]

Having given a brief outline of the history of Tyndale's Testament, we are now in a position to examine into the grounds upon which the ecclesiastical authorities of England condemned it. For this purpose, we need again hardly go beyond the works of Sir Thomas More, who in several of his tracts deals specifically with this subject. " Tyndale's false translation of the New Testament," he says, " was, as he himself confesses, translated with such changes as he has made in it purposely, to the intent that by those changed words the people

---

[1] *English Works*, p. 422.   [2] Dore, 35.

should be led into the opinions which he himself calls true Catholic faith, but which all true Catholic people call very false and pestilent heresies." After saying that for this reason this translation was rightly condemned by the clergy and openly burnt at Paul's Cross, he continues : " The faults are so many in Tyndale's translation of the New Testament, and so spread throughout the whole book, that it were as easy to weave a new web of cloth or to sew up every hole in a net, so would it be less labour to translate the whole book anew than to make in his translation as many changes as there needs must be before it were made a good translation. Besides this, no wise man, I fancy, would take bread which he well knew had once been poisoned by his enemy's hand, even though he saw his friend afterwards sweep it ever so clean. . . . For when it had been examined, considered, and condemned by those to whom the judgment and ordering of the thing belonged, and that false poisoned translation had been forbidden to the people," it would be the height of presumption for any one to encourage the people boldly to resist their prince and disobey their prelates, and give them, as some indeed have, such a poor reason as this, "that poisoned bread is better than no bread." [1]

Further, in speaking with sorrow of the flood of heretical literature which seemed ever growing in volume, Sir Thomas More writes : " Besides the works in Latin, French, and German, there are made in the English tongue, first, Tyndale's New Testament, father of them all, because of his false translations, and after that the five books of Moses, translated by the same man, we need not doubt in what manner, when we know by

[1] *English Works*, p. 849.

whom and for what purpose.   Then you have his introduction to St. Paul's Epistle, with which he intro-
duces his readers to a false understanding of St. Paul,
making them, among many other heresies, believe that
St. Paul held that faith alone was sufficient for salvation, and that men's good works were worth nothing
and could deserve no reward in heaven, though they
were done in grace." [1]

Again, he says : " In the beginning of my *Dyalogue*,
I have shown that Tyndale's translation of the New
Testament deserved to be burnt, because itself showed
that he had translated it with an evil mind, and in such
a way that it might serve him as the best means of
teaching such heresies as he had learnt from Luther,
and intended to send over hither and spread abroad
within this realm.   To the truth of my assertion, Tyndale and his fellows have so openly testified that I need
in this matter no further defence.   For every man sees
that there was never any English heretical book sent
here since, in which one item of their complaint has not
been the burning of Tyndale's Testament.   For of a surety
they thought in the first place that his translation, with
their further false construction, would be the bass and
the tenor wherever they would sing the treble with
much false descant." [2]

To take some instances of the false translations to
which More reasonably objects : First, Tyndale sub-
stitutes for *Church* the word *Congregation*, " a word with
no more signification in Christendom than among the
Jews or Turks."   After protesting that Tyndale has no
right to change the signification of a word, as, for example, to speak of "a football," and to mean "the world,"

---

[1] *English Works*, p. 341.   [2] Ibid., p. 410.

More continues : " Most certainly the word *Congregation*, taken in conjunction with the text, would not, when he translated it first, have served to make the English reader understand by it the Church any more than when he uses the word *idols* for *images*, or *images* for *idols*, or the word *repenting* for *doing penance*, which he also does.   And indeed he has since added to his translation certain notes, viz., that the order of the priesthood is really nothing, but that every man, woman, and child is a priest as much as a real priest, and that every man and woman may consecrate the body of Christ, and say mass as well as a priest, and hear confessions and absolve as well as a priest can ; and that there is no difference between priests and other folks, but that all are one congregation and company without any difference, save appointment to preach."

This enables men to understand " what Tyndale means by using the word *Congregation* in his translation in place of *Church*.   They also see clearly by these circumstances that he purposely changed the word to set forth these his heresies, though he will say he takes them for no heresies.   But, on the other hand, all good and faithful people do, and therefore they call the Church the Church still, and will not agree to change the old *Church* for his new *Congregation*." [1]

In reply to Tyndale's claim to be able to use the word *Congregation* to signify the *Church*, More declares that words must be used in their ordinary signification. " I   say," he writes, " that this is true of the usual signification of these words in the English tongue, by the common custom of us English people that now use these words in our language, or have used them

[1] Ibid., p. 416.

before our days.   And I say that this common custom
and usage of speech is the only way by which we know
the right and proper signification of any word.   So
much so that if a word were taken from Latin, French,
or Spanish, and from lack of understanding the tongue
from which it came, was used in English for something
else than it signified in the other tongue ; then in England, whatsoever it meant anywhere else, it means only
what we understand it.   Then, I say, that in England
this word *Congregation* never did signify the body of
Christian people . . . any more than the word *assembly*, which has been taken from French . . . as
congregation is from the Latin. . . . I say now that
the word Church never has been used to signify in
the ordinary speech of this realm, any other than the
body of all those that are christened.   For this reason,
and more especially because of Tyndale's evil intent, I
said, and still say, that he did wrong to change *Church*
for *Congregation;* a holy word for a profane one, so far
as they have signification in our English tongue, into
which Tyndale made his translation. . . .[1]

   " If Tyndale had done it either accidentally, or purposely merely for pleasure, and not with an evil intent,
I would never have said a word against it.   But inasmuch as I perceive that he has been with Luther, and
was there at the time when he so translated it, and
because I knew well the malicious heresies that Luther
had begun to bring forth, I must needs mistrust him in
this change.   And now I say that even from his own
words here spoken, you may perceive his cankered
mind in his translation, for he says that Demetrius
had gathered a company against Paul for preaching

[1] *Ibid.*, p. 417.

against *images*.   Here the Christian reader may easily
perceive the poison of this serpent.   Every one knows
that all good Christian people abhor the idols of the
false pagan gods, and also honour the images of Christ
and our Lady, and other holy saints.   And as they call
the one sort images, so they call the other sort idols.
Now, whereas St. Paul preached against idols, this good
man comes and says he preached against images.   And
as he here speaks, even so he translates, for in the 15th
chapter of St. Paul to the Corinthians, where St. Paul
says, 'I have written to you that ye company not
together . . . if any that is called a brother be . . . a
worshipper of *idols*'—there Tyndale translates worshipper of *images*.   Because he would have it seem
that the Apostle had in that place forbidden Christian
men to worship images . . . Here you may see the
sincerity and plain meaning of this man's translation." [1] . . .

"As he falsely translated *Ecclesia* into the unknown
word *congregation*, in places where he should have translated it into the known word of *holy Church*, and this
with a malicious purpose to set forth his heresy of the
secret and unknown church wherein is neither good
works nor sacraments, in like manner is it now proved,
in the same way and with like malice, he has translated
idols into *images* . . . to make it seem that Scripture
reprobates the goodly images of our Saviour Himself
and His holy saints. . . . Then he asks me why I have
not contended with Erasmus whom he calls my darling, for translating this word *Ecclesia* into the word
congregatio. . . . I have not contended with Erasmus,
my darling, because I found no such malicious intent

[1] Ibid., p. 419.

with Erasmus, my darling, as I found with Tyndale ;
for had I found with Erasmus, my darling, the cunning
intent and purpose that I found with Tyndale, Erasmus,
my darling, should be no more 'my darling.' But I
find in Erasmus, my darling, that he detests and abhors
the errors and heresies that Tyndale plainly teaches and
abides by, and therefore Erasmus, my darling, shall be
my darling still. . . . For his translation of *Ecclesia* by
congregatio is nothing like Tyndale's, for the Latin
tongue had no Latin word used for Church, but the
Greek word, Ecclesia, therefore Erasmus, in his new
translation gave it a Latin word. But we in our English had a proper English word for it, and therefore
there was no cause for Tyndale to translate it into a
worse. Erasmus, moreover, meant therein no heresy,
as appears by his writings against heretics, but Tyndale,
intended nothing else thereby, as appears by the heresies that he himself teaches and abides by. Therefore,
there was in this matter no cause for me to contend
with Erasmus, as there was to contend with Tyndale,
with whom I contended for putting ' congregation '
instead of ' Church.' " [1]

Further, More blames Tyndale's translation in its
substitution of *senior* or *elder* for the old-established
word *priest*. This word, presbyter, in the Greek, he
says, " as it signifies the thing that men call priest in
English, was sometimes called *senior* in Latin. But
the thing that Englishmen call a priest, and the Greek
church called *presbyter*, and the Latin church also
sometimes called *senior*, was never called elder either
in the Greek church, or the Latin or the English.[2] He
considers, therefore, the change made by Tyndale, in

[1] Ibid., p. 422.   [2] Ibid., p. 424.

the second edition of his translation, from senior into
elder was not only no improvement, but a distinct
and reiterated rejection of the well-understood word
of priest. . . . " I said and say," he continues, " that
Tyndale changed the word priest into senior with the
heretical mind and intent to set forth his heresy, in
which he teaches that the priesthood is no sacrament
. . . for else I would not call it heresy if any one
would translate *presbyteros* a block, but I would say
he was a blockhead. And as great a blockhead were
he that would translate *presbyteros* into an elder instead
of a priest, for this English word no more signifies
an elder than the Greek word *presbyteros* signifies an
elderstick." [1]   " For the same reason he might change
bishop into overseer, and deacon into server, both of
which he might as well do, as priest into elder ; and
then with his English translation he must make us an
English vocabulary of his own device, and so with such
provision he may change chin into cheek, and belly
into back, and every word into every other at his own
pleasure, if all England like to go to school with Tyndale to learn English—but else, not so." [2]

In the same way More condemns Tyndale for
deliberately changing the word " Grace," the meaning
of which was fully understood by Catholic Englishmen,
into " favour," " thinking that his own scoffing is sufficient reason to change the known holy name of virtue
through all Scripture into such words as he himself
liketh." [3]   He says the same of the change of the old
familiar words *Confession* into *knowledge,* and *penance* into
repentance.   " This is what Tyndale means : he would

[1] Ibid., p. 425.   [2] Ibid., p. 427.
[3] Ibid., p. 435.

have all willing confession quite cast away and all penance doing too." [1] And " as for the word *penance*, whatsoever the Greek word be, it ever was, and still is, lawful enough (if Tyndale give us leave) to call any-thing in English by whatever word Englishmen by common custom agree upon. . . . Now, the matter does not rest in this at all. For Tyndale is not angry with the word, but with the matter. For this grieves Luther and him that by *penance* we understand, when we speak of it . . . not mere repenting . . . but also every part of the Sacrament of Penance ; oral confes-sion, contrition of heart, and satisfaction by good deeds. For if we called it the Sacrament of repentance, and by that word would understand what we now do by the word penance, Tyndale would then be as angry with repentance as he is now with penance." [2]

Speaking specially in another place about the change of the old word *charity* into *love* in Tyndale's translation, More declared that he would not much mind which word was used were it not for the evident intention to change the teaching. When it is done consistently through the whole book " no man could deem but that the man meant mischievously. If he called *charity* sometimes by the bare name *love*, I would not stick at that. But since charity signifies in English-men's ears not every common love, but a good virtuous and well-ordered love, he that will studiously flee from the name of good love, and always speak of ' love,' and always leave out ' good,' I would surely say he meant evil. And it is much more than likely. For it is to be remembered that at the time of this translation Huchins (or Tyndale) was with Luther in Wittenberg,

[1] Ibid., p. 437.   [2] Ibid., p. 493.

and put certain glosses in the margins, made to uphold the ungracious sect." . . . And " the reason why he changed the name of *charity* and of the *church* and of *priesthood* is no very great difficulty to perceive. For since Luther and his fellows amongst their other damnable heresies have one that all salvation rests on Faith alone—therefore he purposely works to diminish the reverent mind that men have to charity, and for this reason changes the name of holy virtuous affection into the bare name of love."

In concluding his justification of the condemnation of Tyndale's Testament and his criticism of the translator's *Defence*, Sir Thomas More says : " Every man knows well that the intent and purpose of my *Dyalogue* was to make men see that Tyndale in his translation changed the common known words in order to make a change in the faith. As for example : he changed the word *Church* into this word *congregation*, because he would raise the question which the church was, and set forth Luther's heresy that the church which we should believe and obey is not the common known body of all Christian realms remaining in the faith of Christ and not fallen away or cut off with heresies. . . . But the church we should believe and obey was some secret unknown kind of evil living and worse believing heretics. And he changed *priest* into *senior*, because he intended to set forth Luther's heresy teaching that priesthood is no sacrament, but the office of a layman or laywoman appointed by the people to preach. And he changed *Penance* into *repenting*, because he would set forth Luther's heresy teaching that penance is no sacrament. This being the only purpose of my *Dyalogue*, Tyndale now comes and expressly confesses what I

proposed to show. For he indeed teaches and writes
openly these false heresies so that he himself shows
now that I then told the people the truth . . . his own
writing shows that he made his translation to the intent
to set forth such heresies as I said he did." [1]

John Standish in the tract on the vernacular
Scriptures, published in Queen Mary's reign, uses in
some places the same language as Sir Thomas More
in condemning the translations which had been later
in vogue. " At all times," he writes, " heretics have
laboured to corrupt the Scriptures that they might
serve for their naughty purposes and to confirm their
errors therewith, but especially now in our time. O
good Lord, how have the translators of the Bible into
English purposely corrupted the texts, oft maliciously
putting in such words as in the readers' ears might
serve for the proof of such heresies as they went about
to sow. These are not only set forth in the translations, but also in certain prologues and glosses added
thereunto, and these things they have so handled (as
indeed it is no great mastery to do) with probable
reasons very apparent to the simple and unlearned,
that an infinite number of innocents they have spiritu-
ally poisoned and corrupted within this realm, and
caused them to perish obstinately." [2]

If further proof were wanting that the New Testament as set forth by Tyndale was purposely designed
to overthrow the then existing religious principles held
by English churchmen, it is furnished by works subsequently published by the English Lutherans abroad.
The tract named *The Burying of the Mass*, printed in

[1] Ibid., p. 422.   For examples of other false translations, see also p. 449.
[2] Standish, *A discourse*, &c., *ut supra*, sig. A. iiij.

Germany shortly after the burning of Tyndale's Testament, was, as Sir Thomas More points out, intended as a direct attack upon the Sacrifice of the Mass and the Sacramental system. In it the author poured out the vials of his wrath upon all those who caused Tyndale's translation of the New Testament to be destroyed, saying that they burned it because it destroyed the Mass. " By this," adds More, ".you may see that the author accounted the translation very good for the destruction of the Mass." [1] Moreover, in a book called *The Wicked Mammon*, published by Tyndale himself shortly after this, although he blames the style of the author of *The Burying of the Mass*, he tacitly accepts his assertion that his translation of the New Testament was intended to bring about the abolition of the Sacrifice of the Mass. [2]

In later times, after the experience of the religious changes in the reign of Edward VI., some writers pointed to the evils, religious and social, as evidence of the harm done by the promiscuous reading of the Scriptures. In their opinion, what More had feared and foretold had come to pass. " In these miserable years now past," says Standish of Mary's reign, in this tract on the vernacular Scriptures : " In these miserable years now past, what mystery is so hard that the ignorant with the Bible in English durst not set upon, yea and say they understood it : all was light ! They desired no explanation but their own, even in the highest mysteries. . . . Alas ! experience shows that our own men through having the Bible in English have walked far above their reach, being sundry ways

[1] *English Works*, p. 223.
[2] Ibid., p. 223.

killed and utterly poisoned with the letter of the English Bible." [1]

The spirit in which the study of Sacred Scripture was taken up by many in those days is described by the Marian preacher, Roger Edgworth, already referred to. " Scripture," he says, " is in worse case than any other faculty: for where other faculties take upon them no more than pertaineth to their own science, as (for example) the physician of what pertains to the health of man's body, and the carpenter and smith of their own tools and workmanship—the faculty of Sacred Scripture alone is the knowledge which all men and women challenge and claim to themselves and for their own. Here and there the chattering old wife, the doting old man, the babbling sophister, and all others presume upon this faculty, and tear it and teach it before they learn it. Of all such green divines as I have spoken of, it appeareth full well what learning they have by this, that when they teach any of their disciples, and when they give any of their books to other men to read, the first suggestion why he should labour (at) such books is ' because of this,' say they, ' thou shalt be able to oppose the best priest in the parish, and tell him he lies.' " [2]

The result is patent in the history of the religious confusions which followed, for this much must be allowed, whatever view may be taken of the good or evil which ultimately resulted. Dr. Richard Smith, in 1546, then states the position as he saw it: " In old times the faith was respected, but in our days

[1] Standish, *ut supra*, sig. E. iiij.
[2] Roger Edgworth, *Sermons*, f. 31.

not a few things, and not of small importance, but (alack the more the pity) even the chiefest and most weighty matters of religion and faith, are called in question, babbled about, talked and jangled upon (reasoned, I cannot and ought not to call it)." [1]

Although the cry for the open Bible which had been raised by Tyndale and the other early English reformers generally assumed the right to free and personal interpretation of its meaning, no sooner was the English Scripture put into circulation than its advocates proclaimed the need of expositions to teach people the meaning they should attach to it.   In fact, the marginal notes and glosses, furnished by Tyndale chiefly from Lutheran sources, are evidence that even he had no wish that the people should understand or interpret the sacred text otherwise than according to his peculiar views.   Very quickly after the permission of Henry VIII. had allowed the circulation of the printed English Bible, commentators came forward to explain their views.   Lancelot Ridley, for example, issued many such explanations of portions of the Sacred Text with the object, as he explains, of enabling

---

[1] *The assertion and defence of the Sacrament of the Altar* (1546), f. 3. The amateur theologians and teachers who sprung up so plentifully with the growth of Lutheran ideas in England seem to have been a source of trouble to the clergy.   There was no difficulty in Scripture so hard which these "barkers, gnawers, and railers," as Roger Edgworth calls them, were not ready to explain, and even women were ready to become teachers of God's Word, "and openly to dispute with men."   Speaking in Bristol, in Mary's reign, he advises his audience to stick to their own occupations and leave theology and Scripture alone, "for when a tailor forsaking his own occupation will be a merchant venturer, or a shoemaker will become a grocer, God send him help.   I have known," he says, " many in this town that studying divinity has killed a merchant, and some of other occupations by their busy labours in the Scripture hath shut up the shop windows, and were fain to take sanctuary, or else for mercery and grocery hath been fain to sell godderds, steaves, pitchers, and such other trumpery."

"the unlearned to declare the Holy Scriptures now suffered to all people of this realm to read and study at their pleasure." For the Bible, "which is now undeclared (*i.e.* unexplained) to them, and only had in the bare letter, appears to many rather death than life, rather (calculated) to bring many to errors and heresies than into the truth and verity of God's Word. For this, when unexplained, does not bring the simple, rude, and ignorant people from their ignorant blindness, from their corrupt and backward judgments, false trusts, evil beliefs, vain superstitions, and feigned holiness, in which the people have long been in blindness, for lack of a knowledge of Holy Scripture which the man of Rome kept under latch and would not suffer to come to light, that his usurped power should not have been espied, his worldly glory diminished, and his profit decayed."[1]

Again, in another exposition made eight years later, the same writer complains that still, for lack of teaching what he considers the true meaning of Scripture, the views of the people are still turned towards the "old superstitions" in spite of "the open Bible." "Although the Bible be in English," he says, "and be suffered to every man and woman to read at their pleasures, and commanded to be read every day at Matins, Mass, and Evensong, yet there remain great ignorance and corrupt judgments . . . and these will remain still, except the Holy Scriptures be made more plain to the lay people who are unlearned by some commentary or annotation, so that lay people may understand the Holy Scripture better."[2] Commentaries would help much, he says in

[1] *A Commentary in Englyshe upon Sayncte Paule's Epistle to the Ephesians,* 1540.

[2] *An Exposition in Englysh upon the Epistle of St. Paule to the Colossians,* 1548.

another place, " to deliver the people from ignorance,
darkness, errors, heresy, superstitions, false trusts, and
from evil opinions fixed and rooted in the hearts. of
many for lack of true knowledge of God's Holy Word,
and expel the usurped power of the bishop of Rome
and all Romish dregs." [1]

It is interesting to find that from the first, whilst
objecting to the interpretation of the old teachers of
the Church, and claiming that the plain text of Scripture was a sufficient antidote and complete answer
to them and their traditional deductions, the " new
teachers " found that without teaching and exposition
on their part, the open Bible was by no means sufficient
to wean the popular mind from what they regarded as
superstitious and erroneous ways.   Their attitude in
the matter is at least a confirmation of the contention
of Sir Thomas More and other contemporary Catholic
writers, that the vernacular Scriptures would be useless
without a teaching authority to interpret their meaning.

A brief word may now be said as a summary of
the attitude towards the vernacular Bible taken up by
the ecclesiastical authorities on the eve of the Reformation.   The passages quoted from Sir Thomas More
make it evident that no such hostility on the part of
the Church, as writers of all shades of opinion have too
hastily assumed, really existed.[2]   In fact, though those

[1] *An Exposition*, &c., *upon the Philippians*, 1545.
[2] As an example of the open way in which the reading of the Bible was
advocated, take the following instance.   Caxton's translation of the *Vitæ
Patrum*, published by Wynkyn de Worde in 1495, contained an exhortation
to all his readers to study the Holy Scripture.   " To read them is in part
to know the felicity eternal, for in them a man may see what he ought to do
in conversation . . . oft to read purgeth the soul from sin, it engendereth
dread of God, and it keeps the soul from eternal damnation."   As food
nourishes the body, "in like wise as touching the soul we be nourished by

responsible for the conduct of affairs, both ecclesiastical and lay, at this period objected to the circulation of Tyndale's printed New Testament, this objection was based, not on any dread of allowing the English Bible as such, but on the natural objection to an obviously incorrect translation. It is difficult to see how those in authority could have permitted a version with traditional words changed for the hardly concealed purpose of supporting Lutheran tenets, with texts garbled and marginal explanations inserted for the same end. Those who hold that Tyndale's views were right, and even that his attempt to enforce them in this way was justifiable, can hardly, however, blame the authorities at that time in England, secular or lay, who did not think so, from doing all they could to prevent what they regarded as the circulation of a book calculated to do great harm if no means were taken to prevent it. Men's actions must be judged by the circumstances under which they acted, and it would be altogether unjust to regard the prohibition of the Tyndale Scriptures as a final attempt on the part of the English Church to prevent the circulation of the vernacular Scriptures. To the authorities in those days at least, the book in question did not represent the Sacred Text at all. That it was full of errors, to say the least, is confessed by Tyndale himself; and as to the chief points in his translation which he defended and which Sir Thomas More so roundly condemned, posterity has sided with More and not with Tyndale, for not one of these special characteristics of the trans-

the lecture and reading of Scripture. . . . Be diligent and busy to read the Scriptures, for in reading them the natural wit and understanding are augmented in so much that men find that which ought to be left (undone) and take that whereof may ensue profit infinite " (p. 345).

lation in which so much of Tyndale's Lutheran teaching was allowed to appear, was suffered to remain in subsequent revisions. From this point of view alone, those who examine the question with an unbiassed mind must admit that there was ample justification for the prohibition of Tyndale's printed Testament. If this be so, the further point may equally well be conceded, namely, that the Church on the eve of the Reformation did not prohibit the vernacular Scriptures as such at all, and that many churchmen in common with the king, Sir Thomas More, and other laymen, would, under happier circumstances, have been glad to see a properly translated English Bible.

CHAPTER IX

TEACHING AND PREACHING

IT is very commonly assumed that on the eve of the Reformation, and for a long period before, there was little in the way of popular religious instruction in England. We are asked to believe that the mass of the people were allowed to grow up in ignorance of the meaning of the faith that was in them, and in a studied neglect of their supposed religious practices. So certain has this view of the pre-Reformation Church seemed to those who have not inquired very deeply into the subject, that more than one writer has been led by this assumption to assert that perhaps the most obvious benefit of the religious upheaval of the sixteenth century was the introduction of some general and systematic teaching of the great truths of religion. Preaching is often considered as characterising the reforming movement, as contrasted with the old ecclesiastical system, which it is assumed certainly admitted, even if it did not positively encourage, ignorance as the surest foundation of its authority. It becomes of importance, therefore, to inquire if such a charge is founded upon fact, and to see how far, if at all, the people in Catholic England were instructed in their religion.

At the outset, it should be remembered that the questions at issue in the sixteenth century were not, in

the first place at least, connected with the influence of
religious teaching on the lives of the people at large.
No one contended that the reformed doctrines would
be found to make people better, or would help them
to lead lives more in conformity with Gospel teaching.
The question of what may be called practical religion
never entered into the disputes of the time.   Mr. Brewer
warns the student of the history of this period that he
will miss the meaning of many things altogether, and
quite misunderstand their drift, if he starts his inquiry
by regarding the Reformation as the creation of light
to illuminate a previous period of darkness, or the
evolution of practical morality out of a state of ante-
cedent chaotic corruption.   " In fact," he says, " the
sixteenth century was not a mass of moral corruption
out of which life emerged by some process unknown to
art or nature ; it was not an addled egg cradling a
living bird ; quite the reverse."   For, as the historian of
the German people, Janssen, points out, the truth is that
the entire social order of the Middle Ages " was established on the doctrine of good works being necessary
for the salvation of the Christian soul."   Whilst, as
Mr. Brewer again notes, Luther's most earnest remon-
strances were directed not against *bad* works, but against
the undue stress laid by the advocates of the old religion
upon *good* works.   Moreover, an age which could busy
itself about discussions of questions as to "righteous-
ness," whether of "faith or works," "is not a de-
moralised or degenerate age.   These are not the
thoughts of men buried in sensuality."

Two questions are contained in the inquiry as to
pre-Reformation religious teaching, namely, as to its
extent and as to its character.   There can hardly be

much doubt that the duty of giving instruction to the people committed to their charge was fully recognised by the clergy in mediæval times. In view of the positive legislation of various synods on the subject of regular and systematic teaching, as well as of the constant repetition of the obligation in the books of English canon law, it is obvious that the priests were not ignorant of what was their plain duty. From the time of the constitution of Archbishop Peckham at the Synod of Oxford in 1281, to the time of the religious changes, there is every reason to suppose that the ordinance contained in the following words was observed in every parish church in the country: "We order," says the Constitution, "that every priest having the charge of a flock do, four times in each year (that is, once each quarter) on one or more solemn feast days, either himself or by some one else, instruct the people in the vulgar language simply and without any fantastical admixture of subtle distinctions, in the articles of the Creed, the Ten Commandments, the Evangelical Precepts, the seven works of mercy, the seven deadly sins with their offshoots, the seven principal virtues, and the seven Sacraments."

This means that the whole range of Christian teaching, dogmatic and moral, was to be explained to the people four times in every year; and in order that there should be no doubt about the matter, the Synod proceeds to set out in considerable detail each of the points upon which the priest was to instruct his people. During the fourteenth and fifteenth centuries the great number of manuals intended to help the clergy in the execution of this law attest the fact that it was fully recognised and very generally complied with. When at the close of the latter century, the invention of printing made the multiplication of such manuals easy, the existence both of printed copies of this Constitution of Archbishop Peckham, and of printed tracts drawn up to give every assistance to the parochial clergy in the preparation of these homely teachings, proves that the law was understood and acted upon. In the face of such evidence it is impossible to doubt that, whatever may have been the case as to set sermons and formal discourses, simple, straightforward teaching was not neglected in pre-Reformation England, and every care was taken that the clergy might be furnished with material suitable for the fundamental religious teaching contemplated by the law. As late as 1466, a synod of the York Province, held by Archbishop Nevill, not only reiterated this general decree about regular quarterly instructions of a simple and practical kind, but set out at great length the points of these lessons in the Christian faith and life upon which the parish priests were to insist.

Even set discourses of a more formal kind, though probably by no means so frequent as in these times, when they have to a great extent superseded the simple instructions of old Catholic days, were by no means neglected. Volumes of such sermons in manuscript and in print, as well as all that is known of the great discourses constantly being delivered at St. Paul's Cross, may be taken as sufficient evidence of this. For the conveyance of moral and religious instruction, however, the regular and homely talks of a parish priest to his people were vastly more important than the set orations, and it is with these familiar instructions that the student of this period of our history has chiefly to concern himself. All the available evidence goes to show that the giving of these was not only regarded as an obligation on the pastor ; but attendance at them was looked upon as a usual and necessary portion of the Christian duty. For example, in the examinations of conscience intended to assist lay people in their preparation for the Sacrament of penance, there are indications that any neglect to attend at these parochial instructions was considered sufficiently serious to become a matter of confession. It is, of course, hardly conceivable that this should be so, if the giving of these popular lessons in the duties of the Christian life was neglected by the priests, or if they were not commonly frequented by the laity. To take a few instances. " Also," runs one such examination, " I have been slow in God's service, and negligent to pray and to go to church in due time . . . loth to hear the Word of God, and the preacher of the Word of God. Neither have I imprinted it in my heart and borne it away and wrought thereafter." [1] Again : " I have been setting nought by preaching and teaching of God's Word, by thinking it an idle thing." [2]   And, to take an example of the view taken in such documents as to the priest's duty : " If you are a priest be a true lantern to the people both in speaking and in living, and faithfully and truly do all things which pertain to a priest. Seek wisely the ground of truth and the true office of the priesthood, and be not ruled blindly by the lewd customs of the world. Read God's law and the Expositions of the Holy Doctors, and study and learn and keep it, and when

---

[1] B. Mus. Harl. MS. 172, f. 12ᵇ.
[2] Harl. MS. 115, f. 51.

thou knowest it, preach and teach it to those that are unlearned."[1]

Richard Whitford, the Monk of Sion, in his *Work for Householders*, published first in 1530, lays great stress upon the obligation of parents and masters to see that those under their charge attended the instructions given in the parish church. Some may perhaps regard his greater anxiety for their presence at sermons rather than at Mass, when it was not possible for them to be at both, as doubtful advice. In this, however, he agrees with the author of what was the most popular book of instructions at this period, and the advice itself is proof that the obligation of attending instructions was regarded as sufficiently serious to be contrasted with that of hearing Mass. Speaking of the Sunday duties, Whitford says: "At church on Sundays see after those who are under your care. And charge them also to keep their sight in the church close upon their book and beads. And whilst they are young accustom them always to kneel, stand, and sit, and never walk in the church. And let them hear the Mass quietly and devoutly, much part kneeling. But at the Gospel, the Preface, and at the Paternoster teach them to stand and to make curtesy at the word Jesus, as the priest does. . . . If there be a sermon any time of the day let them be present, all that are not occupied in needful and lawful business ; all other (occupations) laid aside let them ever keep the preachings, rather than the Mass, if, perchance, they may not hear both."

Nothing could possibly be more definite or explicit upon the necessity of popular instructions and upon the duty incumbent upon the clergy of giving proper

[1] Ibid., f. 53.

vernacular teaching to their flocks than the author of *Dives et Pauper*, thé most popular of the fifteenth-century books of religious instruction. In fact, on this point his language is as strong and uncompromising as that which writers have too long been accustomed to associate with the name of Wycliffe. No more unwarranted assumption has ever been made in the name of history than that which classed under the head of Lollard productions almost every fifteenth-century tract in English, especially such as dealt openly with abuses needing correction, and pleaded for simple vernacular teaching of religion. This is what the author of *Dives et Pauper* says about preaching : " Since God's word is life and salvation of man's soul, all those who hinder them that have authority of God, and by Orders taken, to preach and teach, from preaching and teaching God's word and God's law, are manslayers ghostly. They are guilty of as many souls that perish by the hindering of God's word, and namely those proud, covetous priests and curates who can neither teach, nor will teach, nor suffer others that both can and will and have authority to teach and preach of God and of the bishop who gave them Orders, but prevent them for fear lest they should get less from their subjects, or else the less be thought of, or else that their sins should be known by the preaching of God's word. Therefore, they prefer to leave their own sins openly reproved generally, among other men's sins. As St. Anselm saith, God's word ought to be worshipped as much as Christ's body, and he sins as much who hindereth God's word and despiseth God's word, or taketh it recklessly as he that despiseth God's body, or through his negligence letteth it fall to the ground. On this place the gloss showeth

that it is more profitable to hear God's word in preaching than to hear a Mass, and that a man should rather
forbear his Mass than his sermon. For, by preaching,
folks are stirred to contrition, and to forsake sin and
the fiend, and to love God and goodness, and (by it)
they be illumined to know their God, and virtue from
vice, truth from falsehood, and to forsake errors and
heresies. By the Mass they are not so, but if they
come to Mass in sin they go away in sin, and shrews
they come and shrews they wend away. . . . Nevertheless, the Mass profiteth them that are in grace to get
grace and forgiveness of sin. . . . Both are good, but
the preaching of God's word ought to be more discharged and more desired than the hearing of Mass." [1]

In the same way the author of a little book named
The Interpretatyon and Sygnyfycacyon of the Masse, printed
by Robert Wyer in 1532, insists on the obligation of
attending the Sunday instruction. " On each Sunday,"
he says, " he shall also hear a sermon, if it be possible, for if a man did lose or omit it through
contempt or custom, he would sin greatly." [2] And in
The Myrrour of the Church, the author tells those who
desire " to see the Will of God in Holy Scripture," but
being of " simple learning " and " no cunning " cannot
read, that they may do so " in open sermon, or in
secret collation " with those who can. And in speaking of the Sunday duties he tells his readers not to
lie in bed, " but rising promptly you shall go to the
church, and with devotion say your matins without

---

[1] In speaking of the third Commandment, *The art of good lyvyng and
good deyng* (1503) warns people of their obligation to " Layr the holy prech-
yngys, that ys the word of God et the good techyngys, and shoold not go from
the seyd prechyngs " (fol. 8. 2).

[2] Ibid., f. 1.

jangling. Also sweetly hear your Mass and all the
hours of the day. And then if there is any preacher
in the church who proposes to make a sermon, you
shall sweetly hear the Word of God and keep it in
remembrance." [1] And lastly, to take one more example, in Wynkyn de Worde's *Exornatorium Curatorum*,
printed to enable those having the cure of souls to
perform the duties of instruction laid down by Archbishop Peckham's Provincial Constitution, whilst setting
forth a form of examination of conscience under the
head of the deadly sins, the author bids the curate
teach his people to ask themselves : "Whether you
have been slothful in God's service, and specially upon
the Sunday and the holy day whether you have been
slothful to come to church, slothful to pray when you
have been there, and slothful to hear the Word of
God preached.   Furthermore, whether you have been
negligent to learn your *Pater Noster*, your *Ave Maria*,
or your Creed, or whether you have been negligent
to teach the same to your own children or to your
god-children.   Examine yourself also whether you have
taught your children good manners, and guarded them
from danger and bad company." The same book
insists on the need of such examination of conscience
daily, or at least weekly.[2]

The following in this connection is of interest as
being a daily rule of life recommended to laymen
in the English Prymer printed at Rouen in 1538 :
"First   rise   up   at   six   o'clock   in   the   morning

---

[1] *The Myrrour of the Church* (1527), Sig. B4.

[2] *Exornatorium Curatorum*. W. de Worde. In 1518 the Synod of Ely
ordered that all having the cure of souls should have a copy of this book, and
four times a year should explain it in English to their people. (Wilkins,
Concilia, III., p. 712.)

at all seasons, and in rising do as follows : Thank
our Lord who has brought you to the beginning of
the day. Commend yourself to God, to Our Lady
Saint Mary, and to the saint whose feast is kept that
day, and to all the saints in heaven. When you have
arrayed yourself say in your chamber or lodging,
Matins, Prime, and Hours, if you may. Then go to
the church before you do any worldly works if you
have no needful business, and abide in the church the
space of a low mass time, where you shall think on God
and thank Him for His benefits. Think awhile on the
goodness of God, on His divine might and virtue. . . .
If you cannot be so long in the church on account of
necessary business, take some time in the day in your
house in which to think· of these things." . . . Take
your meal " reasonably without excess or overmuch
forbearing of your meat, for there is as much danger
in too little as in too much. If you fast once in a
week it is enough, besides Vigils and Ember days out
of Lent." After dinner rest " an hour or half-an-hour,
praying God that in that rest He will accept your health
to the end, that after it you may serve Him the more
devoutly."

" . . . As touching your service, say up to *Tierce*
before dinner, and make an end of all before supper.
And when you are able say the *Dirge* and *Commendations* for all Christian souls, at least on holy days, and
if you have leisure say them on other days, at least
with three lessons. Shrive yourself every week to your
curate, except you have some great hindrance. And
beware that you do not pass a fortnight unless you
have a very great hindrance. If you have the means
refuse not your alms to the first poor body that asketh

it of you that day.   Take care to hear and keep the Word of God.   Confess you every day to God without fail of such sins you know you have done that day." Think often of our Lord's Passion, and at night when you wake turn your thoughts to what our Lord was doing at that hour in His Passion.   In your life look for a faithful friend to whom you may open "your secrets," and when found follow his advice.   No doubt this "manner to live well" will perhaps hardly represent what people at this time ordinarily did.   But the mere fact that it could be printed as a Christian's daily rule of life as late as 1538, is evidence at any rate that people took at the least as serious a view of their obligations in religious matters as we should.[1]   In the same way *The art of good lyvyng*, quoted above, suggests as the proper way to sanctify the Sunday: Meditations on death, the pains of hell, and the joys of Paradise.   Time should be given to reading the lives of the saints, to saying Matins, and studying the Paternoster and the Creed.   Others should be exhorted to enter into God's service, and fathers of families are bound to see that "their children, servants, and families go to church and hear the preachings."[2]

By far the most interesting and important part of any inquiry on the subject of pre-Reformation instructions, regards of course their nature and effect.   We are asked to believe that the people were allowed to grow up in ignorance of the true nature of religion, and with superstitions in their hearts which the clergy could easily have corrected ; but which they, on the contrary,

[1] *The Prymer of Salisbury Use.*   Rouen : Nicholas le Rour, f. b. vij.
[2] *The art of good lyvyng and good deyng.*   Paris, 1503, f. g. 2.

rather fostered as likely to prove of pecuniary value to themselves. To keep the people ignorant (it is said) was their great object, as it was through the ignorance of the lay folk that the clergy hoped to maintain their influence and ascendency, and, it is suggested, to draw money out of the pockets of the faithful. The reverence which was paid at this time to images of the saints, and in an especial manner to the crucifix, is often adduced as proof that the people were evidently badly instructed in the nature of religious worship ; and the destruction of statues, paintings, and pictured glass by the advanced reformers is thought to be explained, if not excused, by the absolute need of putting a stop once for all to a crying abuse. The explanation given to the people by their religious teachers on the eve of the religious changes on this matter of devotion to the saints, and of the nature of the reverence to be paid to their representations, may be taken as a good sample of the practical nature of the general instructions imparted in those times. The question divested of all ambiguity is really this : Were the people taught to understand the nature of an image or representation, or were they allowed to regard them as objects of reverence in themselves—that is, as *idols ?* The material for a reply to this inquiry is fortunately abundant. The *Dyalogue* of Sir Thomas More was written in 1528, in order to maintain the Catholic teaching about images, relics, and the praying to saints. To this, then, an inquirer naturally turns in the first place for an exposition of the common belief in these matters ; for Sir Thomas claims that in his tract he is defending only " the common faith and belief of Christ's Church." " What this is," he says, " I am very sure ; and perceive it well not only by experience of my own time and the places where I have myself been to, with the common report of other honest men from all other places of Christendom." After having explained that the commandment of God had reference to idols or images worshipped as gods, and not to mere representations of Christ, our Lady, or the Saints,[1] he continues : " but neither Scripture nor natural reason forbids a man to reverence an image, not fixing his final intent on the image, but referring the honour to the person the image represents. In such reverence shown to an image there is no honour withdrawn from God ; but the saint is honoured in his image, and God in His saint. When a man of mean birth and an ambassador to a great king has high honour done to him, to whom does that honour redound, to the ambassador or to the king ? When a man on the recital of his prince's letter puts off his cap and kisses it, does he reverence the paper or his prince ? . . . All names spoken and all words written are no material signs or images, but are made only by consent and agreement of men to betoken and signify such things, whereas images painted, graven, or carved, may be so well wrought and so near to the life and the truth, that they will naturally and much more effectually represent the thing than the name either spoken or written. . . . These two words, *Christus crucifixus*, do not represent to us, either to laymen or to the learned, so lively a remembrance of His bitter Passion as does a blessed image of the crucifix, and this these heretics perceive well enough. Nor do they speak against images in order to further devotion, but plainly with a malicious mind to diminish and

[1] *English Works*, p. 116.

quench men's devotions.   For they see clearly that no
one who loves another does not delight in his image
or in anything of his.   And these heretics who are
so sore against the images of God and His holy saints,
would be right angry with him that would dishonestly
handle an image made in remembrance of one of
themselves, whilst the wretches forbear not to handle
villainously, and in despite cast dirt upon the holy
crucifix, an image made in remembrance of our
Saviour Himself, and not only of His most blessed
Person, but also of His most bitter Passion." [1]

Later on, in the same tract, rejecting the notion
that people did not fully understand that the image
was intended merely to recall the memory of the person
whose image it was, and was not itself in any sense the
thing or person, More says: " The flock of Christ is
not so foolish as those heretics would make them to
be.   For whereas there is no dog so mad that he does
not know a real coney (*i.e.* rabbit) from a coney carved
and painted, (yet they would have it supposed that)
Christian people that have reason in their heads, and
therefore the light of faith in their souls, would think
that the image of our Lady were our Lady herself.
Nay, they be not so mad, I trust, but that they do
reverence to the image for the honour of the person
whom it represents, as every man delights in the image
and remembrance of his friend.   And although every
good Christian man has a remembrance of Christ's
passion in his mind, and conceives by devout meditation a form and fashion thereof in his heart, yet there
is no man I ween so good nor so learned, nor so well
accustomed to meditation, but that he finds himself

[1] *English Works*, p. 117.

more moved to pity and compassion by beholding the holy crucifix than when he lacks it." [1]

In his work against Tyndale, More again takes up this subject in reference to the way in which the former in his new translation of the Bible had substituted the word *idol* for *image*, as if they were practically identical in meaning. "Good folk who worship images of Christ and His saints, thereby worship Christ and His saints, whom these images represent." Just as pagan worshippers of idols did evil in worshipping them, "because in them they worshipped devils (whom they called gods and whom those idols represented), so Christian men do well in worshipping images, because in them they worship Christ and His holy saints." [2]

Roger Edgworth, the preacher, describes at Bristol in Queen Mary's reign how the Reforming party endeavoured to confuse the minds of the common people as to the meaning of the word idol. "I would," he says, "that you should not ignorantly confound and abuse those terms 'idol' and 'image,' taking an image for an idol and an idol for an image, as I have heard many do in this city, as well fathers and mothers (who should be wise) as their babies and children who have learned foolishness from their parents. Now, at the dissolution of the monasteries and friars' houses many images have been carried abroad and given to children to play with, and when the children have them in their hands, dancing them in their childish manner, the father or mother comes and says, 'What nase, what have you there?' The child answers (as she is taught), 'I have here my idol.' Then the father laughs and makes a gay game at it. So says the mother to

<hr />

[1] Ibid., p. 121.   [2] Ibid., p. 420.

another, 'Jugge or Tommy, where did you get that
pretty idol?' 'John, our parish clerk gave it to me,'
says the child, and for that the clerk must have thanks
and shall not lack good cheer. But if the folly were
only in the insolent youth, and in the fond unlearned
fathers and mothers, it might soon be redressed." The
fact is, he proceeds to explain, that the new preachers
have been doing all in their power to obscure the
hitherto well-recognised difference in meaning between
an image and an idol. He begs his hearers to try and
keep the difference in meaning between an image and
an idol clearly before their minds. "An image is a
similitude of a natural thing that has been, is, or may
be," he tells them. "An idol is a similitude of what
never was or may be. Therefore the image of the
crucifix is no idol, for it represents and signifies Christ
crucified as He was in very deed, and the image of St.
Paul with a sword in his hand as the sign of his martyrdom is no idol, for the thing signified by it was a
thing indeed, for he was beheaded with a sword." [1]

In another part of the *Dialogue* Sir Thomas More
pointed out that what the reforming party said against
devotion to images and pilgrimages could be summed
up under one of three heads. They charge the people
with giving "to the saints, and also to their images,
honour like in kind to what they give to God Himself"; or (2) that "they take the images for the things
themselves," which is plain idolatry; or (3) that the
worship is conducted in a "superstitious fashion with
a desire of unlawful things." Now, as to these three
accusations, More replies: "The first point is at once
soon and shortly answered, for it is not true. For

[1] *Sermons,* fol. 40.

though men kneel to saints and images, and incense them also, yet it is not true that they for this reason worship them in every point like unto God. . . . They lack the chief point (of such supreme worship). That is, they worship God in the mind that He is God, which intention in worship is the only thing that maketh it *latria*, and not any certain gesture or bodily observance." It would not be supreme or divine worship even if " we would wallow upon the ground unto Christ, having in this a mind that He were the best man we could think of, but not thinking Him to be God. For if the lowly manner of bodily observance makes *latria*, then we were in grave peril of idolatry in our courtesy used to princes, prelates, and popes, to whom we kneel as low as to God Almighty, and kiss some their hands and some our own, ere ever we presume to touch them ; and in the case of the Pope, his foot ; and as for incensing, the poor priests in every choir are as well incensed as the Sacrament. Hence if *latria*, which is the special honour due to God, was contained in these things, then we were great idolaters, not only in our worship of the saints and of their images, but also of men, one to another among ourselves." Though indeed to God Almighty ought to be shown as " humble and lowly a bodily reverence as possible, still this bodily worship is not *latria*, unless we so do it in our mind considering and acknowledging Him as God, and with that mind and intention do our worship ; and this, as I think," he says, " no Christian man does to any image or to any saint either."

" Now, as touching the second point—namely, that people take the images for the saints themselves, I trust there is no man so mad, or woman either, that they do not know live men from dead stones, and a tree from flesh and bone. And when they prefer our Lady at one pilgrimage place before our Lady at another, or one rood before another, or make their invocations and vows some to the one and some to the other, I ween it easy to perceive that they mean nothing else than that our Lord and our Lady, or rather our Lord for our Lady, shows more miracles at the one than the other. They intend in their pilgrimages to visit, some one place and some another, or sometimes the place is convenient for them, or their devotion leads them ; and yet (this is) not for the place, but because our Lord pleases by manifest miracles to provoke men to seek Him, or His Blessed Mother, or some Holy Saint of His, in these places more especially than in some others."

"This thing itself proves also that they do not take the images of our Lady for herself. For if they did, how could they possibly in any wise have more mind to one of them than to the other ? For they can have no more mind to our Lady than to our Lady. More-over, if they thought that the image at Walsingham was our Lady herself then must they needs think that our Lady herself was that image. Then, if in like manner they thought that the image at Ipswich was our Lady herself, and as they must then need think that our Lady was the image at Ipswich, they must needs think that all these three things were one thing. . . . And so by the same reason they must suppose that the image at Ipswich was the self-same image as at Walsingham. If you ask any one you take for the simplest, except a natural fool, I dare hold you a wager she will tell you ' nay ' to this. Besides this, take the simplest fool you can find and she will tell you our Lady herself is in heaven. She will also call an image an image, and she will tell you the difference between an image of a horse and a horse in very deed. And this appears clearly whatever her words about her pilgrimage are, calling, according to the common manner of speech, the image of our Lady, our Lady. As men say, ' Go to the King's Head for wine,' not meaning his real head, but the sign, so she means nothing more in the image but our Lady's image, no matter how she may call it. And if you would prove she neither takes our Lady for the image, nor the image for our Lady—talk with her about our Lady and she will tell you that our Lady was saluted by Gabriel ; that our Lady fled into Egypt with Joseph ; and yet in the telling she will never say that ' our Lady of Walsingham,' or ' of Ipswich,' was saluted by Gabriel, or fled into Egypt. If you would ask her whether it was ' our Lady of Walsingham,' or ' our Lady of Ipswich,' that stood by the cross at Christ's Passion, she will, I warrant you, make answer that it was neither of them ; and if you further ask her, ' which Lady then,' she will name you no image, but our Lady who is in heaven. And this I have proved often, and you may do so, too, when you will and shall find it true, except it be in the case of one so very a fool that God will give her leave to believe what she likes. And surely, on this point, I think in my mind that all those heretics who make as though they had found so much idolatry among the people for mistaking (the nature) of images, do but devise the fear, to have some cloak to cover their heresy, wherein they bark against the saints them-selves, and when they are marked they say they only mean the wrong beliefs that women have in images." [1]

As regards the third point—namely, that honour is sometimes shown to the saints and their images in " a superstitious fashion with a desire of unlawful things," More would be ready to blame this as much as any man if it could be shown to be the case.   " But I would not," he says, " blame all things which are declared to be of this character by the new teachers. For example, to pray to St. Apollonia for the help of our teeth is no witchcraft, considering that she had her teeth pulled out for Christ's sake.   Nor is there any superstition in other suchlike things."   Still, where abuses can be shown they ought to be put down as abuses, and the difference between a lawful use and an unlawful abuse recognised.   But because there may be abuses done on the Sunday, or in Lent, that is no reason why the Sunday observance, or the fast of Lent, should be swept away. [2]   " In like manner it would not be right that all due worship of saints and reverence of relics, and honour of saints' images, by which good and devout folk get much merit, should be abolished and put down because people abuse " these things. " Now, as touching the evil petitions," he continues, " though they who make them were, as I trust they are not, a great number, they are not yet so many that ask evil petitions of saints as ask them of God Himself.   For whatsoever such people will ask of a good saint, they will ask of God Himself, and where as the worst point it is said, ' that the people do idolatry in that they take the images for the saints them-

---

[1] *English Works*, pp. 196-7.
[2] Ibid., p. 198.

selves, or the rood for Christ Himself,—which, as I
have said, I think none do ; for some rood has no
crucifix thereon, and they do not believe that the cross
which they see was ever at Jerusalem, or that it was
the holy cross itself, and much less think that the
image that hangs on it is the body of Christ Himself.
And though some were so mad as to think so, yet it
is not 'the people' who do so.   For a few doddering
dames do not make the people." [1]

It is hard to imagine any teaching about the use
and abuse of images clearer than that which is contained in the foregoing passages from Sir Thomas
More's writings.   The main importance of his testimony, however, is not so much this clear statement
of Catholic doctrine on the nature of devotion to
images, as his positive declaration that there were not
such abuses, or superstitions, common among the
people on the eve of the religious changes, as it suited
the purpose of the early reformers to suggest, and of
later writers with sectarian bias to believe.

For evidence of positive and distinct teaching on
the matter of reverence to be shown to images, and
on its nature and limits, we cannot do better than
refer to that most popular book of instruction in the
fifteenth and early sixteenth centuries, already referred
to, called *Dives et Pauper*, a treatise on the Ten Commandments.   It was multiplied from the beginning
of the fifteenth century in manuscript copies, and
printed editions of it were issued from the presses of
Pynson, Wynkyn de Worde, and Thomas Berthelet.
These editions published by our early printers are
sufficient to attest its popularity, and the importance

[1] Ibid., p. 199.

attached to it as a book of instruction by the ecclesiastical authorities on the eve of the Reformation.

This is how the teacher lays down the general principle of loving God : "The first precept of charity is this : Thou shalt love the Lord God with all thy heart, with all thy soul, and with all thy mind, with all thy might. When He saith thou shalt love thy God with all thy heart, He excludeth all manner of idolatry that is forbidden by the first commandment ; that is, that man set not his heart, nor his faith, nor his trust in any creature more than in God, or against God's worship. . . . God orders that thou shouldst love Him with all thy heart, that is to say, with all thy faith, in such a way that thou set all thy faith and trust in Him before all others, as in Him that is Almighty and can best help thee in thy need." Later on, under the same heading, we are taught that : "by this commandment we are bound to worship God, who is the Father of all things, who is called the Father of mercies and God of all comfort. He is our Father, for He made us of nought : He bought us with His blood, He findeth us all that we need, and much more, He feedeth us. He is our Father by grace, for by His grace He hath made us heirs of heavenly bliss. Was there ever a father so tender of his child as God is tender of us ? He is to us both father and mother, and therefore we are bound to love Him and worship Him above all things." [1]

Under the first commandment the whole question as to images, and the nature of the reverence to be paid to them, is carefully considered, and the matter put so plainly, that there is no room for doubt as to

[1] Ed. W. de Worde, 1496.

the nature of the instructions given to the people in pre-Reformation days. Images, the teacher explains, are ordered for three great ends, namely: "To stir men's minds to meditate upon the Incarnation of Christ and upon His life and passion, and upon the lives of the saints;" secondly, to move the heart to devotion and love, "for oft man is stirred more by sight than by hearing or reading;" thirdly, they "are intended to be a token and a book to the ignorant people, that they may read in images and painting as clerks read in books."

And in reply to a question from *Dives*, who pretended to think that it would be difficult to read a lesson from any painting, *Pauper* explains his meaning in calling them "books to the unlearned." "When thou seest the image of the crucifix," he says, "think of Him that died on the cross for thy sins and thy sake, and thank Him for His endless charity that He would suffer so much for thee. See in images how His head was crowned with a garland of thorns till the blood burst out on every side, to destroy the great sin of pride which is most manifested in the heads of men and women. Behold, and make an end to thy pride. See in the image how His arms were spread abroad and drawn up on the tree till the veins and sinews cracked, and how His hands were nailed to the cross, and streamed with blood, to destroy the sin that Adam and Eve did with their hands when they took the apple against God's prohibition. Also He suffered to wash away the sin of the wicked deeds and wicked works done by the hands of men and women. Behold, and make an end of thy wicked works. See how His side was opened and His heart cloven in two by the sharp spear, and how it shed blood and water, to show that if He had had more blood in His body, more He would have given for men's love. He shed His blood to ransom our souls, and water to wash us from our sins."

But whilst the instructor teaches the way in which the crucifix may be a book full of deep meaning to the unlearned, he is most careful to see that the true signification of the image is not misunderstood. In language which for clearness of expression and simplicity of illustration cannot be excelled, he warns *Dives* not to mistake the real nature of the reverence paid to the symbol of our redemption. "In this manner," he says, "read thy book and fall down to the ground and thank thy God who would do so much for thee. Worship Him above all things—not the stock, nor the stone, nor the wood, but Him who died on the tree of the cross for thy sins and thy sake. Thou shalt kneel if thou wilt before the image, but not to the image. Thou shalt do thy worship before the image, before the thing, not to the thing; offer thy prayer before the thing, not to the thing, for it seeth thee not, heareth thee not, understandeth thee not: make thy offering, if thou wilt, before the thing, but not to the thing: make thy pilgrimage not to the thing, nor for the thing, for it may not help thee, but to Him and for Him the thing represents. For if thou do it for the thing, or to the thing, thou doest idolatry."

This plain teaching as . to the only meaning of reverence paid to images, namely, that it is relative and intended for that which the image represents, our author enforces by several examples. Just as a priest when saying mass with a book before him, bends down, holds up his hands, kneels, and performs other external signs of worship, not to the book, but to God, " so should the unlettered man use his book, that is images and paintings, not worshipping the thing, but God in heaven and the saints in their degree. All the worship which he doth before the thing, he doth, not to the thing, but to Him the thing represents."

The image of the crucified Saviour on the altar is specially intended, our author says, to remind all that " Mass singing is a special mind-making of Christ's passion."   For this reason, in the presence of the crucifix, the priest says " his mass, and offers up the highest prayer that Holy Church can devise for the salvation of the quick and the dead.   He holds up his hands, he bows down, he kneels, and all the worship he can do, he does—more than all, he offers up the highest sacrifice and the best offering that any heart can devise—that is Christ, the Son of the God of heaven, under the form of bread and wine.   All this worship the priest doth at mass before the thing—the crucifix ; and I hope there is no man nor woman so ignorant that he will say that the priest singeth his mass, or maketh his prayer, or offers up the Son of God, Christ Himself, to the thing. . . . In the same way, unlettered men should worship before the thing, making prayer before the thing, and not to the thing."

One of the special practices of the mediæval church to which the English reformers objected, and to which they gave the epithet " superstitious," was the honour shown to the cross on Good Friday, generally known as " the creeping to the cross."   The advocates of change in insisting upon this time-honoured ceremony being swept away, claimed that in permitting it the

Church had given occasion to wrong ideas of worship
in the minds of the common people, and that the
reverence shown to the symbol of our redemption on
that occasion amounted practically to idolatry. In
view of such assertions, it is not without interest to
see how *Pauper* in this book of simple instructions
treats this matter. " On Good Friday especially," says
Dives, " men creep to the cross and worship the cross."
" That is so," replies the instructor, " but not in the
way thou meanest. The cross that we creep to and
worship so highly at that time is Christ Himself, who
died on the cross on that day for our sin and our
sake. . . . He is that cross, as all doctors say, to
whom we pray and say, '*Ave crux, spes unica*,' ' Hail,
thou cross, our only hope.' " But rejoins *Dives*,
" On Palm Sunday, at the procession the priest draweth
up the veil before the rood and falleth down to the
ground with all the people, saying thrice thus, '*Ave
Rex noster*,' ' Hail, be Thou our King.' In this he worships the thing as King! *Absit!*" "God forbid!"
replies *Pauper*, " he speaks not to the image that the
carpenter hath made and the painter painted, unless
the priest be a fool, for the stock and stone was never
king. He speaketh to Him that died on the cross
for us all—to Him that is King of all things . . . For
this reason are crosses placed by the wayside, to remind
folk to think of Him who died on the cross, and to
worship Him above all things. And for this same
reason is the cross borne before a procession, that
all who follow after it or meet it should worship Him
who died upon a cross as their King, their Head, their
Lord and their Leader to Heaven."

Equally clear is the author of *Dives et Pauper* upon

the distinction between the worship to be paid to God and the honour it is lawful to give to His saints. It is, of course, frequently asserted that the English pre-Reformation church did not recognise, or at least did not inculcate, this necessary difference, and consequently tolerated, even if it did not suggest, gross errors in this matter. No one who has examined the manuals of instruction which were in use on the eve of the Reformation can possibly maintain an opinion so opposed to the only evidence available. In particular, the real distinction between the supreme worship due to God alone, and the honour, however great, to be paid to His creatures is drawn out with great care and exactness in regard to the devotion paid to our Lord's Blessed Mother. Thus, after most carefully explaining that there are two modes of "service and worship" which differ not merely in degree, but in kind and nature, and which were then, as now, known under the terms *latria* and *dulia*, our author proceeds, "Latria is a protestation and acknowledgment of the high majesty of God; the recognition that He is sovereign goodness, sovereign wisdom, sovereign might, sovereign truth, sovereign justice; that He is the Creator and Saviour of all creatures and the end of all things; that all we have we have of Him, and that without Him we have absolutely nothing; and that without Him we can neither have nor do anything, neither we nor any other creature. This acknowledgment and protestation is made in three ways: by the heart, and by word, and by deed. We make it by the heart when we love Him as sovereign goodness; when we love Him as sovereign wisdom and truth, that may not deceive nor be deceived;

when we hope in Him and trust Him as sovereign might that can best help us in need ; as sovereign greatness and Lord, who may best yield us our deserts ; and as sovereign Saviour, most merciful and most ready to forgive us our misdeeds. . . . Also the acknowledgment is done in the prayer and praise of our mouths. . . . For we must pray to Him and praise Him as sovereign might, sovereign wisdom, sovereign goodness, sovereign truth ; as all-just and merciful as the Maker and Saviour of all things, &c.

"And in this manner we are not to pray to or praise any creature. Therefore, they who make their prayers and their praises before images, and say their *Paternoster* and their *Ave Maria* and other prayers and praises commonly used by holy Church, or any such, if they do it to the image, and speak to the image, they do open idolatry. Also they are not excused even if they understand not what they say, for their lights, and their other wits, and their inner wit also, showeth them well that there ought that no such prayer, praise, or worship be offered to such images, for they can neither hear them, nor see them, nor help them in their needs."

Equally definite and explicit is another writer, just on the eve of the Reformation. William Bond, the brother of Sion, in 1531 published his large volume of instructions called *The Pilgrymage of Perfeccyon*, to which his contemporary, Richard Whitford, refers his readers for the fullest teaching on sundry points of faith and practice. In setting forth the distinction between an *image* and an *idol* this authority says, "Many nowadays take the Scripture wrongly, and thereby fall into heresy as Wycliffe did with his followers, and now this abominable heretic, Luther, with his adherents. . . . And (as I suppose) the cause of their error is some of these following :—First, that they put no difference between an idol and an image; secondly, that they put no difference between the service or high adoration due to God, called in the Greek tongue *latria*, and the lower veneration or worship exhibited and done to the saints of God, called in Greek *dulia*. . . . The veneration or worship that is done to the images (as Damascene, Basil, and St. Thomas say) rest not in them, but redound unto the thing that is represented by such images : as for example, the great ambassador or messenger of a king shall have the same reverence that the king's own person should have if he were present.   This honour is not done to this man for himself, or for his own person, but for the king's person in whose name he cometh, and all such honour and reverence so done redoundeth to the king and resteth in him. . . . So it is in the veneration or worshipping of the images of Christ and His saints.   The honour rests not in the image, nor in the stock, nor in the stone, but in the thing that is represented thereby."   According to St. Thomas, he says the images in churches are intended to " be as books to the rude and unlearned people." and to " stir simple souls to devotion." [1]

Bond then draws out most carefully the distinction which the Church teaches as to the kinds of honour to be given to the saints.   " Our lights, oblations, or Paternosters and creeds that we say before images of saints," he says, " are as praisings of God, for His

---

[1] William Bond, *The Pilgrymage of Perfeccyon*, Wynkyn de Worde, 1531, fol. 192.

graces wrought in His saints, by whose merits we
trust that our petitions shall be the sooner obtained
of God. . . . We pray to them, not as to the granters
of our petitions, but as means whereby we may the
sooner obtain the same." [1]

Speaking specially of the reverence shown to the
crucifix, our author uses the teaching of St. Thomas
to explain the exact meaning of this honour. " The
Church in Lent, in the Passion time," he continues,
" worships it, singing, ' *O crux ave, spes unica*,' ' Hail,
holy cross, our only hope.' That is to be understood
as ' Hail, blessed Lord crucified, Who art our only
hope '—for all is one worship and act. Christ, our
Maker and Redeemer, God and man in one person,
is of duty worshipped with the high adoration only due
to God, called *latria*. His image also, or his similitude,
called the crucifix, is to be worshipped, just as the
Blessed Sacrament is adored with the worship of
latria." [2]

To this testimony may be added that of another
passage from Sir Thomas More. He was engaged in
refuting the accusation made by Tyndale against the
religious practices of pre-Reformation days, to which
charges, unfortunately, people have given too much
credence in later times. " Now of prayer, Tyndale
says," writes More, " that we think no man may pray
but at church, and that (*i.e.* the praying before a crucifix or image) is nothing but the saying of a *Paternoster*
to a post. (Further) that the observances and ceremonies of the Church are vain things of our own
imagination, neither needful to the taming of the flesh,
nor profitable to our neighbour, nor to the honour of

[1] Ibid., fol. 196.   [2] Ibid.

God.   These lies come in by lumps ; lo ! I dare say
that he never heard in his life men nor women say
that a man might pray only in church.   Just as true
is it also that men say their *Paternosters* to the post, by
which name it pleases him of his reverent Christian
mind to call the images of holy saints and our Blessed
Lady, and the figure of Christ's cross, the book of His
bitter passion.   Though we reverence these in honour
of the things they represent, and in remembrance of
Christ do creep to the cross and kiss it, and say *Paternoster* at it, yet we say not our *Paternoster* to it, but to
God ; and that Tyndale knows full well, but he likes to
rail." [1]

Finally a passage on the subject of pre-Reformation
devotion to the saints and angels, from the tract *Dives et
Pauper*, may fitly close this subject.   " First," says the
author, " worship ye our Lady, mother and maid, above
all, next after God, and then other saints both men and
women, and then the holy angels, as God giveth the
grace.   Worship ye them not as God, but as our
tutors, defenders and keepers, as our leaders and
governors under God, as the means between us and
God, who is the Father of all and most Sovereign
Judge, to appease Him, and to pray for us, and to
obtain us grace to do well, and for forgiveness of
our misdeeds. . . . And, dear friend, pray ye heartily
to your angel, as to him that is nearest to you and
hath most care of you, and is, under God, most busy
to save you.   And follow his governance and trust
in him in all goodness, and with reverence and purity
pray ye to him faithfully, make your plaints to him,
and speak to him homely to be your helper, since he

[1] *English Works*, p. 408.

is your tutor and keeper assigned to you by God.   Say oft that holy prayer, *Angele qui meus est,* &c."

This prayer to the Guardian Angel, so highly commended, was well known to pre-Reformation Catholics. Generations of English mothers taught it to their children ; it is found frequently recommended in the sermons of the fifteenth century, and confessors are charged to advise their penitents to learn and make use of it.   For the benefit of those of my readers who may not know the prayer, I here give it in an English form, from a Latin version in the tract *Dextra Pars Oculi,* which was intended to assist confessors in the discharge of their sacred ministry—

> " O angel who my guardian art,
>   Through God's paternal love,
> Defend, and shield, and rule the charge
>   Assigned thee from above.
>
> From vice's stain preserve my soul,
>   O gentle angel bright,
> In all my life be thou my stay,
>   To all my steps the light."

It is, of course, impossible here to do more than refer to the books of instruction, and those intended to furnish the priests on the eve of the Reformation with material for the familiar teaching they were bound to give their people.   Such works as Walter Pagula's *Pars Oculi Sacerdotis,* and the *Pupilla Oculi* of John de Burgo, both fourteenth-century productions, were in general use during the fifteenth century among the clergy. The frequent mention of these works in the inventories and wills of the period shows that they were in great demand, and were circulated from hand to hand, whilst an edition of the latter, printed in 1510 by Wolffgang,

at the expense of an English merchant, William Bretton, attests its continued popularity.   In a letter from
the editor, Augustine Aggeus, to Bretton, printed on
the back of the title-page, it is said that the *Pupilla* was
printed solely with the desire that the rites and sacraments of the church might be better understood and
appreciated, and to secure " that nowhere in the English Church " should there be any excuse of ignorance
on those matters.[1]

The contents of the first-named tract, the *Pars
Oculi Sacerdotis*, show how very useful a manual it must
have been to assist the clergy in their ministrations.   It
consists of three parts : the first portion forms what
would now be called the *praxis confessarii*, a manual for
instructing priests in the science of dealing with souls,
and giving examples of the kind of questions that should
be asked of various people, for example, of religious,
secular priests, merchants, soldiers, and the like.   This
is followed by a detailed examination of conscience,
and pious practices are suggested for the priest to
recommend for the use of the faithful.   For example,
in order that the lives of lay people might be associated
in some way with the public prayer of the church, the
Divine office, the priest is advised to get his penitents
to make use of the Pater and Creed, seven times a
day, to correspond with the canonical hours.   Those
having the cure of souls are reminded that it is their

[1] The full title of this book is : *Pupilla oculi omnibus presbyteris precipue
Anglicanis necessaria*.   It is clear from the letter that W. Bretton had already
had other works printed in the same way, and it is known that amongst those
works were copies of Lynwode's *Provinciale* (1505), *Psalterium et Hymni*
(1506), *Horæ*, &c. (1506), *Speculum Spiritualium*, and Hampole, *De Emen-
datione Vitæ* (1510), (cf. *Ames*, Ed. Herbert, iii. p. 16).   Pepwell the London
publisher, at "the sign of the Holy Trinity," was the same who published many
books printed abroad, and had dealings with Bishops Stokesley and Tunstall.

duty to see that all at least know the Lord's Prayer, the Creed, and the Hail Mary by heart, and they are urged to do all in their power to inculcate devotions to our Lady, Patron Saints, and the Guardian Angels.

The second part of the *Dextra Pars Oculi* deals minutely and carefully with the instructions which a priest should give his people in their religion, and this includes not only points of necessary belief and Christian practice, but such matters as the proper decorum and behaviour in Church, and the cemetery, &c. The materials for these familiar instructions are arranged under thirty-one headings, and following on these are the explanations of Christian faith and practice to be made in the simple sermons the clergy were bound to give to their people quarterly. The third part, called the *Sinistra Pars Oculi*, is an equally careful treatise on the sacraments. The instructions on the Blessed Eucharist are excellent, and in the course of them many matters of English religious practice are touched upon and the ceremonies of the Mass are fully explained.[1]

---

[1] For further information upon popular religious instruction in England, see an essay upon the teaching in the fourteenth and fifteenth centuries in my *The old English Bible, and other Essays.* The Rev. J. Fisher, in his tract on *The Private Devotions of the Welsh* (1898), speaking of the vernacular prayer-books, says, "they continued to be published down to the end of Henry's reign, and, in a modified form, even at a later date. Besides these prymers and the oral instruction in the principal formulæ of the Church, the scriptorium of the monastery was not behind in supplying, especially the poor, with horn-books, on which were, as a rule, written in the vulgar tongue the Lord's Prayer, the Creed, and the Hail Mary." In 1546 appeared a prymer in Welsh in which, amongst other things, the seven capital or deadly sins and their opposite virtues are given and analysed. This book, consequently, besides being a prayer-book afforded popular instruction to the people using it. The prymers in Welsh, we are told, were usually called " Matins' Books," and continued to be published long after the change of religion. A copy published in 1618 is called the fifth edition, and copies of it are recorded under the years 1633 and 1783. " It is rather a curious fact," writes Mr. Fisher, "that nearly all the Welsh manuals of devotion and instruction, of

It is obvious that much of the real religious instruction in pre-Reformation days, as indeed in all ages, had to be given at home by parents to their children. The daily practices by which the home life is regulated and sanctified are more efficacious in the formation of early habits of solid piety and the fear of God in the young than any religious instructions given at school or at Church. This was fully understood and insisted upon in pre-Reformation books of instruction. Such, for example, is the very purpose of Richard Whitford's book, called *A werke for Housholders, or for them that have the guyding or governance of any company*, printed by Wynkyn de Worde in 1534, and again by Robert Redman in 1537. After reminding his readers that life is short, and that it is impossible for any man to know when he shall be called upon to give an account

any size, published in the second half of the sixteenth and the first half of the seventeenth century, were the productions of Welsh Roman Catholics, and published on the Continent. In Dr. Gruffydd Roberts's Welsh Grammar, published at Milan in 1567, will be found poetical versions of the Apostles' Creed, the Lord's Prayer, the Hail Mary, the Ten Commandments and the Seven Sacraments. This work was followed by the *Athravaeth Gristnogavl*, a short catechism of religious doctrine, translated or compiled by Morys Clynog, the first Rector of the English College in Rome. It was published at Milan in 1568, and contains the Creed, the Lord's Prayer, the Hail Mary, the Ten Commandments, &c., in Welsh, with expositions."

The above, with the prayer-books of 1567, 1586, 1599, were all the works of religious instruction and devotion (private and public) that appeared in Welsh down to the end of the sixteenth century. I might add that there is in the Earl of Macclesfield's collection a large folio volume of *Miscellanea* (Shirburn MS. 113, D. 30), written between 1540 and 1560, which contains a prymer occupying several pages. There is also in the Swansea Public Library a Welsh-Latin MS. of the sixteenth and seventeenth centuries, written in different hands and in the South Walian dialect, which forms a manual of Roman Catholic devotion, containing in Welsh devotions for Mass, the usual meditations and prayers for various occasions, instructions, &c.

With the seventeenth century there is a good crop of manuals of devotion and instruction, such as the catechisms of Dr. Rosier Smith (1609–1611) and Father John Salisbury (1618 *tacito nomine*), both Welsh Roman Catholics (pp. 24–26).

of his stewardship, he turns to the consideration of the Christian's daily life. Begin the day well, he says; on first awakening, turn your thoughts and heart to God, " and then use by continual custom to make a cross with your thumb upon your forehead or front, whilst saying these words, *In nomine Patris;* and another cross upon your mouth, with these words, *Et filii;* and then a third cross upon your breast, saying, *Et spiritus Sancti.*" After suggesting a form of morning and evening prayer, and urging a daily examination of conscience, he continues : Some may object that all this is very well for religious, or people secluded from the world, " but we lie two or three sometimes together, and even in one chamber divers beds, and so many in company, that if we should use these things in the presence of our fellows some would laugh us to scorn and mock at us." But to this objection Whitford in effect replies that at most it would be a nine days' wonder, and people would quickly be induced to follow an example of such a good Christian practice if set with courage and firmness.[1]

Speaking of the duty of instructing others, " the wretch of Syon," as Whitford constantly calls himself, urges those who can read to use their gifts for the benefit of others not so fortunate. They should get their neighbours together on holidays, he says, especially the young, and teach them the daily exercise, and in particular the " things they are bound to know or can say : that is the *Paternoster,* the *Ave,* and the *Creed.*" Begin early to teach those that are young, for " our English proverb saith that the young cock croweth as he doth hear and learn of the old." Parents, above all things, he urges to look well after their children

---

[1] *A Werke for Housholders.* London, R. Redman, 1537, sig. A. 8.

and to take care of the company they keep. Teach them to say their grace at meals. "At every meal, dinner or supper, I have advised, and do now counsel, that one person should with loud voice say thus, 'Paternoster,' with every petition paraphrased and explained, and the Hail Mary and Creed likewise. This manner of the Paternoster, Ave, and Creed," he says, "I would have used and read from the book at every meal, or at least once a day with a loud voice that all the persons present may hear it." People are bound to see that all in their house know these prayers and say them.[1]

Very strongly indeed does Whitford in this volume write against belief in charms and giving way to superstitions. There is no question about his strong condemnation of anything, however slight, which might savour of reliance on these external things, and as an instance of what he means, he declares that the application of a piece of bread, with a cross marked upon it, to a tooth to cure its aching, savours of superstition, as showing too great a reliance on the material cross. In the same place our author urges parents to correct their children early for any use of oaths and strong expressions. "Teach your children," he says, "to make their additions under this form: 'yea, father,' 'nay, father,' 'yea, mother,' 'nay, mother,' and ever to avoid such things as 'by cock and pye,' and 'by my hood of green,' and such other."[2]

Finally, to take but one more example of the advice given in this interesting volume to parents and others having the charge of the young, Whitford says: "Teach your children to ask a blessing every night,

---

[1] Ibid., sig. B. i.   [2] Ibid., sig. C. 8.

kneeling, before they go to rest, under this form:
'Father, I beseech you a blessing for charity.'" If the
child is too stubborn to do this, he says let it "be well
whisked." If too old to be corrected in this way, let it
be set out in the middle of the dining-room and made
to feed by itself, and let it be treated as one would
treat one who did not deserve to consort with its
fellows. Also teach the young "to ask a blessing
from every bishop, abbot, and priest, and of their god-
fathers and godmothers also." [1]

In taking a general survey of the books issued by
the English presses upon the introduction of the art of
printing, the inquirer can hardly fail to be struck with
the number of religious, or quasi-religious, works which
formed the bulk of the early printed books. This fact
alone is sufficient evidence that the invention which at
this period worked a veritable revolution in the intellectual life of the world, was welcomed by the ecclesiastical authorities as a valuable auxiliary in the work of
instruction. In England the first presses were set up
under the patronage of churchmen, and a very large
proportion of the early books were actually works of
instruction or volumes furnishing materials to the clergy
for the familiar and simple discourses which they were
accustomed to give four times a year to their people.
Besides the large number of what may be regarded as
professional books chiefly intended for use by the
ecclesiastical body, such as missals, manuals, breviaries,
and horæ, and the prymers and other prayer-books used
by the laity, there was an ample supply of religious
literature published in the early part of the sixteenth
century. In fact, the bulk of the early printed English

[1] Ibid., sig. D. 5.

books were of a religious character, and as the publication of such volumes was evidently a matter of business on the part of the first English printers, it is obvious that this class of literature commanded a ready sale, and that the circulation of such books was fostered by those in authority at this period. Volumes of sermons, works of Instruction on the Creed and the Commandments, lives of the saints, and popular expositions of Scripture history, were not only produced but passed through several editions in a short space of time. The evidence, consequently, of the productions of the first English printing-presses goes to show not only that religious books were in great demand, but also that so far from discouraging the use of such works of instruction, the ecclesiastical authorities actively helped in their diffusion.

In considering the religious education of the people in the time previous to the great upheaval of the sixteenth century, some account must be taken of the village mystery plays which obviously formed no inconsiderable part in popular instruction in the great truths of religion. The inventories of parish churches and the churchwardens' accounts which have survived show how very common a feature these religious plays formed in the parish life of the fifteenth century, and the words of the various dramas, of which we still possess copies, show how powerful a medium of teaching they would have been among the simple and unlettered villagers of Catholic England, and even to the crowds which at times thronged great cities like Coventry and Chester, to be present at the more elaborate plays acted in these traditional centres of the religious drama.

As to their popularity there can be no question. Dramatic representations of the chief events in the life of our Lord, &c., were commonly so associated with the religious purposes for which they were originally produced, that they were played on Sundays and feast days, and not infrequently in churches, church porches, and churchyards. " Spectacles, plays, and dances that are used on great feasts," says the author of *Dives et Pauper*, quoted above, " as they are done principally for devotion and honest mirth, and to teach men to love God the more, are lawful if the people be not thereby hindered from God's service, nor from hearing God's word, and provided that in such spectacles and plays there is mingled no error against the faith of Holy Church and good living. All other plays are prohibited, both on holidays and work days (according to the law), upon which the gloss saith that the representation in plays at Christmas of Herod and the Three Kings, and other pieces of the Gospel, both then and at Easter and other times, is lawful and commendable."

A few examples of the kind of teaching imparted in these plays will give a better idea of the purpose they served in pre-Reformation days than any description. There can be no reasonable doubt that such dramatic representations of the chief mysteries of religion and of scenes in the life of our Lord or of His saints served to impress these truths and events upon the imaginations of the audiences who witnessed them, and to make them vivid realities in a way which we, who are not living in the same religious atmosphere, find it difficult now to understand. The religious drama was the handmaid of the Church, and was intended to assist in instructing the people at large in the truths and duties of religion, just as the paintings upon the walls of the sacred buildings were designed to tell their own tale of the Bible history, and form " a book " ever open to the eyes of the unlettered children of the Church, easy to be understood, graphically setting forth events in the story of God's dealings with men, and illustrating truths which often formed the groundwork for oral instruction in the Sunday sermon.

Whatever we may be inclined to think of these simple plays as literary works, or however we may be inclined now to smile at some of the characters and " situations," as to the pious spirit which dictated their composition and presided over their production there can be no doubt. " In great devotion and discretion," says the monk and chronicler, " Higden published the story of the Bible, that the simple in their own language might understand." [1]

This was the motive of all these mediæval religious plays. As a popular writer upon the English drama says : " There is abundant evidence that the Romish ecclesiastics in the mystery plays, especially that part of them relating to the birth, passion, and resurrection of Christ, had the perfectly serious intention of strengthening the faith of the multitude in the fundamental doctrines of the Church, and it seems the less extraordinary that they should have resorted to this expedient when we reflect that, before the invention of printing, books had no existence for the people at large." [2]

The subjects treated of in these plays were very

[1] B. Mus. Harl. MS. 2125, f. 272.
[2] *Penny Cyclopædia*.   Art., " English Drama."

varied, although those which were performed at the great feasts of Christmas and Easter generally had some relation to the mystery then celebrated. In fact, the mystery plays of the sacred seasons were only looked upon as helping to make men realise more deeply the great drama of the Redemption, the memory of which was perpetuated in the sequence of the great festivals of the Christian year. In such a collection as that known as the *Towneley Mysteries*, and published by the Surtees Society, we have examples of the subjects treated in the religious plays of the period. The collection makes no pretence to be complete, but it comprises some three and thirty plays, including such subjects as the Creation, the death of Abel, the story of Noah, the sacrifice of Isaac and other Old Testament histories, and a great number of scenes from the New Testament, such as the Annunciation, the Visitation, Cæsar Augustus, scenes from the Nativity, the Shepherds and the Magi, the Flight into Egypt, various scenes from the Passion and Crucifixion, the parable of the Talents, the story of Lazarus, &c.

Any one who will take the trouble to read these plays as they are printed in this volume cannot fail to be impressed not only with the vivid picture of the special scene in the Old or New Testament that is presented to the imagination, but by the extensive knowledge of the Bible which the production of these plays must have imparted to those who listened to them, and by the way in which, incidentally, the most important religious truths are conveyed in the crude and rugged verse. Again and again, for instance, the entire dependence of all created things upon the Providence of Almighty God is declared and illustrated. Thus, the confession of God's Omni-potence, put into the mouth of Noah at the beginning of the play of " Noah and his Sons," contains a profession of belief in the Holy Trinity and in the work of the three Persons : it describes the creation of the world, the fall of Lucifer, the sin of our first parents, and their expulsion from Paradise. In the story of Abraham, too, the prayer of the patriarch with which it begins :

> "Adonai, thou God very,
> Thou hear us when to Thee we call,
> As Thou art He that best may,
> Thou art most succour and help of all,"

gives a complete résumé of the Bible history before the days of Abraham, with the purpose of showing that all things are in the hands of God, and that complete obedience is due to Him by all creatures whom He has made.

The same teaching as to the entire dependence of the Christian for all things upon God's Providence appears in the address of the soul to its Maker in the " morality " of Mary Magdalene, printed by Mr. Sharpe from the Digby Manuscript collection of religious plays :—

> "*Anima :* ' Sovereign Lord, I am bound to Thee ;
> When I was nought, Thou made me thus glorious ;
> When I perished through sin, Thou saved me ;
> When I was in great peril, Thou kept me, Christus ;
> When I erred, Thou reduced me, Jesus ;
> When I was ignorant, Thou taught me truth ;
> When I sinned, Thou corrected me thus ;
> When I was heavy, Thou comforted me by truth
>   (*i.e.* Thy mercy) ;
> When I stand in grace, Thou holdest me that tide ;
> When I fall, Thou raisest me mightily ;

When I go well, Thou art my guide ;
When I come, Thou receivest me most lovingly ;
Thou hast anointed me with the oil of mercy ;
Thy benefits, Lord, be innumerable :
Wherefore laud endless to Thee I cry ;
Recommending me to Thy endless power endurable.'"

The more these old plays which delighted our forefathers are examined, the more clear it becomes that, although undoubtedly unlearned and unread, the people in pre-Reformation days, with instruction such as is conveyed in these pious dramas, must have had a deeper insight into the Gospel narrative, and a more thorough knowledge of Bible history generally, not to speak of a comprehension of the great truths of religion, than the majority of men possess now in these days of boasted enlightenment. Some of the plays, as for example that representing St. Peter's fall, exhibit a depth of genuine feeling, of humble sorrow, for instance, on the part of St. Peter, and of loving-kindness on the part of our Lord, which must have come home to the hearts as well as to the minds of the beholders. At the same time, the lesson deduced by our Saviour from the apostle's fall, namely, the need of all learning by their own shortcomings to be merciful to the trespasses of others, must have impressed itself upon them with a force which would not easily have been forgotten.

In that most popular of all representations—that of Doomsday—"people learnt that before God there is no distinction of persons, and that each individual soul will be judged on its own merits, quite apart from any fictitious human distinctions of rank, wealth, or power." Thus, as types, appear a *saved* pope, emperor, king and queen, and amongst the *damned* we also find a pope, emperor, king and queen, justiciar and merchant." And the words of thankfulness uttered by the Pope that has obtained his crown betrays "no self-satisfaction at the attainment of salvation ; on the contrary, the true ring of Christian humility betokens a due appreciation of God's unutterable holiness, and our unworthiness to stand before His face till the uttermost blemish left by sin has been wiped away" by the healing fires of Purgatory. No less clearly is the full doctrine of responsibility taught in the lament of the Pope, who is represented as having lost his soul by an evil life, and as being condemned to eternal punishment. The mere fact of a pope being so represented was in itself, when the Office was held in the highest regard, a lesson of the highest importance in the teaching of the true principles of holiness. In a word, these mystery plays provided a most useful means of impressing upon the minds of all the facts of Bible history, the great truths of religion, and the chief Christian virtues. The people taught in such a school and the people who delighted in such representations, as our forefathers in pre-Reformation days unquestionably did, cannot, even from this point of view alone, be regarded as ignorant of scriptural or moral teaching.

CHAPTER X

PARISH LIFE IN CATHOLIC ENGLAND

To understand the attitude of men's minds to the ecclesiastical system on the eve of the great religious changes of the sixteenth century, some knowledge of the parochial life of Catholic England is necessary. Under present conditions, when unity has given place to diversity, and three centuries of continuous wrangling " over secret truths which most profoundly affect the heart and mind " have done much to coarsen and deaden our spiritual sense ; when the religious mind of England manifests every shade of belief and unbelief without conscious reflection on the logical absurdity of the position, it is by no means easy to realise the influence of a state of affairs when all men, from the highest to the lowest, in every village and hamlet throughout the length and breadth of the land, had but one creed, worshipped their Maker in but one way, and were bound together with what most certainly were to them the real and practical ties of the Christian brotherhood. It is hardly possible to overestimate the effect of surroundings upon individual opinion, or the influence of a congenial atmosphere both on the growth and development of a spirit of religion and on the preservation of Christian morals and religious practices generally. When all, so far as religious faith is concerned, thought the same, and when all, so far as religious observance is concerned, did the same, the very atmosphere of unity was productive of that spirit of common brotherhood, which appears so plainly in the records of the period preceding the religious revolt of the sixteenth century. Those who will read below the surface and will examine for themselves into the social life of that time must admit, however much they feel bound to condemn the existing religious system, that it certainly maintained up to the very time of its overthrow a hold over the minds and hearts of the people at large, which nothing since has gained. Religion overflowed, as it were, into popular life, and helped to sanctify human interests, whilst the affection of the people was manifested in a thousand ways in regard to what we might now be inclined to consider the ecclesiastical domain. Whether for good or evil, religion in its highest and truest sense, at least as it was then understood, was to the English people as the bloom upon the choicest fruit. Whatever view may be taken as to advantage or disadvantage which came to the body politic, or to individuals, by the Reformation, it must be admitted that at least part of the price paid for the change was the destruction of the sense of corporate unity and common brotherhood, which was fostered by the religious unanimity of belief and practice in every village in the country, and which, as in the main-spring of its life, and the very central point of its being, centred in the Church with its rites and ceremonies.

A Venetian traveller at the beginning of the six-teenth century bears witness to the influence of religion upon the English people of that time. His opinion is all the more valuable, inasmuch as he appeals to the experience of his master, who was also the companion of his travels, to confirm his own impressions, and as he was fully alive to the weak points in the English character, of which he thus records his opinion : " The English are great lovers of themselves and of every-thing belonging to them ; they think that there are no other men but themselves and no other world but England. Whenever they see a handsome foreigner they say that ' he looks like an Englishman,' or that ' it is a great pity that he should not be an English-man,' and when they partake of any delicacy with a foreigner they ask him whether such a thing is made in his country." [1] In regard to the religious practices of the people, this intelligent foreigner says, " They all attend mass every day, and say many *Paternosters* in public. The women carry long rosaries in their hands, and any who can read take the Office of Our Lady with them, and with some companion recite it in Church verse by verse, in a low voice, after the manner of churchmen. On Sundays they always hear Mass in their parish church and give liberal alms, because they may not offer less than a piece of money of which fourteen are equivalent to a golden ducat. Neither do they omit any form incumbent on good Christians." [2]

In these days perhaps the suggestion that the English people commonly in the early sixteenth century were present daily at morning Mass is likely to be received with caution, and classed among the strange tales proverbially told by travellers, then as now. It is, however, confirmed by another Venetian who visited

[1] *A Relation of the Island of England* (Camden Society), p. 20.
[2] Ibid., p. 23.

England some few years later, and who asserts that every morning " at daybreak he went to Mass arm-in-arm with some English nobleman or other." [1]   And, indeed, the same desire of the people to be present daily at the Sacrifice of the Mass is attested by Archbishop Cranmer when, after the change had come, he holds up to ridicule the traditional observances previously in vogue.   What he specially objected to was the common practice of those who run, as he says, "from altar to altar, and from sacring, as they call it, to sacring, peeping, tooting, and gazing at that thing which the priest held up in his hands . . . and saying, 'this day have I seen my Maker,' and 'I cannot be quiet except I see my Maker once a day.' " [2]

If there were no other evidence of the affection of the English people on the eve of the Reformation for their religion, that of the stone walls of the churches would be sufficient to prove the sincerity of their love. In the whole history of English architecture nothing is more remarkable than the activity in church building manifested during the later half of the fifteenth and the early part of the sixteenth centuries.   From one end of England to the other in the church walls are to be seen the evidences of thought and skill, labour and wealth, spent freely upon the sacred buildings during a period when it might not unnaturally have been thought that the civil dissensions of the Wars of the Roses, and the consequent destruction of life and property, would have been fatal to enterprise in the field of church building and church decoration and enrichment.   It is not in any way an exaggeration to

[1] *Venetian Calendar*, ii. p. 91.
[2] *Works on the Supper* (Parker Society), p. 229.

say that well-nigh every village church in England can show signs of this marvellous activity, whilst in many cases there is unmistakable evidence of personal care and thought in the smallest details.

No less remarkable than the extent of this movement is the source from which the money necessary for all the work upon the cathedrals and parish churches of the country came. In previous centuries, to a great extent churches and monastic buildings owed their existence and embellishment mainly to the individual enterprise of the powerful nobles or rich ecclesiastics; but from the middle of the fifteenth century the numerous, and, in many cases, even vast operations, undertaken in regard to ecclesiastical buildings and ornamentation, were the work of the people at large, and were mainly directed by their chosen representatives. At the close of the fifteenth century, church work was in every sense of the word a popular work, and the wills, inventories, and churchwardens' accounts prove beyond question that the people generally contributed generously according to their means, and that theirs was the initiative, and theirs the energetic administration by which the whole was accomplished.[1] Gifts of money and valuables, bequests of all kinds, systematic collections by parish officials, or by directors of guilds, often extending over considerable

---

[1] To take one instance : the church of St. Neots possessed many stained glass windows placed in their present positions between the years 1480 and 1530. Almost all of them were put in by individuals, as the inscriptions below testify. In the case of three of the lights it appears that groups of people joined together to beautify their parish church. Thus below one of the windows in the north aisle is the following : "*Ex sumptibus juvenum hujus parochiæ Sancti Neoti qui istam fenestram fecerunt anno domini millessimo quingentessimo vicessimo octavo.*" Another window states that it was made in 1529, "*Ex sumptibus sororum hujus parochiæ*"; and a third in 1530, "*Ex sumptibus uxorum.*"

periods, and the proceeds of parish plays and parish feasts, were the ordinary means by which the sums necessary to carry out these works of building and embellishment were provided.   Those who had no money to give brought articles of jewellery, such as rings, brooches, buckles, and the like, or articles of dress or of domestic utility, to be converted into vestments, banners, and altar hangings to adorn the images and shrines, to make the sacred vessels of God's house, or to be sold for like purposes.   For the same end, and to secure the perpetuity of lamps before the Blessed Sacrament, or lights before the altars of saints, people gave houses and lands into the care of the parish officials, or made over to them cattle and sheep to be held in trust, which, when let out at a rent, formed a permanent endowment for the furtherance of these sacred purposes.

Undoubtedly the period with which we are concerned was not merely an age of building, but an age of decoration, and of decoration which may almost be described as " lavish."   The very architecture of the time is proof of the wealth of ornament with which men sought to give expression to their enthusiastic love of the Houses of God, which they had come to regard as the centre of their social no less than of their religious life.   Flowing lines in tracery and arch moulding gave place to straight lines, groined roofs were enriched by extra ribs, and panels of elaborate work covered the plain surfaces of former times ; the very key-stones of the vaulting became pendants, and the springers branched out like palm trees, forming that rich and entirely English variety of groin called "fan-tracery," such as we see at Sherborne, Eton,

King's College, Cambridge, and Henry VII.'s Chapel at Westminster. "In other respects," says a modern writer, "the architects of the fifteenth century were very successful. Few things can be seen more beautiful than the steeples of Gloucester Cathedral and St. Mary's, Taunton. The open roofs, as for example that of St. Peter Mancroft, Norwich, are superb, and finally they have left us a large number of enormous parish churches all over the country, full of interesting furniture and decoration."

The fact is, that this was the last expression of Gothic as a living art. The builders and beautifiers of the English churches on the eve of the religious changes spoke still a living language, and their works still tell us of the fulness of the hearts which planned and executed such works. It is somewhat difficult for us to understand this, when living in an age of imitation, and at a time when architecture has no longer a language of its own. "Imitation," writes Mr. Ferguson, "is in fact all we aim at in the architectural art of the present day. We entrust its exercise to a specially educated class, most learned in the details of the style they are called upon to work in, and they produce buildings which delight the scholars and archæologists of the day, but which the less educated classes neither understand nor appreciate, and which will lose their significance the moment the fashion which produced them has passed away.

"The difference between this artificial state of things and the practice of a true style will not be difficult to understand. When, for instance, Gothic was a living art in England, men expressed themselves in it as in any other part of the vernacular. Whatever was done was a part of the usual, ordinary every-day life, and men had no more difficulty in understanding what others were doing than in comprehending what they were saying. A mason did not require to be a learned man to chisel what he had carved ever since he was a boy, and what alone he had seen being done during his lifetime, and he adapted new forms just in the same manner and as naturally as men adapt new modes of expression in language as they happen to be introduced, without even remarking it. At that time any educated man could design in Gothic Art, just as any man who can read and write can now compose and give utterance to any poetry or prose that may be in him.

"Where art is a true art, it is naturally practised and as easily understood, as a vernacular literature of which, indeed, it is an essential and most expressive part, and so it was in Greece and Rome, and so, too, in the Middle Ages. But with us it is little more than a dead corpse, galvanised into spasmodic life by a few selected practitioners for the amusement and delight of a small section of the specially educated classes. It expresses truthfully neither our wants nor our feelings, and we ought not to be surprised how very unsatisfactory every modern building really is, even when executed by the most talented architects as compared with the productions of our village mason or parish priest at an age when men sought only to express clearly what they felt strongly, and sought to do it only in their natural mother tongue, untrammelled by the fetters of a dead or familiar foreign form of speech." [1]

To any one who will examine the churchwardens' accounts of the period previous to the religious changes,

[1] *History of Modern Architecture*, pp. 37, 87.

the truth of the above quotation will clearly appear. Then, if ever, ecclesiastical art and architecture was the living expression of popular feeling and popular love of religion, and the wholesale destruction of ancient architectural monuments throughout the land, the pulling down of rood and screen and image, the casting down of monuments sacred to the memory of the best and holiest and most venerated names in the long roll of English men of honour, the breaking up of stone-work and metal-work upon which the marks of the chisel of the mason and graver were yet fresh, the whitewash daubed over paintings which had helped to make the parish churches objects of beauty and interest to the people, the ruthless smashing of the pictured window lights, and the pillage of the sacred vessels and vestments and hangings, which the people and their fathers had loved to provide for God's service—all this and much more of the same kind, the perhaps inevitable accompaniments of the religious change, was nothing less to the people than proscription by authority of the national language of art and architecture, such as they had hitherto understood it.   And never probably had the language been more truly the language of the people at large.   For reasons just assigned, the work of church building and church decoration, and the provision of vestments and plate, the care of the fabric and the very details of things necessary for the church services, were in the hands of the people.   The period in question had given rise to the great middle class, and here, as in Germany, the burgher folk, the merchants and traders, began literally to lavish their gifts in adornment of their parish churches, and to vie one with another in the profusion of their generosity.

It is somewhat difficult for us, as we look upon the generally bare and unfurnished churches that have been left to us as monuments of the past about which we are concerned, to realise what they must have been before what a modern writer has fitly called " the great pillage" commenced. All, from the great minsters and cathedral churches down to the poorest little village sanctuary, were in those days simply overflowing with wealth and objects of beauty which loving hands had gathered together to adorn God's house, and to make it the best and brightest spot in their little world, and so far as their means would allow the very pride of their hearts. This is no fancy picture. The inventories of English churches in this period when compared, say, with those of Italy, reveal the fact that the former were in every way incomparably better furnished than the latter. The Venetian traveller in England in 1500 was impressed by this very thing during his journeyings throughout the country. He notes and comments upon the great sums of money regularly given to the church as a matter of course by Englishmen of all sorts. Then after speaking of the important wealth of the country as evidenced by the silver plate possessed by all but the poorest in the land, he continues : " But above all are their riches displayed in the church treasures, for there is not a parish church in the kingdom so mean as not to possess crucifixes, candlesticks, censers, patens and cups of silver, nor is there a convent of mendicant friars so poor as not to have all these same articles in silver, besides many other ornaments worthy of a cathedral church in the same metal. Your magnificence may therefore imagine what the decorations of those enormously rich Benedictine, Carthusian, and Cistercian monasteries must be. . . . I have been informed that amongst other things many of these monasteries possess unicorns' horns of an extraordinary size. I have also been told that they have some splendid tombs of English saints, such as St. Oswald, St. Edmund, and St. Edward, all kings and martyrs. I saw, one day being with your magnificence, at Westminster, a place out of London, the tomb of that saint, King Edward the Confessor, in the church of the foresaid place, Westminster; and indeed, neither St. Martin of Tours, a church in France, which I have heard is one of the richest in existence, nor anything else that I have ever seen, can be put into comparison with it. The magnificence of the tomb of St. Thomas the Martyr, Archbishop of Canterbury, surpasses all belief."

Our present concern, however, is not with the greater churches of the kingdom, but with the parish churches which were scattered in such profusion all over the country. An examination of such parochial accounts as are still preserved affords an insight into the working of the parish, and evidences the care taken by the people to maintain and increase the treasures of their churches. What is most remarkable about the accounts that remain, which are, of course, but the scanty survivals from the wreck, is their consistent tenor. They one and all tell the same story of general and intelligent interest taken by the people as a whole in the beautifying and supporting of their parish churches. In a very real sense, that seems strange to us now, it was *their* church; their life centred in it, and they were intimately concerned in its working and management. The articles of furniture and plate, the vestments and hangings had a well-known history, and were regarded as—what in truth they were—the common property of every soul in the particular village or district. Such accounts as we are referring to prove that specific gifts and contributions continued to flow in an ample stream to the churches from men and women of every sort and condition up to the very eve of the great religious changes.

From these and similar records we may learn a good deal about parochial life and interests in the closing period of the old ecclesiastical system. The church was the common care and business. Its welfare was the concern of the people at large, and took its natural place in their daily lives. Was there any building to be done, a new peal of bells to be procured, the organs to be mended, new plate to be bought, or the like, it was the parish as a corporate body that decided the matter, arranged the details, and provided for the payment. At times, say for example when a new vestment was in question, the whole parish would be called to sit in council in the church house upon this matter of common interest, and discuss the cost, and stuff, and make.

To take some examples : the inventory of Cranbrook parish church for 1509 shows that all benefactors were regularly noted down on a roll of honour, that their gifts might be known and remembered. The presents, of course, vary greatly in value : thus, there was a monstrance of silver and gilt of the "value of £20, of Sir Robert Egelonby's gift ; which Sir Robert was John Roberts' priest thirty years, and he never had other service nor benefice ; and the said John Roberts was father to Walter Roberts, Esquire." And the foresaid Sir Robert gave also to the common treasury of the parish " two candlesticks of silver and twenty marks of old nobles." Again John Hendely " gave three copes of purple velvet, whereof one was of velvet upon velvet with images broidered," and, adds the inventory, " for a perpetual memory of this deed of goodness to the common purposes of the parish church, his name is to be read out to the people on festival days." " He is grandfather of Gervase Hendely of Cushorn, and of Thomas of Cranbrook Street." Or once more, it is recorded that " old mother Hopper " gave the " two long candlesticks before Our Lady's altar, fronted with lions, and a towel on the rood of Our Lady's chancel."

So, too, the inventory of the church goods of St. Dunstan's, Canterbury, includes a wonderful list of furniture, plate, and vestments to which the names of the donors are attached. Thus, the best chalice was the gift of one " Harry Bole " ; the two great candlesticks of laten of John Philpot ; and " a kercher for Our Lady and a chapplet and a powdryd cap for her Son," the gift of Margery Roper.

The memory of these gifts was kept alive among the people by the " bede-roll " or list of those for whom the parish was bound to pray in return for their benefactions to the public good. Thus to take an example : at Leverton, in the county of Lincoln, the parson, Sir John Wright, presented the church with a suit of red purple vestments, " for the which," says the note in the churchwardens' accounts, " you shall all specially pray for the souls of William Wright and Elizabeth his wife (father and mother of the donor), and for the soul of Sir William Wright, their son, and for the soul of Sir John, sometime parson of this place, and for the souls of

Richard Wright and Isabel his wife, John Trowting and Helen his wife, and for all benefactors, as well them that be alive as them that be departed to the mercy of God, for whose lives and souls are given here (these vestments) to the honour of God, His most blessed Mother, Our Lady Saint Mary, and all His Saints in Heaven, and the blessed matron St. Helen his patron, to be used at such principal feasts and times as it shall please the curates as long as they shall last. For all these souls and all Christian souls you shall say one Paternoster." [1]

In this way the memory of benefactors and their good deeds was ever kept alive in the minds of those who benefited by their gifts. The parish treasury was not to them so much stock, the accumulation of years, without definite history or purpose ; but every article, vestment, banner, hanging, and chalice, and the rest called for the affectionate memories of both the living and the dead. On high day and festival, when the church was decked with all that was best and richest in the parochial treasury, the display of the parish ornaments recalled to the mind of the people assembled within its walls the memory of good deeds done by neighbours for the common good. " The immense treasures in the churches," writes Dr. Jessop, " were the joy and boast of every man and woman and child in England, who day by day and week by week assembled to worship in the old houses of God which they and their fathers had built, and whose every vestment and chalice and candlestick and banner, organs and bells and picture and image and altar and shrine, they looked upon as their own and part of their birthright." [1]

---

[1] *Archæologia*, vol. xli. p. 355.

[1] *Parish Life in England before the Great Pillage* ("Nineteenth Century," March 1898), p. 433.

What seems so strange about the facts revealed to us in these church accounts of bygone times is that, where now we might naturally be inclined to look for poverty and meanness, there is evidence of the contrary, so far as the parish church is concerned. Even when the lives of the parishioners were spent in daily labours to secure the bare necessities of life, and the village was situated in the most out-of-the-way part of the country, the sordid surroundings of a hard life find no counterpart in the parish accounts so far as the church is concerned, but even under such unfavourable circumstances there is evidence of a taste for things of art and beauty, and of both the will and power to procure them. To take some examples : Morebath was a small uplandish parish of no importance lying within the borders of Devon, among the hills near the sources of the river Exe. The population was scanty, and worldly riches evidently not abundant. Morebath may, consequently, be taken as a fair sample of an obscure and poor village community. For this hamlet we possess fairly full accounts for the close of the period under consideration, namely, from the year 1530. At this time, in this poor place, there were no less than eight separate accounts kept of money intended for the support of different altars, or for carrying out definite decorations, such as, for example, the chapels of St. George and Our Lady, and the guilds of the young men and maidens of the parish. To the credit of these various accounts, or "stores," as they are called, are entered numerous gifts of money, or articles of value, and even of kind, like cows and swarms of bees. Most of them are possessed of cattle and sheep, the proceeds from the rent of which form a considerable portion of their endowment. The accounts as a whole furnish abundant evidence of active and intelligent interest in the support and adornment of the parish church on the part of the people at large. Voluntary rates to clear off obligations contracted for the benefit of the community, such as the purchase of bells, the repair of the fabric, or even the making of roads and bridges, were raised. Collections for Peter's pence, for the support of the parish clerk, and for various other church purposes, are recorded, and the spirit of self-help is evidenced in every line of these records. In 1528 the vicar gave up his rights to certain wool tithes in order to purchase a complete set of black vestments, which were only finished and paid for, at the cost of £6, 5s. od., in 1547. In the year 1538, the parish made a voluntary rate to purchase a new cope, and the collection for the purpose secured £3, 6s. 8d. When in 1534 the silver chalice was stolen, "ye yong men and maydens of ye parysshe dru themselffe together, and at ther gyfts and provysyon they bought in another chalice without any charge of the parysshe." Sums of money big and small, specific gifts in kind, the stuff or ornaments needed for vestments, were apparently always forthcoming when occasion required. Thus at one time a new cope is suggested, and Anne Tymwell of Hayne gave the churchwardens her "gown and ring," Joan Tymwell a cloak and girdle, and Richard Norman "seven sheep and three shillings and four pence in money," towards the expenses. At another time it is a set of black vestments ; at another a chalice ; at another a censer ; but whatever it was, the people were evidently ready and desirous of taking their share in the common work of the parish. In 1529 the wardens state that Elinor Nicoll gave to the store of St. Sydwell her wedding-ring—"the which ring," they add, "did help to make Saint Sydwell's shoes." Then she gave to "the store of Jesus" a little silver cross, parcel gilt, of the value of 4d. In 1537 there is one item which deserves to be noted, as it records the arrival of a piece of spoil from Barlinch Abbey Church, which was dissolved by the king's orders the previous year. "Memorandum," runs the entry, "Hugh Poulett gave to the church one of the glass windows of the Barlinch, with the iron and stone and all the price" for setting it up.[1]

To understand the working of the pre-Reformation parish, it is necessary to enter in detail into some one of the accounts that are still preserved to us. We may conveniently take those of Leverton in Lincolnshire, printed in the *Archæologia*, which commence in the year 1492. It is well to note, however, that the same story of self-help and the same evidence of a spirit of affection for the parish church and its services, is manifested in every account of this kind we possess. It must be remembered that it was popular government in a true sense that then regulafed all parochial matters. Every adult of both sexes had a voice in this system of self-government, and what cannot fail to strike the student of these records is that, in the management of the fabric, in the arrangements for the services, and all things necessary for the due performance of these, diocesan authorities evidently left to the parish itself a wise discretion. No doubt the higher ecclesiastical officials could interfere in theory, but in practice such interference was rare. If the means necessary to carry out repairs and keep the church in an efficient state, both

---

[1] *Churchwardens' Accounts* (Somerset Record Soc.), ed. Bishop Hobhouse, p. 200, *seqq.*

as to fabric and ornaments, were apparently never wanting, it must be borne in mind that it was then regarded as a solemn duty binding on the conscience of each parishioner to maintain the House of God and the parochial services. Bishop Hobhouse, from an examination of the churchwardens' accounts for some parishes in Somerset, is able to describe the various ways in which the parochial exchequer was replenished. First, there were the voluntary rates, called "setts," and these, though voluntary in the sense that their imposition depended on the will of the people at large, when once the parish had declared for the rate, all were bound to pay. Then the mediæval church authorities cultivated various methods of eliciting the goodwill of the people, and after prohibiting work on Sundays and certain festivals, busied themselves with the finding of amusements. Amongst these were the parish feasts and church ales, at which collections for various public purposes were made, which, together with the profits made from such entertainments by those who managed them for the benefit of the public purse, formed one of the chief sources of parochial income. Beyond this, the principle of association was thoroughly understood and carried out in practice in the village and town communities. People banded themselves together in religious guilds and societies, the *raison d'être* of which was the maintenance of special decorations at special altars, the support of lamps and lights, or the keeping of obits and festivals. These societies, moreover, became the centres of organisation of any needed special collections, and from their funds, or "stores" as they were called, they contributed to the general expenses of maintaining the fabric and the services. Popular bounty was, moreover, elicited by means of the "bede-roll," or list of public benefactors, for whom the prayers of the parishioners were asked in the church on great festivals. On this list of honour, all—even the poorest—were anxious that their names should appear, and that their memory be kept and their souls prayed for in the House of God which they had loved in life. Even more than money, which in those days, especially in out-of-the-way places, was not over plentiful, the churchwardens' accounts show that specific gifts of all kinds, either to be sold for the profit of the purpose for which they were bestowed, or to form a permanent part of the church treasury, were common in pre-Reformation times.

Added to these sources of income were the profits of trade carried on in the "church house." Besides the church itself, the wardens' accounts testify to the existence of a church house, if not as a universal feature in mediæval parish life, at least as a very common one. It was the parish club-house—the centre of parochial life and local self-government; the place where the community would assemble for business and pleasure. It was thus the focus of all the social life of the parish, and the system was extending in influence and utility up to the eve of the great religious changes which put an end to the popular side of parochial life. At Tintinhull, a small village in Somerset, for example, the accounts help us to trace the growth of this parish club-house. Beginning as a place for making the altar bread, it developed into a bakery for the supply of the community. It then took up the brewing of beer to supply the people and the church ales and similar parish festivals. This soon grew into the brewing of beer to supply those who required a supply, and at the same time the oven and brewing utensils were let out to hire to private persons. In the reign of Henry VII. a house was bought by the wardens for parish purposes, and one Agnes Cook was placed in it to manage it for the common benefit. In 1533 it was in full swing as a parish club-house, used for business and plesaure.[1] The "ale"—the forerunner of the wardens' "charity dinner"—was the ordinary way of raising money to meet extraordinary expenses ; and as an incidental accompaniment came invitations to other parishes in the neighbourhood, and we find items charged for the expenses of church-wardens attending at other parochial feasts, and the sums they there put into the collection plate.

Beyond this, the parish, as a corporate body gene-rally, if not invariably, possessed property in land and houses, which was administered by the people's wardens for the public good. The annual proceeds lightened the common burdens, as indeed it was intended that they should. A further source of occasional income was found in the parish plays which were managed for the common profit. Very frequently the production was entrusted to some local guild, and the expenses of mounting were advanced by the parochial authorities, who not infrequently had amongst the church treasures the dress and other stage properties necessary for the proper productions. At Tintinhull, in Somerset, for instance, in 1451, five parishioners got up a Christmas play for the benefit of the fund required for the erection of the new rood loft. At Morebath there was an Easter play representing the Resurrection of our Lord, to defray the expenses incurred by the parish on some extensive repairs.[2]

---

[1] Ibid., p. xxi.   [2] Ibid., p. xii.

With this general notion of the working of pre-Reformation parochial accounts, we are now in a position to turn by way of a particular example to those of Leverton. The village is situated about six miles from Boston. The church, until the neglect of the past three hundred years had disfigured it, must have been very beautiful when decked with the furniture and ornaments which the loving care of the people of the neighbourhood had collected within its walls. When first the accounts open in 1492, the parish was beginning to be interested, as indeed, by the way, so many parishes were at this period, in the setting up of a new peal of bells. The people had evidently made a great effort to get these, and they contributed most generously. The rector promised ten shillings and sixpence —which sum, by the way, some one paid for him—but the whole arrangement for the purchase and hanging of the bells was in the hands of the churchwardens. The bell chamber was mended and timber was bought to strengthen the framework. When this was ready, the great bell was brought over from the neighbouring town, and money is disbursed for the carriage and the team of horses, not forgetting a penny for the toll in crossing a bridge. One William Wright of Benington came over professionally to superintend the hanging and " trossyng " of this great service bell. We may judge, however, that it was not altogether satisfactory, for in 1498 the two wardens made a " move " to " the gathering of the township of Leverton in the kirk," in which they collected £4, 13s. 0d., and they forthwith commenced again the building of a steeple for another set of bells. The stone was given to them, but they had to see to the work of quarrying it, and to all the business of collecting material and of building. Trees in a neighbouring wood were bought, were cut and carried, and sawn into beams and boards, and poles were selected for scaffolding. Lime was burnt and sand was dug for the mortar, and tubs were purchased to mix it in, whilst Wreth, the carpenter, was retained to look after the building in general, and the timber-work of the new belfry in particular.

This seems to have exhausted the parish exchequer for a year or two, but in 1503 the two wardens attended at Boston to see their bell "shot," and to provide for its transport to Leverton. Here Richard Messur, the local blacksmith, had prepared the necessary bolts and locks to fasten it to the swinging beam, and he was in attendance professionally to see the bell hung, with John Red, the bellmaker of Boston, who, moreover, remained for a time to teach the parish men how to ring a peal upon their new bells.

As the sixteenth century progressed, a great deal of building and repairs was undertaken by the parish authorities. In 1503, a new font was ordered, and a deputation went to Frieston, about three miles from Leverton, to inspect and pass the work. The lead for the lining was procured, and it was cast on the spot. In 1517, repairs on the north side of the church were undertaken, and these must have been extensive, judging from the cost of the timber employed to shore up the walls during the progress of the work. Two years later, on the completion of these extensive building operations, which had been going on for some time, the church and churchyard were consecrated at a cost to the public purse of £3. In 1526, the rood loft was decorated, and the niches intended for images of the saints, but which had hitherto been vacant, were filled. One of the parishioners, William Frankish, in that year left a legacy of 46s. 8d. for the purpose. The wardens hired a man, called sometimes "the alabaster man," and sometimes "Robert Brook the carver," and in earnest for the seventeen images of alabaster of the rood loft they gave him a shilling. At the same time a collection was made for the support of the artist during his stay; some of the parishioners gave money, but most of them apparently contributed "cheese" for his use.

So much with regard to the serious building operations which were continued up to the very eve of the Reformation. They by no means occupied all the energies of the parish officials. If the books required binding, a travelling workman was engaged on the job, and leather, thread, wax, and other necessary materials were purchased for the work; the binder's wife was paid extra for stitching, and he was apparently lodged by one of the townspeople as a contribution to the common work. Then there were vestments to be procured, and surplices and other church linen to be made, washed, and marked; the very marks, by the way, being given in the accounts. So entirely was the whole regarded as the work of the people, that just as we have seen how the parish paid for the consecration of their parish church and graveyard, so did they pay a fee to their own vicar for blessing the altar linen and the new vestments, and entering the names of benefactors on the parish bede-roll.[1]

Details such as these, which might be multiplied to any extent, make it abundantly clear that the church was the centre and soul of village life in pre-Reformation times, and that up to the very eve of the religious

---

[1] *Archæologia*, vol. xli., p. 333 *seqq.*

revolution it had not lost its place in the hearts of the people. In this connection it is useful to bear in mind, though somewhat difficult to realise, inasmuch as it is now too foreign to our modern experience, that in the period about which we are concerned the "parish" meant the whole community of a well-defined area "organised for church purposes and subject to church authority." In such a district, writes Bishop Hobhouse, "every resident was a parishioner, and, as such, owed his duty of confession and submission to the official guidance of a stated pastor. There was no choice allowed. The community was completely organised with a constitution which recognised the rights of the whole and of every adult member to a voice of self-government when assembled for consultation under" their parish priest.[1] In this way the church was the centre of all parish life, in a way now almost inconceivable. "From the font to the grave," says an authority on village life at this time, "the greater number of the people lived within the sound of its bells. It provided them with all the consolations of religion, and linked itself with such amusements as it did not directly supply."[2]

The writer of the above words was specially interested in the accounts of the parish of St. Dunstan in the city of Canterbury, and some few notes on those accounts founded upon his preface may usefully be added to what has already been said. The parochial authorities evidently were possessed of considerable power either by custom or consent over the inhabitants. In St. Dunstan's, for example, somewhere about 1485,

---

[1] *Somerset Record Soc.*, preface, p. xi.
[2] J. W. Cowper, *Accounts of the Churchwardens of St. Dunstan's, Canterbury* (*Archæologia Cantiana*, 1885).

there was some disagreement between a man named Baker and the parish, and an item of 2½d. appears in the accounts as spent on the arbitration that settled it.   Later on, two families fell out, and the vicar and a jury of four parishioners met in council to put an end to what was considered a scandal.   A parish so managed had necessarily some place in which the inhabitants of the district could meet, and this in St. Dunstan's is called the *church house*, and sometimes the *parish house*.   It is frequently mentioned in the matters of repairs, &c., and two dozen trenchers and spoons, the property of the parish, were placed there for use at the common feasts, and for preparation of food distributed to the poor. The annual dinner is named in the accounts, and there is no doubt the young people too had dancing, bowling, and other games, while "the ancients sat gravely by."

The money needed for the repairs of the fabric and for parish work generally was here collected by the various brotherhoods connected with the church. Some wore "scutchons" or badges to show that they were authorised to beg.   These brotherhoods were possessed of more than money; malt, wheat, barley, besides parish sheep and parish cows let out to the highest bidder, are mentioned in the accounts as belonging to them.   One Nicholas Reugge, for example, left four cows to the people of the parish to free them for ever from the cost of supplying the "paschal," or great Easter candle.   These four cows were valued by the churchwardens at 10s. apiece, and were each let at a rent of 2s. a year.   In 1521, one John Richardson rented five-and-twenty of the parish sheep, and the wardens received rent of lambs, wool, &c.   The chief of the brotherhoods connected with St. Dunstan's was that named the " Schaft," and it had the principal voice in the ultimate management of parochial affairs. Besides this, however, there were many other associations, such as that of St. Anne for women and that of St. John for youths, and various wardens were appointed to collect the money necessary to keep the various lights, such as St. Anne's light, St. John's light, St. Katherine's light, and the light of the Holy Rood. " These things," writes the editor of these interesting accounts, " all go to show what life and activity there was in this little parish, which never wanted willing men to devote their time and influence to the management of their own affairs."

The parish was small, numbering perhaps hardly more than 400 souls. " But if small," says the same authority, " it was thoroughly efficient, and the religious and intellectual work was as actively carried on as the social." At the close of the reign of Henry VIII. the church possessed a library of some fifty volumes. Of these about a dozen were religious plays, part, no doubt, of the Corpus Christi mystery plays, which were carried out at St. Dunstan's with undiminished splendour till the advent of the new ideas in the reign of Edward VI.

These parish accounts prove that many cases of disagreement and misunderstanding, which in modern times would most likely lead to long and protracted cases in the Law Courts, were not infrequently settled by arbitration, or by means of a parish meeting or a jury of neighbours. Sometimes, undoubtedly, the law had to be invoked in defence of parochial rights. A case in point is afforded in the accounts of St. Dunstan's, Canterbury. Nicholas Reugge, as we have said above, had left money to purchase four cows as an endowment for the Paschal candle and the Font taper. Things went well, apparently, till 1486, when William Belser, who rented the stock, died, and his executors either could not or would not, or, at any rate, did not pay. To recover the common property, the churchwardens, as trustees for the parish, had to commence a suit at law. Chief-Justice Fineux and Mr. Attorney-General John Roper were two of the parishioners, and the parish had their advice, it may be presumed gratuitously. The case, however, seems to have dragged on for five years, as it was finally settled only in 1491, when the parish scored a pyrrhic victory, for although they recovered 30s., the value of three of the cows, their costs had mounted up to 35s. 2d., and as they never could get more than a third of that amount from the defendants, on the whole they were out of pocket by their adventure with the law.

For the most part, however, the parish settled its own difficulties in its own way. Documents preserved almost by chance clearly show that a vast number of small cases—police cases we should call them— were in pre-Reformation days arranged by the ecclesi- astical authority. Disputes, brawls, libels, minor im- moralities, and the like, which nowadays would have to be dealt with by the local justices of the peace or by the magistrates at quarter sessions, or even by the judges at assizes, were disposed of by the parson and the parish. It may not have been an ideal system, but it was patriarchal and expeditious. The Sunday pulpit was used not only for religious instruction, properly so called, and for the " bedes-bidding," but for the pub- lication of an endless variety of notices of common interest. The church was, as we have said, the

centre of popular life, and it was under these circumstances the natural place for the proclamation of
the commencement of some inquiry into a local suit,
or one in which local people were concerned.   It was
here, in the house of God, and at the Sunday service
at which all were bound to be present, that witnesses
were cited and accused persons warned of proceedings
against them.   Here was made the declaration of the
probate of wills of deceased persons, and warning given
to claimants against the estate to come forward and
substantiate their demands.   Here, too, were issued
proclamations against such as did not pay their just
debts or detained the goods of others ; here those who
had been guilty of defamation of character were ordered
to restore the good name of those they had calum-
niated ; and those who, having been joined in wedlock,
had separated without just and approved cause, were
warned of the obligations of Christian marriage.   The
transactions of business of this kind in the parish church
by the parish officials made God's house a practical
reality and God's law a practical code in the ordinary
affairs of life, and gave religion a living importance
in the daily lives of every member of every parish
throughout the country.

CHAPTER XI

PRE-REFORMATION GUILD LIFE

IT would be impossible to fully understand the conditions of life on the eve of the Reformation without some knowledge of the working and purposes of mediæval guilds. These societies or brotherhoods were so common, formed such a real bond of union between people of all ranks and conditions of life, and fulfilled so many useful and even necessary purposes before their suppression under Edward VI., that a study of their principles of organisation and of their practical working cannot but throw considerable light on the popular social life of the period. To appreciate the position, it is necessary to bear in mind the very real hold the Gospel principles of the Christian brotherhood had over the minds of all in pre-Reformation days, the extinction of the general sense that man did not stand alone being distinctly traceable to the tendencies in regard to social matters evolved during the period of turmoil initiated by the religious teachings of the Reformers. What M. Siméon Luce says about the spirit of common life existing in the villages of Normandy in the fourteenth century might be adopted as a picture of English life in the fifteenth and early sixteenth centuries. "Nobles, priests, religious clerks, sons of the soil who laboured at various manual works," he writes, "lived then, so to say, in common, and they are found continually together in all their daily occupations. So far from this community of occupations, this familiar daily intercourse, being incompatible with the great inequality of conditions which then existed, in reality it resulted from it. It was where no strict line of demarcation divided the various classes that they ordinarily affected to keep at a distance one from the other."[1]

There can be no doubt as to the nature of the teaching of the English Church in regard to the relation which, according to true Christian principles, should exist between all classes of society. In particular is this seen in all that pertained to the care of the poorer members of the Christian family. The evidence appears clear and unmistakable enough in pre-Reformation popular sermons and instructions, in formal pronouncements of Bishops and Synods, and in books intended for the particular teaching of clergy and laity in the necessary duties of the Christian man. Whilst fully recognising as a fact that in the very nature of things there must ever be the class of those who "have," and the class of those who "have not," our Catholic forefathers in pre-Reformation days knew no such division and distinction between the rich man and the poor man as obtained later on, when pauperism, as distinct from poverty, had come to be recognised as an inevitable consequence of the new era. To the Christian moralist, and even to the bulk of Catholic Englishmen, whether secular or lay, in the fifteenth century, those who had been blessed by God's providence with worldly wealth were regarded not so much as the fortunate possessors of personal riches, their own to do with what they listed, and upon which

---

[1] Siméon Luce, *Histoire de Bertrand du Guesclin*, p. 19.

none but they had right or claim, as in the light of stewards of God's good gifts to mankind at large, for the right use and ministration of which they were accountable to Him who gave them.

Thus, to take one instance: the proceeds of ecclesiastical benefices were recognised in the Constitutions of Legates and Archbishops as being in fact as well as in theory the *eleemosynæ et spes pauperum*—the alms and the hope of the poor. Those ecclesiastics who consumed the revenues of their cures on other than necessary and fitting purposes were declared to be " defrauders of the rights of God's poor," and " thieves of Christian alms intended for them ;" whilst the English canonists and legal professors who glossed these provisions of the Church law gravely discussed the ways in which the poor of a parish could vindicate their right to their share in the ecclesiastical revenues of the Church.

This *"jus pauperum,"* which is set forth in such a text-book of English Law as Lyndwood's *Provinciale*, is naturally put forth more clearly and forcibly in a work intended for popular instruction such as *Dives et Pauper.* " To them that have the benefices and goods of Holy Church," writes the author, " it belonged principally to give alms and to have the cure of poor people." To him who squanders the alms of the altar on luxury and useless show, the poor may justly point and say: " It is ours that you so spend in pomp and vanity ! . . . That thou keepest for thyself of the altar passing the honest needful living, it is raveny, it is theft, it is sacrilege." From the earliest days of English Christianity the care of the helpless poor was regarded as an obligation incumbent on all ; and in 1342, Archbishop Stratford, dealing with *appropriations,* or the assignment of ecclesiastical revenues to the support of some religious house or college, ordered that a portion of the tithe should always be set apart for the relief of the poor, because, as Bishop Stubbs has pointed out, in England, from the days of King Ethelred, "a third part of the tithe" which belonged to the Church was the acknowledged birthright of the poorer members of Christ's flock.

That there was social inequality is as certain as it was inevitable, for that is in the very constitution of human society. But this, as M. Luce has pointed out in regard to France, and Professor Janssens in regard to Germany, in no way detracted from the frank and full acknowledgment of the Christian brotherhood. Again and again in the sermons of the fifteenth century this truth, with all its practical applications, was enforced by the priest at the altar, where both poor and rich alike met on a common footing—"all, poor and rich, high and low, noble and simple, have sprung from a common stock and are children of a common father, Adam :" "God did not create a golden Adam from whom the nobles are descended, nor a silver Adam from whom have come the rich, and another, a clay Adam, from whom are the poor ; but all, nobles, rich and poor, have one common father, made out of the dust of the earth." These and similar lessons were constantly repeated by the religious teachers of the pre-Reformation English Church.

Equally definite is the author of the book of popular instruction, *Dives et Pauper*, above referred to. The sympathy of the writer is with the poor, as indeed is that of every ecclesiastical writer of the period. In fact, it is abundantly clear that the Church of England in Catholic days, as a *pia mater*, was ever ready to open wide her heart to aid and protect the poorer members of Christ's mystical body.   This is how *Pauper* in the tract in question states the true Christian teaching as to the duties of riches, and impresses upon his readers the view that the owners of worldly wealth are but stewards of the Lord : " All that the rich man hath, passing his honest living after the degree of his dispensation, it is other men's, not his, and he shall give full hard reckoning thereof at the day of doom, when God shall say to him, ' Yield account of your bailywick.'   For rich men and lords in this world are God's bailiffs and God's reeves, to ordain for the poor folk and to sustain them." Most strongly does the same writer insist that no property gives any one the right to say *" this is mine "* and that is *" thine,"* for property, so far as it is of God, is of the nature of governance and dispensation, by which those who, by God's Providence "have," act as His stewards and the dispensers of His gifts to such as " have not." [1]

It would, of course, be affectation to suggest that

---

[1] The words of Pope Leo XIII. as to the Catholic teaching most accurately describe the practical doctrine of the English pre-Reformation Church on this matter : " The chiefest and most excellent rule for the right use of money," he says, " rests on the principle that it is one thing to have a right to the possession of money and another to have the right to use money as one pleases. . . . If the question be asked, How must one's possessions be used ? the Church replies, without hesitation, in the words of the same holy doctor (St. Thomas), *Man should not consider his outward possessions as his own, but as common to all*, so as to share *them without difficulty when others are in need.* When necessity has been supplied and one's position fairly considered, it is a duty to give to the indigent out of that which is over.   It is a duty, not of justice (except in extreme cases) but of Christian charity . . . (and) to sum up what has been said, Whoever has received from the Divine bounty a large share of blessings . . . has received them for the purpose of using them for the perfecting of his own nature, and, at the same time, that he may employ them, as the minister of God's Providence, for the benefit of others."

poverty and great hardness of life were not to be found in pre-Reformation days, but what did not exist was pauperism, which, as distinguished from poverty, certainly sprung up plentifully amid the ruins of Catholic institutions, overthrown as a consequence—perhaps as a necessary and useful consequence—of the religious changes in the sixteenth century. Bishop Stubbs, speaking of the condition of the poor in the Middle Ages, declares that "there is very little evidence to show that our forefathers in the middle ranks of life desired to set any impassable boundary between class and class. . . . Even the villein, by learning a craft, might set his foot on the ladder of promotion. The most certain way to rise was furnished by education, and by the law of the land, 'every man or woman, of what state or condition that he be, shall be free to set their son or daughter to take learning at any school that pleaseth him within the realm.'" Mr. Thorold Rogers, than whom no one has ever worked so diligently at the economic history of England, and whom none can suspect of undue admiration of the Catholic Church, has also left it on record that during the century and a half which preceded the era of the Reformation the mass of English labourers were thriving under their guilds and trade unions, the peasants were gradually acquiring their lands and becoming small freeholders, the artisans rising to the position of small contractors and working with their own hands at structures which their native genius and experience had planned. In a word, according to this high authority, the last years of undivided Catholic England formed "the golden age" of the Englishman who was ready and willing to work.

" In the age which I have attempted to describe," writes the same authority, " and in describing which I have accumulated and condensed a vast amount of unquestionable facts, the rate of production was small, the conditions of health unsatisfactory, and the duration of life short.   But, on the whole, there were none of those extremes of poverty and wealth which have excited the astonishment of philanthropists and are exciting the indignation of workmen.   The age, it is true, had its discontents, and these discontents were expressed forcibly and in a startling manner.   But of poverty which perishes unheeded, of a willingness to do honest work and a lack of opportunity there was little or none.   The essence of life in England during the days of the Plantagenets and Tudors was that every one knew his neighbour, and that every one was his brother's keeper." [1]

In regard to the general care of the poorer brethren of a parish in pre-Reformation England, Bishop Hobhouse, after a careful examination of the available sources of information, writes as follows : " I can only suppose that the brotherhood tie was so strongly realised by the community that the weaker ones were succoured by the stronger, as out of a family store. The brotherhood tie was, no doubt, very much stronger then, when the village community was from generation to generation so unalloyed by anything foreign, when all were knit together by one faith and one worship and close kindred ; but, further than this, the guild fellowships must have enhanced all the other bonds in drawing men to share their worldly goods as a common stock.   Covertly, if not overtly, the guildsman

[1] *The Economic Interpretation of History*, p. 63.

bound himself to help his needy brother in sickness and age, as he expected his fellow-guildsman to do for him in his turn of need, and these bonds, added to a far stronger sense of the duty of children towards aged parents than is now found, did, I conceive, suffice for the relief of the poor, aided only by the direct alms-giving which flowed from the parsonage house, or in favoured localities from the doles or broken meat of a monastery." [1]

To relieve the Reformation from the odious charge that it was responsible for the poor-laws, many authors have declared that not only did poverty largely exist before, say, the dissolution of the monastic houses, but that it would not long have been possible for the ancient methods of relieving the distressed to cope with the increase in their numbers under the changed circumstances of the sixteenth century. It is of course possible to deal with broad assertions only by the pro-duction of a mass of details, which is, under the present circumstances, out of the question, or by assertions equally broad, and I remark that there is no evidence of any change of circumstances, so far as such changes appear in history, which could not have been fully met by the application of the old principles, and met in a way which would never have induced the degree of distressing pauperism which, in fact, was produced by the application of the social principles adopted at the Reformation. The underlying idea of these latter was property in the sense of absolute ownership in place of the older and more Christian idea of property in the sense of stewardship.

Most certainly the result was not calculated to

[1] *Churchwardens' Accounts* (Somerset Record Soc.), p. xxiv.

improve the condition of the poorer members of the community. It was they who were made to pay, whilst their betters pocketed the price. The well-to-do classes, in the process, became richer and more prosperous, whilst the " masses " became, as an old writer has it, " mere stark beggars." As a fact, moreover, poverty became rampant, as we should have expected, immediately upon the great confiscations of land and other property at the dissolution of the religious houses. To take one example : Dr. Sharpe's knowledge of the records of the city of London enables him to say that " the sudden closing of these institutions caused the streets to be thronged with the sick and poor."

" The devil," exclaims a preacher who lived through all these troublous times—" the devil cunningly turneth things his own way." " Examples of this we have seen in our time more than I can have leisure to express or to rehearse. In the Acts of Parliament that we have had made in our days what godly preambles hath gone afore the same ; even *quasi oraculum Apollinis*, as though the things that follow had come from the counsel of the highest in heaven ; and yet the end hath been either to destroy abbeys or chauntries or colleges, or such like, by the which some have gotten much land, and have been made men of great possessions. But many an honest poor man hath been undone by it, and an innumerable multitude hath perished for default and lack of sustenance. And this misery hath long continued, and hath not yet (1556) an end. Moreover, all this commotion and fray was made under pretence of a common profit and common defence, but in very deed it was for private and proper lucre." [1]

---

[1] Roger Edgeworth, *Sermons*, London, R. Caly, 1557, p. 309.

In the sixty years that followed the overthrow of the old system, it was necessary for Parliament to pass no less than twelve acts dealing with the relief of distress, the necessity for which, Thorold Rogers says, "can be traced distinctly back to the crimes of rulers and agents." I need not characterise the spirit which is manifested in these acts, where poverty and crime are treated as indistinguishable.

Dr. Jessop writes : " In the general scramble of the *Terror* under Henry the Eighth, and of the *anarchy* in the days of Edward the Sixth . . . the monasteries were plundered even to their very pots and pans. The almshouses, in which old men and women were fed and clothed, were robbed to the last pound, the poor almsfolk being turned out in the cold at an hour's warning to beg their bread. The splendid hospitals for the sick and needy, sometimes magnificently provided with nurses and chaplains, whose very *raison d'être* was that they were to look after the care of those who were past caring for themselves, these were stripped of all their belongings, the inmates sent out to hobble into some convenient dry ditch to lie down and die in, or to crawl into some barn or house, there to be tended, not without fear of consequences, by some kindly man or woman, who could not bear to see a suffering fellow-creature drop down and die at their own doorposts." [1]

Intimately connected with the subject of the care of the poor in pre-Reformation days is obviously that of the mediæval guilds which, more than anything else, tended to foster the idea of the Christian brotherhood up to the eve of the religious changes.

---

[1] *Parish Life in England before the Great Pillage* (" Nineteenth Century," March 1898), p. 432.

It would probably be a mistake to suppose that these societies existed everywhere throughout the country in equal numbers. Mr. Thorold Rogers, it is true, says—and the opinion of one who has done so much work in every kind of local record must carry great weight—that " few parishes were probably without guild lands." But there is certainly no distinct evidence that this was the case, especially in counties say like Hampshire, always sparsely populated as compared with other districts in the east of England, and where the people largely depended on agricultural pursuits for a living. It was in the great centres of trade and manufacture that the guilds were most numerous and most important, for it was precisely in those parts that the advantages of mutual help and co-operation outside the parish bond were most apparent and combination was practically possible.

An examination of the existing records leads to a general division of mediæval guilds into two classes— *Craft* or *Trade* associations, and *Religious* or, as some prefer now to call them, *Social* guilds. The former, as their name implies, had, as the special object of their existence, the protection of some work, trade or handicraft, and in this for practical purposes we may include those associations of traders or merchants known under the name of " guild-merchants." Such, for instance, were the great companies of the city of London, and it was in reality under the plea that they were trading societies that they were saved in the general destruction which overtook all similar fraternities and associations in the sixteenth century. The division of guilds into the two classes named above is, however, after all more a matter of convenience than a real distinction founded on fact. All guilds, no matter for what special purpose they were founded, had the same general characteristic of brotherly aid and social charity ; and no guild was divorced from the ordinary religious observances commonly practised by all such bodies in those days.

It is often supposed that, for the most part, what are called religious guilds existed for the purpose of promoting or encouraging the religious practices, such as the attendance at church on certain days, the taking part in ecclesiastical processions, the recitations of offices and prayers, and the like. Without doubt, there were such societies in pre-Reformation days—such as, for example, the great Guild of Corpus Christi, in the city of York, which counted its members by thousands. But such associations were the exception, not the rule. An examination of the existing statutes and regulations of ancient guilds will show how small a proportion these purely *Ecclesiastical* guilds formed of the whole number of associations known as Religious guilds. The origin of the mistaken notion is obvious. In mediæval days— that is, in times when such guilds flourished—the word " religious " had a wider, and what most people who reflect will be inclined to think, a truer signification than has obtained in later times. Religion was then understood to include the exercise of the two commandments of charity—the love of God and the love of one's neighbour—and the exercises of practical charity to which guild brethren were bound by their guild statutes were considered as much religious practices as attendance at church or the taking part in an ecclesiastical procession. In these days, as Mr. Brentano in his essay *On the History and Development of Guilds* has pointed out, most of the objects, to promote which the guilds existed, would now be called social duties, but they were then regarded as true objects of Christian charity. Mutual assistance, the aid of the poor, of the helpless, of the sick, of strangers, of pilgrims and prisoners, the burial of the dead, even the keeping of schools and schoolmasters, and other such like works were held to be " exercises of religion." [1]

If the word "religious" be thought now to give a wrong impression about the nature of associations, the main object of which was to secure the performance of duties we should now call " social," quite as false an impression would be conveyed by the word " social " as applied to them. A " social " society would inevitably suggest to many in these days an association for convivial meetings, and this false notion of the nature of a mediæval guild would be further strengthened by the fact that in many, if not most, of them a yearly, and sometimes a more frequent feast existed under an item in their statutes. This guild feast, however, was a mere incident in the organisation, and in no case did it form what we might consider the end or purpose of the association.

By whichever name we call them, and assuming the religious basis which underlay the whole social life in the fifteenth century, the character and purpose of these mediæval guilds cannot in reality be misunderstood. Broadly speaking, they were the benefit societies and the provident associations of the middle ages. They undertook towards their members the duties now frequently performed by burial clubs, by hospitals, by almshouses, and by guardians of the

English Gilds (Early English Text-Society), pp. lxxx.–civ.

poor. Not infrequently they acted for the public good of the community in the mending of roads and the repair of bridges, and for the private good of their members, in the same way that insurance companies to-day compensate for loss by fire or accident. The very reason of their existence was the affording of mutual aid and assistance in meeting the pecuniary demands which were constantly arising from burials, legal exactions, penal fines and all other kinds of payments and compensations. Mr. Toulmin Smith thus defines their object: "The early English guild was an institution of local self-help which, before the poor-laws were invented, took the place in old times of the modern friendly or benefit society, but with a higher aim ; while it joined all classes together in the care of the needy and for objects of common welfare, it did not neglect the forms and practice of religion, justice, and morality,"[1] which I may add was, indeed, the mainspring of their life and action.

"The guild lands," writes Mr. Thorold Rogers, "were a very important economical fact in the social condition of early England. The guilds were the benefit societies of the time from which impoverished members could be, and were, aided. It was an age in which the keeping of accounts was common and familiar. Beyond question, the treasurers of the village guild rendered as accurate an annual statement of their fraternity as a bailiff did to his lord. . . . It is quite certain that the town and country guilds obviated pauperism in the middle ages, assisted in steadying the price of labour, and formed a permanent centre for those associations which fulfilled the function that

[1] Ibid., p. xiv.

in more recent times trades unions have striven to satisfy."[1]

An examination of the various articles of association contained in the returns made into the Chancery in 1389, and other similar documents, shows how wide was the field of Christian charity covered by these "fraternities." First and foremost amongst these works of religion must be reckoned the burial of the dead ; regulations as to which are invariably to be found in all the guild statutes. Then, very generally, provisions for help to the poor, sick, and aged. In some, assistance was to be given to those who were overtaken by misfortune, whose goods had been damaged or destroyed by fire or flood, or had been diminished by loss or robbery ; in others, money was found as a loan to such as needed temporary assistance. In the guild at Ludlow, in Shropshire, for instance, "any good girl of the guild had a dowry provided for her if her father was too poor to find one himself." The "guild-merchant" of Coventry kept a lodging-house with thirteen beds, "to lodge poor folk coming through the land on pilgrimage or other work of charity," with a keeper of the house and a woman to wash the pilgrims' feet. A guild at York found beds and attendance for poor strangers, and the guild of Holy Cross in Birmingham kept almshouses for the poor in the town. In Hampshire, the guild of St. John at Winchester, which comprised men and women of all sorts and conditions, supported a hospital for the poor and infirm of the city.

The very mass of material at hand makes the task of selecting examples for illustrating some of the objects

[1] *The Economic Interpretation of History*, p. 306.

for which mediæval guilds existed somewhat difficult. I take a few such examples at haphazard. The organisation of these societies was the same as that which has existed in similar associations up to the time of our modern trades unions. A meeting was held at which officers were elected and accounts audited ; fines for non-acceptance of office were frequently imposed, as well as for absence from the common meeting. Often members had to declare on oath that they would fulfil their voluntary obligations, and would keep secret the affairs of the society. Persons of ill-repute were not admitted, and members who disgraced the fraternity were expelled. For example, the first guild statutes printed by Mr. Toulmin Smith are those of Garlekhithe, London. They begin : " In worship of God Almighty our Creator and His Mother Saint Mary, and all Saints, and St. James the Apostle, a fraternity is begun by good men in the Church of St. James, at Garlekhith in London, on the day of Saint James, the year of our Lord 1375, for the amendment of their lives and of their souls, and to nourish greater love between the brethren and sisters of the said brotherhood." Each of them has sworn on the Book to perform the points under-written.

" First : all those that are, or shall be, in the said brotherhood shall be of good life, condition, and behaviour, and shall love God and Holy Church and their neighbours, as Holy Church commands." Then, after various provisions 'as to meetings and payments to be made to the general funds, the statutes order that " if any of the foresaid brethren fall into such distress that he hath nothing, and cannot, on account of old age or sickness, help himself, if he has been in the brotherhood

seven years, and during that time has performed all
duties, he shall have every week after from the common
box fourteen pence (*i.e.* about £1 a week of our money)
for the rest of his life, unless he recovers from his
distress." [1]   In one form or other this provision for the
assistance of needy members is repeated in the statutes
of almost every guild.   Some provide for help in case
of distress coming " through any chance, through fire
or water, thieves or sickness, or any other haps."   Some,
besides granting this kind of aid, add : " and if so befall
that he be young enough to work, and he fall into distress, so that he have nothing of his own to help himself with, then the brethren shall help him, each with a
portion as he pleases in the way of charity." [2]   Others
furnish loans from the common fund to enable brethren
to tide over temporary difficulties : " and if the case
falleth that any of the brotherhood have need to borrow a
certain sum of silver, he (can) go to the keepers of the
box and take what he hath need of, so that the sum be
not so large that any one may not be helped as well as
another, and that he leave a sufficient pledge, or else
find a sufficient security among the brotherhood." [3]
Some, again, make the contributions to poor brethren
a personal obligation on the members, such as a farthing
a week from each of the brotherhood, unless the distress
has been caused by individual folly or waste.   Others
extend their Christian charity to relieve distress beyond
the circle of the brotherhood—that is, of all " whosoever falls into distress, poverty, lameness, blindness,
sent by the grace of God to them, even if he be a thief
proven, he shall have seven pence a week from the

---

[1] *English Gilds* (Early English Text-Society), p. 3.
[2] Ibid., p. 6.   [3] Ibid., p. 8.

brothers and sisters to assist him in his need." [1]   Some of the guilds in seaside districts provide for help in case of " loss through the sea," and there is little doubt that in mediæval days the great work carried on by such a body as the Royal Lifeboat Society would have been considered a work of religion, and the fitting object of a religious guild.

It would be tedious to multiply examples of the purposes and scope of the old fraternities, and it is sufficient to repeat that there was hardly any kind of social service which in some form or other was not provided for by these voluntary associations.   As an illustration of the working of a trade or craft guild, we may take that of the " Pinners " of the city of London, the register of which, dating from A.D. 1464, is now in the British Museum.[2]   These are some of the chief articles approved for the guild by the Mayor and Corporation of the city of London : (1) No foreigner to be allowed to keep a shop for the sale of pins.   (2) No foreigner to take to the making of pins without undergoing previous examinations and receiving the approval of the guild officers.   (3) No master to receive another master's workman.   (4) If a servant or workman who has served his master faithfully fall sick he shall be kept by the craft.   (5) Power to the craft to expel those who do ill and bring discredit upon it.   (6) Work at the craft at nights, on Saturdays, and on the eves of feasts is strictly prohibited.   (7) Sunday closing is rigidly enforced.

It is curious to find, four hundred years ago, so many of the principles set down as established, for which in our days trades unions and similar societies

---

[1] Ibid., p. 48.   [2] Egerton MS., 142.

are now contending. It has been remarked above, that
even in the case of craft guilds, such as this Society of
Pinners undoubtedly was, many of the ordinary purposes of the religious guilds were looked to equally
with the more obvious object of protecting the special
trade or handicraft of the specific society. The accounts
of this Pinners' Guild fully bear out this view. For
example: We have the funeral services for departed
brethren, and the usual *trentals*, or thirty masses, for
deceased members. Then we find: " 4d. to the wax
chandlers' man for setting up of our lights at St. James."
One of the members, William Clarke, borrowed 5s. 10d.
from the common chest, to secure which he placed a
gold ring in pledge. There are also numerous payments for singers at the services held on the feast days
of the guild, and for banners and other hangings for
processions.

Of payments for the specific ends of the guild
there are, of course, plenty of examples. For instance:
spurious pins and " other ware " are searched for and
burnt by the craft officers, and this at such distances
from London as Salisbury and the fair at Stourbridge,
near Cambridge, the great market for East Anglia and
the centre of the Flanders trade. " William Mitchell is
paid 8d. for pins for the sisters, on Saint James' day."
In 1466, a man is fined 2s. for setting a child to
work before he had been fully apprenticed ; and
also another had to pay 2s. for working after seven
o'clock on a winter night. Later on in the accounts
we have a man mulcted for keeping a shop before he
was a " freeman " of the society, and another " for
that he sold Flaundres pynnes for English pynnes."
At another time, a large consignment of no less than

12,000 "pynnes of ware" were forfeited to the craft, and sold by them for 8s., which went to the common fund. These accounts show also the gradual rise in importance and prosperity which the Pinners' Guild, under the patronage of St. James, manifested. At first, the warden and brethren at their yearly visit to Westminster were content to hire an ordinary barge upon the Thames, but after a few years they had started " a keverid boote " of their own at the cost of half-a-crown, in place of the sixpence formerly paid. So, too, in the early days of their incorporation they had their annual dinner and audited their accounts at some London tavern — the "Mayremayde in Bread Street" and "the brew house atte the Sygne of the Rose in Old Jury" are two of the places named. Later on they met in some hall belonging to another guild, such as the "Armourers'" Hall, and later still they built their own Guild Hall and held their banquet there. This building made a great demand upon their capital, and the officers evidently began to look more carefully after the exaction of fines. For late working at this time one of the brethren was mulcted in the sum of twenty pence : another was fined twopence for coming late to the guild mass, and several others had to pay for neglecting to attend the meeting. From the period of starting their own hall, ill-fortune seems to have attended the society. About the year 1499, they got involved in a great lawsuit with one Thomas Hill, upon which was expended a large sum of money. A special whip was made to meet expenses and keep up the credit of the guild ; for what with counsel's fees, the writing of bills, and the drawing of pleas, the general fund was unable to find the necessary munitions of war to continue the suit. To the credit of the members, most of them apparently responded generously to this call, and, in consequence of this unfortunate litigation, to many subsequent demands which the empty ex-chequer necessitated.

There would be no difficulty whatever in multiplying the foregoing illustrations of the working of these mediæval societies. The actual account books of course furnish us with the most accurate knowledge, even to minute details, and any one of them would afford ample material.

The funds at the disposal of the guilds were derived chiefly from voluntary subscriptions, entrance fees, gifts, and legacies of members. Frequently these societies became in process of time the trustees of lands and houses which they either held and administered for the purposes of the guilds, or for some specific purpose determined by the will of the original donor. Thus, to take one or two examples from the account rolls of the Guild of Tailors in the city of Winchester. In the time of King Richard II.—say 1392—the usual entrance fee for members was 3s. 4d., and the annual subscription was 1s. There were 106 members at that time, seven of whom had been enrolled during the previous year. Among others who had thus entered was one Thomas Warener, or Warner, a cousin of Bishop William of Wykeham, and the Bishop's bailiff of the Soke ; his payment was 4s. 8d. instead of the usual entrance fee. In the same year we find the names of Thomas Hampton, lord of the manor of Stoke Charity, and Thomas Marleburgh, who was afterwards Mayor of Winchester. In the following year, seventeen new members were enrolled, one of them being a baker of Southampton, called Dunster. Turning over these accounts, we come upon examples of presents either in kind or money made to the society. Thus in one place Thomas Marleburgh makes a present of a hooded garment which was subsequently sold for eighteen pence; and in another, one Maurice John Cantelaw presented for the service of the guild, "a chalice and twelve pence in counted money," requesting the members "to pray for his good estate, for the souls of his parents, friends, benefactors, and others for whom he was bound to pray." In return for this valuable present, the guild granted that it should be accounted as Cantelaw's life-subscription.

Having spoken of the sources of income, which were practically the same in all guilds, something must be said as to the expenditure over and above the purposes for which the guilds existed. This may be illustrated from the accounts of this same fraternity of tailors of Winchester.[1] In the first place, as in almost every similar society, provision was made for the funerals of members and for the usual daily mass for thirty days after the death of the deceased members. The sum set down is 2s. 6d. for each trental of thirty masses. Then we find mention of alms to the poor and sick; thus in 1403, the sum of 36s., about one-tenth of the annual revenue, was spent upon this object. This, of course, was charity of a general kind, and wholly unconnected with the assistance given by rule to necessitous members of the guild.[2]

---

[1] The existence of which I know from Mr. Francis Joseph Baigent, who with his usual generosity allowed me to examine and take my notes from the copies which he has among his great collection of materials for the history of Hampshire.

[2] One example of this latter, or as I might call it, ordinary expense of the society, is worth recording. In 1411, and subsequent years, an annual pay-

One expense, very common in these mediæval guilds, was the preparation for taking a fitting part in the great annual religious pageant or procession on Corpus Christi day. In the case of this Tailors' Guild at Winchester, we find sums of money charged for making wax torches and ornamenting them with flowers and red and blue wax, with card shields and parchment streamers, or "pencils," as they are called. The members of the guild apparently carried small tapers ; but the four great torches were borne by hired men, who received a shilling each for their trouble. It is somewhat difficult for us nowadays to understand the importance attached to these great ecclesiastical pageants by our ancestors four hundred years or so ago.   But as to the fact, there can be no doubt. Among the documents in the municipal archives of Winchester there exists an order of the Mayor and Corporation as to the disposition of this solemn procession in 1435.   It runs thus : " At a convocation holden in the city of Winchester the Friday next after the Feast of Corpus Christi in the thirteenth year of the reign of King Harry the Sixth, after the conquest ; it was ordained by Richard Salter, mayor of the city of

ment of 13s. 4d. is entered on the accounts as made to one Thomas Deverosse, a tailor, and apparently a member of the fraternity. The history of this man's poverty is curious. When Bishop William of Wykeham, desiring to build Winchester College, purchased certain lands for the purpose, amongst the rest was a field which a tailor of Winchester, this Thomas Deverosse, subsequently claimed ; and to make good his contention, brought a suit of ejectment against the Bishop. The case was tried in the King's Bench, and the tailor not only lost, but was cast in costs and so ruined. With some writers, William of Wykeham's good name had been allowed to suffer most unjustly for his share in the misfortunes of the unlucky tailor ; for the Bishop not only undertook to pay the costs of the suit himself, but agreed that the college should make the unfortunate claimant a yearly allowance of 8d. to assist him in his poverty. The Tailors' Guild secured to him a pension of 13s. 4d.

Winchester, John Symer and Harry Putt, bailiffs of the city aforesaid, and also by all the citizens and commonalty of the same city : It is agreed of a certain general procession on the Feast of Corpus Christi, of divers artificers and crafts within the said city : that is to say the carpenters and felters shall go together first ; smiths and barbers, second ; cooks and butchers, third ; shoemakers with two lights, fourth ; tanners and japanners, fifth ; plumers and silkmen, sixth ; fishers and farriers, seventh ; taverners, eighth ; weavers, with two lights, ninth ; fullers, with two lights, tenth ; dyers, with two lights, eleventh ; chaundlers and brewers, twelfth ; mercers, with two lights, thirteenth ; the wives with one light and John Blake with another light, fourteenth ; and all these lights shall be borne orderly before the said procession before the priests of the city. And the four lights of the brethren of St. John's shall be borne about the Body of our Lord Jesus Christ, the same day in the procession aforesaid."

The brethren of St. John's just named, as the chief object of their association, kept a hospital for the poor and sick in the city. They paid a chaplain of their own, as indeed did most of the guilds, and had a master and matron to look after the comfort of the poor. They provided bed and bedding, and carefully administered not only their own subscriptions, but the sums of money freely bequeathed to them to be spent on charity. At every market held within the precincts of Winchester an officer, paid by the society, attended and claimed for the support of the poor a tax of two handfuls of corn from every sack exposed for sale. The mayor and bailiffs were apparently the official custodians of this guild, and numerous legacies in wills,

even in the reign of Henry VIII., attest its popularity.
For example, on February 19, 1503, John Cornishe,
alias Putte, late Mayor of Winchester, died and left to
the guardians his tenements and gardens under the
penthouse in the city for the charity, on condition that
for ten years they would spend 6s. 8d. in keeping his
annual obit.   In 1520, a draper of London, named
Calley, bequeathed ten shillings to the hospital for
annually repairing and improving the bedding of the
poor.   The accounts of this Fraternity of St. John's
Hospital for a considerable period in the fourteenth
century are still in existence.   They show large re-
ceipts, sometimes amounting to over £100, from lands,
shops, houses, and from the sale of cattle and farm
produce, over and above the annual subscriptions of
members.   On the other side, week by week we have
the payments for food provided for the service of the
poor : fish, flesh, beer, and bread are the chief items.
One year, for instance, the bread bought for the sick
amounted to 36s. 6d. ; beer to 36s. 8d. ; meat to 32s. 2d. ;
fish to 28s. 3½d., &c.   Besides this seven shillings were
expended in mustard, and 3s. 6d. for six gallons of
oil.   This same year the guardians also paid 2s. 2d. for
the clothes and shoes for a young woman named Sibil
" who nursed the poor in the hospital."   The above represents only the actual money expended over the sick
patients, and from the same source, most minute and
curious information might be added as to the other expenses of the house, including, for instance, even the
purchase of grave-clothes and coffins for the dead poor,
the wages and clothing of the matron and servant, and
the payment of the officer who collected the handfuls of
corn in the market-place.   At times we have evidence

of the arrival and care of strange poor people—we should perhaps call them "tramps" in our day. For instance, here is one heading : " The expenses of three poor strangers in the hospital for 21 days and nights, 15¾d. ; to each of whom is given ¾d. *Item :* the expenses of one other for 5 days, 3¾d. *Item :* the expenses of the burial of the said sick person, 3d. *Item :* the expenses of four pilgrims lodged for a night, 2d. *Item :* new straw to stuff the beds of the sick, 8d. *Item :* paid to the laundress for washing the clothes of the sick during one year, 12d."

To speak of guilds without making any mention of the feasts—the social meetings—which are invariably associated with such societies, would be impossible. The great banquets of the city companies are proverbial, and, in origin at least, they arose out of the guild meeting for the election of officers, followed by the guild feast. As a rule, these meetings took place on the day on which the Church celebrated the memory of the Saint who had been chosen as patron of the society, and were probably much like the club dinners which are still cherished features of village life in many parts of England.[1]

---

[1] Here is the bill for the annual feast in the Guild of Tailors of Winchester in 1411. The association was under the patronage of St. John the Baptist, and they kept their feast on the Day of the beheading of the Saint, August 29. In this year, 1411, the 29th of August fell upon a Saturday, which in mediæval times, as all know, was a day of abstinence from flesh-meat. It is to be noticed, consequently, that provision is made for a fish dinner : " 6 bushels of wheat at 8½d. the bushel ; for grinding of the same, 3d. ; for baking the same, 6d. ; ready-made bread purchased, 12d. ; beer, 7s. 1d. ; salt fish bought of Walter Oakfield, 6s. 8d. ; mullet, bass, ray, and fresh conger bought of the same Walter, 6s. 8d. ; fresh salmon of the same, 8s. ; eels, 10½d. ; fresh fish bought of John Wheller, ' fisher,' 2s. ; ditto, of Adam Frost, 9s. ; ditto, bought of a stranger, 2s. 8d. ; beans purchased, 9d. ; divers spices, *i.e.* saffron, cinnamon, sanders, 12½d. ; salt, 2d. ; mustard, 2½d. ; vinegar, 1d. ; tallow, 2d. ; wood, 18d. ; coals, 3½d. ; paid to Philip the cook, 2s. ; to four labourers,

It has been said that the wardens of guilds were frequently named in mediæval wills as trustees of money for various charitable purposes. As an example of property thus left to a guild, take the Candlemas Guild, established at Bury St. Edmunds : the society was established in the year 1471, and a few years later one of the members made over to the brethren considerable property for the common purposes of the guild and other specified objects. His name was John Smith, a merchant of Bury, and he died, we are told, on " St. Peter's even at Midsummer, 1481." His will, which is witnessed by the Abbot and Prior of St. Edmund's Abbey, provides, in the first place, for the keeping of an obit " devoutly." The residue of the income was to accumulate till the appointment of each new abbot, when, on the election, the entire amount was to be paid over to the elect in place of the sum of money the town was bound to pay on every such occasion. Whatever remained over and above this was to be devoted to the payments of any tenth, fifteenth, or other tax, imposed upon the citizens by royal authority. This revenue was to be administered by the guardians of the guild, who were bound at the yearly meeting at Candlemas to render an account of their stewardship. Year by year John Smith's will was read out at the meeting, and proclamation was made before the anniversary of his death in the following manner : " Let us all of charity pray for the soul of John. We put you in remembrance that you shall not miss the keeping of

---

2s. 6d. ; to three minstrels, 3s. 4d. ; for rushes to strew the hall, 4d. ; three gallons and one pint of wine, 19d. ; cheese, 8d." Making in all a total of £3, 4s. 3½d. This, no doubt, represented a large sum in those days, but it is as well to remember that at this time the guild consisted of 170 men and women, and the cost of the feast was not one-sixth part of the annual income.

his *Dirge* and also of his Mass." Round about the town the crier was sent to recite the following lines :—

" We put you in remembrance all that the oath have made,
  To come to the Mass and the *Dirge* the souls for to glade :
  All the inhabitants of this town are bound to do the same,
  To pray for the souls of John and Anne, else they be to blame :
  The which John afore-rehearsed to this town hath been full kind,
  Three hundred marks for this town hath paid, no penny unpaid behind.
  Now we have informed you of John Smith's will in writing as it is,
  And for the great gifts that he hath given, God bring his soul to
    bliss. Amen." [1]

The example set by this donor to the Candlemas Guild at Bury was followed by many others in the later part of the fifteenth century. For instance, a " gentlewoman," as she calls herself, one Margaret Odom, after providing by will for the usual obit and for a lamp to burn before " the holie sacrament in St. James's Church," desires that the brethren of the guild shall devote the residue of the income arising from certain houses and lands she has conveyed to their keeping, to paying a priest to " say mass in the chapel of the gaol before the prisoners there, and giving them holy water and holy bread on all Sundays, and to give to the prisoners of the long ward of the said gaol every week seven faggots of wood from Hallowmass (November 1) to Easter Day." [2]

Intimately connected with the subject of the guilds is that of the fairs, which formed so great a feature in mediæval commercial life, and at which the craft guilds were represented. For the south of England, the great fair held annually at Winchester became the

---

[1] Harl. MS. 4626, f. 26.
[2] Ibid., f. 29. This was confiscated to the Crown on the dissolution of the Guilds and Fraternities under Edward VI.

centre of our national commerce with France. The following account of it is given in Mr. W. J. Ashley's most interesting *Introduction to English Economic History* : "A fair for three days on the eastern hill outside Winchester was granted to the bishop by William II.; his immediate successors granted extension of time, until by a charter of Henry II. it was fixed at sixteen days, from 31st August to 15th September. On the morning of 31st August 'the justiciars of the pavilion of the bishop' proclaimed the fair on the hilltop, then rode on horseback through the city proclaiming the opening of the fair. The keys of the city and the weighing machine in the wool market were taken possession of, and a special mayor and special bailiffs were appointed to supersede the city officials during the fair time. The hilltop was quickly covered with streets of wooden shops : in one, the merchants from Flanders ; in another, those of Caen or some other Norman town ; in another, the merchants from Bristol. Here were placed the goldsmiths in a row, and there the drapers, &c., whilst around the whole was a wooden palisade with guarded entrance, a precaution which did not always prevent enterprising adventurers from escaping payment of the toll by digging a way in for themselves under the wall. . . . In Winchester all trade was compulsorily suspended, and within 'a seven league circuit,' guards being stationed at outlying posts, on bridges and other places of passage, to see that the monopoly was not infringed. At Southampton nothing was to be sold during the fair time but victuals, and even the very craftsmen of Winchester were bound to transfer themselves to the hill and there carry on their occupations during the fair. There was a graduated scale of tolls and duties : all merchants of London, Winchester, or Wallingford who entered during the first week were free from entrance tolls. . . . In every fair there was a *court of pie-powder* (of dusty feet) in which was decided by merchant law all cases of dispute that might arise, the ordinary jurisdiction being for a time suspended in the town ; at Winchester this was called the Pavilion Court. Hither the bishop's servants brought all the weights and measures to be tested ; here the justices determined on an assize, or fixed scale, for bread, wine, beer, and other victuals, adjudging to the pillory any baker whose bread was found to be of defective weight ; and here every day disputes between merchants as to debts were decided by juries upon production and comparison of the notched wooden tallies." [1]

A few words must be said about the final destruction of the English guilds. At the close of the reign of Henry VIII. an act of Parliament was passed vesting the property of colleges, chantries, fraternities, brotherhoods and guilds in the Crown (38 Hen. VIII., c. 4). The king was empowered to send out his commissioners to take possession of all such property, on the plea that it might be " used and exercised to more godly and virtuous purposes." Henry died before the provisions of the act could be complied with, and a second act was passed through the first Parliament in the reign of Edward VI. (1 Ed. VI., c. 14). This went beyond the former decree of destruction, for after providing for the demolition of colleges, free chapels, and chantries, it proceeded not only separately by name to grant to the king all sums of money devoted " by any manner of corporations, guilds, fraternities, companies or fellow-

---

[1] *Introduction to English Economic History* (2nd ed.), i. pp. 100–101.

ships or mysteries or crafts," to the support of a priest, obits or lights (which may be taken under colour of religion), but to hand over to the crown " all fraternities, brotherhoods and guilds, being within the realm of England and Wales and other the king's dominions, and all manors, lands, tenements, and other hereditaments belonging to them, other than such corporations, guilds, fraternities, &c., and the manors, lands, &c., pertaining to the said corporations, &c., above mentioned."

The Parliament of Henry VIII. assigned as a reason for this seizure of the property of the corporate bodies the need " for the maintenance of these present wars," and cleverly put into one group " colleges, free chapels, chantries, hospitals, fraternities, brotherhoods, and guilds." " The act of Edward VI.," writes Mr. Toulmin Smith, " was still more ingenious, for it held up the dogma of purgatory to abhorrence, and began to hint at grammar schools. The object of both acts was the same. All the possessions of all the guilds (except what could creep out as being mere trading guilds, which saved the London guilds) became vested by these two acts in the Crown ; and the unprincipled courtiers who had advised and helped the scheme gorged themselves out of this wholesale plunder of what was, in every sense, public property." [1]

It is clear that in seizing the property of the guilds the Crown destroyed far more than it gained for itself. A very large proportion of their revenues was derived from the entrance fees and the annual subscriptions of the existing members, and in putting an end to these societies the State swept away the organisation by which

[1] *Old Crown House*, p. 36, cf. pp. 37–39.

these voluntary subscriptions were raised, and this not in one or two places, but all over England. In this way far more harm was in reality done to the interests of the poor, sick, and aged, and, indeed, to the body politic at large, than the mere seizure of their comparatively little capital, whether in land or money.

It is not, of course, meant to imply that the injury to the poor and sick was not fully recognised at the time of these legal confiscations. People deeply resented the idea that what generations of benefactors had intended for the relief of distress should thus be made to pass into the pocket of some " new" man who had grown great upon the spoils. The literature of the period affords abundant evidence of the popular feeling. Crowley, for instance, wrote about 1550— just at this very time—and although no one would look for any accurate description of facts in his rhyming satires, he may be taken as a reliable witness as to what the people were saying. This is what he writes on the point :—

> "A merchant, that long time
>   Had been in strange lands
> Returned to his country,
>   Which in Europe stands.
>
> And in his return
>   His way lay to pass
> By a spittle house not far from
>   Where his dwelling-house was.
>
> He looked for this hospital,
>   But none could he see,
> For a lordly house was built
>   Where the hospital should be.

' Good Lord !' (said the merchant),
  ' Is my country so wealthy
That the very beggars' houses
  Are built so gorgeously ? '

Then by the wayside
  Him chanced to see
A poor man that craved
  Of him for charity.

' Why ' (quoth the merchant),
  ' What meaneth this thing ?
Do ye beg by the way,
  And have a house for a king ? '

' Alas ! sir ' (quoth the poor man),
  ' We are all turned out,
And lie and die in corners
  Here and there about.' "

It has frequently been asserted that although grave
injury was undoubtedly done to the poor of the land
by this wholesale confiscation, it was done unwittingly
by the authorities, or that, at the worst, the portions
of revenue derived from the property which had been
intended for the support of the sick, aged, &c., was
so bound up with those to which religious obligations
(now declared superstitious and illegal) were attached,
that it was impossible to distinguish the latter from
the former, and all perished together, or rather passed
undistinguished into the royal pocket. Such a view is
not borne out by facts, and however satisfactory it
might be to believe that this robbery of the poor and
sick by the Crown was accidental and unpremeditated,
the historian is bound by the evidence to hold that the
pillage was fully premeditated and deliberately and con-
sciously carried out. It is of course obvious, that some
may regard it as proper that funds given for the support

of priests to say masses or offer prayers for the souls of the departed should have been confiscated, although it would have been better had the money been devoted to some purpose of local utility rather than that it should have been added to the Crown revenues or have gone to enrich some royal favourite. For example it may, for the sake of argument, be admitted that the two fields at Petersfield in Hampshire thus taken by the royal commissioners—one called *White field*, in the tenure of Gregory Hill, the rent of which was intended to keep a perpetual light burning in the parish church, and the other held by John Mill, given to support a priest " called the Morrow Masse priest " (*i.e.* the priest employed to say the early morning mass for the convenience of people going to work)—were under the circumstances fair articles of plunder for the royal officials, when the mass was prohibited and the doctrine symbolised by the perpetual light declared superstitious. But this will not apply to the money intended for the poor. It might have been easy to justify the Crown's action in taking the priest's portion, and even the little pittance intended for the serving clerk, but the seizure of the benefactions to the poor cannot be defended. It was not accidental ; for an examination of the original documents relating to the guilds and chantries now in the Record Office will show not only that the Royal Commissioners were as a rule careful to distinguish between the portions intended for religious purposes and those set aside for perpetual charity to the sick and poor, but in many cases they actually proposed to the Court of Augmentation to protect the latter and preserve them for the objects of Christian charity intended by the original donors. In every such case the document reveals the fact that this suggestion in the interest of common justice was rejected by the ultimate Crown officials, and a plain intimation is afforded on the face of the documents that even those sums intended by the original donors for the relief of poverty were to be confiscated.

The destruction of the guilds is, from any point of view, a sad and humiliating story, and, perhaps fortunately, history has so far permitted the thick veil of obscurity drawn over the subject at the time to remain practically undisturbed. A consideration of the scope and purposes of English mediæval guilds cannot but raise our opinion of the wisdom of our forefathers who fostered their growth, and convince us that many and useful ends were served by these voluntary societies. This opinion we can hold, wholly apart from any views we may entertain about the religious aspects of these societies generally.   Socialistic they were, but their socialism, so far from being adverse to religion, as the socialism of to-day is generally considered to be, was transfused and directed by a deeply religious spirit, carried out into the duties of life, and manifesting itself in practical charities of every kind.

One or two points suggested by consideration of the working of mediæval guilds may be emphasized. The system of these voluntary societies would be, of course, altogether impossible and out of place in this modern world of ours. They would not, and could not, meet the wants and needs of these days ; and yet their working is quite worth studying by those who are interested in the social problems which nowadays are thrusting themselves upon the public notice and demanding a solution. The general lessons taught by these voluntary associations may be summed up under one or two heads suggested by Mr. Ashley's volume already referred to : (1) It is obvious that, unlike what we find to-day in the commercial enterprises of the world, capital played but a very small part in the handicrafts of those times ; skill, perseverance, and connection were more important. (2) The middle ages had no knowledge of any class of what may be called permanent wage-labourers. There was no working-class in our modern sense : if by that is meant a class the greater portion of which never rises. In the fourteenth century, a few years of steady work as a journeyman meant, in most cases, that a workman was able to set up as a master craftsman. Every hardworking apprentice expected as a matter of course to be able to become in time a master. The collisions between capital and labour to which we are so much accustomed had no place in the middle ages. (3) There was no such gulf between master and man as exists in our days. The master and his journeyman worked together side by side, in the same shop, at the same work, and the man could earn fully half as much as his master. (4) If we desire to institute a comparison between the status of the working-classes in the fourteenth century and to-day, the comparison must be between the workman we know and the old master craftsman. The shop-keeping class and the middleman were only just beginning to exist. The consumer and producer stood in close relation, and public control was exercised fully, as the craft guilds were subject to the supervision and direction of the municipal or central authority of the cities in which they existed.

CHAPTER XII

MEDIÆVAL WILLS, CHANTRIES, AND OBITS

THE value of side-lights in an historical picture is frequently overlooked, or not duly appreciated. The main facts of a story may be presented with accuracy and detail, and yet the result may be as unlike the reality as the fleshless skeleton is to the living man. More especially are these side-lights requisite when the object of the inquirer is to ascertain the tone and temper of minds at some given time, and to discover what men, under given circumstances, were doing and thinking about. In trying, therefore, to gauge the mental attitude of Englishmen towards the ecclesiastical system existing on the eve of the Reformation, it is important not to neglect any faint glimmer of light which may be reflected from the records of the past, the brightness of which in its setting has been obscured only too well by the dark storm-clouds of controversy and prejudice.

Not the least valuable among what may be described as the minor sources of information about the real feeling of the people generally towards their religion on the eve of the Reformation are the wills, of which we have abundant examples in the period in question. It may, of course, appear to some that their spirit was in great measure dictated by what they now hold to be the· erroneous opinions then in vogue as to Purgatory and the efficacy of prayer for the dead. That these doctrines of the Church had a firm hold on the minds and hearts of the people at large is certain.   The evidence that this was so is simply overwhelming, and it may be taken to prove, not merely the existence of the teaching, but the cordial and unhesitating way in which it was accepted as a necessary part of the Christian faith. But this, after all, is merely a minor point of interest in the wills of the fifteenth and sixteenth centuries.   What clearly appears in these documents, however, is the Catholic tone which pervades them, and enables the reader to realise perhaps more than he is able to do from any other class of document, the strong hold their religion must have had on the love and intelligence of the people of those days.   The intelligences may not, indeed, have been of any very high order, but the souls were certainly penetrated by true Christian ideals.   To those who penned those early wills, Faith was clearly no mere intellectual apprehension of speculative truth.   Religion, and religious observance, was to them a practical reality which entered into their daily lives.   The kindly Spirit that led them, brought them strength to bear their own and others' burdens, in sickness and health, in adversity and prosperity, from childhood till their eyes closed in their last sleep.   If we may judge from these last aspirations of the Christian soul as displayed in mediæval wills, we must allow that religion was very real indeed to our English forefathers in the sixteenth century, and that in reality the whole social order was founded upon a true appreciation of the Christian brotherhood in man, and upon the doctrine of the efficacy of good works for salvation.   These truths of the social order were not indeed taught perhaps scientifically, and we might look in vain for any technical expression of them in the books of religious instruction most used during this period, but they formed none the less part of the traditional Christian teaching of the Middle Ages founded on the great principles of the Bible which then dominated popular thought.[1]

Those who would understand what this Christian spirit meant and the many ways in which it manifested itself, need only compare the wills of the late fifteenth and the early sixteenth centuries with those, say, of the later years of Queen Elizabeth, when the religious revolution had been accomplished, and note the obvious difference in tone and purpose.   The comparison need not be searching or entail much study ; the change is patent and striking, and lies on the very surface.

Some examples of notes taken from pre-Reformation wills may be here given from the collection of Northern wills published by the Surtees Society under the title *Testamenta Eboracensia,* the fourth volume of which contains many wills made during the period in question. It may be useful to remark that one and all of these documents manifest the same spirit of practical Christianity, though of course in various degrees.   Most of them contain bequests to churches with which the donors were chiefly connected ; money is frequently left to the fabric, or to some special altar, or for the purchase of vestments, or to furnish some light

---

[1] See the remarks in regard to France of M. Charles de Ribbe, *La Société Provençale à la fin du moyen age,* 1898, p. 60.   Speaking of the fifteenth-century wills, he says : " Nous en avons lu un grand nombre, et nous avons été frappé de la haute inspiration, parfois meme du talent, avec lesquels des notaires de village savaient traduire les élans de foi et de piété dont ils étaient les interprètes chez leurs clients. . . . Cette foi et cette piété ; trouvé d'abord leur expression dans le vénérable signe de la sainte croix (lequel est plus d'une fois figuré graphiquement).   Suit la recommandation de l'âme à Dieu Créateur du ciel et de la terre, au Christ rédempteur, à la Vierge Marie," &c. (p. 91).

to burn before the Blessed Sacrament, the rood or some image, to which the deceased had a particular devotion. Specific gifts of silks, rich articles of clothing and embroidered hangings fitted to adorn the Church of God, to make chasubles and copes, or altar curtains and frontals, are common. Practical sympathy with the poor is manifested by provision for distributions of doles at funerals and at anniversaries, and by gifts of cloaks and other articles of clothing, to those of the parish who were engaged in carrying torches at the burial, or had promised to offer up prayers for the soul of the testator. Besides these general features of interest, the wills in question show us that building operations of great magnitude were being carried on at this time in the parish churches of the North, and they thus furnish an additional proof of the very remarkable interest thus taken by the people at large in the rebuilding and adornment of the parish churches of England right up to the very overthrow of the old ecclesiastical system. These particular wills also bear a singular testimony to the kindly feelings which existed at this time between the general body of the clergy and the regular orders. Nearly every will of any cleric of note contains bequests of money to monks, nuns, and friars, whilst, in particular, those of the canons and officials of the great metropolitan church of York bear testimony to the affection and esteem in which they held the Abbot and monks of St. Mary's Abbey in the same city, which from its close proximity to the minster might in these days have been regarded as its rival.

As an illustration of the religious spirit which pervades these documents, we may take the following pre-

face to the will of one John Dalton of Hull, made in
1487. " In nomine Patris et Filii et Spiritus Sancti.
Amen. I, John Dalton of the Kingstown upon Hull—
considering and remembering, think in my heart that
the days of man in this mortal life are but short, that
the hour of death is in the hand of Almighty God, and
that He hath ordained the terms that no man may pass.
I remember also that God hath ordained man to die,
and that there is nothing more uncertain than the hour
of death. I seeing princes and (men of) great estates
die daily, and men of all ages end their days, and that
death gives no certain respite to any living creature, but
takes them suddenly. For these considerations, I, being
in my right wit and mind, loved be God, whole not
sick, beseech Almighty God that I may die the true son
of Holy Church and of heart truly confessed, with contrition and repentance, of all my sins that ever I did
since the first hour I was born of my mother into
this sinful world, to the hour of my death. Of these
offences I ask and beseech Almighty God pardon and
forgiveness ; and in this I beseech the Blessed Virgin
Mary and her blessed Son Jesu, our Saviour, that
suffered pain and passion for me and all sinful
creatures, and all the holy company of Paradise to
pray for me. . . . For these causes aforesaid, I, being
alive of whole mind and memory, loved be God, dispose and ordain such goods as God hath lent me mov-
able and immovable by my testament, and ordain this
my last will in the form and manner that followeth :
First, I recommend in humble devotion, contrition, and
true repentance of my faults and sins, praying and
craving mercy of our Saviour Jesus Christ . . . my
soul to our Lord Jesus Christ when it shall depart from

my body, and to our Lady St. Mary, Saint Michael, St. John the Baptist, St. John the Evangelist, St. Katherine and St. Barbara, and to all the whole company and saints of heaven : and my body I will to the earth whereof it came."

The testator then proceeds to direct that his executors shall give his wife a third of his property, and his children another third.   The rest he wishes to be bestowed in charity as they may think best "to the pleasure of God and the health of my soul" . . . "as they shall answer before God at the dreadful day of doom.   (Especially) I will them to pay my debts, charging them before God to discharge me and my soul ; and in this let them do for me as they would I did for them, as I trust they will do." [1]

Of much the same character is the briefer Latin preface to the will of a sub-dean of York in 1490.   "I protest before God Almighty, the Blessed Mary, and all saints, and I expressly proclaim that, no matter what infirmity of mental weakness may happen to me in this or any other sickness, it is not my intention in anything to swerve from the Catholic faith.   On the contrary I firmly and faithly believe all the articles of faith, all the sacraments of the Church ; and that the Church with its sacraments is sufficient for the salvation of any one however guilty." [2]

To take one more example of the same spirit. Thomas Dalton, merchant of Hull—probably son of the John Dalton whose will is quoted above—died in 1497.   After charging his wife, whom he leaves his executrix, to pay all his debts, he adds : " And I will

---

[1] *Testamenta Eboracensia* (Surtees Society), vol. iv. p. 21.
[2] Ibid., p. 127.

and give my mother forty shillings, beseeching her
meekly to pray for me and to give me her daily blessing,
and that she will forgive me all trespasses and faults
done by me to her since I was born of her, as she will
be forgiven before God at the great day of judgment." [1]

Much the same spirit evidently dictated the following clause in the will of John Sothill of Dewsbury, 1502 :
" Also I pray Thomas my son, in my name and for the
love of God, that he never strive with his mother, as he
will have my blessing, for he will find her courteous to
deal with." [2]

Other examples of the catholicity of these mediæval
wills may be here added as they are taken from the
volume almost at haphazard.   In 1487, a late mayor
of the city of York leaves money to help in the repairs
of many churches of the city and its neighbourhood.
He charges his executors to provide for the maintenance of lamps and lights in several places, and specially
names a gold ring with a diamond in it, which he desires
may be hung round the neck of Our Lady's statue in
York Minster, and another with a turquoise " round our
Lord's neck that is in the arms of the said image of Our
Lady."   After making provision for several series of
masses to be said, as for example one of thirty in
honour of the Holy Trinity, another in honour of the
Holy Cross, a third in that of Our Lady, &c., the testator bequeaths a large sum of money to dower fifteen
poor girls, and to find fifty complete sets of beds and
bedding for the poor, as well as other extensive charities.[3]

Thomas Wood, a draper of Hull, was sheriff in
1479 and died in 1490.   By will he left to his parish

----

[1] Ibid., p. 127.   [2] Ibid., p. 170.

[3] Ibid., p. 27.

church a piece of worked tapestry, and the clause by which the bequest was conveyed shows that the church already possessed many costly hangings of this kind. It runs thus : " To the Trinity Church one of my best beds of Arras work, upon condition that after my decease the said bed shall yearly cover my grave at my *Dirge* and Mass, done in the said Trinity Church with note (in singing) for ever more. Also I will that the said bed be yearly hung in the said church on the feast of St. George the Martyr among other worshipful beds, and when the said bed be taken down and delivered, then I will that the same bed be re-delivered into the vestry and there to remain with my cope of gold." [1]

The same kind of gift appears in the last testament of William Rowkshaw, Rector of Lowthorpe, in 1504. " I leave," he says, " to the Church of Catton a bed-covering worked with great figures to lie in front of the High Altar on the chief feasts. And I leave also a bed-covering (worked) with the image of a lion (a blue lion was the family arms) to place in front of the altar in the parish church of Lowthorpe on the chief feasts." Also in the will of William Graystoke of Wakefield, executed in 1508, there is made a gift to the parish church of " a cloth of arras work sometime hanging in the Hall." [2]

Poor scholars at the universities were not forgotten in the wills of the period. Mr. Martin Collins, Treasurer of York, for instance, in 1508 charges his executors to pay for a scholar at either Oxford or Cambridge for seven years to study canon law, or the arts. The only condition is that they are to choose him from the " poor and very needy, and even from the poorest and

[1] Ibid., p. 60.   [2] Ibid., p. 335.

most necessitous." [1]   So, too, William Copley in 1489 leaves money to support two poor priests for the purpose of study at Cambridge.   Archbishop Rotheram in his long and most Christian will, executed in June 1500, makes provision for the education of youth.   He founds a college in the place of his birth—the College of Jesus at Rotheram—in thanksgiving for God's providence in securing his own education.   " For," he says, " there came to Rotheram, I don't know by what chance, but I believe by the special grace of God, a teacher of grammar, who taught me and other youths, and by whose means I and others with me rose in life.   Wherefore desirous of returning thanks to our Saviour, and to proclaim the reason, and lest I might seem ungrateful and forgetful of God's benefits and from whence I have come, I have determined first of all to establish there for ever a grammar master to teach all gratuitously. And because I have seen chantry priests boarding with lay people, one in one place one in another, to their own scandal and in some places ruin, I have desired, in the second place, to make them a common dwelling-house.   For these reasons I have commenced to build the college of Jesus, where the head shall teach grammar and the others may board and sleep."   Moreover, as he has seen, he says, many unlettered and country folk from the hills (*rudi et montani*) attracted to church by the very beauty of ceremonial, he establishes at Rotheram a choir-master and six singing boys to add to the attraction of the services, and for such of these boys, who may not want to become priests, he endows a master to teach them the art of writing and arithmetic. [2]

A merchant of Holme, one John Barton, after

---

[1] Ibid., p. 277.   [2] Ibid., p. 139, *seqq.*

leaving legacies to his parish church, charges his executors to pay the king's taxes for all people of the town assessed at 4d. and under, for two years after his death.   John Barton was a merchant of the staple, and had made his wealth by the wool trade.   At Holme he built "a fair stone house and a fair chapel like a parish church," and to remind his descendants of the source whence their means had come, and in humble acknowledgment of God's goodness to him, he set in the windows of his home the following posie—

> "I thank God, and ever shall,
> It is the sheep hath payed for all." [1]

As an example of specific bequests for pious purposes, we may take the following: Sir Gervase Clifton in 1491 gives many sums of money to churches in Yorkshire and to various chantries in Southwell Minster.   For the use of these latter also, he directs that "all the altar cloths of silk, a bed of gold bawdkyne and another bed of russet satin, which belonged to (Archbishop Boothe of York) be delivered to make vestments." [2]   In 1493–4, John Vavasour, Justice of the Common Pleas, leaves £100 in money to the monastery of Ellerton, to which he says he had previously given all his vestments.   He names the Priors of Ellerton and Thorneholme his executors, and tells them that the Prior of the Charterhouse of Axholme has £800 of his in his keeping, and also that a chest of his plate is in charge of the London Carthusians. [3]

Again Agnes Hildyard of Beverley, in 1497–8, leaves "an old gold noble to hang round the neck of

---

[1] Ibid., p. 61 and *note*.   [2] Ibid., p. 69.

[3] Ibid., p. 89.

the image of Our Lady in the church of Beverley," some money to purchase a mantle for the statue of the Blessed Virgin at Fisholme, and another gold piece for the statue at Molescroft.[1]   About the same time Lady Scrope of Harling left "to the Rood of Northdor my heart of gold with a diamond in the midst.   To Our Lady of Walsingham, ten of my great gold beads joined with silk of crimson and gold, with a button of gold, tasselled with the same. . . . To Our Lady of Pew ten of the same beads ; to St. Edmund of Bury ten of the same ; to St. Thomas of Canterbury, ten of the same ; to my Lord Cardinal, ten aves with two *Paternosters* of the same beads ; to Thomas Fynchman ten aves and two *Paternosters* of the same beads."[2]   Again, in 1502, Elizabeth Swinburne bequeathed to the Carmelites of Newcastle a piece of silver to make a crown for the image of Our Lady at her altar "where my mother is buried," and to Mount Grace a rosary, "fifty beads of gold, a hundred of corall, with all the gaudys of gold," on condition that she and her mother might be considered *consorores* of the house, and that thirteen poor people might be fed on the day of her burial.[3]   So, too, a chain of gold is left to make a cup for the Blessed Sacrament, velvet and silk dresses to make vestments,[4] plate to make a new chrismatory, crystal beads to adorn the monstrance used on Corpus feast day."[5]

William Sheffield, Dean of York, whose will is dated 1496, after some few bequests to friends, leaves the residue to the poor, and he thus explains the reason : "Also I will that the residue of my goods be distri- buted among the poor parishioners in each of the bene-

[1] Ibid., p. 132.   [2] Ibid., p. 149.   [3] Ibid., p. 208.
          [4] Ibid., p. 215.   [5] Ibid., p. 230.

fices I have held, according to the discretion of my executors, so that they may be bestowed more or less in proportion to the time of my living and keeping hospitality in them ; for the goods of the church are the riches of the poor, and so the distribution of church goods is a serious matter of conscience, and on those badly disposing of them Jesus have mercy."[1]

The Vicar of Wighill, William Burton, in 1498–9, left a sum of money to remain in the hands of his successors for ever "to ease poor folk of the parish, for to pay their farms with, so that the said people set not their goods at wainworth (*i.e.* cartloads—what they would fetch), and that they have a reasonable day to pay the said silver again duly and truly to the Vicar for the time being, and the said Vicar to ask and keep eyes (aye) to the same intent, as he will answer for it at the dreadful day of judgment betwixt God and the devil ; and he shall not lend the foresaid money for any tax or tallage, nor for any common purpose of the town, but only to the said poor men." With kindly thought for the young among his old flock, the Vicar adds a bequest of 4d. "to every house poor and rich among the children."[2]

The above is not by any means an isolated instance of a sum, or sums, of money being left to assist the poorer members of the Christian brotherhood, represented by the parish, with temporary loans. One document sets out the working of such a common parish chest under the supervision of the priest. The original chest and the necessary funds for starting this work of benevolence were furnished by one of the parishioners. In order to maintain "this most pious

---

[1] Ibid., p. 119. [2] Ibid., p. 160.

object," as it is called, the rector undertakes to read out the name of the original donor at the "bedes-bidding" on principal feasts, together with those of all who may subsequently add to the capital sum by alms or legacies, in order that people might be reminded of their duty to offer up prayers for the eternal welfare of their benefactors.   The chest was to have three locks, the keys being kept by the rector and the two wardens. Those who might need to borrow temporarily from the common stock to meet their rent, purchase of seed or stock, or for any other purpose, were to bring pledges to the full value of the loan, or else to find known sureties for the amount.   No single person was to be surety for more than six shillings and eightpence, and for wise and obvious reasons the parish priest was not to be allowed to stand security under any circumstances. The loan was for a year, and if at the end of that time the pledge was not redeemed, it was to be sold, but all that it might fetch over and above the amount of the original loan was to be returned to the borrower.[1]

In close connection with the subject of wills in pre-Reformation times is that of chantries and obits. Both these two institutions of the later mediæval church in England have been commonly much misunderstood and misrepresented.   Most writers regard them only in the light of the doctrine of Purgatory, and as illus-trating the extent to which the necessity of praying for the dead was impressed upon the people by the eccle-siastical authorities, and that with a view to their own profit.   It has come, therefore, to be believed that a "chantry" only meant a place (chapel or other locality) connected with the parish church, where masses were

---

[1] B. Mus. Harl. MS. 670, f. 77b.

offered for the repose of the soul of the donor, and other specified benefactors. No doubt there were such chantries existing, but to imagine that all followed this rule is wholly to mistake the purpose of such foundations. Speaking broadly, the chantry priests were the assistant priests or, as we should nowadays say, the curates of the parish, who were supported by the foundation funds which benefactors had left or given for that purpose, and even not infrequently by the contributions of the inhabitants. To speak the language of our own time the system held the place of the "additional curates" or "pastoral aid" societies. For the most part the *raison d'être* of these chantry priests was to look after the poor of the parish, to visit the sick, and to assist in the functions of the parish church. By universal custom, and even by statute law of the English Church, every chaplain and chantry priest, besides the fulfilment of the functions of his own special benefice, was bound to be at the disposition of the parish priest in the common services of the parish church. His presence was required in the choir, vested in a surplice or other ecclesiastical dress proper to his station, or as one of the sacred ministers of the altar, should his services be so required. In this way the existence of guild chaplains, chantry priests, and others, added to the dignity of the ecclesiastical offices and the splendour of the ceremonial in most parish churches throughout the country, and afforded material and often necessary assistance in the working of the parish.

It will give, perhaps, a better idea of the functions of a chantry priest on the eve of the Reformation than can be obtained by any description, to take an example of the foundation made for a chantry at the altar of Saint Anne in the church of Badsworth.   It was founded in 1510 to pray for the soul of Isabella, wife of William Vavasour, and daughter of Robert Urswick. The charter deed ordains that the chaplain shall be a secular priest, without other benefice, and that he should say a Requiem each week with *Placebo* and *Dirige*.   At the first lavatory of the Mass he is to turn to the people and exhort them to pray for the soul of the founder, saying *De Profundis* and the prayer *Inclina Domine*. Once every year there is to be an anniversary service on Tuesday in Easter week, when ten shillings and eightpence is to be distributed to the poor under the direction of the rector.   The chaplain is to be learned in grammar and plain song, and should be present in the choir of the parish church at Matins, Mass, Vespers, and Compline, with other divine services on Sundays and feasts, when he is to take what part the rector shall ordain.   He is not to be absent for more than a month, and then only with leave of the rector, by whom, for certain specified offences, he may be deprived of his office.[1]

In these chantries were established services for the dead commonly called " obits."   These were not, as we have been asked to believe, mere money payments to the priest for anniversary services, but were, for the most part, bequests left quite as much for annual alms to the poor as for the celebration of those services.   A few examples will illustrate this better than any explanation. In the town of Nottingham there were two chantries connected with the parish church of St. Mary, that of our Lady and that called Amyas Chantry.   The former,

[1] *Yorkshire Chantry Surveys* (Surtees Soc.), ii., preface, p. xiv.

according to the record, was founded "to maintain the services and to be an aid to the Vicar and partly to succour the poor;" the latter, to assist in "God's service," and to pray for William Amyas the founder. When the commissioners, in the first year of Edward VI., came to inquire into the possession of these chantries, they were asked to note that in this parish there were "1400 houseling people, and that the vicar there had no other priests to help but the above two chantry priests." They were not, of course, spared on this account, for within two years the property, upon which these two priests were supported, had been sold to two speculators in such parcels of land—John Howe and John Broxholme.

Then again, in the parish of St. Nicholas, in the same town, we find from the returns that the members of the Guild of the Virgin contributed to the support of a priest. In that parish there were more than 200 houseling people, and as the living was very poor, there was absolutely no other priest to look after them but this one, John Chester, who was paid by the guild. The king's officials, however, did not hesitate on this account to confiscate the property. It is needless to adduce other instances of this kind, some scores of which might be given in the county of Nottingham alone. As an example of "obits" and the purposes for which they were intended, the following instances may be given, which it must be remembered could be multiplied to any extent. From the returns of the commissioners in Nottinghamshire we find that in the parish of South Wheatley there were parish lands let out to farm which produced eighteenpence a year, say from eighteen shillings to a pound of our money. Of this sum, one shilling was for the poor, and sixpence for church lights ; that is two-thirds, or, say, 16s. of our money, was for the relief of the distressed.   So in the parish of Tuxford, the church "obit" lands produced £1, 5s. 4d., or about £16 a year ; of which 16s. 4d. was for the poor and 9s. for the church services.

Mr. Thorold Rogers, speaking of the endowments left by generations of Englishmen for the support of chantries, obits, &c., says : "The ancient tenements which are still the property of the London companies were originally burdened with masses for donors.   In the country, the parochial clergy undertook the services of these chantries . . . and the establishment of a mass or chantry priest at a fixed stipend in a church with which he had no other relation, was a common form of endowment.   The residue, if any, of the revenue de-rivable from these tenements was made the common property of the guild, and as the continuity of the service was the great object of its establishment, the donor, like the modern trustee of a life income, took care that there should be a surplus from the founda-tion.   The land or house was let, and the guild consented to find the ministration which formed the motive of the grant." [1]

This is very true, but it is questionable whether Mr. Thorold Rogers appreciated the extent to which these chantry funds were intended to be devoted to purposes other than the performance of the specified religious services.   A couple of examples have been given in Nottinghamshire, and to these may be added one in the south of England.   In connection with the parish church of Alton, in Hampshire, there were, on the eve

[1] *The Economic Interpretation of History*, p. 306.

of the Reformation, six foundations for obits. The following is the account of these taken from the chantry certificates made by the king's commissioners in the first year of the reign of Edward VI.: (1) " Issues of land for an obit for John Pigott, growing and coming out of certain houses and lands in Alton for to maintain for ever a yearly obit there, in the tenure of Thomas Mathew, of the yearly value of 23s. 4d. ; whereof to the poor 15s. 4d., to the parish priest and his clerk 8s.   (2) The same for an obit for William Reding, of the annual value of 15s., of which the poor were to have 10s. and the priest and his clerk 5s.   (3) The same for Alice Hacker, of the yearly value of 10s., of which the poor were to get 7s. 8d. and the priest 2s. 4d.   (4) Another of the value of 4s., the poor to get 2s. 10d. and the priest 1s. 2d.   (5) Another for the soul of Nicholas Bailey, worth annually 11s., and of this 7s. 8d. was intended for the poor and 3s. 4d. for the clergy. (6) Another for Nicholas Crushelon, worth annually 4s. 4d., the poor to have 3s. 1d. and the priest 1s. 3d."   In this parish of Alton, therefore, these six foundations for " obits " or anniversaries produced a total of 77s. 8d., but so far from the whole sum being spent upon priests' stipends, lights, and singing men, we find that considerably more than half, namely 46s. 7d., was bestowed upon the relief of the poor of the parish.   Or if we take the value of money in those days as only twelve times that of our present money, out of a total of £36, 12s. some £27, 19s. went to the support of the poor.

It is obvious that the general advantages derived by a parish from the foundation of these chantries and obits have been commonly overlooked, and the notion that they were intended for no other purpose than pro-

curing prayers for the dead, and that in fact they served
no other end, is altogether misleading and erroneous.
Without the assistance of the clergy, so supported by
the generosity of those who left money for these foundations, the religious services in many of the parish
churches of England in pre-Reformation times could
not have been so fittingly or even adequately provided
for.   Wherever information is available this view is
borne out, and it is altogether to mistake the true bearing of facts to suppose that in suppressing the chantries
and appropriating the endowment of obits the officials of
Edward VI. merely put an end to superstitious prayers
for the souls in Purgatory.   In reality they deprived
the poor of much property left by deceased persons for
their relief, and took away from every parish in England
the assistance of the unbeneficed clergy who had hitherto
helped to support the dignity of God's worship and look
after the souls of the people in the larger districts.

One instance may be given to illustrate how far the
chantry clergy actually took part in the work of the
parish.   At Henley on Thames, on the eve of the
Reformation, there were seven chapels or chantries—
namely, those of Our Lady, St. Katherine, St. Clement,
St. Nicholas, St. Ann, St. John, and St. Leonard.   These
were all supported by various bequests, and the four
priests who served them all resided in a common house
situated in the churchyard known as " the chapel-house,"
or "the four priest chambers."   The disposition of the
services of these chaplains was apparently in the hands
of the " Warden and the commonalty " of the township,
and for the convenience of the people they arrange, for
example, that the chaplain of the Lady altar shall say
his mass there every day at six in the morning, and that

the priest in charge of St. Katherine's shall always begin his at eight.[1]

"To maintain God's service" is perhaps the most common reason assigned to King Edward's commission for the existence of a chantry, or chantries, in connection with a parish church. Thus at Edwinstowe, in Nottinghamshire, there was a chantry chapel a mile from the parish church known as Clipston Chantry. The priest was John Thompson, and he had £5 a year, and "hath no mansion but a parlour under the chapel."[2] At Harworth in the same county there was the hospital of St. Mary's of Bawtree, founded by Robert Morton to serve the people two miles from the parish church. The priest had a mansion and close, "and had to say Mass every morning before sunrise, for such as be travellers by the way and to maintain God's service there, which towne is also a thoroughfare towne."[3]   At Hayton, still in the same county, also two miles from the parish church, was the chantry of Tilne, founded for a priest to serve the villages of North and South Tilne "to celebrate mass and minister the sacraments to the inhabitants adjoining, for that they for the greatness of the waters cannot divers times in the year repair to the parish church." For "the water doth abound so much within the said hamlets that the inhabitants thereof can by no means resort into their parish church of Hayton, being two miles distant from the said chapel, neither for christening, burying, nor other rights."[4]

[1] J. S. Burn, *History of Henley on Thames*, pp. 173–175.
[2] R. O. Chantry Certificate, No. 13 (account for year 37 H. VIII.), No. 17.
[3] Ibid., No. 30 and No. 95, M. 6.
[4] Ibid., No. 37, M. 12; also No. 95, M. 7; and No. 13 (38) Mins. Accts. 2, 3, Ed. VI., shows that the king received £11, 19s. 8d. for the property of this chapel, which was granted to Robert Swift and his brother.

The purposes which these chantry priests were intended to serve is seen to be the same all over England.   To take Suffolk for example : at Redgrave, near Eye, or rather at Botesdale, a hamlet about a mile and a half from Redgrave, there was a chapel of " ancient standing for the ease of the inhabitants of the said street, which was first built at their cost, whereunto do belong no other than the chapel yard." The " street " consisted of forty-six householders, and by estimation a hundred and sixty houselings. It was " a common thoroughfare and hath a liberty of market." These matters " the poor inhabitants " submitted to the King ; it is unnecessary to say without success.[1]   At Levenham the alderman of St. Peter's Guild held certain lands to find a priest who was to teach the children of the town, and was to be " secondary to the curate, who without help of another priest is not able to serve the cure there," as there were two thousand souls in the district.[2]   So, too, at Mildenhall there was a chantry established, as the parish was long and populous, " having a great number of houseling people and sundry hamlets, divers of them having chapels distant from the parish church one mile or two miles, where the said priest did sing Mass sundry festival days and other holy days, and also help the curate to minister the Sacraments, who without help were not able to discharge his cure." [3] At Southwold were four cottages left by one John Perce for an " obit." The property produced twenty shillings a year, and of this sum ten shillings were to be distributed to the poor ; eight shillings to maintain the town and pay the taxes of the poor, and two shillings to be

---

[1] R. O. Chantry Certificate, No. 45 (m. i. d.).
[2] Ibid.   [3] Ibid.

paid to the parson and his clerk for their services in church.   There was also in the same town a tenement called Skilman's, intended to supply a stipendiary priest for sixteen years to the parish, and after that to go to the town.   The sixteen years were up when the royal commissioners visited the town, and the whole sum was then being spent on the town.   In vain the people pleaded that " it was to be considered that the said town of Southwold is a very poor town, whereupon the sea lies beating daily, to the great ruin and destruction of the said town, if that the power and violence of the same were not broken by the maintenance of jetties and piers there, and that the maintenance of the haven and bridge of the same town is likewise very chargeable." The marsh belonging to the said tenement, called Skilman's, is let to the poor inhabitants of the same town, every man paying for his cowgate by the year 20d. only " to the great relief of the poor." [1]

So, too, the Aldermen of the Guild of the Holy Ghost in Beccles held lands to supply a priest to assist in the parish for ninety-nine years, to find money to pay the tenths, fifteenths, and other taxes, and for other charitable purposes.   The property brought in £10, 9s. 4d., and each year the poor received forty shillings ; thirty shillings went to pay for the taxes, and the rest—some £6—to the priest.   In order to induce the king to leave this fund untouched, the commissioners of 1547 are asked to note " that Beccles is a great and populous town," there being eight hundred houselings, " and the said priest is aiding unto the curate there, who without help is not able to discharge the said cure." [2]

---

[1] Ibid. (18).   [2] Ibid. (20).

The case of Bury St. Edmunds is particularly distressing. Amongst other charities, lands had been left by will or given by various benefactors to find priests to serve St. Mary's, to sing " the Jesus Mass," and to act as chaplain at the Lady altar. Property also was given in charge of St. Nicholas Guild of the annual value of 25s. 4d., of which sum 22s. was to be distributed to the poor of the town, and the rest was to go to the annual anniversary services for members of the guild. More property, too, had been left by one Margaret Oldham for a priest to say Mass in the church of St. James on the week days, and in the jail on the Sundays, and to find the poor prisoners in wood for a fire during winter months.   There were several other similar bene-factions of the same kind, and the parishioners of St. James's church " gathered weekly of their devotion " the stipend of a priest paid to say "the morrow Mass " —that is, the Mass at daybreak intended for those who had to go early to their daily work.   When the royal commissioners came on behalf of the said Edward VI. to gather in these spoils at Bury, they were asked to forward to the authorities in London the following plea for pity: " It is to be considered that the said town of Bury is a great and populous town, having in it two parish churches, and in the parishes of the same above the number of 3000 houseling persons, and a great number of youth.   And the king's majesty hath all the tithes and all the profits yearly coming and growing within the same parishes,[1] finding two parish priests there.   And the said two parish priests are not able to serve and discharge the said cures without aid and help of other priests.   And further, there is no

---

[1] This was owing to the recent dissolution of the Abbey.

school, nor other like foundation, within the said town, nor within twenty miles of it, for the virtuous education and bringing up of youth, nor any hospital or other like foundation for the comfort and relief of the poor, of which there is an exceeding great number within the said town other than what are before mentioned, of which the said incumbents do now take the whole [1] yearly revenues and profits, and distribute no part thereof to the aid and comfort or relief of the said poor people.

"In consideration whereof it may please the king's majesty of his most charitable benignity, moved with pity in that behalf, to convert the revenues and profits of the sum of the said promotions into some godly foundation, whereby the said poor inhabitants, daily there multiplying, may be relieved, and the youth instructed and brought up virtuously, or otherwise, according to his most godly and discreet wisdom, and the inhabitants shall daily pray to God for the prosperous preservation of his most excellent majesty, long to endure." [2]

It is hardly necessary to say that the petition had no effect. At Bury, as indeed all over England, the claims of the sick and poor were disregarded and the money passed into the possession of the crown. The hospitals that mediæval charity had erected and sup-

---

[1] In one case it is said : "*Mem.:* The decay of rent is caused by the fact that most came from lands in possession of the abbey ; since the dissolution these have been sold, and the purchasers do not allow that they are liable to pay." The hospital called St. Parvell's, without the south gate, also had been dissolved by Henry VIII., and the property granted to Sir George Somerset (6th July, 37 H. VIII.). It had produced £16, 13s. 4d. a year, with £5, 10s. "paid out of the late abbey of Bury to the sustentation of the poor." The whole charity, of course, by the dissolution of the abbey and the grant of the remaining property as above, had come to an end.

[2] Ibid. (No. 44).

ported were destroyed ; the youth remained untaught ; the poor were deprived of the charity which had been, as it was supposed, secured to them for ever by the wills of generations of Catholic benefactors ; the poor prisoners in the jail at Bury had to go without their Sunday Mass and their winter fire ; whilst the money that had hitherto supported chaplains and chantry priests to assist the parish priests in the care of their districts was taken by the crown.

For Yorkshire the certificates of the commissioners have been published by the Surtees Society.   The same impression as to the utility and purpose of the chantry and other assisting priests may be gathered from almost every page.   For example, the chantry of St. Katherine in the parish church of Selby : " The necessity thereof is to do divine service, and help the parish priest in time of necessity to minister sacraments and sacramentals and other divine ser-vices." . . . For "the said parish of Selby is a great parish, having but one curate, and in the same parish is a thousand houseling people ; and the said curate has no help in time of necessity but only the said chauntry priest." [1]

Again : " Two chantries of our Lady in the parish church of Leeds, 'founded by the parishioners there to serve in the choir and to minister sacraments and other divine service, as shall be appointed by the vicar and other honest parishioners there, which they do. . . . The necessity thereof is to do divine service, to help the curate, and minister the Sacraments, having 3000 houseling people.' " [2]

---

[1] *Yorkshire Chantry Surveys* (Surtees Soc.), p. 213.
[2] Ibid., p. 214.

In the same parish church, the chantry of St. Mary
Magdalene was "founded by William Evers, late vicar
of Leeds, to pray for the soul of the founder and all
Christian souls, to minister at the altar of St. Mary
Magdalene, to keep one yearly obit, with seven shillings
to be distributed, and to serve in the choir at divine
service all holy days and festival days, as appears by
the foundation deed thereof, dated A.D. 1524." [1]

One more example may be taken out of the hundreds
in these volumes: "The chantry, or donative, within
the chapel of Holbecke in the parish of Leeds, 'the
incumbent is used to say daily mass there and is taken
for a stipendiary priest paying tithes. And there is a
great river between the said parish church and the
chapel, whereby they can by no means often pass to
the said church. . . . The said chantry is distant from
the said parish church one mile. The necessity thereof
is to do divine service according to the foundation.'" [2]

A few words enforcing the lesson to be learned
from these extracts taken from the preface to the second
part of these interesting Yorkshire records may be here
given. Mr. Page, the editor, says: "Up to the time of
the Reformation nearly all education was maintained
by the church, and when the chantries were dissolved
practically the whole of the secondary education of the
country would have been swept away, had not some
provision for the instruction of the middle and lower
classes been made by continuing, under new ordinances,
some of the educational endowments which pious
founders had previously provided." [3]

"The next most important class of foundations,

[1] Ibid., p. 215.   [2] Ibid., p. 216.
                    [3] Ibid., p. 11.

some of which were continued under the commission
. . . consisted of the chapels of ease, which were much
required in extensive parishes with a scattered population, and had been generally founded by the parishioners
for their own convenience.   It seems, therefore, that
the dissolution of these chapels was a peculiar hardship.
As early as 1233, the Pope granted licence to the archbishop of York to build oratories or chapels and to
appoint to them priests, in places so distant from the
parish churches that the people could with difficulty
attend divine service, and the sick died before the priest
could get to them to administer the last sacraments.
The necessity for these chapels of ease was especially
felt in Yorkshire, where the inhabitants of so many
outlying hamlets were cut off from their parish churches
in winter time by impassable roads and flooded rivers,
which is the reason time after time assigned by the commissioners, for the necessity of the existence of such
chapels ; and yet comparatively few of them were recommended for continuance by Sir Walter Mildmay and
Robert Kelway in the returns to the commission.
Possibly, it was the loss of the endowments of Ayton
chapel which occasioned the insurrection at Leamer
. . . which chapel the inhabitants so piously kept up
afterwards at their own expense." [1]

   " In most cases, the chantry priest seems to have
acted in much the same capacity in a parish as that
now occupied by the curate ; he assisted the parish
priest in performing mass, hearing confessions and
visiting the sick, and also helped in the ordinary
services of the church; the few only were licensed to
preach, like the schoolmaster at Giggleswick.   In the

[1] Ibid., p. 12.

Cathedral Church at York, besides praying for the soul of his founder and all Christian souls, each chantry priest had to be present in the choir in his habit of a parson on all principal and double feast days, Sundays, and nine lections, at Matins, Mass, Evensong, and processions, when he had to read lessons, begin anthems, and to minister at the high altar as should be appointed to him by the officers of the choir. Besides these purely ecclesiastical duties, very many of the chantry priests were bound to teach a certain number of the children of the neighbourhood, which was the origin of most of our Grammar schools." [1]

[1] Ibid., p. 13.

CHAPTER XIII

PILGRIMAGES AND RELICS

PILGRIMAGES and the honour shown to relics are frequently pointed out as, with Indulgences, among the most objectionable features of the pre-Reformation ecclesiastical system. It is assumed that on the eve of the religious changes the abuses in these matters were so patent, that no voice was, or indeed could have been, raised in their defence, and it is asserted that they were swept away without regret or protest as one of the most obvious and necessary items in the general purification of the mediæval church initiated in the reign of Henry VIII. That they had indeed been tolerated at all even up to the time of their final overthrow was in part, if not entirely, due to the clergy, and in particular to the monks who, as they derived much pecuniary benefit from encouraging such practices, did not scruple to inculcate by every means in their power the spiritual advantages to be derived from them. That the objectionable features of these so-called works of piety had long been recognised, is taken for granted, and the examinations of people suspected of entertaining Wyclifite opinions are pointed to as proof that earnest men were alive to these abuses for more than a century before religion was purified from them. As conclusive evidence of this, the names, too, of Chaucer for early times, and of Erasmus for the Reform period, are given as those whose condemnation and even scornful rejection of such practices cannot be doubted. It becomes important, then, for a right understanding of the mental attitude of the people generally to the existing ecclesiastical system at the time of its overthrow, to see how far the outcry against pilgrimages and the devotion to relics was really .popular, and what were the precise objections taken to them by the innovators.

It is difficult to exaggerate the importance attached to pilgrimages by our pre-Reformation forefathers. From very early times the practice was followed with eagerness, not to say with devotion, and included not merely visits to the shrines situated within the country itself, but long and often perilous journeys into foreign lands—to Compostella, Rome, and to the Holy Land itself. These foreign pilgrimages of course could be undertaken only by the rich, or by those for whom the requisite money was found by some one unable to undertake the journey in person. Not infrequently the early English wills contain injunctions upon the executors to defray the cost of some poor pilgrim to Spain, to Rome, or to some of the noted shrines on the Continent. The English love for these works of piety in nowise showed any sign of decadence even right up to the period of change. Books furnishing intending pilgrims with necessary information, and vocabularies, even in Greek, were prepared to assist them in their voyages. The itineraries of William Wey, printed by the Roxburghe Club, give a very good idea of what these great religious pilgrimages must have been like at the close of the fifteenth century. In 1462 Wey was in the Holy Land, and describes how joyfully the pilgrims on landing at Jaffa sang the

"*Urbs beata Jerusalem* in faburthyn." In 1456 he took part in a large English pilgrimage to St. James of Compostella, leaving Plymouth with a shipload of English fellow-pilgrims on May 17. William Wey's ship was named the *Mary White*, and in company with them six other English ships brought pilgrims from Portsmouth, Bristol, Weymouth, Lymington, and a second from Plymouth. They reached Corunna on May 21st, and Compostella for the great celebration of Trinity Day. Wey was evidently much honoured by being pointed out to the church officials as the chief Englishman of note present, and he was given the post of first bearer of the canopy in the procession of the Blessed Sacrament. Four out of the six poles were carried by his countrymen, whom he names as Austill, Gale, and Fulford.

On their return the pilgrims spent three days at Corunna. They were not allowed to be idle, but religious festivities must have occupied most of their time. On Wednesday, the eve of Corpus Christi day, there was a procession of English pilgrims throughout the city and a mass in honour of the Blessed Virgin. On Corpus Christi itself their procession was in the Franciscan church, and a sermon was preached in English by an English Bachelor in Theology on the theme, *Ecce ego; vocasti me.* " No other nation," says William Wey, somewhat proudly, " had these special services but the English." In the first port there were ships belonging to English, Welsh, Irish, Norman, French, and Breton, and the English alone had two and thirty.

Such journeys were not, of course, in those days devoid of danger, especially from sickness brought on, or developed in the course of the travels. Erasmus, in his *Colloquy on Rash Vows,* speaks of losing three in a company. "One dying on the way commissioned us to salute Peter (in Rome) and James (at Compostella) in his name. Another we lost at Rome, and he desired that we should greet his wife and children for him. The third we left behind at Florence, his recovery entirely despaired of, and I imagine he is now in heaven." That this account of the mortality among pilgrims is not exaggerated is shown in the diary of Sir Richard Torkington, Rector of Mulbarton, in Norfolk. In 1517 he made a pilgrimage to Jerusalem, and records on "the 25th of August, that was Saynt Bertolmew's day, deceased Robert Crosse of London, and was buried in the churchyard of Salyus (in the island of Cyprus); and the 27th day of August deceased Sir Thomas Tappe, a priest of the West country, and was cast over the board ; as were many more whose souls God assoyl; and then there remained in the ship four English priests more."[1]

If Englishmen went abroad to the celebrated shrines, foreigners in turn found their way to the no less renowned places of pilgrimage in England. Pilgrims' inns and places of rest were scattered over the great roads leading to Glastonbury, Walsingham, and Canterbury, and other "holy spots" in this island, and at times these places were thronged with those who came to pay their devotion. At one time we are told that more than a hundred thousand pilgrims were together in the city of Canterbury to celebrate one of the Jubilee celebrations of the martyr St. Thomas; whilst the road to Walsingham was so much frequented, that

---

[1] *Gentleman's Magazine,* vol. lxxxii., ii. 318.   Quoted in J. Gough Nichol's *Pilgrimages,* &c.   Introduction, xcv.

in the common mind the very "milk way" had been set by Providence in the heaven to point the path to Our Lady's shrine.

With the very question of pilgrimages, Sir Thomas More actually deals in the first portion of his *Dyalogue*, and it would be difficult to find any authority who should carry greater weight. He first deals with the outcry raised by the followers of Luther against the riches which had been lavished upon the churches, and in particular upon the shrines containing the relics of saints.

Those who so loudly condemn this devotion shown by the church to the saints should know, he says "that the church worships not the saints as God, but as God's servants, and therefore the honour that is done to them redoundeth principally to the honour of their Master ; just as by common custom of people we sometimes, for their master's sake, reverence and make great cheer for people to whom perhaps except for this we would not have said 'good morrow.'

"And sure if any benefit or alms, done to one of Christ's poor folk for his sake, be reputed and accepted by His high goodness, as done unto Himself: and if whosoever receiveth one of His apostles or disciples re-ceives Himself, every wise man may well think that in like manner he who honours His holy saints for His sake, honours Himself, except these heretics think that God were as envious as they are themselves, and that He would be wroth to have any honour done to any other, though it thereby redoundeth unto Himself.   In this matter our Saviour Christ clearly declares the con-trary, for He shows Himself so well content that His holy saints shall be partakers of His honour that He promises His apostles that at the dreadful doom (when He shall come in His high majesty) they shall have their honourable seats and sit with Himself upon the judgment of the world. Christ also promised that Saint Mary Magdalene should be worshipped through the world and have here an honourable remembrance because she bestowed that precious ointment upon His holy head. When I consider this thing it makes me marvel at the madness of these heretics that bark against the old ancient customs of Christ's church, mocking at the setting up of candles, and with foolish facetiousness (fallacies) and blasphemous mockery demand whether God and His saints lack light, or whether it be night with them that they cannot see without a candle. They might as well ask what good did that ointment do to Christ's head ? But the heretics grudge the cost now as their brother Judas did then, and say it were better spent on alms upon a poor folk, and thus say many of them who can neither find in their heart to spend on the one nor the other. And some spend sometimes on the one for no other intent, but the more boldly to rebuke against and rail against the other."

After pointing out how riches were lavished on the temple by God's special ordinance, Sir Thomas More continues : " If men will say that the money were better spent among poor folk by whom He (*i.e.* God) setteth more store as the living temples of the Holy Ghost made by His own hand than by the temples of stone made by the hand of men, this would perhaps be true if there were so little to do it with that we should be driven by necessity to leave the one undone. But God gives enough for both, and gives divers men divers

kinds of devotion, and all to His pleasure. Luther, in a
sermon of his, wished that he had in his hand all the
pieces of the holy cross, and said if he had he would
throw them where the sun should never shine on them.
And for what worshipful reason would the wretch do
such villainy to the cross of Christ ?   Because, as he
says, there is so much gold now bestowed on the garnishing of the pieces of the cross that there is none left
for poor folks.   Is not this a high reason ?   As though
all the gold that is now bestowed about the pieces of
the holy cross would not have failed to be given to poor
men if they had not been bestowed on the garnishing
of the cross ; and as though there was nothing lost
except what is bestowed about Christ's cross.   Take
all the gold that is spent about all the pieces of Christ's
cross through Christendom (albeit many a good Christian
prince and other godly people have honourably garnished
many pieces of it), yet if all the gold were gathered
together it would appear a poor portion in comparison
with the gold that is bestowed upon cups—what do we
speak of cups for ? in which the gold, though it is not
given to poor men, is saved, and may be given in alms
when men will, which they never will; how small a
portion, ween we, were the gold about all the pieces of
Christ's cross, if it were compared with the gold that is
quite cast away about the gilding of knives, swords, &c."

Our author then goes on to put in the mouth of the
" objector " the chief reasons those who were then the
advocates of the religious changes were urging against
pilgrimages to the shrines of saints and to special places
of devotion to our Blessed Lady.   Protesting that he
had, of course, no desire to see the images of the saints
treated in any way disrespectfully, the objector declares

that " yet to go in pilgrimages to them, or to pray to them, not only seemed vain, considering that (if they can do anything) they can do no more for us among them all than Christ can Himself alone who can do all things, nor are they so ready to hear (if they hear us at all) as Christ that is everywhere." . . . Moreover, to go a pilgrimage to one place rather than to another " seems to smell of idolatry," as implying that God was not so powerful in one place as He is in another, and, as it were, making God and His saints " bound to a post, and that post cut out and carved into images. For when we reckon we are better heard by our Lord in Kent than at Cambridge, at the north door of Paul's than at the south door, at one image of our Lady than at another," is it not made plain that we " put our trust and confidence in the image itself, and not in God and our Lady," and think of the image and not of what the image represents.

Further, " men reckon that the clergy gladly favour these ways, and nourish this superstition under the name and colour of devotion, to the peril of people's souls for the lucre and temporal advantage that they themselves receive from the offerings " (p. 120).

Lest it may be thought that these objections to places of pilgrimage were merely such as Sir Thomas More invented to put into the mouth of the " objector " in order to refute them, the reader may like to have the words of a known advocate of the new ideas. Lancelot Ridley, in his expositions of some of the Epistles, states his views very clearly. " Ignorant people," he writes, " have preferred the saints before God, and put more trust, more confidence, (look for) more help and succour, in a saint than in God. Yea, I fear me that

many have put their help and succour in an image made
of stone or of wood by men's hand, and have done
great honour and reverence to the image, believing
that great virtue and great holiness was in that image
above other images.   Therefore that image must have
a velvet coat hanged all over with brooches of silver,
and much silver hanged about it and on it, with much
light burning before it, and with candles always burning
before it.   I would no man (should put out the light)
in contempt of the saint whose image there is, but I
would have this evil opinion out of the simple hearts
that they should esteem images after the value they are,
and put no more holiness in one image than in another,
no more virtue in one than in another.   It holds the
simple people in great blindness, and makes them put
great trust and (esteem) great holiness in images, because
one image is called our Lady of Grace, another our
Lady of Pity, another our Lady of Succour or Comfort ;
the Holy Rood of such a place, &c."   And this he maintained, though he did not condemn images generally
in churches.   These he thought useful to remind people
of God's saints and their virtues, and "to stir up our
dull hearts and slothful minds to God and to goodness."
What he objected to chiefly was the special places of
pilgrimage and special images to which more than
ordinary devotion was shown.[1]

[1] Lancelot Rydley. *Exposition in the Epistell of Jude.* London,
Thomas Gybson, 1538, sig. B. v.   In sermons and writings, pre-Reformation ecclesiastics strove to impress upon the minds of the people the true
principles of devotion to shrines and relics of the saints. To take one
example beyond what is given above.   In *The Art of Good Lyvyng and
Good Deyng*, printed in 1503, the writer says : " We should also honour the
places that are holy, and the relics of holy bodies of saints and their images,
not for themselves, but for that in seeing them we show honour to what it
represents, the dread reverence, honour and love of God, after the intention
of Holy Church, otherwise it were idolatry " (fol. 6).

In another of his *Expositions,* printed in 1540, Ridley again states his objections to the places of pilgrimage. " Some think," he writes, " that they have some things of God, and other part of saints, of images, and so divide God's glory, part to God and part to an image, of wood or of stone made by man's hand. This some ignorant persons have done in times past, and thanked God for their health and the blessed Lady of Walsingham, of Ipswich, St. Edmund of Bury, Etheldred of Ely, the Lady of Redbourne, the Holy Blood of Hayles, the Holy Rood of Boxley, of Chester, &c., and so other images in this realm to the which have been much pilgrimage and much idolatry, supposing the dead images could have healed them or could have done something for them to God. For this the ignorant have crouched, kneeled, kissed, bobbed and licked the images, giving them coats of cloth, of gold, silver, and of tissue, velvet, damask, and satin, and suffered the living members of Christ to be without a russet coat or a sackcloth to keep them from the cold." [1]

Again in another place he says that his great objection to images is not that they may not be good in themselves and as a reminder of the holiness of the saints, but that they are used as a means of making money. " Who can tell," he writes, " half the ways they have found to get, yea to extort money from men by images, by pardons, by pilgrimages, by indulgences, &c. . . . all invented for money." The above passages may be taken as fair samples of the outcry against shrines and pilgrimages raised by the English followers of Luther and the advocates of the religious changes generally. It will be noticed that the ground

[1] *A Commentary in Englyshe upon the Ephesians,* 1540, sig. A. ii.

of the objections was in reality only the same as that which induced them to declare against any honour shown to images, whether of Christ or His saints. There is no suggestion of any special abuses connected with particular shrines and places of pilgrimage, such as is often hinted at by those who refer to Chaucer and Erasmus. In addition to the general ground of objection, the only point raised in regard to pilgrimages by the advocates for their suppression was that money was spent upon them which might have been bestowed more profitably on the poor, and that the clergy were enriched by the offerings made at the shrines visited. Sir Thomas More's reply to the latter suggestion has been already given, and elsewhere his views as to the general question of the danger of people mistaking the nature of the honour shown to images of the saints have been stated at length. With regard to his approval of the principle of pilgrimages there is no room for doubt.

" If the thing were so far from all frame of right religion," he says, " and so perilous to men's souls, I cannot perceive why the clergy, for the gain they get thereby, would suffer such abuses to continue. For, first, if it were true that no pilgrimage ought to be used, no image offered to, nor worship done nor prayer offered to any saint, then—if all these things were all undone (if that were the right way, as I wot well it were wrong), then to me there is little question but that Christian people who are in the true faith and in the right way Godward would not thereby in any way slack their good minds towards the ministers of His church, but their devotion towards them would more and more increase. So that if by this way they now get a penny they would not then fail to receive a groat ; and so should no lucre be the cause to favour this way if it be wrong, whilst they could not fail to win more by the right."

" Moreover, look through Christendom and you will find the fruit of those offerings a right small part of the living of the clergy, and such as, though some few places would be glad to retain, yet the whole body might easily forbear without any notable loss. Let us consider our own country, and we shall find that these pilgrimages are for the most part in the hands of such religious persons or of such poor parishes as have no great authority in the convocations. Besides this you will not find, I suppose, that any Bishop in England has the profit of even one groat from any such offering in his diocese. Now, the continuance or breaking of this manner and custom stands them specially in the power of those who take no profit by it. If they believed it to be (as you call it) superstitious and wicked they would never suffer it to continue to the perishing of men's souls (something whereby they themselves would destroy their own souls and get no commodity either in body or goods). And beyond this, we see that the bishops and prelates themselves visit these holy places and pilgrimages, and make as large offerings and (incur) as great cost in coming and going as other people do, so that they not only take no temporal advantage, but also bestow their own money therein. And surely I believe this devotion so planted by God's own hand in the hearts of the whole Church, that is to say, not the clergy only, but the whole congregation of all Christian people, that if the spirituality were of the mind to give it up, yet the temporality would not suffer it."

It would be impossible, without making extensive quotations, to do justice to Sir Thomas More's argument in favour of the old Catholic practice of pilgrimages. He points out that the whole matter turns upon the question whether or no Almighty God does manifest His power and presence more in one place of His world than in another. That He does so, he thinks cannot be questioned ; why He should do so, it is not for us to guess, but the single example of the Angel and the pool of Bethsaida related in St. John's Gospel is sufficient proof of the fact—at least to Sir Thomas More's intelligence. Moreover, he thinks also that in many cases the special holiness of a place of pilgrimage has been shown by the graces and favours, and even miracles, which have been granted by God at that particular spot, and on the "objector" waiving this argument aside on the plea that he does not believe in modern miracles, More declares that what is even more than miracles in his estimation is the "common belief in Christ's Church" in the practice.

As to believing in miracles ; they, like every other fact, depend on evidence and proof. It is unreasonable in the highest degree to disbelieve everything which we have not seen or which we do not understand. Miracles, like everything else, must be believed on the evidence of credible witnesses. What in their day, he says, is believed in by all would have been deemed impossible a century or two before ; for example, that the earth is round and "sails in mid-air," and that "men walk on it foot to foot" and ships sail on its seas "bottom to bottom." Again, "It is not fifty years ago," he says, "since the first man, as far as men have heard, came to London who ever parted the silver gilt from the silver, consuming shortly the silver into dust with a very fair water." At first the gold and silver smiths laughed at the suggestion as absurd and impossible. Quite recently also More had been told that it was possible to melt iron and make it " to run as silver or lead doeth, and make it take a print." More had never, he says, seen this, but he had seen the new invention of drawing out silver into thread-like wires. The " objector " was incredulous, and when More went on to tell him that if a piece of silver had been gilded, it could be drawn out with the gilding into gilt wires, he expressed his disbelief in the possibility of such a thing, and was hardly more satisfied that he was not being deceived when the process was shown to him the next day.

These and such like things, argues More, show us that our knowledge is, after all, very limited, and that while some supposed miracles may be doubted, it is most unreasonable to doubt or deny the possibility of miracles generally. If nature and reason tell us there is a God, the same two prove that miracles are not impossible, and that God can act when He wills against the course of nature. Whether He does in this or that case is plainly a matter of evidence. The importance of Sir Thomas More's opinion on the matter of Pilgrimage does not, of course, rest upon the nature of his views, which were those naturally of all good Catholic sons of Holy Church, but upon the fact that, in face of the objections which were then made and which were of the kind to which subsequent generations have been accustomed, so learned and liberal a man as he was, did not hesitate to treat them as groundless, and to defend the practice as it was then known in England.

That there may have been "abuses" he would have no doubt fully admitted, but that the "abuses" were either so great or so serious as to be any reasonable ground against the "use" he would equally have indignantly denied.

No less clear and definite are his opinions as to "relics" and the honour shown them. The "adversary" in the *Dyalogue* takes up the usual objections urged against the reverence shown to the remains of the saints, and in particular to the wealth which was lavished upon their shrines. "May the taking up of a man's bones," he says, "and setting his carcase in a gay shrine, and then kissing his bare scalp, make a man a saint? And yet are there some unshrined, for no man knoweth where they lie. And men doubt whether some ever had any body at all or not, but to recompense that again some there are who have two bodies, to lend one to some good fellow that lacketh his. For . . . some one body lies whole in two places asunder, or else the monks of the one be beguiled. For both places plainly affirm that it lieth there, and at either place they show the shrine, and in the shrine they show a body which they say is *the* body, and boldly allege old writings and miracles also for the proof of it. Now must he confess that either the miracles at the one place be false and done by the devil, or else that the same saint had indeed two bodies. It is therefore likely that a bone worshipped for a relic of some holy saint in some place was peradventure 'a bone (as Chaucer says) of some holy Jew's sheep.'" More's "adversary" then goes on to say that our Lord in reproving the Pharisees for "making fresh the sepulchres of the prophets" condemns the "gay golden shrines made for saints' bodies, especially when we have no certainty that they are saints at all." [1]

What all this really amounts to, replies More, is not that your reasons would condemn honour and worship to true relics of the saints, but that " we may be deceived in some that we take for saints—except you would say that if we might by any possibility mistake some, therefore we should worship none." Few people would say this, and " I see," says More, " no great peril to us from the danger of a mistake. If there came, for example, a great many of the king's friends into your country, and for his sake you make them all great cheer ; if among them there come unawares to you some spies that were his mortal enemies, wearing his badge and seeming to you and so reported as his familiar friends, would he blame you for the good cheer you made his enemies or thank you for the good cheer you gave his friends ? " He then goes on at great length to suggest that, as in the case of the head of St. John the Baptist in which portions only existing in each place are each called " the head," so, very frequently, only a portion of the body of a saint is called " the body." He mentions having himself been present at the abbey of Barking thirty years before (*i.e.* in 1498), when a number of relics were discovered hidden in an old image, which must have been put there four or five hundred years since " when the abbey was burned by the infidels." He thinks that in this way the names of relics are frequently either lost or changed. But he adds, " the name is not so very requisite but that we may mistake it without peril, so that we nevertheless have the relics of holy men in reverence."

[1] p. 190.

In replying to Tyndale also, More declares that he had never in all his life held views against relics of the saints or the honour due to their holy images. Tyndale had charged him with being compromised by the words used by Erasmus in the *Encomium Moriæ*, which was known to have been composed in More's house, and was commonly regarded as almost the joint work of the two scholars. If there were anything like this in the *Moriæ*—any words that could mean or seem to mean anything against the true Catholic devotion to relics and images—then More rejects them from his heart. But they are not my words, he adds, " the book being made by another man, though he were my darling never so dear " (p. 422). But the real truth is that in the *Moriæ* Erasmus never said more or meant more than to " jest upon the abuses of such things."

In this regard it is of interest to understand what was the real opinion of Erasmus in regard to devotions to particular saints and their images and relics. This is all the more important, as most people regard the account of his two pilgrimages to Walsingham and to Canterbury as full and conclusive evidence of his sentiments. In his tract *Enchiridion Militis Christiani*, published at Louvain in 1518, his views are stated with absolute clearness. " There are some," he says, " who honour certain saints with some special ceremonies. . . One salutes St. Christopher each day, and only in presence of his image. Why does he wish to see it ? Simply because he will then feel safe that day from any evil death. Another honours Saint Roch—but why ? Because he thinks that he will drive away infection from his body. Others murmur prayers to St. Barbara or St. George, so as not to fall into the hands of any enemy. One man fasts for St. Apollonia, not to have toothache. Some dedicate a certain portion of their gains to the poor so that their merchandise is not destroyed in shipwreck," &c.[1]

Our author's point is that in these and such-like things people pray for riches, &c., and do not think much about the right use of them; they pray for health and go on living evil lives. In so far such prayers to the saints are mere superstitions, and do not much differ from the pagan superstitions; the cock to Æsculapius, the tithe to Hercules, the bull to Neptune. "But," he says, "I praise those who ask from St. Roch a life protected from disease if they would consecrate that life to Christ. I would praise them more if they would pray only for increased detestation of vice and love virtue. I will tolerate infirmity, but with Paul I show the better way." He would think it, consequently, a more perfect thing to pray only for grace to avoid sin and to please God, and to leave life and death, sickness, health and riches to Him and His will.

"You," he says farther on, "venerate the saints, you rejoice to possess their relics, but you despise the best thing they have left behind them, namely, the example of a pure life. No devotion is so pleasing to Mary as when you imitate her humility ; no religion is so acceptable to the saints and so proper in itself as striving to copy their virtue. Do you wish to merit the patronage of Peter and Paul ? Imitate the faith of the one and the charity of the other and you will do more than if you had made ten journeys to Rome. Do you wish to do something to show high honour to St. Francis ? You are proud, you are a lover of riches,

[1] *Opera omnia* (ed. Leclerc), tom. v., col. 26.

you are quarrelsome ; give these to the saint, rule your
soul and be more humble by the example of Francis ;
despise filthy lucre, and covet rather the good of the
soul. Leave contentions aside and overcome evil by
good. The saint will receive more honour in this way
than if you were to burn a hundred candles to him.
You think it a great thing if clothed in the habit of St.
Francis you are borne to the grave. This dress will
not profit you when you are dead if, when alive, your
morals were unlike his."

"People," he continues, "honour the relics of St.
Paul, and do not trouble to listen to his voice still
speaking. They make much of a large portion of one
of his bones looked at through a glass, and think little
of honouring him really by understanding what he
teaches and trying to follow that." It is the same so
often with the honour shown to the crucifix. " You
honour," he says, "the representation of Christ's face
fashioned of stone or of wood or painted in colours,
the image of His mind ought to be more religiously
honoured, which, by the work of the Holy Spirit, is
set forth in the gospels. No Apelles ever sketched the
form and figure of a human body in such a perfect
way as to compare with the mental image formed in
prayer."

Erasmus then passes on to speak at length of what
should lie at the foundation of all true devotion to the
saints. The spirit which actuates is that which matters.
To put up candles to images of the saints and not
to observe God's laws ; to fast and to abstain and not to
set a guard on the tongue, to give way to detraction
and evil speaking of all kinds ; to wear the religious
habit and to live the life of a worldling under it ; to

build churches and not to build up the soul; to keep Sunday observances externally but not to mind what the spirit gives way to—these are the things that really matter. "By your lips you bless and in your heart you curse. Your body is shut up in a narrow cell, and in thought you wander over the whole world. You listen to God's word with the ears of your body; it would be more to the purpose if you listened inwardly. What doth it profit not to do the evil which you desire to accomplish? What doth it profit to do good outwardly and to do the opposite inwardly? Is it much to go to Jerusalem in the body when in the spirit it is to thee but Sodom and Egypt and Babylon?"[1]

In his tract *De amabili Ecclesiæ concordia*, printed in 1533, Erasmus lays down the same principle. It is, he writes, a pious and good thing to believe that the saints who have worked miracles in the time of their lives on earth, can help us now that they are in heaven. As long as there is no danger of real superstition, it is absurd to try to prevent people invoking the saints. Though superstition in the cultus of the saints is, of course, to be prevented, " the pious and simple affection is sometimes to be allowed even if it be mixed with some error." As for the representations of the saints in churches, those who disapprove of them should not for that reason " blame those who, without superstition, venerate these images for the love of those they represent, just as a newly-married woman kisses a ring or present left or sent by her absent spouse out of affection for him." Such affection cannot be displeasing to God, since it comes not from superstition, but from an abundance of affectionate feeling, and exactly the same

[1] Col. 37.

view should be taken of the true devotion shown to the relics of the saints, provided that it be ever borne in mind that the highest honour that can be paid to them consists in imitation of their lives.

Considering the importance of "indulgences" or "pardons," as they were frequently called, in the Reformation controversies, it is curious that very little is made of them in the literature of the period preceding the religious changes. If we except the works of professed followers of Luther, there is hardly any trace of serious objection being raised to the fundamental idea of "indulgences" in their true sense. Here and there may be found indications of some objection to certain abuses which had been allowed to creep into the system, but these proceeded from loyal sons of the Church rather than from those ill affected to the existing ecclesiastical authority, or those who desired to see the abolition of all such grants of spiritual favours. The lawyer Saint-German, for instance, may be taken as an example of the acute layman, who, although professing to be a Catholic and an obedient son of the Church, was credited by his contemporaries with holding advanced if not somewhat heterodox views on certain matters of current controversy. What he has to say about "pardons" and "indulgences" is neither very startling nor indeed very different from what all serious-minded churchmen of that day held. He considered that the people generally were shocked at finding "the Pope and other spiritual rulers" granting "pardons" for the payment of money. This, he considered, had been brought prominently into notice at the time he was writing, by the indulgences granted to those who should contribute to the building of St.

Peter's when "it has appeared after, evidently that it has not been disposed to that use. And that has caused many to think that the said pardons were granted rather of covetousness than of charity, or for the health of the souls of the people. And thereupon some have fallen in a manner into despising "pardons" as though pardons "granted upon such covetousness would not avail . . . and verily it were a great pity that any misliking of pardons should grow in the hearts of the people for any misdemeanour in the grantor or otherwise, for they are right necessary. And I suppose that if certain pardons were granted freely without money, for the saying of certain appointed prayers, then all misliking of pardons would shortly cease and vanish away." [1]

Christopher Saint-German speaks much in the same way as to the evil of connecting payment of money with the granting of indulgences, in the work in connection with which his name is chiefly known, *A Dyaloge in English between a Student and a Doctor of Divinity*. "If it were so ordered by the Pope," he writes, "that there might be certain general pardons of full remission in diverse parts of the realm, which the people might have for saying certain orisons and prayers without paying any money for it, it is not unlikely that in a short time there would be very few that would find any fault with 'pardons.' For verily it is a great comfort to all Christian people to remember that our Lord loved His people so much that to their relief and comfort leave behind Him so great a treasure as is the power to grant pardons, which, as I suppose,

---

[1] *A treatise concerning the division between the spiritualitie and the temporalitie.* London, R. Redman (1532 ?), fol. 27.

next unto the treasure of His precious body in the
Sacrament of the altar, may be accounted among the
greatest, and therefore he would labour greatly to his
own hurt and to the great heaviness of all others also
who would endeavour to prove that there was no such
power left by God." [1]

In the literature of the period, it must be remembered, there is nothing to show that the true nature of
a "pardon" or indulgence was not fully and commonly
understood. There is no evidence that it was in any
way interpreted as a remission of sin, still less that any
one was foolish enough to regard it as permission to
commit this or that offence against God. Tyndale,
indeed, had suggested that by purchasing an indulgence
"thou mayest quench almost the terrible fire of hell for
three halfpence." But Sir Thomas More meets the
point directly. "Nay, surely," he says, "that fire is
not so lightly quenched that folk upon the boldness of
pardons should stand out of the fear of purgatory. For
though the sacrament of penance is able to put away
the eternal (nature) of the pain, yet the party for all
that has cause to fear both purgatory and hell too, lest
some default on his own part prevented God working
such grace in him in the Sacrament as should serve for
this. So, though the pardon be able to discharge a
man of purgatory, yet there may be such default in the
party to whom the pardon is granted that although
instead of three halfpence he gives three hundred
pounds, still he may receive no pardon at all, and
therefore he cannot be out of fear of purgatory, but
ever has cause to fear it. For no man without a
revelation can be sure whether he be partaker of the

[1] *Dyaloge in Englyshe*, 1531. Part 3, fol. 23.

pardon or not, though he may have and ought to have both in that and every good thing good hope."[1]

Bishop Gardiner in 1546, in writing against George Joye, incidentally makes use of some strong expressions about the granting of pardons for the payment of money, and blames the friars as being instrumental in spreading them.   He has been asserting that by every means in his power the devil, now in one way and now in another, attempts to prevent men from practising the good works necessary for salvation.   " For that purpose," he says, " he procured out pardons from Rome, wherein heaven was sold for a little money, and to retail that merchandise the devil used friars for his ministers.   Now they be all gone with all their trumpery ; but the devil is not yet gone, for now the cry is that ʻheaven needs no works at all, but only belief, only, only, and nothing else.ʼ "[2]

This, after all, was very little more than the abuse which previously was pointed out by the cardinal who, conjointly with Cardinal Caraffa, afterwards Pope Paul IV., had been directed to draw up suggestions for improvement of ecclesiastical discipline.   The document drawn up by Caraffa himself was submitted to the Pope by his command, and amongst the points which were declared to need correction were the granting of indulgences for money payments and permission given to travelling collectors, such as the Questors of the Holy Spirit, &c., to bestow " pardons " in return for subscriptions.   This, in the judgment of the four cardinals, is likely to lead to misunderstandings as

---

[1] English Works, p. 476.

[2] Stephen Gardiner.   *A declaration of such true articles as George Joye hath gone about to confute as false.*   1546, f. 2.

to the real nature of the indulgences granted, to deceive rustic minds, and to give rise to all manner of superstitions.[1]

Cardinal Sadolet, one of the four cardinals who formed the Papal Commission just referred to, in an appeal to the German princes makes the same adverse criticism about the money payments received for the granting of indulgences. "The whole of Germany," he says, "has been convulsed by the indulgences granted by Pope Leo. X. to those who would contribute to the building of St. Peter's. These indulgences," he says, "and consequently the agents in distributing them, I do not now defend. And I remember that, as far as my position and honour would then allow, I spoke against them when those decrees were published, and when my opinion had no effect I was greatly grieved." He did not, he continued, doubt the power of the Pope in granting the indulgences, but held that "in giving them, the manner now insisted on with every care by the supreme Pontiff, Paul III., ought to be maintained, namely, that they should be granted freely, and that there should be no mention of money in regard to them. The loving-kindness and mercy of God should not be sold for money, and if anything be asked for at the time, it should be requested as a work of piety."[2]

The above will show that earnest-minded men were fully alive to the abuses which might be connected with the granting of indulgences, and no condemnation could have been stronger than that formulated by the Council of Trent. At the same time, it is clear that the abuses

---

[1] *Consilium de emendanda ecclesia* (Ed. 1538), sig. B. 4.
[2] Jacobi Sadoletti, *Opera Omnia*, Verona (1737). Tom ii., p. 437.

of the system were, so far as England at least is concerned, neither widespread nor obvious. The silence of Sir Thomas More on the matter, and the very mild representations of his adversary, Christopher Saint-German, show that this is the case. Saint-German's objection was not against the system, but against the same kind of abuses against which subsequently the Fathers of Trent legislated. The reformers attacked not the abuses only but the whole system, and their language has quite unjustly been frequently interpreted by subsequent writers as evidence of the existence everywhere of widespread abuses. In this regard it is well to bear in mind that the translation of the works of the German reformers into English cannot be taken as contemporary evidence for England itself.

The cry of the advanced party which would sweep away every vestige of the old religious observances was certainly not popular. One example of a testimony to the general feeling in London is given in a little work printed by one of the reforming party in 1542, when it was found that Henry VIII. did not advance along the path of reformation marked out by the foreign followers of Luther as quickly as his rejection of papal supremacy and the overthrow of the religious houses had caused some people to hope. The tract in question is called *The lamentation of a Christian against the Citie of London, made by Roderigo Mors*,[1] and some quotations from it will show what view an ardent reformer took of the spirit of Londoners towards the new doctrines. "The greater part of these inordinate rich, stiff-necked citizens," he writes, "will not have in their houses that

---

[1] It is said to be "printed at Jericho in the land of Promes, by Thomas Treuth."

lively word of our souls [1] nor suffer their servants to
have it, neither yet (will they) gladly read it or hear it
read, but abhors and disdains all those who would
live according to the Gospel, and instead thereof they
set up and maintain idolatry and other innumerable
wickedness of man's invention daily committed in the
city of London."

"The greatest part of the seniors and aldermen, with
the multitude of the inordinate rich . . . with the
greatest multitude of thee, O city of London, take the
part and be fully bent with the false prophets, the
bishops and other strong, stout, and sturdy priests of
Baal, to persecute unto death all and every godly person
who either preaches the word or setteth it forth in writing . . . O Lord! how blind are these citizens who
take so good care to provide for the dead which is not
commanded of them nor availeth the dead.[2] . . . When
they feel themselves worthily plagued, which comes of
Thee only, then they will run a-gadding after their false
prophets through the streets once or twice a week, crying and calling to creatures of the Creator, or with *ora
pro nobis*, and that in a tongue which the greatest part
of them understand not, unto Peter, Paul, James and
John, Mary and Martha : and I think within a few years
they will (without Thy great mercy) call upon Thomas
Wolsey, late Cardinal, and upon the unholy (or as they
would say holy) maid of Kent. Why not, as well as
upon Thomas Becket ? What he was, I need not write.
It is well known.[3]

"And think ye not that if the Blessed Virgin Mary
were now upon earth and saw her Son and only Redeemer

---

[1] The English Testament.
[2] Sig. A. 3.   [3] Ibid., sig. A. 4.

robbed of His glory, which glory, you blind citizens give to her, would she not rend her clothes like as did the Apostles, for offering oblations with their forefathers' kings' heads unto the Queen of Heaven ? How many queens of Heaven have ye in the Litany ? O ! dear brethren, be no longer deceived with these false prophets your bishops and their members." [1]

" The great substance which you bestow upon chantries, obits, and such like dregs of . . . Rome, which most commonly ye give for three causes, as ye say, first, that you will have the service of God maintained in the church to God's honour, and yet by the same service is God dishonoured, for the Supper of the Lord is perverted and not used after Christ's institution . . . and the holy memory turned into a vain superstitious ceremonial Mass, as they call it, which Mass is an abominable idol, and of all idols the greatest ; and never shall idolatry be quenched where that idol is used after antichrist's institution . . . which no doubt shall be reformed when the time is come that God hath appointed, even as it is already in divers cities of Germany, as Zurich, Basle, and Strasburg and such other."

" The second cause is for redeeming your souls and your friends, which is also abominable. . . . The idolator nowadays, if he set a candle before an image and idol, he says he does not worship the image, but God it represents. For say they, who is so foolish as to worship an image ? The third cause of your good intent is that the profit of your goods may come to the priests ; as though they were the peculiar people of God and only beloved ; as indeed to those who preach the Gospel the people are bound to give sufficient living . . . but not

[1] Ibid., sigs. A. 5 d., A. 6 d.

that their prayers can help the dead no more than a
man's breath blowing a sail can cause a great ship to
sail. So is this also become an abomination, for those
be not Christ's ministers, but the ministers of a rabble
of dirty traditions and popish ceremonies, and you find
a sort of lusty lubbers who are well able to labour for
their living and strong to get it with the sweat of their
face." [1]

" . . . O ye citizens, if ye would turn but even the
profits of your chantries and obits to the finding of the
poor, what a politic and goodly provision ! whereas now
London being one of the flowers of the world as touching worldly riches hath so many, yea innumerable poor
people, forced to go from door to door and to sit openly
in the streets begging, and many not able to do otherwise but lie in their houses in most grievous pains and
die for lack of the aid of the rich, to the great shame of
thee, oh London ! " [2]

After exclaiming against the amount of money spent
by the authorities of the city of London on civic entertainments, and railing against the support given to " the
Mass of Scala cœli, of the Five wounds, and other such
like trumpery," our author continues : " Have you not
slain the servants of the Lord, only for speaking against
the authority of the false bishop of Rome, that monstrous
beast, whom now you yourselves do, or should, abhor ?
I mean all his laws being contrary to Christ and not His
body, and yet you see that a few years past you burnt
for heretics abominable those who preached or wrote
against his usurped power, and now it is treason to
uphold or maintain any part of his usurped power,

[1] Ibid., sig. B. i.
[2] Ibid., sig. B. ii.

and he shall die as a traitor who does so, and well worthy." [1]

After declaiming against the Mass and confession, and declaring that the bishops and cathedral churches should be despoiled of their wealth as their " companions and brethren in antichrist, the abbots" had been, the author of the tract goes on : " God gave the king a heart to take the wicked mammon from you, as he may rightfully do with the consent of the Commons by Act of Parliament, so that it may be disposed of according to God's glory and the commonwealth, and to take himself as portion, as (say) eight or ten of every hundred, for an acknowledgment of obedience and for the maintenance of his estate. The rest politically to be put into a commonwealth, first distributed among all the towns in England in sums according to the quantity and number of the occupiers and where most need is, and all the towns to be bound to the king so that he may have the money at his extreme need to serve him, he rendering it again. And also a politic way (should be) taken for provision of the poor in every town, with some part to the marriage of young persons that lack friends." [2]

The bishops the writer considers to be the greatest obstacles to the reformation of religion in England on the model of what had already taken place in Germany. "You wicked mammon," he continues, "your inordinate riches was not of your heavenly Father's planting ; therefore it must be plucked up by the roots with the riches of your other brethren of the Romish church or church malignant, which of late were rightfully plucked up. I would to God that

---

[1] Ibid., sig. B. viii.   [2] Sig. D. vii.

the distribution of the same lands and goods had been as godly distributed as the act of the rooting up was ; which distribution of the same I dare say all Christian hearts lament. For the fat swine only were greased, but the poor sheep to whom that thing belonged had least or nothing at all. The fault will be laid to those of the Parliament House, especially to those who bear the greatest swing. Well, I touch this matter here, to exhort all that love God's word unfeignedly to be diligent in prayer only to God to endue the Lords, Knights, and Burgesses of the next Parliament with His spirit, that the lands and goods of these bishops may be put to a better use, as to God's glory, the wealth of the commonalty and provision for the poor." [1]

The above lengthy extracts will show what the advanced spirits among the English followers of Luther hoped for from the religious revolution which had already, when the tract was written, been begun. It will also serve to show that even in London, which may be supposed to have been in the forefront of the movement, the religious changes were by no means popular ; but the civic authorities and people clung to the old faith and traditions, which the author well and tersely describes as " the Romish religion."

THE readers of the foregoing pages will see that no attempt has been made to draw a definite conclusion from the facts set down, or expound the causes of the ultimate triumph of the Reformation principles in England. It has already been pointed out that the time for

[1] Ibid., sig. D. viii.

a satisfactory synthesis is not yet come ; but it may not be unnecessary to deprecate impatience to reach an ultimate judgment.

The necessary assumption which underlies the inherited Protestant history of the Reformation in the sixteenth century is the general corruption of manners and morals no less than of doctrine, and the ignorance of religious truths no less than the neglect of religious precepts on the part of both clergy and people. On such a basis nothing can be easier and simpler than to account for the issue of the English religious changes. The revival of historical studies and the alienation of the minds of many historians from traditional Christianity, whether in its Catholic or Protestant form, has, however, thrown doubt on this great fundamental assumption—a doubt that will be strengthened the more the actual conditions of the case are impartially and thoroughly investigated.   Many of the genuine sources of history have only within this generation become really accessible ; what was previously known has been more carefully examined and sifted, whilst men have begun to see that if the truth is to be ascertained inquiries must be pursued in detail within local limits, and that it does not suffice to speak in general terms of " the corrupt state of the Church."

If we are to know the real factors of the problem to be solved, separate investigations have to be pursued which lead to very varying conclusions as to the state of the Church, the ecclesiastical life and the religious practices of the people in different countries.   It is already evident that the corruptions or the virtues prevailing in one quarter must not straightway be credited to the account of another ; that the reason why one country has become Protestant, or another remained Catholic, has to be sought for in each case, and that it may be safely asserted that the maintenance of Catholicity or the adoption of Protestantism in different regions, had comparatively little to do with prevalence or absence of abuses, or as little depended on the question whether these were more or less grievous.

Unquestionably those who desire to have a ready explanation of great historical movements or revolutions, find themselves increasingly baulked in the particular case of the Reformation by the new turn which modern historical research has given to the consideration of the question.   Recent attempts to piece up the new results with the old views afford a warning against precipitation, and have but shown that the explanation of the successful issue of the Reformation in England is a problem less simple or obvious than many popular writers have hitherto assumed.   The factors are clearly seen now to be many—sometimes accidental, sometimes strongly personal—whilst aspirations after worldly commodities, though destined not to be realised for the many, were often and in the most influential quarters a stronger determinant to acquiescence or active co-operation in the movement than thirst after pure doctrine, love of the open Bible, or desire for a vernacular liturgy.   The first condition for the understanding of the problem at all is the most careful and detailed examination possible of the state of popular religion during the whole of the century which witnessed the change, quite apart from the particular political methods employed to effect the transition from the public teaching of the old faith, as it was professed in the closing years of the reign

of Henry VIII., and the new as it was officially practised a dozen years after Elizabeth had held the reins
of power.

The interest of the questions discussed in the
present volume is by no means exclusively, perhaps
to some persons is even by no means predominantly,
a religious one. It has been insisted upon in the
preceding pages that religion on the eve of the Reformation was intimately bound up with the whole social
life of the people, animating it and penetrating it at
every point. No one who is acquainted with the
history of later centuries in England can doubt for a
moment that the religion then professed presented in
this respect a contrast to the older faith ; or as some
writers may put it, religion became restricted to what
belongs to the technically " religious" sphere. But this
was not confined to England, or even to Protestant
countries. Everywhere, it may be said, in the centuries
subsequent to the religious revolution of the sixteenth
century, religion became less directly social in its
action ; and if the action and interference of what is
now called the State in every department of social
life is continually extending, this may not inaptly be
said to be due to the fact that it has largely taken up
the direct social work and direction from which the
Church found herself perhaps compelled to recede, in
order to concentrate her efforts more intensely on
the promotion of more purely and strictly religious
influences. It is impossible to study the available
sources of information about the period immediately
preceding the change without recognising that, so far
from the Church being a merely effete or corrupt agency
in the commonwealth, it was an active power for popular

good in a very wide sense.   At any rate, whatever view
we may take of the results of the Reformation, to
understand rightly the conditions of religious thought
and life on the eve of the religious revolution, is a
condition of being able really to read aright our own
time and to gauge the extent to which present tendencies
find their root or their justification in the past.

INDEX